I0824316

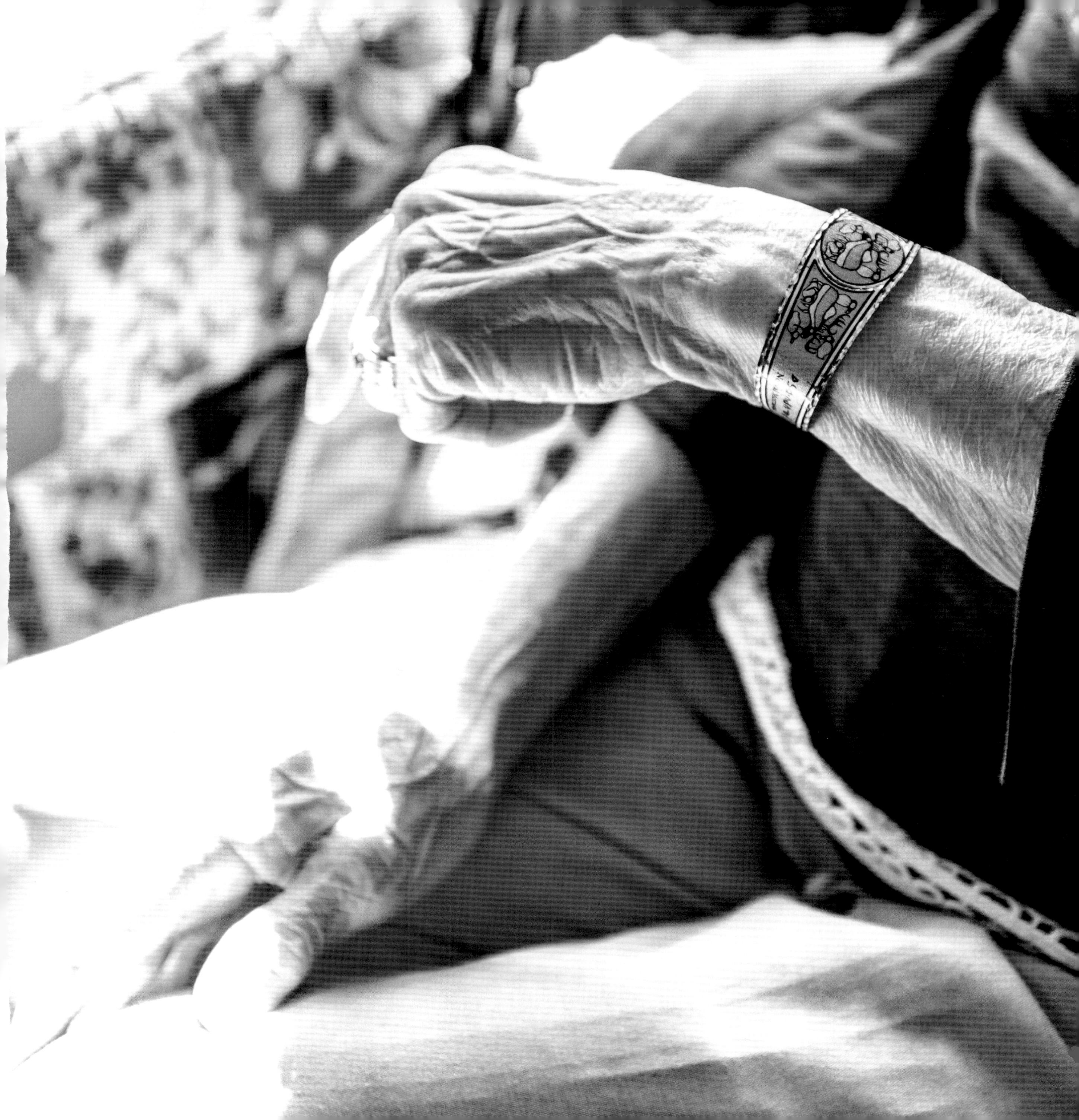

STILL HERE

PRESERVING OUR LEGACY

Historical research by MARY McCARTHY

Poetry by THANDIWE McCARTHY

Photography by GARY WEEKES

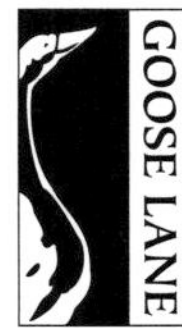

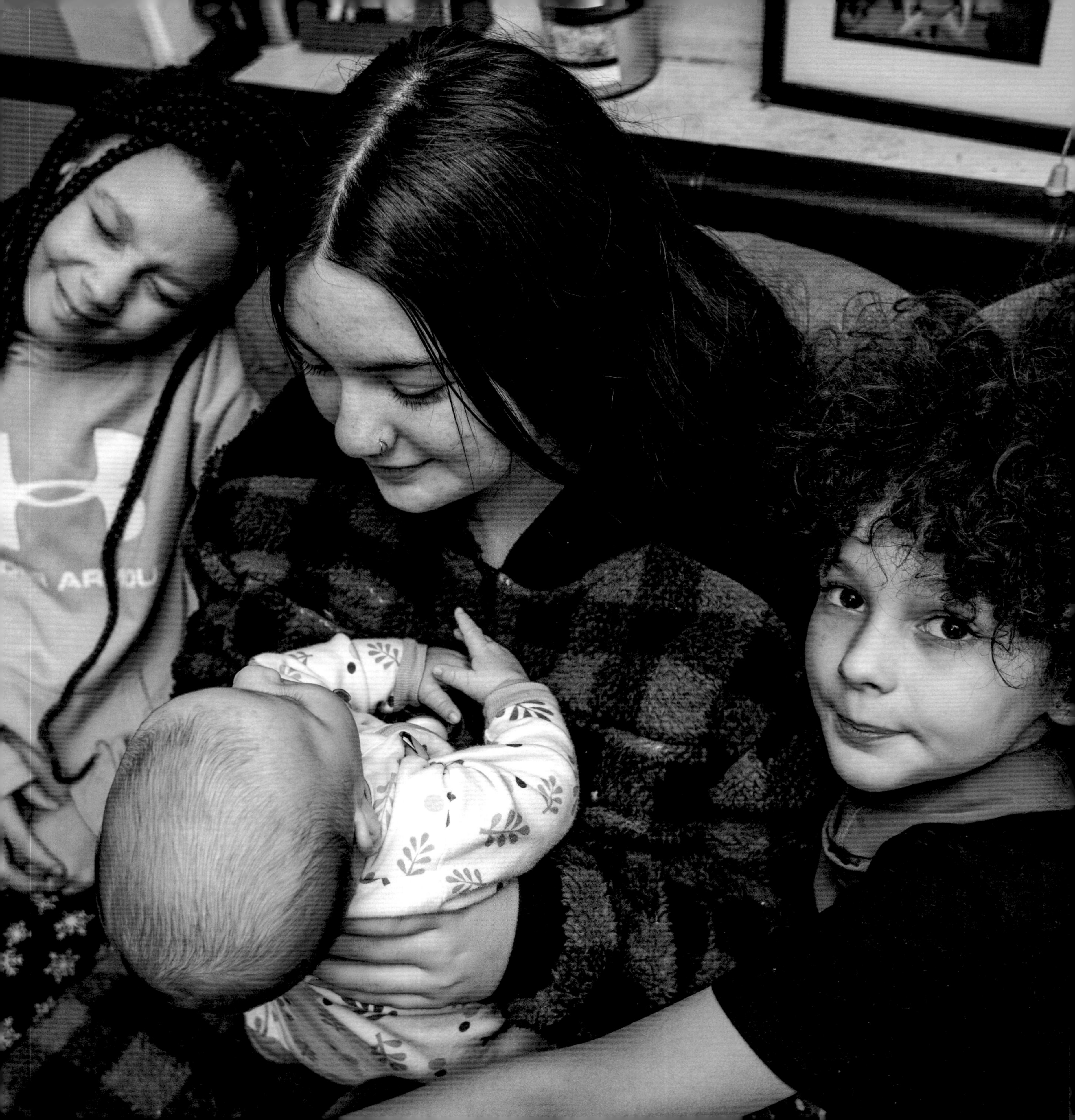

Contents

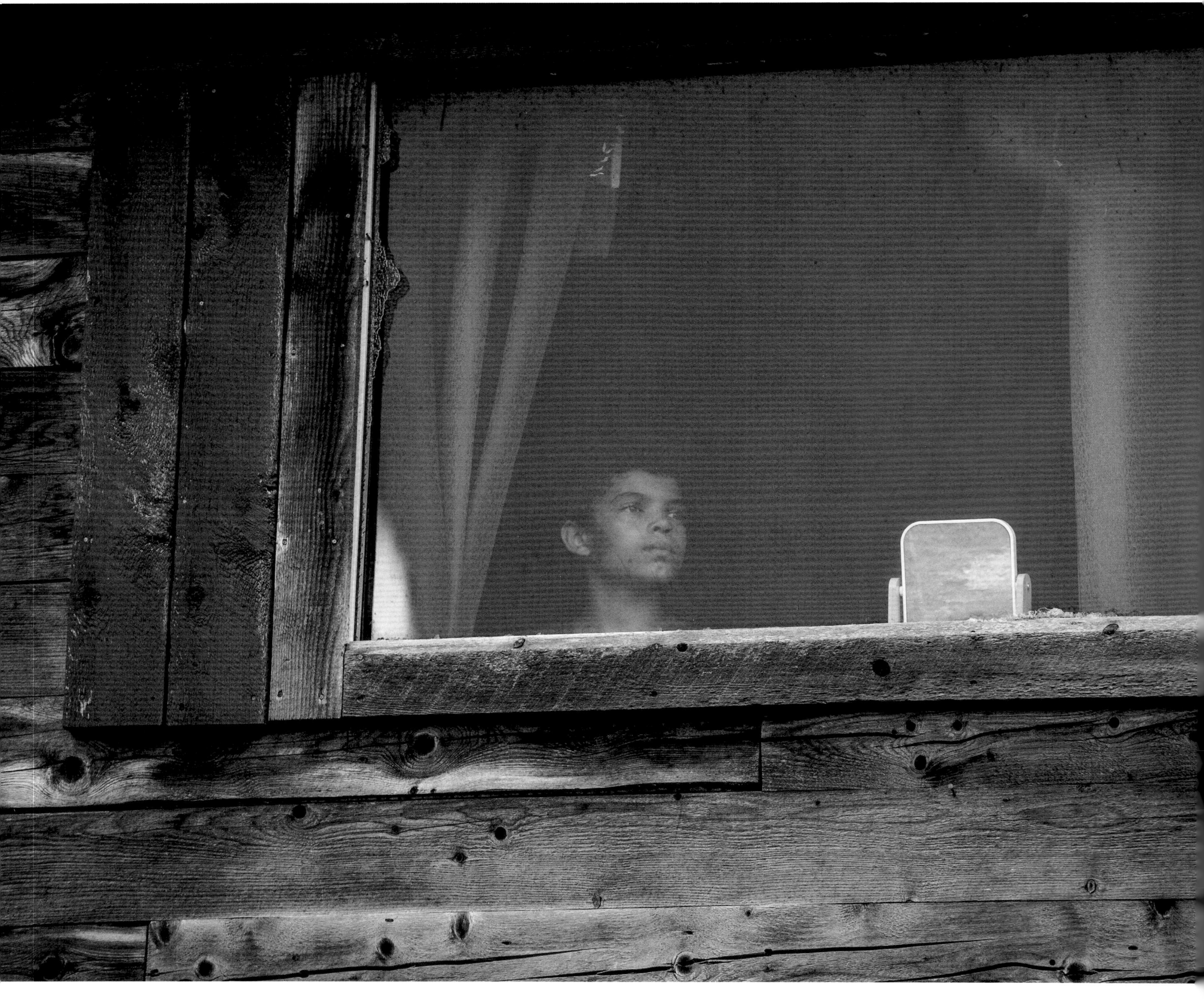

Foreword

Still Here is an incredibly significant addition to the literature about Black New Brunswick history. Thandiwe McCarthy, Mary McCarthy, and Gary Weekes illuminate the story of Black New Brunswickers as they show the depth, nuance, and agency of past generations. There could be no better authors for this book thanks to their deep roots in the Black New Brunswick community. Mary McCarthy is an expert in Black history. Her historical timeline is informative for those new to the saga of Black New Brunswick, but it also contains nuggets of evidence and wisdom for experienced historians including myself. In his poetry, Thandiwe McCarthy captures the soul and spirit of a community that underlines the very apt title of this book, *Still Here: Preserving Our Legacy*. His poetry is dynamic, moving, and fulfilling. Gary Weekes is a master of communicating history through photography. He takes the most mundane daily event and turns it into a treasure trove of family photographic history. Taken together, these intellectuals have given us a book that will serve as a starting point for anyone interested in the history of Black people in New Brunswick.

As a historian of slavery in North America, I am impressed with Mary McCarthy's overview of New Brunswick Black history. It gives scholars and everyday people alike a starting place for future research. This timeline is one of the most important pieces published about Black New Brunswick history, along with W.A. Spray's seminal *The Blacks in New Brunswick*. Of course, the difference is that Mary grew up in the Black community, experienced its trials and tribulations, and those experiences shape the way she writes this history. Starting with the Loyalist influx (though there were Black people in New Brunswick prior to 1783), McCarthy highlights the experience of both free Black people and their enslaved counterparts. Thandiwe McCarthy's poetry is interspersed with the timeline and captures the bittersweet experience of the Black Loyalists. He shows that, despite being emancipated, the Black Loyalists did not enjoy meaningful freedom: "Never fish, never wheat. The sweat of your back never got you seated at the feast."

Mary McCarthy also carefully captures the development of Black New Brunswick history in the nineteenth century. She centres the experience of people like William Flood and other Black refugees who petitioned the government for aide in settling land near Saint John. These refugees were exhibiting agency in claiming the right to settle the land just like White inhabitants. Toward the end of the century, McCarthy highlights the story of Abraham Beverley Walker, the first Black Canadian lawyer and editor of the short-lived magazine, *Neith*, which was an academic publication that showed local White people that Black New Brunswickers were intellectual equals—crucial at a time when most universities in North America taught racialized science that imagined Black people as biologically inferior to Whites. But the timeline does not stop at the end of the nineteenth century, taking readers all the way to the declaration of Emancipation Day in New Brunswick in 2022, and seamlessly weaving individual stories of courage with the history of various organizations that fought to secure equal rights in New Brunswick.

The fifteen families profiled in the second half of *Still Here* present a beautiful tapestry of the lives of contemporary Black New Brunswickers. Gary Weekes's photographs capture Black joy, something it is easy to forget about when we discuss the totality of the African North American experience. The author of *Invisible Man*, Ralph Ellison, once noted that Black history was more than the sum of its brutalization. Ellison meant that Black history could not be reduced to slavery, segregation, racism, and trauma. It is and always has been more. The photographs of the fifteen families remind us of this important fact. Ultimately, *Still Here: Preserving Our Legacy* belongs at every Canadian library and on bookshelves throughout the country.

Still Here asks very serious questions about history and the production of historical knowledge, being understandably concerned with how Black New Brunswickers understand themselves. In discussing the achievements of the Black community in their introduction, the authors ask, "How do most of us never know about them . . . [and] who advocates for these stories to be added to provincial history curriculums? Who tells these stories to the wider community?" This book provides the framework to begin to answer these questions—the heartfelt stories in this volume should be widely read by historians and genealogists throughout Canada and the United States.

—Harvey Amani Whitfield
Centennial Carnegie Chair in the History of Slavery in Canada
University of King's College

Introduction

How far would you go to set right what has gone wrong? As Black Canadians, we have found ourselves asking that question a lot lately. Our federal and provincial governments have often been quick to promote Canada as the standard for diversity and inclusion, citing examples like the abolition of slavery and the Underground Railroad. Yet the federal government only designated August 1 as Emancipation Day in 2021, and—thanks to the tireless advocacy of the Black community—New Brunswick followed a year later. Emancipation Day was declared in the province 188 years after the abolition of slavery in Canada and the British Empire—188 years of Black New Brunswickers being officially kept out of the conversations of their right to celebrate our core values. *Still Here* is an attempt to repair a few of the injustices and oversights by showcasing the rich past and present of everyday Black New Brunswick life. The project started as a fire in Thandiwe McCarthy's belly before it crystalized into an idea in his mind.

As a seventh-generation Black Canadian, Thandiwe grew up in New Brunswick without any knowledge of heritage or history. Oh, he could articulate injustice for hair touches, debate differences between combs, picks, and hairbrushes. Yet never could he define anything he attempted to defend. Decades of knowing that something was wrong, of feeling like justice had to be done, led him here.

Thandiwe's experience isn't rare. In fact, it is typical of his generation (born in the 1980s) that he was among the few racialized groups in public school and thus forced to wear the hats of both educator and ambassador for the entire African diaspora. It doesn't work out so well for the kids, and they have all the receipts from Effexor to Ritalin, from therapist to counsellor, all detailing the trauma of not knowing who they are while at the same time feeling extreme pressure to both teach and advocate for their identity.

An' so Thandiwe did what he suspects many Black people do: he reached for Black history as a way to help process trauma. From childhood, we feel voids throughout our identity, and so we look to history for the puzzle pieces to help fill these gaps. Why are children not empowered to know their heritage?

If we do not prioritize telling the local stories to the people closest to us, they disappear. A quick look back through a few generations of Black history makes that clear as day.

Thandiwe's generation participated in the Black Lives Matter movement—a 2020 cry to the world that we won't be kept in the dark corners of society, only to be let out for others' entertainment. This led to the establishment of many activist and advocacy organizations, such as the New Brunswick Black Artists Alliance, among others.

Thandiwe's mother Mary's generation was filled with organizations dedicated to bringing Black people together. For instance, in the 1960s the New Brunswick Association for the Advancement of Coloured People had goals such as "to encourage the educational, social, physical, and cultural standards of coloured people in New Brunswick" and "to advocate a better relationship with other members of society and to take an active part in community activities."

Thandiwe's grandparents' generation came of age during the Second World War, in which many Black Canadians served, including his grandfather Arthur McCarthy. Although the women did not serve overseas, they played a crucial role taking over work on the home front—and often relinquished these roles once peace returned. This generation also had the wildest parties at Elm Hill, a Black settlement as old as Nova Scotia's Africville. The community had a post office, a church, a school, and a lake to swim in in the summer and to skate on in the winter. During events there were two dance floors because all the surrounding towns would drive over to boogie.

Thandiwe's great-grandparents' generation experienced the First World War. Many Black New Brunswickers served in the all-Black No. 2 Construction Battalion. Prior to the war, Canada's first Black-owned Magazine, *Neith*, was founded in Saint John, promoting Black writers and poets and speaking out on issues such as slavery, diversity, and the state of race relations.

Thandiwe's great-great-grandparents' generation (born in the 1850s and '60s) organized giant emancipation dinners with politicians whose names now adorn university buildings. This generation included those who had escaped slavery, started businesses, and then fundraised to buy back family members from Down South. One woman, Georgina Whetsel of Saint John, was good friends with the wife of Frederick Douglass and eventually sold her business for $33,000—well over $1.2 million today—making her one of the richest women in North America.

All of these events happened right here in New Brunswick. How do most of us never know about them? Why is the legacy of all this advocacy and organization only amnesia, ignorance, and apathy? Can someone please explain how we went from being so successful at business—that entire Black sports leagues were funded; that dinners were hosted for leaders of the province; that Black-owned magazines were printed and sold; that three-day-weekend parties, complete with chartered bus rides from neighboring cities, were funded; and that a Black New Brunswick woman was one of the richest women in North America—to what we have now?

Now, the Black community knows justice. Give your attention to any of our greatest movies, songs, or stories, and the theme sticks out bright as day. As a culture, we know when we've been dealt a bad hand, and we are internationally respected for our ways of expressing injustice. We set the gold standard for offense—if anyone has a mind to hurt the Black community, they know our spirits will attack. An' buried you will be, in an avalanche of literature, rhythm, and research. But after the crisis is over, we are terrible at recording and sharing over generations the memory of our resistance. We are awesome at winning, but awful at defence.

Imagine Thandiwe's surprise that there are historians who still do not know about Black New Brunswick history. Then imagine his surprise at finding out that not only were there published and documented cases of slavery in the province, but there were activists, all the way back to Frederick Douglass, who visited early New Brunswick Black communities. Here was Thandiwe struggling on his personal journey of identity, desperate for any mention of community, and silently struggling with a sense of injustice. But in the 1960s the Black community in New Brunswick had civil rights marches in the streets and massive picnics in the parks. These stories are preserved by our historians and archivists. But who advocates for these stories to be added to provincial history curriculums? Who tells these stories to the wider community?

Now, people proudly claim that there was no history of slavery in our province. Now, Elm Hill, our Black historic community, as old as Africville, is one generation away from being a field of tall grass. Now, Black children go through school not knowing who they are, surrounded by heroes from every heritage but their own.

How, how, how did we go from every generation being the best at bringing the families together to forgetting to share the stories that bind past strengths to present struggles?

•••

Thandiwe needed a way to make permanent change in this issue. But such impact doesn't come easily, so he built a team of experts. He knew words alone wouldn't cut it; he knew that pictures are windows into moments but lack the sharp spirituality of poetry. *Still Here* had to be multidisciplinary, a combination of exceptional poetry, history, photography, and archival work. No one genre could accomplish what needed to be done on its own, because the truth is none ever have. History books are read only by historians. The documents at the archives are visited mostly by academics. Poetry is read by poets. Photography books are bought and sit unopened on coffee tables. How could we create something that will be read, shared, and celebrated again and again, while also preserving our Black history? And so, with an open mind and a fantastic team we blended the best of everything into a book: *Still Here*.

While *Still Here* raises awareness of Black history, this is not the goal of the book. The goal is to inspire a stronger connection to sharing an' preserving our history within and between families. The stories of our great-aunts and great-uncles have real power to heal and strengthen us against our anxieties, and their families are the best people to research and share these stories. Our greatest historians are often related by blood.

Thandiwe's first step in researching the history of Black New Brunswickers was to visit the provincial archives. His early days in the archives were filled with wonder over how much was there. He encountered dozens of images alongside hundreds of documents and newspapers clippings. Upon looking through the material, he realized most of the documents related to arrests and court cases. Is this surprising when the compilers of the archives have largely been White historians, who were focused on their stories? It seemed the only things of Black heritage worth archiving were the negative moments. So, Thandiwe turned to the New Brunswick Black History Society. As an organization dedicated to preserving Black New Brunswick history, surely this would be a one-stop shop for his research. An' while he was delighted to see a wonderful timeline of Black New Brunswick history, filled with an all-star cast, he found something lacking there, too. What was missing was the family element, the day-to-day love and labour of those who didn't win medals or receive honours from royalty. It seemed that no one was talking about family; it was all social struggles or heroic individuals. (Of course, these individuals are crucial parts of the story, and you will find some of them in the first half of the book, but they are not the whole story.) It seemed that if we wanted the community story, the family heritage, we would have to go to the source. So, we did. It is unacceptable to us that anyone trying to piece together their own heritage would have to go through all these steps. So why not put a little of everything all in one place? Let's build the big picture, gaps included.

That's why you're holding this book. This is our response to these historical gaps in the provincial narrative of Black New Brunswickers. We have been here for at least two hundred years. We have been here for over two hundred years. We have aimed to create something that will last another two hundred years.

•••

This book could not happen without the families who are still here. Mary, Thandiwe, and Gary have blended methods across the creative and academic spectrum, but the families are the life of this project. They have helped shape *Still Here*, and they walk with us, equally motivated to make sure that years from now people know our heritage and our faces. They tell their own stories in a way no academic or artist could. Everyone in this project adds to the brilliance the families have shared, in our own voices, using our own disciplines. Thandiwe's poetry, Gary's photography, Mary's academic rigour, and all of our project partners helped bring this to life. We have become an orchestra, with the lead vocals given to the fifteen families who are Still Here preserving their legacy.

How did we choose the fifteen families? We did not choose them—they chose us. We approached many Black families, and these fifteen trusted us with their families' histories, photos, and family anecdotes. The emotions, experiences we shared as we completed the fifteen interviews. Of course, there are many more Black families in New Brunswick—those who have been here for generations and those who are recent arrivals—and *Still Here* is meant as a sampling to demonstrate the depth of Black life in the province rather than an encyclopedic exercise.

Historian and elder Mary McCarthy led the historical research and interviews. Mary is a sixth generation Black New Brunswicker, who traces her ancestors back to a plantation in Virginia in 1783. She remembers attending, as a child, the Black picnics at both Elm Hill and French Lake with her Dymond cousins and her Uncle Charlie and Aunt Florence. These picnics were always great afternoons of Black communities gathering and celebrating. Mary has been a storyteller throughout her life, evolving into a historian and eventually becoming the first Black woman to be president of the New Brunswick Black History Society. In a province where Acadian and British settler stories are well documented, Mary felt the need to advocate and stand up for the descendent Black community and the ancestors who helped build this province. Mary embraced history and storytelling as a gift that was bestowed on her by her ancestors. As she states, "I feel their presence, I lean on my gifts that were bestowed on me to tell their stories, to uplift our beautiful Black community." If left to current history and historians, our ancestors are diminished as unnamed servants and farmers. History needs to be told, discussed, and written about to educate the next generation and correct the wrongs of the past. In Mary's words, "It is my breath and purpose to highlight the lives of the early Black settlers of this beautiful province of New Brunswick!"

Mary felt blessed and honoured to be able to interview the fifteen families. Fourteen of the interviews were done virtually, and one was completed in a half-ton truck, while driving around the city of Saint John. These interviews laid the foundations for the Still Here team to visit the families in person, documenting their visits through poetry and photographs. The experience of speaking to and interviewing family representatives was, for Mary, the highlight of the research. Mary began forming family trees in her head as she got deeper and deeper into the interviews. Mary felt thrilled and at times speechless to hear the stories of their families from the family representatives.

• • •

Gary grew up as part of a large family in the UK. Hanging with his cousins, aunts, and uncles was a regular occurrence that he always looked forward to, and Gary misses the shared secrets, the bickering, and the moments of collusion that arose from family gatherings. Being part of these gatherings as a kid filled Gary with wonderment, looking at his older cousins and thinking how cool they were, while trying to escape or tease his younger cousins. When we visited the families, Gary was shooting as someone who misses those family gatherings of his childhood and who no longer experiences family gatherings as regularly now that his own daughters have grown up.

Gary's formative years were spent in London and New York City, living in predominantly Black neighborhoods. He was acutely aware of Black History and achievement growing up in the US, and always surrounded by Black excellence in the UK, and so the marginalization of Black success stories in New Brunswick became very apparent. Without the work of the likes of Mary McCarthy and the New Brunswick Black History Society, he would not have known about the incredible stories of Black achievement in the province, and—more importantly—nor would the people of New Brunswick. The Provincial Archives of New Brunswick reflected this dearth of information and reflection about generational Black families, making Gary realize how powerful a project this could become through the combination of images, words, and research. By documenting contemporary images of Black family life, we can begin to offset the years of negative and stereotypical documentation of Black history.

Entering the homes of such a diverse group of Black families was somewhat surreal; city folks, country folks, and everyone in between provided Gary with a wealth of imagery about how we live and how complex a culture we are. He photographed hunting families, professionals, educators, and children—providing a rich narrative of how Black New Brunswickers live and always have done so. Gary's photography revealed everyday living that differed from what is highlighted by the media as he had known it in both the UK and US.

Visiting the families and taking photos of them in situ was extremely important to Gary and the whole team. Capturing each of our fifteen families at family gatherings allowed Gary to show everyone as they were on that day, free from the artifice that usually attends studio portraiture. The opportunity to observe a family over two to three hours, revealing how they communicated and interacted with each other, was essential for Gary, who, as part of his artistic discipline, observes intentionally and intently.

Over the time shared, Gary created a group photograph, individual portraits of each family member in attendance, and candid images that captured the family as they went about their day. From the very first family visit, there was a feeling that we were experiencing something magical and producing something that would connect the disconnected.

Each welcome we received on entering, and each hug we received as we departed, was deeply moving. For Gary, this was an incredible opportunity to see a part of Black New Brunswick life that he would never have experienced otherwise. The commonalities with his own family, found in the eyes and attitudes of our fifteen families, hit him with unbridled joy. "Living away" has left Gary longing to be a part of a greater collective, where we all endeavour to be the best father, mother, son, or daughter that we could possibly become. All while striving to keep our family's name intact, respected, and passed on, thus adding to the rich layers of history. He has been forever affected.

Exactly 174 individuals accepted us as members of their extended family for three hours of their lives. We all showed up as our authentic selves, not knowing that the time we spent together would become another memory, to be shared with future family members. Some family members are no longer with us; but this document of that moment in time will remain forever.

•••

As you read through this book, you may notice some gaps that leave you asking questions—this is intentional. The families featured in *Still Here* were not employees or research subjects. They were not on the hook for us to mine their memories and mementos for the project's benefit. These are our friends. At times there were questions they didn't want to answer, or information they wanted to keep out of the book.

We want you to have questions. We want you to reflect on all the pieces—the timeline and the archival documents, the poetry, photography, historical paragraphs, and the first-person stories from the family representatives. We want you to experience the gaps as every Black person in New Brunswick does. These are not mere stories. They are seeds of resilience planted in the souls of every child that will sprout into a forest of confidence. An' each of those trees covered with leaves of courage will protect future generations from ignorance about their ancestors but also from forgetting themselves. Think of that as you read the histories, look at these moments, sit with the poetry.

Then look to your own family heritage, and ask if there are similar gaps. What will you do about it?

With love and respect,
Mary, Thandiwe, and Gary

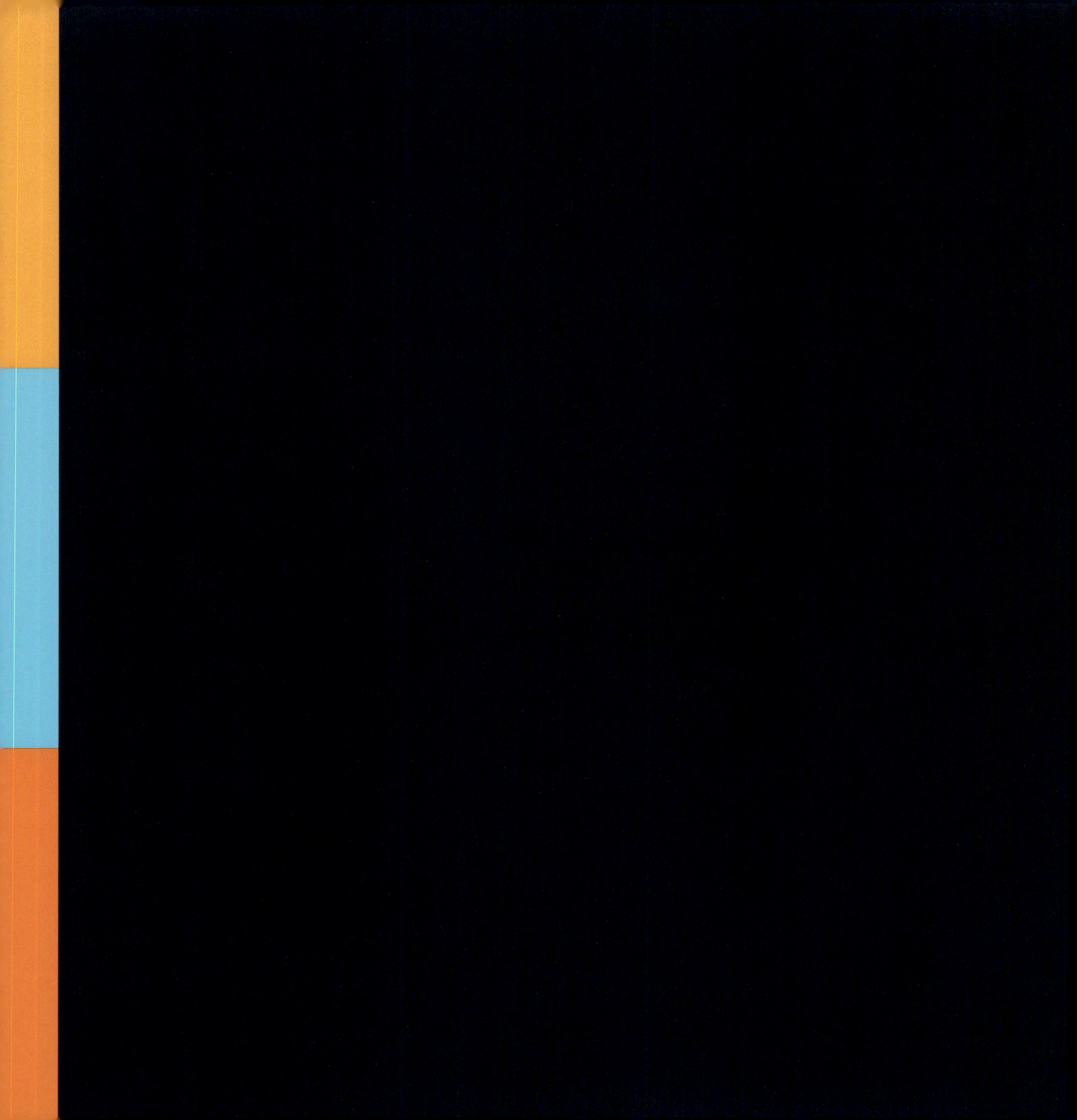

A Brief Overview of Black New Brunswick History

Free Blacks transported on board the Royal Navy ship *Clinton* from New York to Saint John, late July–early September 1783 (David Bell, *American Loyalists to New Brunswick*, 181–82)

Adult males

Saml Hutchins
Benj Elliott
John Cox
Joe Stone
Andw Cole
Stepney Hancock
Benj Bush
Fras Patrick
Antny Randall
Isaac White
Antny Stephens
Dick Richards
Job Christeen
John Sparrow
James Nickens
Thos Stevens
Moses Jessup
Willm Keeling
Saml Hunter
Robt Flemming
Bristol Mitchell
Andw Randall
Adam Randall
Joshua Thompson
Richd Henry
Saml Sampson
Danl Herring
Saml Flemming
Robt Johnson
James Jackson
Robt Roberts
Peter Scott
Christr Clumwell [?]
Josiah Hewlet
John James
Richd Wheeler
Henry VanRiper
Abram Smith
John Francis
John Strong
John Smith
Randall Steward
Saml Thomas
Mark Anthony
Thos Malby
John Richards
Philp Woodly
Robt Smallwood
Fras Marshall
Danl Stewart
John Manuel
James Hogwood
John Cato
Antny Demarest
Caesar Kingsland
Thos Mason
James Richards
Willm Holmes
John Savage
Nathl Wanzey
Jeremiah

Adult females

Dolly Bush
Barbara Hancock
Ann Randall
Ann Sparrow
Ann Johnson
Pendore Keeling
Hannah Moore
Jenny Hunter
Phebe Randall
Sarah Stevens
Judith Christeen
Peggy Richard
Elizth White
Nancy Elliot
Mary Coles
Sally Williams
Phillis Crutchley
Elanor Flemming
Rachael Johnson
Peggy Jackson
Hannah Flemming
Nancy Mead
Thama [?] Steward
Polly Richards
Jenny Coddimus
Tillah Mosely
Nelly Smallwood
Jane Marshall
Mary Smith or Savage [sic]
Susannah VanRiper
Dinah Strong
Mary VanRiper
Lydia Sally
Betsey Holmes
Sarah Flee
Rachel Dey
Suckey Smith
Dinah Kingsland
Patty Mosely
Sarah Hutchins
Jane Francis
Chloe Johnson

Children 10 and above

Esther Richards 12
Lucy Marshall 11
Sarah Kingsland 12

"Negro Children under 10 years old"

Robt Hancock 6
Andw Johnson 18mo
Thos McLeod 3
Moses Stevens 3
Dick Richards 4
Andw Cox 6mo
Peggy Cox 3
Jacob Crutchley 5
John Flemming 4
James Johnson 3
Rachel Jackson 8
Lydia Jackson 6
Ann Jackson 1
Peter Scarborough 8mo
Charlotte Steward 8
Nancy Steward 4
Jacob Steward 6mo
John Coddimus 6
Harry Coddimus 2
Elizth Marshall 3mo
Thos Strong 7
John VanRiper 18mo
Willm Holmes 3
Jenny Mosely 2mo
Rose Hutchins 7mo
Jenny Francis 6
Ralph Francis 4
Sarah Francis 18mo

[**A variant list shows the following additional persons bound for St. John Harbour, or who may have been bound there, rather than for Annapolis Royal.**]

Jacob Adams (drowned 27 Aug.); Jerh Smith, Benj Lightfoot, Saml Saunders, Hannah Bummell, Sarah Steward, Judith Jackson (all discharged while still at NY); Bob Johnson (died 28 Aug.); Nelly Cox (died 31 Aug.); Polly Edwards 9 (died 30 Aug.); Hannah Holmes 8 mo (died 31 Aug.); James Richards 2 (died 29 Aug.); Thos Williams 3 mo (died 31 Aug.)

Note: This list is of unusual value in that it names all family members and even gives children's ages. Spelling of names sometimes varies considerably from the parallel list in the Book of Negroes: G.R. Hodges, ed., *Black Loyalist Directory: African Americans in Exile after the American Revolutio*n (Garland Pub. in association with the New England Historic Genealogical Society, 1996), 89–103.

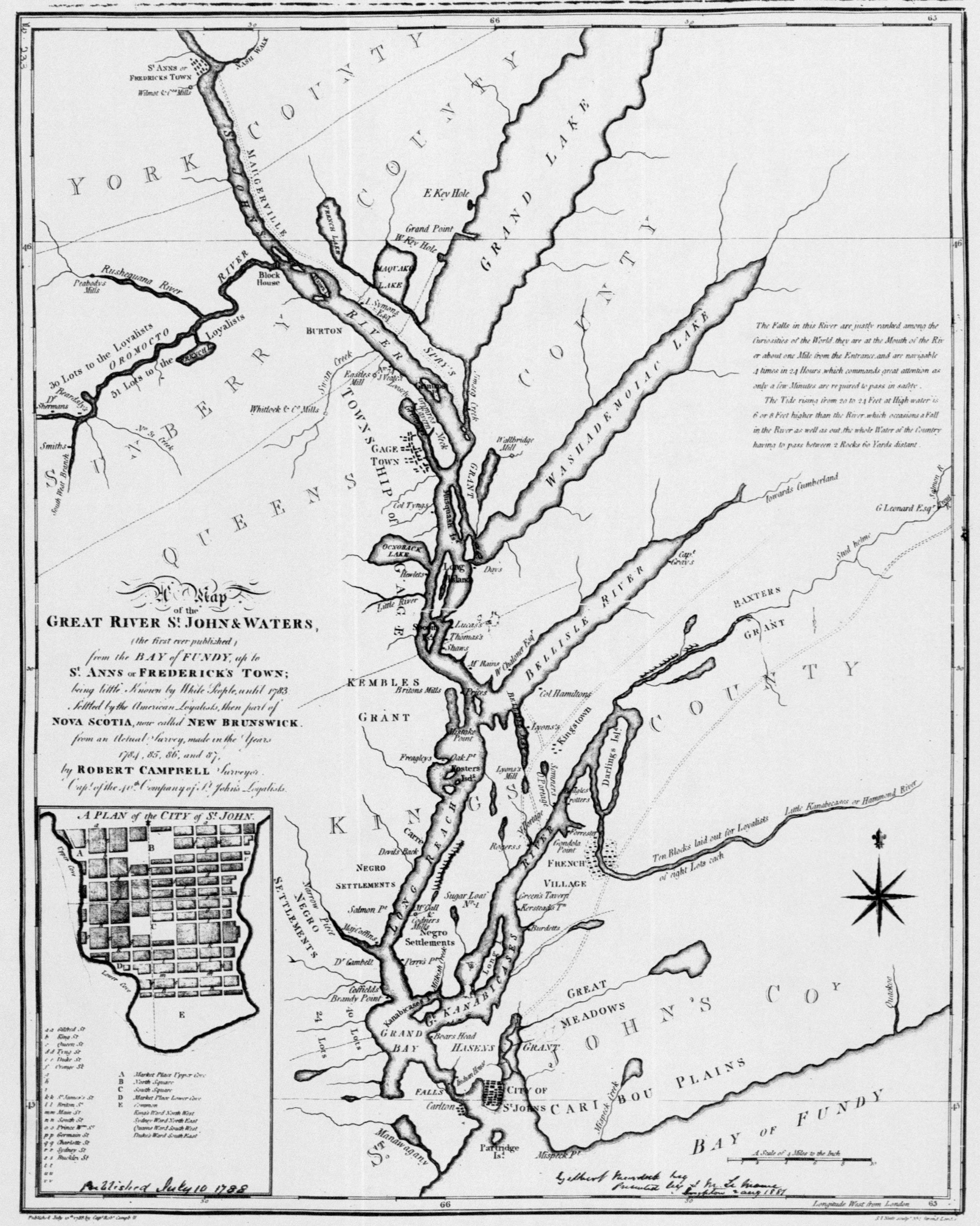

A Map of the GREAT RIVER St. JOHN & WATERS,
(the first ever published)
from the BAY of FUNDY, up to
St. ANNS or FREDERICK'S TOWN;
being little Known by White People, until 1783.
Settled by the American Loyalists, then part of
NOVA SCOTIA, now called NEW BRUNSWICK.
from an Actual Survey, made in the Years
1784, 85, 86, and 87,
by ROBERT CAMPBELL Surveyor.
Capt. of the 40th Company of St. John's Loyalists.
A PLAN of the CITY of St. JOHN.
The Falls in this River are justly ranked among the Curiosities of the World, they are at the Mouth of the River or about one Mile from the Entrance, and are navigable 4 times in 24 Hours which commands great attention as only a few Minutes are required to pass in safety.
The Tide rising from 20 to 24 Feet at High water is 6 or 8 Feet higher than the River, which occasions a Fall in the River as well as out, the whole Water of the Country having to pass between 2 Rocks 60 Yards distant.
YORK COUNTY
SUNBERRY COUNTY
QUEENS COUNTY
KINGS COUNTY
St. JOHN'S COY
St. Anns or Fredricks Town
Nashwalk
Maugerville
Grand Lake
Washademoiac Lake
Bellisle River
Oromocto
Burton
Gage Town
Kembles Grant
Baxters Grant
Negro Settlements
Long Reach
Kanabicases
Grand Bay
French Village
Great Meadows
Hasens Grant
City of St. Johns
Carlton
Falls
Caribou Plains
Partridge Is.
Bay of Fundy
Ten Blocks laid out for Loyalists of eight Lots each
Little Kanabecasis or Hammond River
Published July 10 1788
Longitude West from London

The Royal Vow

In 1776 war sparked to life.
The banshee screams of revolution
Howled flames across British America.
The King needed more cannon fodder
To season and secure his empire.
Enslaved Africans craved only freedom.
An' so there was a promise.
The deal was forged by blood and broken bones
That should any shackled African back the Crown
They'd taste freedom, inhale liberty, and dance on their own land
As supremely valued — and prestigious — British citizens.
They need only trade chains for firing guns, fixed bayonets
Need only stab, rip, and kill.
The meat of liberty was to be chewed
Off the bones of war.
Washed down with their oppressors' blood.
Only then could once-slaves become liberated citizens.
That was the promise.

(opposite) Robert Campbell, surveyor, *A Map of the Great River St. John & Waters*, 1788 (PANB MC3326-1301)

1783 Over 3,500 Blacks, free and enslaved, arrived in the Maritimes with the United Empire Loyalists. As many as 1,500 settled in what became the province of New Brunswick in 1784. Many Black Loyalists settled around Saint John, although the land they were granted (marked as "Negro Settlements" in the 1788 map on page 20, near the modern town of Grand Bay–Westfield, as well as on the Kingston Peninsula and Loch Lomond) was a long way outside Saint John and often unsuitable for farming. The Black settlers had few resources to assist them (Spray 2021, 3–33).

Sales at Auction,
By JAMES HAYT,
On THURSDAY 14th inſtant,
At his AUCTION ROOM:
A VARIETY of Ironmongery and Cutlery neatly aſſorted and in the beſt order,
20 Kegs choice Crackers,
A hogſhead Madeira Wine of an excellent quality,
6 Barrels very good Sugar,
2 Puncheons Rum,
2 Caſks Coffee,
And a variety of DRY GOODS as uſual.

JAMES HAYT,
HAS FOR SALE,
A BLACK BOY, fourteen years of age, in full vigor of health, very active, has a pleaſing countenance and every ability to render himſelf uſeful and agreeable in a family. The title for him is indiſputable.

Slavery advertisements in the *Royal Gazette*, September 12, 1786 (above), and September 11, 1787 (Provincial Archives of New Brunswick/PANB)

1785 Sir Guy Carleton, Governor General of British North America, issued instructions that votes by Black residents were not to be counted or included in the General Assembly elections.

TO BE SOLD,
A Likely, healthy negro wench, of about 17 years of age, is well calculated for the country, and ſold for want of employ.—The title indiſputable. If not ſold within 8 days from the date hereof by private ſale, ſhe will be ſold at public auction.—Enquire of THOMAS MALLARD.

When the United Empire Loyalists arrived in New Brunswick, they brought their property — including enslaved peoples — with them. Slavery was a reality in New Brunswick for the first fifty years of the province's history. It was abolished on August 1, 1834, through Britain's Slavery Abolition Act, 1833, the anniversary of which is celebrated as Emancipation Day (Spray 2021, 16–28).

New-Brunswick.

SAINT JOHN,
TUESDAY, February 18.

Laſt week the Hilary Term of the Supreme Court was held at Fredericton, at which we underſtand there were few cauſes agitated of any conſequence excepting one upon an Habeas Corpus brought by a Negro Woman claimed as a ſlave by Captain Jones of Fredericton, in order to procure her liberation. The queſtion of Slavery upon general principles was diſcuſſed at great length, by the Counſel on both ſides, and we underſtand the Court were divided in their opinions, the Chief Juſtice and Judge Upham being of opinion that by the exiſting Law of this Province, Negroes may be held as Slaves here, and Judge Allen and Judge Saunders being of opinion, that the Law upon that ſubject is the ſame here as in England and therefore that Slavery is not recognized by the Laws of this Province.—The Court being thus divided, no judgment was entered.

Slavery and habeas corpus in the *Royal Gazette*, February 18, 1800 (PANB)

1792 After eight years of promises of land grants broken by the British government, 1,096 Blacks, under the leadership of Thomas Peters, left Nova Scotia and New Brunswick for Sierra Leone in West Africa. There they helped in the development of the community of Freetown, today the capital and largest city in Sierra Leone (Fergusson, 1971; Walker, 1976; Wilson, 1976).

1800–1860 During the nineteenth century, tens of thousands of Black Americans escaped slavery via the Underground Railroad and came to Canada. One branch of the Underground Railroad went through Maine to Carlingford, New Brunswick. Life was still dangerous even upon reaching New Brunswick — slave catchers were searching for any solitary Black persons, with the aim of capturing them and returning them for a reward to slave owners in the Southern United States. For a Black person living alone without any protection, the nineteenth century was a frightening time to be free in rural New Brunswick.

The Tomlinson Lake Hike to Freedom happens every October in Carlingford, New Brunswick, the site of the northernmost terminus of the Underground Railroad. The 2.75 km hike commemorates the enslaved peoples who travelled from the South to Fort Fairfield, Maine, and crossed into New Brunswick. The enslaved peoples were told, “Follow the path and when you see water”—Tomlinson Lake—“you are in Canada and safe and free.” Our knowledge of the Tomlinson Lake terminus owes much to Ruth and Art Mraz’s research into the history of the Friends Church, Fort Fairfield, Maine, and the 1995 discovery of a hiding place in the church.

1806 The Black community of Elm Hill was founded near Otnabog Lake by freed slaves from New York. In its day, Elm Hill was a thriving community with a school, church, and community hall.

Today, the community is small, with less than fifty year-round residents, although some descendants have put mini homes or trailers on their heritage property and spend summers in this picturesque area of New Brunswick (Spray 2021, 42–51).

Exodus

1791.
Hear this, Black Loyalist!
Eight years of false freedom have meant
Sleeping in the ground, no better than a mole.
Always starving.
And so you plotted on farm plots
To seed independence and cultivate pride.
Instead, you got ambushed by surveyors and pushed
Onto barren rock, or into swamps.
All soils impossible to plough.
And when you failed, and had to beg for crumbs.
The palefaces cursed you as "lazy" and a "burden."

Well, perhaps there was hope in religion?
A pathway to freedom through unwavering belief in that gospel.
You walked ten hours to baptize your children.
Because "taking the waters" was as good as voting
Yourself into the Equality, that Caucasian Christians
Belted out, chapter and verse, in hymnals and law books.

Instead, your congregation suffered segregation.
If a Black preacher was caught baptizing a white believer,
Hellish men would rampage through their church
And publicly beat the pastor into suddenly bloody floorboards.
Which reduced your own hymns to a hum.
You gnawed the worst rations, cornmeal and molasses.
Never fish, never wheat.
The sweat of your back never got you seated at the feast.

Slave twice as long as whites to be paid half as much.
But your cheap-bought labour outraged white workers.
Who, scared and jealous, trampled down Black settlements at night.
Burning, bashing, and slashing all those they blamed
For taking bread out of their mouths.
And so you lost your appetite for King and Crown.

The Empire was fed up with Black Loyalist spirituals
And petitions.
The Crown now barked: "Back to Africa with y'all!"
If you'd sail away under the Royal Navy flag
There'd be free land, seeds, hoes, ploughs, tents, and huts.
To sweeten the deal, the redcoats kidnapped and drugged
Fifty white women.
Forcing them to marry any Black Loyalist who agreed to leave.
And so you and almost half of the Black Atlantic Maritimers
Elected to step aboard the boats, bitter and distrustful
Yet still hoping that you'd finally arrive to find
The Promised Land at last.

1813 Between September 1813 and August 1816, approximately two thousand Black refugees from the War of 1812 arrived in the Maritimes, some five hundred settling in New Brunswick and the remainder in Nova Scotia.

Their settlement was full of difficulties. Discrimination in land grants, jobs, and supplies was rampant as the refugees tried to make their livings and provide better lives for their families.

1817 Black refugee William Flood petitioned the House of Assembly on behalf of a number of refugees who had been granted land at Willow Grove, an area outside of Saint John near Loch Lomond. The refugees were seeking financial assistance to cover the costs of surveying the land and settling it, as they had barely any money to support themselves. The government refused Flood's petition, and the settlers had to pay the costs themselves, with the help of the judge who'd heard the petition. It was only when the judge advanced part of the money to the refugees that the government reimbursed the judge (although the money the refugees paid themselves was not reimbursed).

Three hundred and seventy-one Black refugees eventually settled at Willow Grove. They were granted three-year occupation licences for fifty acres of land per family but were not given official title. It was only in 1836 that those settlers who remained on the land were able to buy titles to the land for twenty shillings (Spray 2021, 44–51).

Descendants from those land grants still live in Willow Grove today. Although the Gothic revival church that was built in the 1870s was destroyed by fire in 1931, there is a small replica of the church at the Black Settlement Burial Ground that tells the story and history of this beautiful Black settlement.

One member of the McCarty Peters family recently bought land outside of Saint John, the original (non-Indigenous) owner of which was Hannah Flood, who was granted title in 1837. It is possible that Hannah may have been related to William Flood, who originally petitioned for a land grant at Willow Grove in 1817.

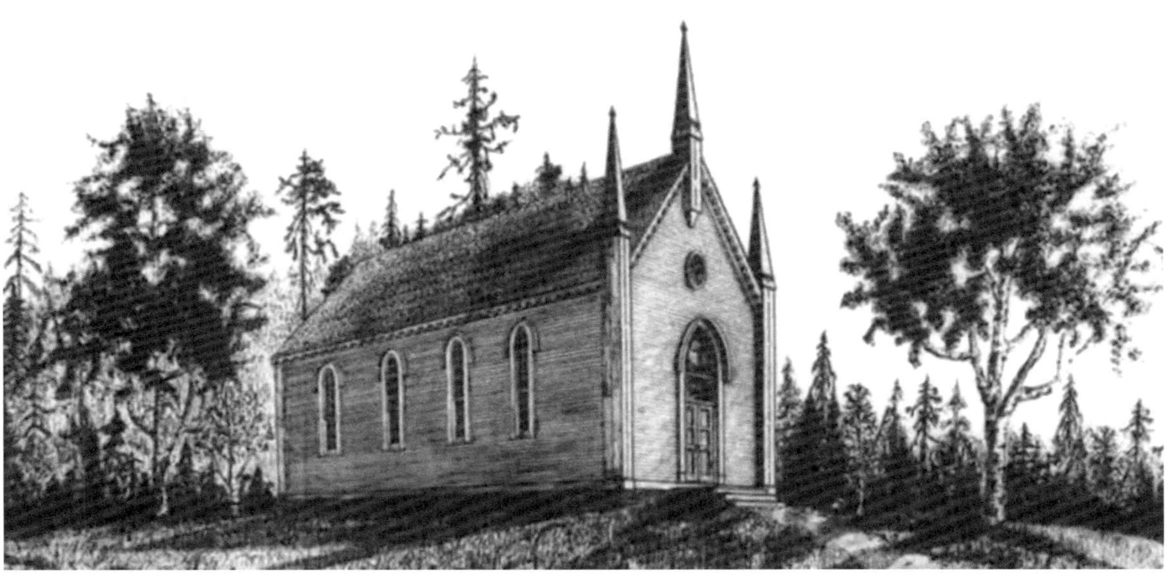

Willow Grove Church (Ralph Thomas / New Brunswick Black History Society)

1820 The African School in Saint John opens in August, the first school for Black children in the province. Further schools opened at Loch Lomond / Willow Grove in 1825, at Fredericton in 1826, and at Kingsclear in 1831. These schools were established because Black children were often prevented from going to school with White children. Funding for these schools was precarious, and they often slipped in and out of existence. A Black school in Saint John still existed in the twentieth century (Spray 2021, 54).

1833 The Slavery Abolition Act was passed by the British government, coming into effect on August 1, 1834.

1848 The Negro Day School was reopened in Loch Lomond under the legislation of the New Brunswick Government.

The Pit of Loyalty

1785
Freedom, Can you imagine it?
To be Black and loyal
Meant a mountain-sized leap
From being tasked to slave fifteen-hour, back-breaking days
Beaten and whipped under heavy sun.
To suddenly you, your partner, and children, are free.
Now a British citizen of New Brunswick.
Loyal to a King who legalized and got stinking rich off your dirty work.
The selling off of wives, husbands, and children
To rapists, torturers, and slave drivers.
But now you and your family are free.
An' standing on land granted you for your service.
But it is way farther north, and cold.

Shovels bounce off the frozen ground as if they'd struck steel.
Sparks of frustration freeze instantly. Then melt ashen into despair.
Yet you are free, so you refuse to freeze.
By order of the King, crates got packed with blankets
Shipped north to New Brunswick from New York.
So that Black Loyalists would feel the warmth of the Empire.
Yet every single blanket was polka-dotted with holes.
Nor were planks and nails provided to raise up a home.
An' so you dig
Into the steel earth.

This small square hole in the ground
Covered in sticks and secured with stones.
Is where you an' your family will sleep.
Wrapped around each other.
Wrapped in the tattered leftovers of loyalty.
This is how you and your family will outlast winter.
Blasted by frostbite, scurvy, and gangrene
An left starving.
For the promise.

Family Slavery

In early New Brunswick, 1787,
You could legally own a human being.
Like a Christmas tree, you could be brought to someone's home
gift-wrapped in rope, tinsel-drizzled with chains.

The husband who bought your life would yell.
Hollering everyone into the living room.
He'll begin to sing how much easier their lives will be.
Praising your boundless good temper, your unbounded skills.

The wife will bark orders, and daily you will
Nurture the garden
Hustle up meals, bustle to serve,
Scour dishes, swish brooms across floors,
Feed infants your very nipples.
But nothing will ever be good enough.

The children will force you to play. Thinking that that's your real work.
Then you will crawl into the cold root cellar
Under the warm house.
Where you will snooze, cobwebbed in iron,
Kicking at the rats hungry to gnaw at your toes.

You dream of running away.
Of seeking freedom
Seeking anything resembling
The promise.

To the Lovers of Freedom.

There will be a Soiree held at Union Hall, Horsefield Street, this evening, the 15th, at half-past seven o'clock, for the purpose of raising funds to purchase the son of George and Easter Lewis, who is now a slave in Richmond Va. We hope that all friends to humanity and lovers of freedom will attend on the occasion. The Rev. Mr. Ferrie, and Rev. Mr. Bill, who have taken an active part in the subject will address the audience; there will also be several other gentlemen who will in the course of the evening, deliver some interesting remarks upon Slave Life.—As a part of the purchase money is already reised, it is expected there will be a gcoh attendance, so that the proceeds will furnish a good addition to the amount already in hand. The Refreshments will be served up in good style by Mr. C. Sparrow, and Mr. Whetsel. Tickets 2s 6d; each.—*Communicated.*

1850–1861 The Fugitive Slave Act was passed by the US Congress in 1850, leading to a significant increase of Black migration to Canada via the Underground Railroad. Between 1851 and 1861, New Brunswick's Black population doubled to nearly 1,600 (having previously declined significantly, as many of the initial influx of refugees from the War of 1812 emigrated from Canada).

Among those who came to New Brunswick was Robert Patterson, who arrived in 1852. Patterson had escaped slavery in Virginia and was living in Boston when the Fugitive Slave Act was passed. In 1860, he was made a freeman of the city, allowing him to operate a business—a privilege afforded to few Blacks in the city. Patterson kept an eating house, located on the west side of Germain Street above King, and supported the refounding of the Black school in Saint John. The school was in the South End, on the second floor of St. Philip's African Methodist Episcopal Church, near the corner of Pitt and Queen Streets.

When escaped and freed slaves arrived in the province, the scars and hardships of slavery remained visible, and power imbalances and discrimination remained. Many new arrivals had abandoned old relationships and needed to find work to provide for their families and care for their own small plots of land. These inequities and imbalances of power still persist today.

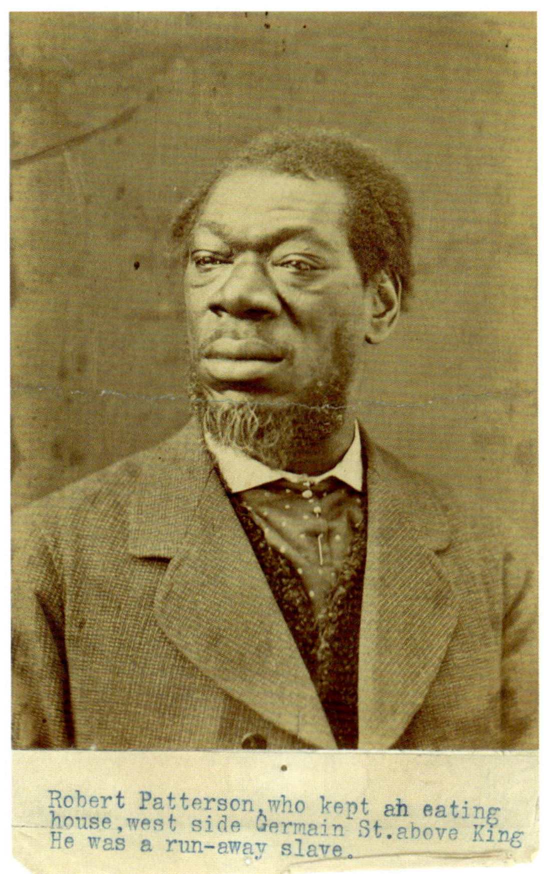

(above) "To the Lovers of Freedom," *The Christian Visitor*, September 15, 1858 (PANB)

(right) Robert Patterson, ca. 1872–76 (PANB P256-510)

Underground Railroad

1842.
You are one of three million enslaved Africans in the United States of America.
An' your priceless life carries the value of a house.
By encouraging and supporting escape, the antislavery Abolitionists hoped
To bankrupt the cruel institution, so that the very idea of slavery would rust.

An' so on a Mississippi plantation an Abolitionist pamphlet finds your work-weary eyes.
A wealthy New York tycoon begs you to flee north. Quotes him saying,
"The Abolitionist knows no more grateful employment than that of
Carrying the dog-and-rifle-hunted slave to Canada."

So you run.

The Dixie-to-North-Star Underground Railroad is a death march.
Study the hidden codes on the clothes lines. The drying quilts tell you
When to rest and when to go.
But you're never safe, and there are thousands of miles left.

You're gonna have to crawl in mud, swim exhausted up rivers.
But mostly you will sprint night and day through the trees.
Barking dogs and horseback bounty hunters hounding you, haunting you.
You will be too terrified to sleep, desperate to eat.

So you run.

You arrive in the city of Baltimore, decades after the 1808 ruling.
Importing Africans to slave in shackles was now illegal.
No problem, now lining every Baltimore street are shops
That double as prisons for those born in chains.
And all over Maryland breeding camps grow like cancerous capitalist tumors.
To ensure America's shackled labour force never dies out.

True to their word, the Abolitionists find and hide you
In a carriage northbound for New York.
You then journey to Maine to reach the most northerly part
of the Underground Railroad:
Tomlinson Lake, New Brunswick, Canada.
At the end of your two-thousand-mile odyssey,
You will breathe a sigh of relief,
Excited to embrace
The promise.

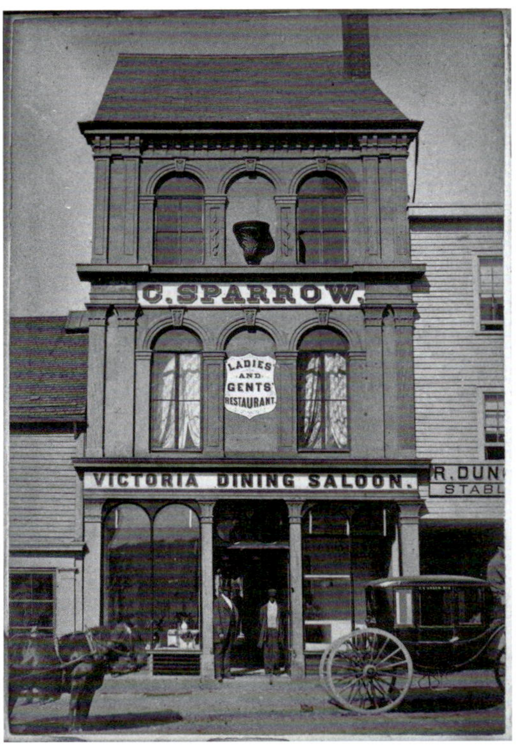

1862 Cornelius Sparrow opened his first restaurant, the Royal Saloon, at 18 Charlotte Street in Saint John. His establishment carried foreign and domestic fruit. Born in Norfolk, Virginia in 1824, Sparrow came to Saint John in 1851, having escaped slavery, along with his wife, thanks to the help of the Boston Vigilance Committee, an abolitionist organization.

In 1874, Sparrow moved his business to 8 Germain Street. His brother George teamed up with him in 1877, and they started a new business, the Victoria Dining Saloon. After they moved the business to 35 Germain Street, the building was destroyed in the Great Fire of 1877. They reopened the saloon a year later (*Rediscovering the Roots of Black New Brunswickers*).

(left) Cornelius Sparrow's dining saloon, ca. 1870–77 (PANB P338-293)

Eliza (1783–1888) was born into slavery in Virginia. At an early age, she was brought to Bermuda and later to Saint John, where she became a servant to the Gagetown lawyer James Peters. After fifteen years of service, Eliza fled and married James Taylor of French Village. Eliza and her husband were among the original settlers of Willow Grove. In later life, Eliza was a well-known figure on the corner of Sydney Street and King's Square in Saint John, where she peddled household wares and was known as the Belle of Willow Grove for her choice of brightly coloured, flowing gowns and lavish hats (*Rediscovering the Roots of Black New Brunswickers*).

(right) Eliza Taylor, ca. 1872–76 (PANB P256-641)

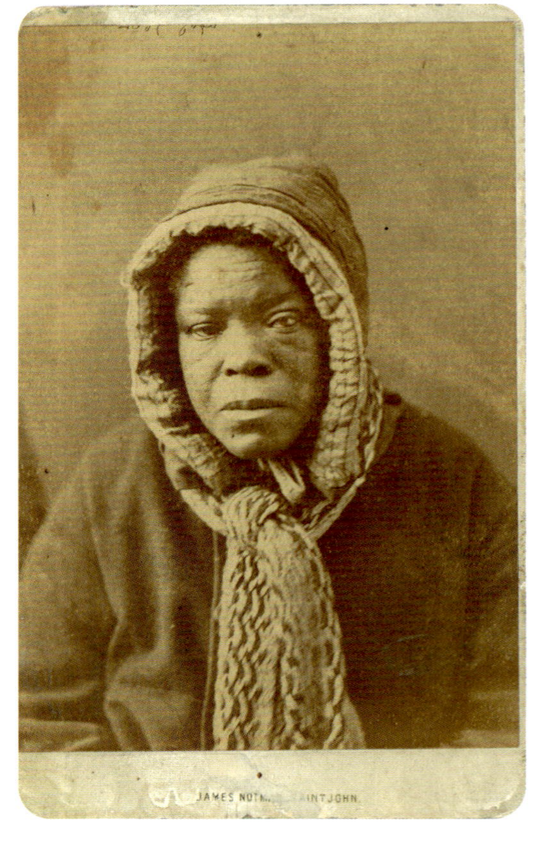

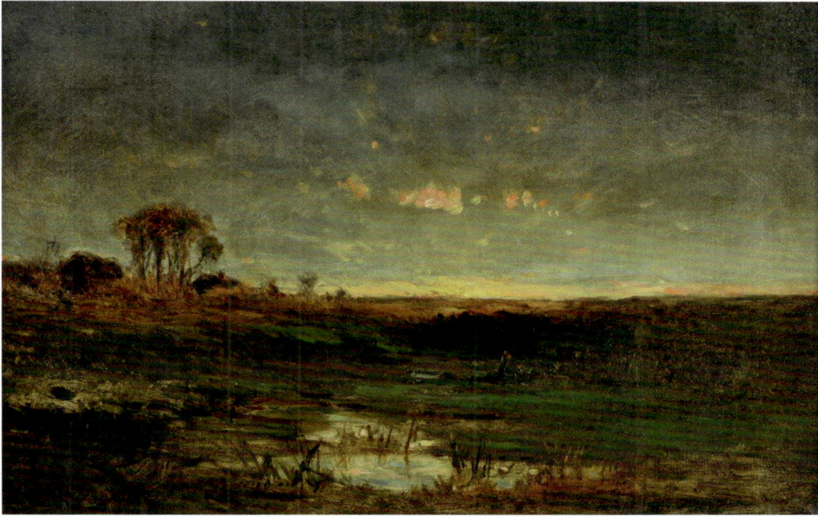

Edward Mitchell Bannister, *Landscape with Swamps and Trees*, 1881
New Brunswick Museum—Musée du Nouveau-Brunswick, www.nbm-mnb.ca A59.46

1876 Edward Mitchell Bannister of Saint Andrews became the first Black person to win a major art prize in North America when he won the first-prize bronze medal for his enormous painting *Under the Oaks* at the Philadelphia Centennial Exposition.

Bannister had moved to Boston in 1848, where he worked as a barber before becoming a painter. In 1870, he moved from Boston to Rhode Island, where he became a widely respected artist. He was an original board member of the Rhode Island School of Design and was instrumental in establishing the closely affiliated Providence Art Club (*Rediscovering the Roots of Black New Brunswickers*; Manthey, Nelson, Whitfield, and Woods, 2026).

1882 Abraham Beverley Walker became the first Canadian-born Black lawyer in Canada. Born on the Kingston Peninsula to a family of Black Loyalists, Walker studied law at the Saint John Law School (now the Faculty of Law at the University of New Brunswick) and was called to the New Brunswick bar in 1882. Walker experienced racial discrimination while working as a lawyer, particularly when he was passed over for appointment as a QC.

In 1903, Walker created *Neith*, the first Black literary magazine in Canada. Named after the Egyptian goddess of war and hunting, *Neith* sadly had a short run of only five issues. Despite suffering from discrimination during his legal career, Walker was posthumously honoured with the Order of New Brunswick in 2019 (Little, 2019).

NEITH

CONTENTS FOR FEBRUARY, 1903.

Cover designed by A. J. Charlton.	
W. P. Dole, B. A., LL. D.	Frontispiece
Prefatory Remarks	1
The Late Coal Strike	1
Hayti and its Enemies	2
The Archbishop of Canterbury	3
Emile Zola	4
Lost Israel Found	5
The Art Exhibition in St. John.	5
Negrophobes Should be Kept out of Africa	6
Treat Boer and Black Alike	6
England and Her Negro Subjects	6
None but White Republicans are Wanted in the South	7
A Most Rabid Negrophobe	7
President Roosevelt on the Appointment of Negroes to Office	8
Industrial Schools for British Negroes	8
An Imperial Zollverein	12
Let the Natives of South Africa Have Justice and Education	13
Tillmanism, or Mob Rule in the South	16
The Negro Problem, and How to Solve it. No. 1. Part 1	22
The Museum Shell — By Charles Campbell	26
The Negro in New Brunswick — By the Rev. W. O. Raymond, M. A., LL. D.	27
The Canadian Outlook — By the Rev. Robert Wilson, Ph. D.	35
The Progress of Canada — By the Hon. H. A. McKeown, B. A., LL. B., K. C., M. P. P.	39
Pleasures of the Imagination — By Geo. G. Walker.	46
Fidei Responsa — By W. P. Dole, B. A., LL. D.	51
Literary Notes	53
Editorial Announcements	59

Issued monthly: 10c. a single copy: $1.00 a year.

N. B.—The $1.00 a year applies only to subscribers who reside in Canada or in the United States. In all other Countries the subscription price is $1.50 a year.

Advertising rates on application.

All money should be sent by Express, or Post Office Order, or Registered Letter, addressed to A. B Walker, Editor of NEITH, St. John, N. B., Canada.

Printed by Paterson & Co., 107 Germain Street, St. John, N. B., Canada.

(left) The table of contents of the February 1903 edition of *Neith* (PANB A004198-F14898)

1883 Arthur Richardson became the first Black person in New Brunswick to graduate from the University of New Brunswick (*Rediscovering the Roots of Black New Brunswickers*).

1886 William Gosman graduated from the New Brunswick Normal College—the first Black person to do so—and began teaching at the Elm Hill School. This school served not only as a school for Black children, but also as the community Sunday school (Marshall Smith, 2010, 46).

Georgina Whetsel was a Saint John businesswoman who inherited an ice business from her husband, following his death in 1884. She was also a social justice advocate, who wrote often to the Daily Telegraph to protest racial discrimination, sexism, and local displays of blackface. In 1895, Whetsel was featured in Women's Era, a Boston-based monthly newspaper, which was the first national newspaper published by and for African American women. When Whetsel sold her company in the early 1900s, she was believed to be the wealthiest Black woman in North America (*Rediscovering the Roots of Black New Brunswickers*).

Mrs. R. [Georgina] Whetsel, "Fair Play to a Woman," *Daily Telegraph* (Saint John), March 1, 1889 (PANB)

Fair Play to a Woman.

To the Editor of the Telegraph:—

A few words from Mrs. Whetzel concerning yesterday's carnival: I think the way they represented my business in their street procession, yesterday, was not at all fair, and for fear some one would think I had something to do with getting it up, I simply say I had not, and if I had it would have been far more creditable. I think that all the intelligent people of St. John will agree with me that I do my ice business in a way that ought not to be ridiculed. I spend a great deal of money every year to keep the wagons, horses, harness, everything in regards to my business in keeping with our nice city. I I think I can safely say they were never kept looking in the past as well. I do not know what firm represented my business, but who ever they were, they know very little about it. I see they represent my business with all blackened faces, but I may tell them that I hire as many poor white men as I do poor colored men. It makes no difference to me as long as they can do their work what color they are. But one noticeable feature in the St. John procession was that the larger part was taken up with the African caricatures, and always in the lowest and most degraded state. This may be a mark of culture and refinement, bnt pardon me if I don't think so.

MRS. R. WHETZEL.

St. John, Feb. 28.

(clockwise from right)
Children at Browns Flat in the early twentieth century (PANB P338-1768). Browns Flat is on the Saint John River at Long Reach.

Charlie Diggs, Indiantown, 1913 (PANB P551-333). "Indiantown" was located near the mouth of the river in Saint John.

Black settlers near Grand Bay–Westfield, late nineteenth century (New Brunswick Black History Society)

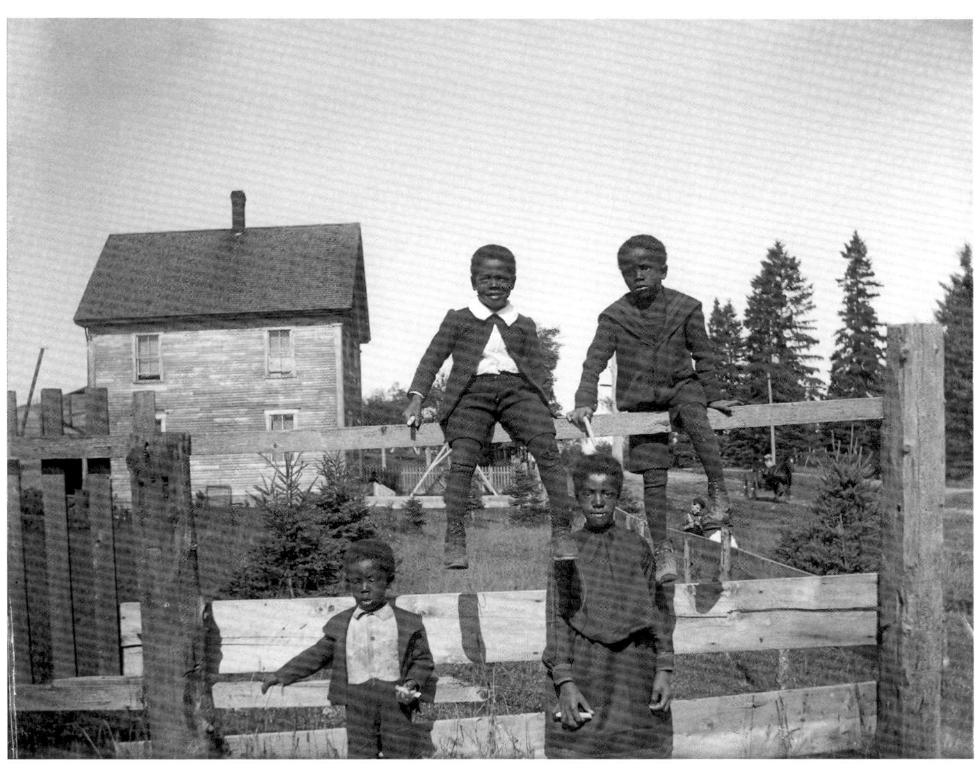

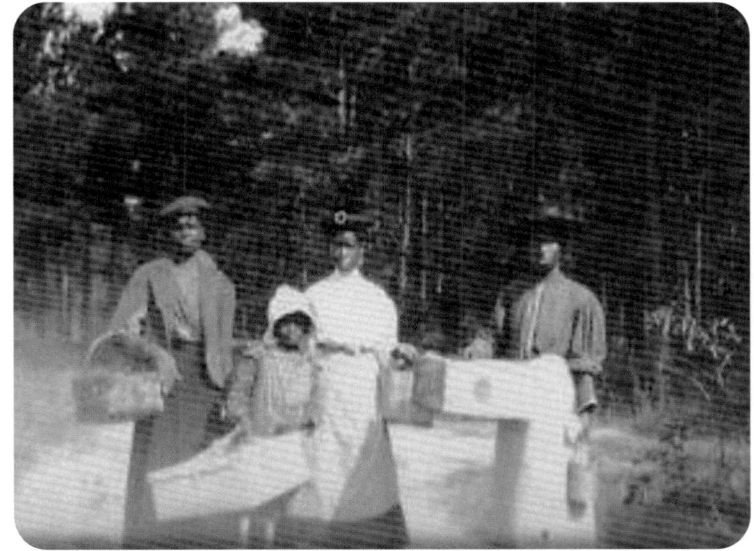

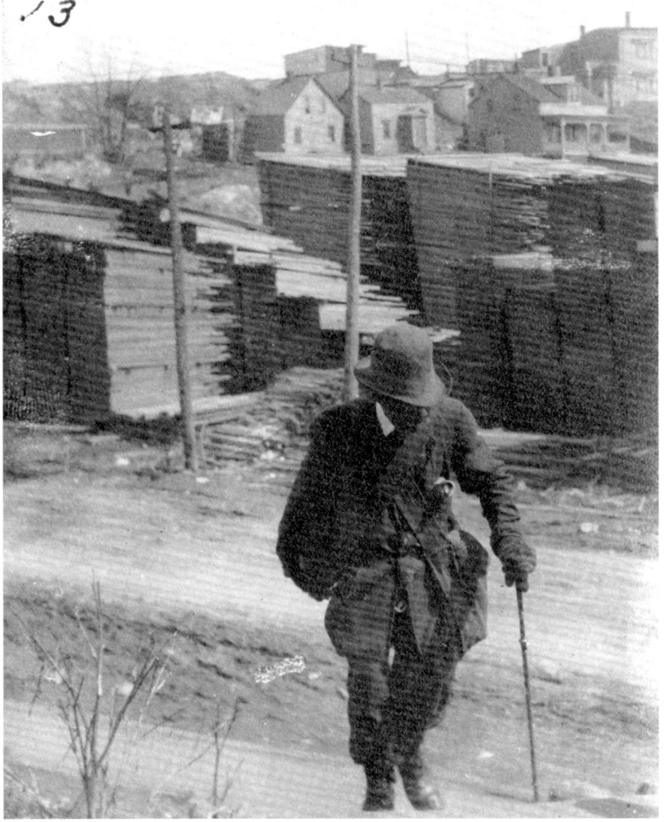

1905 Mary Matilda "Tillie" Winslow became the first Black woman to graduate university in New Brunswick. Winslow earned honours in classics, ranking at the top of her class. Even though Winslow received such high academic standing, sadly she could not find work in her home province. She subsequently moved to the United States and worked as a teacher, including at the well-known Tuskegee Institute, founded by Booker T. Washington, a former runaway slave. Her children and grandchildren still live in the US today (*Rediscovering the Roots of Black New Brunswickers*).

That same year, Saint John athlete Eldridge Eatman set a Canadian record of 9.8 seconds for the 100-yard sprint. Eatman was one of the first Black sprinters in North America to compete with White athletes. He later served in the First World War and then toured as a singer using the name "the Sprinting Songster."

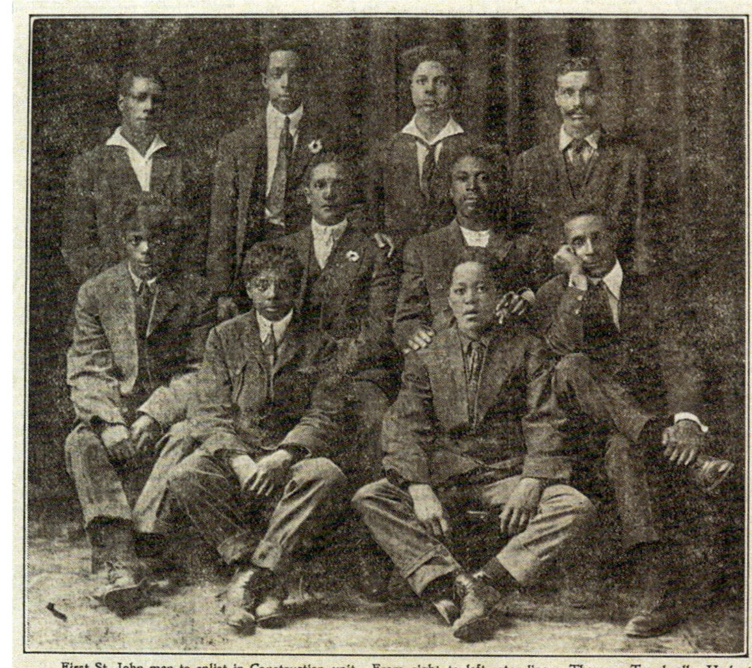

First St. John men to enlist in Construction unit. From right to left—standing: Thomas Treadwell, Herbert Nichols, Roy Hayes, Robert Bushfan; back row, sitting: Charles Williams, James Holmes, Percy Ritchie, Elijah Tyler. In front: A. C. Austin, Harold McCarthy.

1914 The First World War began. Although Black New Brunswickers were keen to serve their country, they were not allowed to operate military machinery or guns and were often barred from serving with White soldiers. The No. 2 Construction Battalion was composed of Black volunteers from New Brunswick and Nova Scotia. The men worked as a construction group, digging trenches and gutters at the front line for the White Canadian soldiers to shoot from.

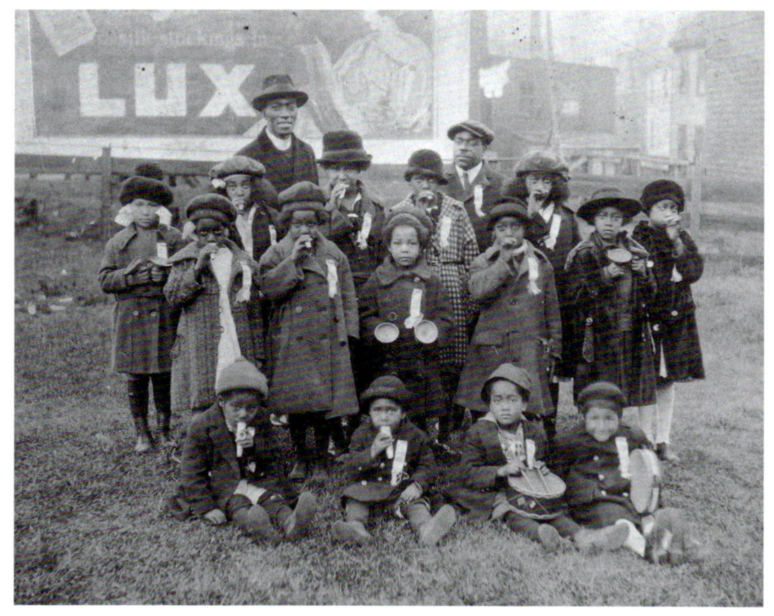

(top to bottom)
No. 2 Construction Battalion coloured soldiers, *Daily Telegraph and Sun* (Saint John), August 17, 1916 (PANB)

Rev. C. Stewart Junior Band, AME churchyard, 1920s (PANB P338-4)

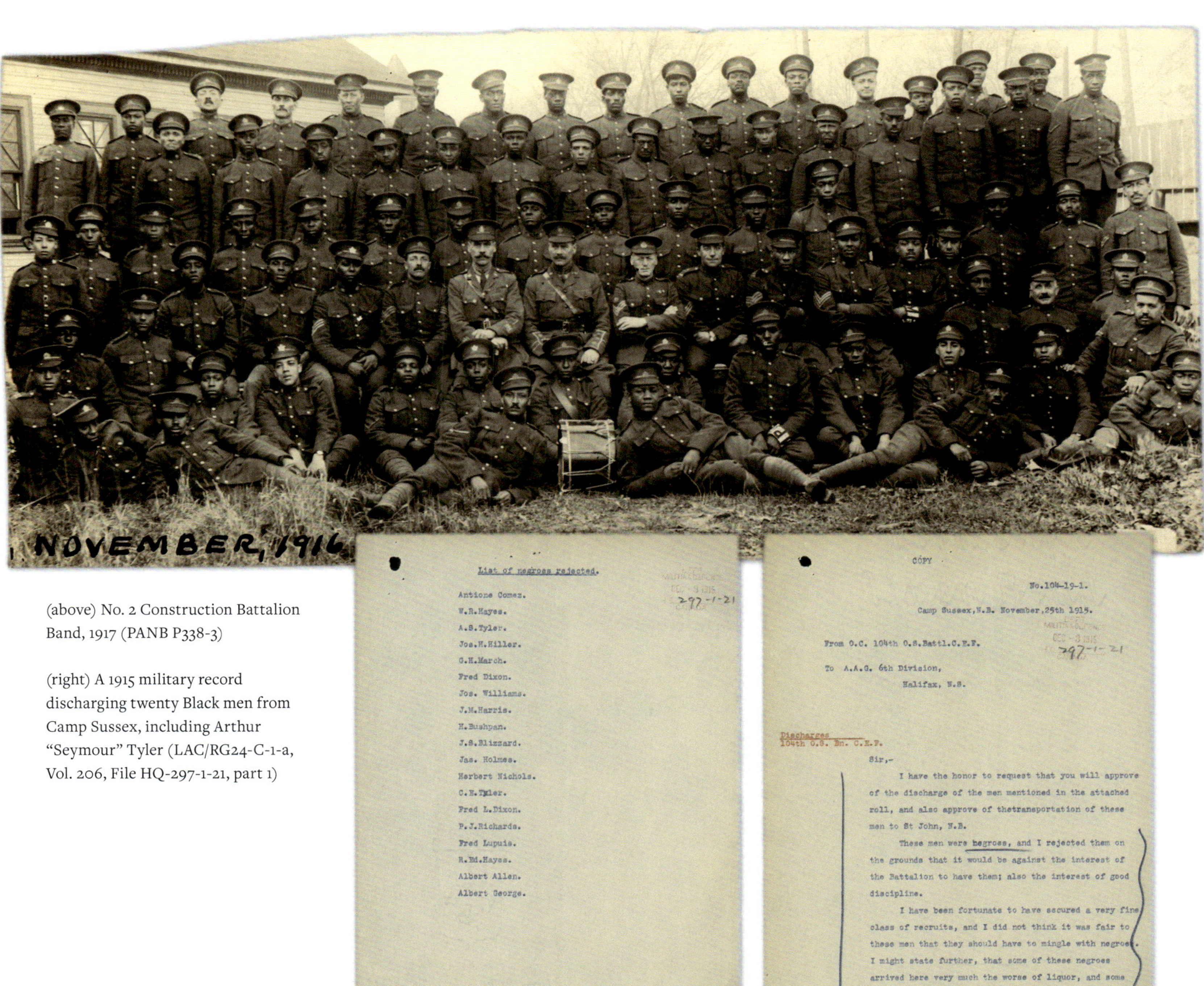

List of negroes rejected.

Antione Comez.
W.R.Hayes.
A.S.Tyler.
Jos.H.Hiller.
G.H.March.
Fred Dixon.
Jos. Williams.
J.M.Harris.
H.Bushpan.
J.S.Blizzard.
Jas. Holmes.
Herbert Nichols.
C.E.Tyler.
Fred L.Dixon.
P.J.Richards.
Fred Lupuis.
R.Ed.Hayes.
Albert Allen.
Albert George.

297-1-21

38

COPY

No.104-19-1.

Camp Sussex, N.B. November, 25th 1915.

From O.C. 104th O.S.Battl.C.E.F.

To A.A.G. 6th Division,
Halifax, N.S.

297-1-21

Discharges
104th O.S. Bn. C.E.F.

Sir,-

I have the honor to request that you will approve of the discharge of the men mentioned in the attached roll, and also approve of thetransportation of these men to St John, N.B.

These men were negroes, and I rejected them on the grounds that it would be against the interest of the Battalion to have them; also the interest of good discipline.

I have been fortunate to have secured a very fine class of recruits, and I did not think it was fair to these men that they should have to mingle with negroes. I might state further, that some of these negroes arrived here very much the worse of liquor, and some of them very insolent and were not proper men to become members of the Battalion.

I have the honour to be,
Sir,
Your obedient servant,

(SIGNED) Geo.W.Fowler, Lt. Col.
Commdg. 104th O.S. Battl.C.E.F.

39

(above) No. 2 Construction Battalion Band, 1917 (PANB P338-3)

(right) A 1915 military record discharging twenty Black men from Camp Sussex, including Arthur "Seymour" Tyler (LAC/RG24-C-1-a, Vol. 206, File HQ-297-1-21, part 1)

During the 1920s and 1930s, Black cultural life thrived, with a proliferation of sports clubs, bands, and other community organizations. The Saint John Royals, an all-Black baseball team, dominated the Saint John South End league, while athlete Clifford "Nick" Skinner set regional records in the hundred-yard dash, high jump, and broad jump (a standing long jump). Yet this thriving cultural life existed alongside subtle, and sometimes overt, displays of racism. Musical groups regularly performed in blackface in Fredericton, and the Ku Klux Klan flourished in the province.

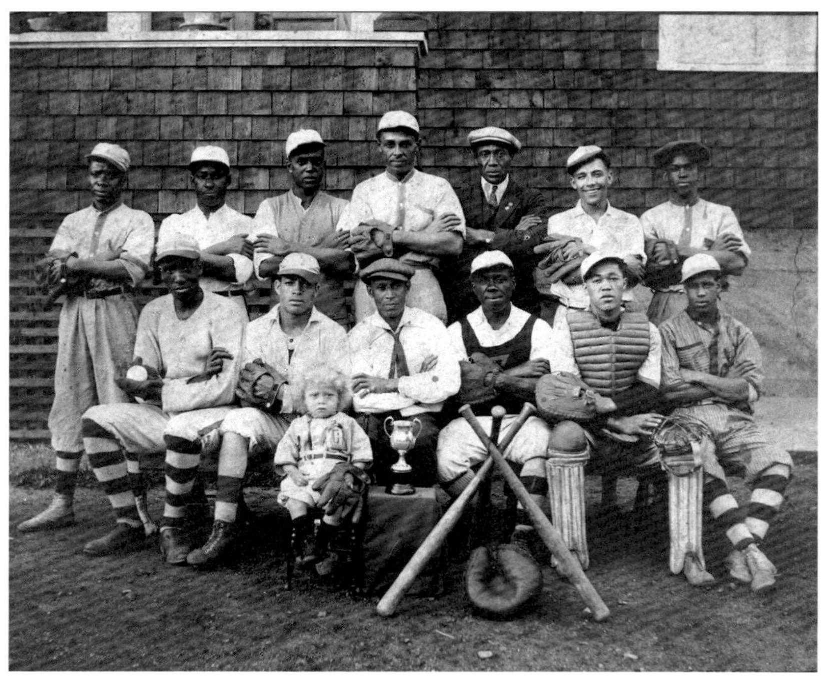

(above) The Saint John Royals, Royal Baseball Intermediate Champions, Saint John, 1922 (PANB P338-2)

(below) Report of a Ku Klux Klan meeting at Barkers Point, *Daily Gleaner*, August 10, 1931 (PANB)

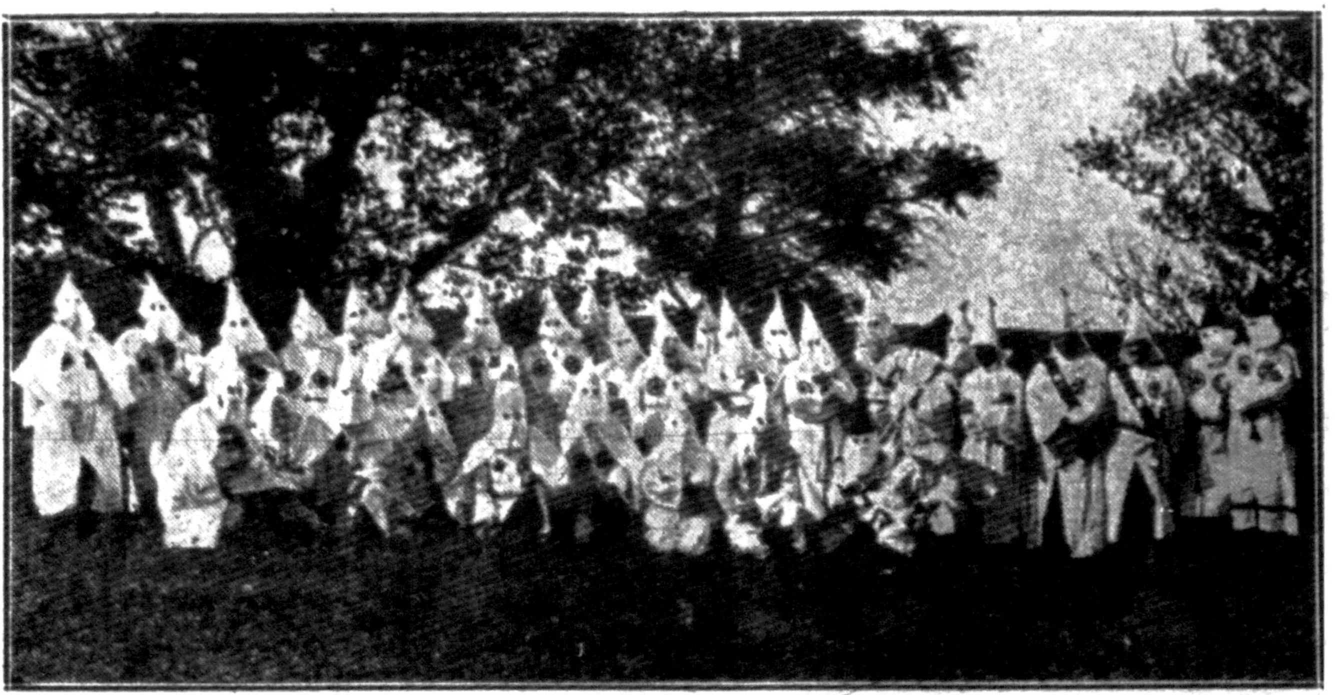

Above is shown a group picture taken at Barker's Point Saturday afternoon, shortly before opening of Provincial Field Day of Order of Ku Klux Klan. The group was formed largely of male members of order, but a few women also are in the party. The Nashwaak River is at the rear of the party posing.

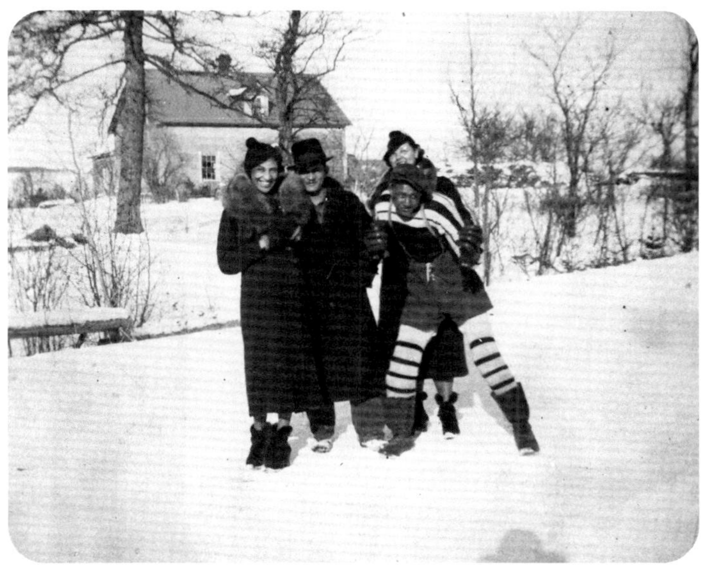

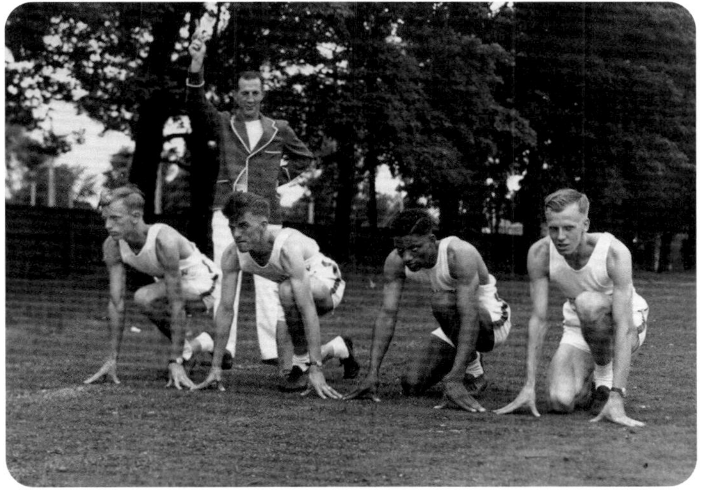

(top to bottom)
Dorothy McCarty, Ralph McCarty, Phyllis McIntyre, and Manny McIntyre, ca. 1950–70 (PANB P498-050)

Carl Howe (third from left) with the Fredericton track team, 1950 (PANB P654-122)

1946 Vincent "Manny" McIntyre became the first Black Canadian to play professional baseball when he debuted for the Sherbrooke Canadiens, a farm team for the St. Louis Cardinals. McIntyre also played hockey for the Sherbrooke Saints, where, with brothers Herb and Ozzie Carnegie, he was part of the famed "Black Aces," the first all-Black line in professional hockey. Officials, fellow players, and fans widely agreed that, had it not been for racial prejudice in sports, the Black Aces would have been able to compete at any level, including the National Hockey League (NHL). McIntyre was inducted into the New Brunswick Sports Hall of Fame in 1977 and, posthumously, into the Canadian Sports Hall of Fame in 2015.

1947 Carl Howe was part of the Fredericton team who won the one-mile relay in the Canadian Junior Track and Field Championships. Born in Devon, on Fredericton's north side, Howe was an outstanding athlete who also played rugby and hockey, as well as being a gifted musician who played with the Golden Bel-Aires and, for twelve years, with the Royal Canadian Artillery Band. In 1971, he became the first Black man to be elected to Fredericton City Council and served as a councillor until 1978.

1958 Fredericton-born Willie O'Ree breaks the colour barrier in the NHL when he debuts for the Boston Bruins. (*Rediscovering the Roots of Black New Brunswickers*).

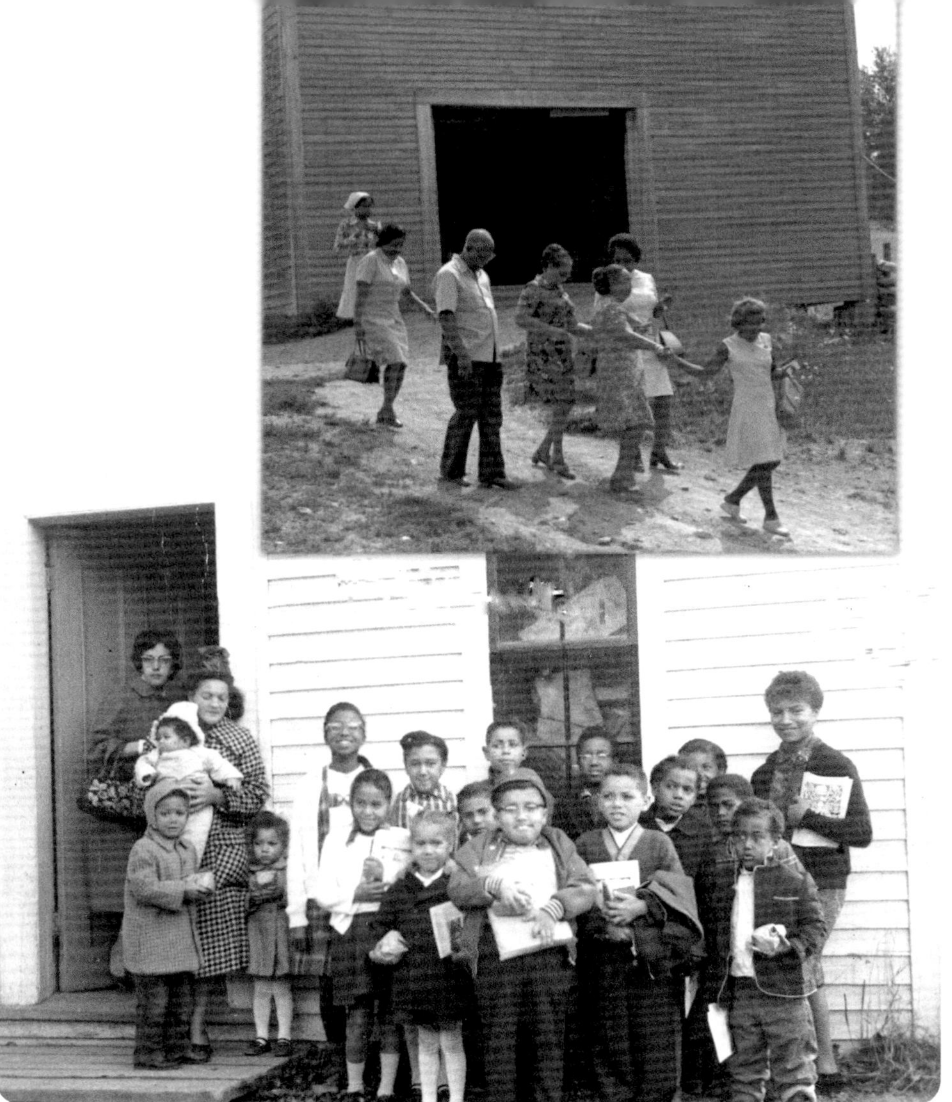

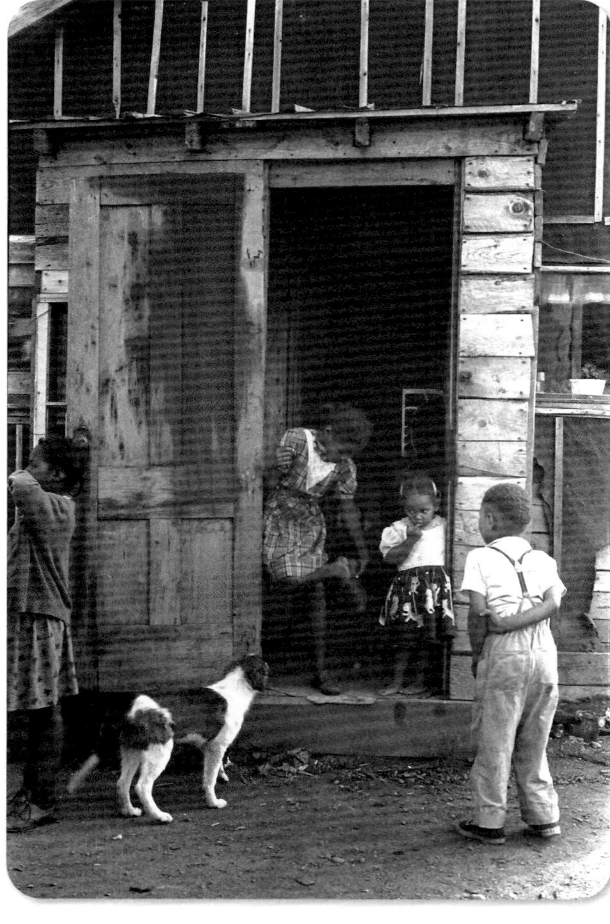

(clockwise from above)
Elm Hill School, 1965 (PANB P365-90). The school was the centre of the community, serving as community school and church Sunday school.

French Lake, 1970s (PANB P348-F328-17)

Palmer children at French Lake, 1963 (PANB P348-F117-5; PANB F117-8)

The Claybourne family, Barkers Point, Fredericton, 1958 (PANB P342-3662.1)

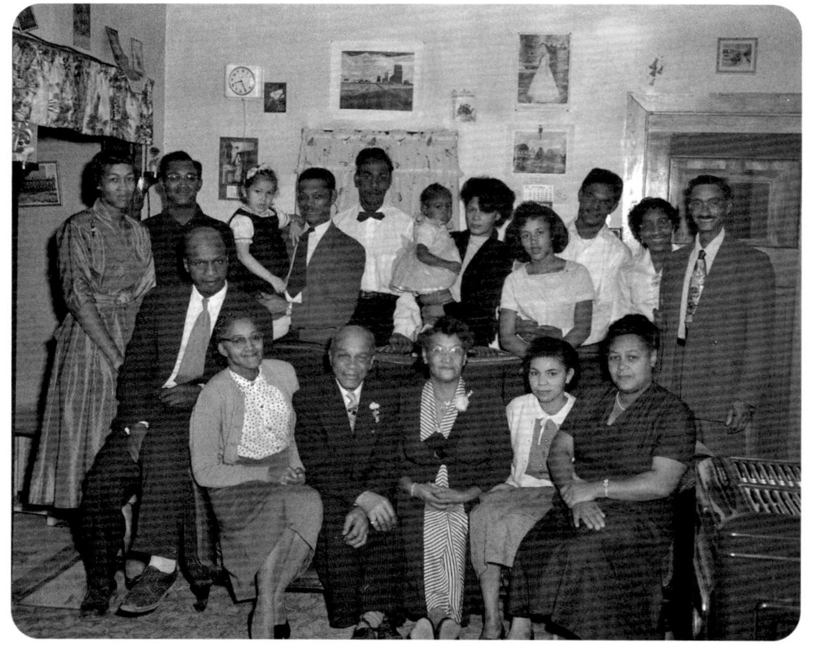

1959 The New Brunswick Association for the Advancement of Coloured People was founded by Walter Peters, Frederick Hodges, Joseph Drummond, Garfield Skinner, and Ovid Machett. This organization led the fight against discrimination in housing sales and rentals within the province.

1962 The first Black picnic was held in Rockwood Park, Saint John, in the summer of 1962, organized by Joseph Drummond and Frederick Hodges.

1965 The Women's Auxiliary of the Black Community (WABC) took over the organization of the annual Black picnic in Saint John. In addition to organizing the annual picnic, the WABC provided year-round outreach, such as helping parents with school supplies, offering bursaries to graduating high school students, and organizing children's parties and Christmas baskets.

1969 Saint John, New Brunswick, native Hartley Gosline became one of the first Black Canadians to serve in the Royal Canadian Mounted Police. Constable Gosline's first posting was to New Glasgow, Nova Scotia.

1969 Saint John, New Brunswick's Shirley Brown became the first Black teacher in Saint John schools. Born in 1947, Brown was the daughter of Harry and Doris (Skinner) Brown. She was employed in District 8 and taught in the local system for thirty-four years, retiring in 2003.

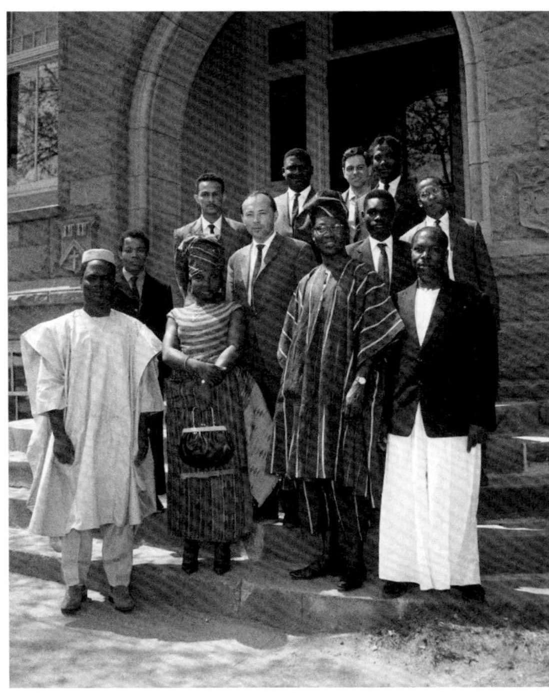

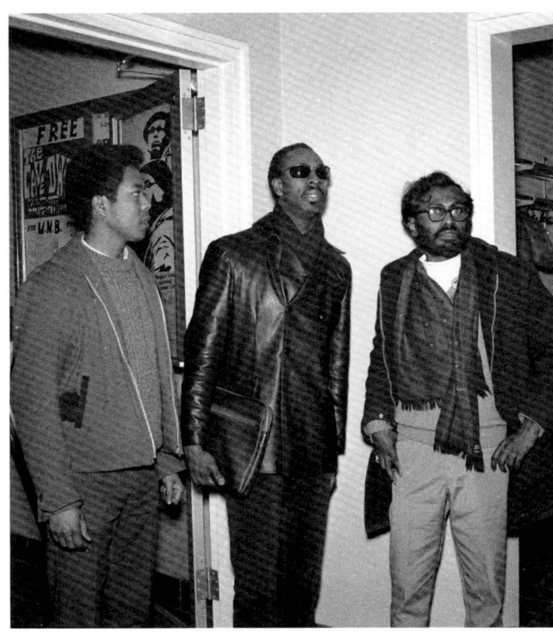

(top to bottom)
African student graduates at UNB, 1966. In the second half of the twentieth century, international students and scholars began arriving at UNB to study and work. (PANB P14-2-9852)

UNB Black Panthers, 1970 (PANB P14-2-12749-1)

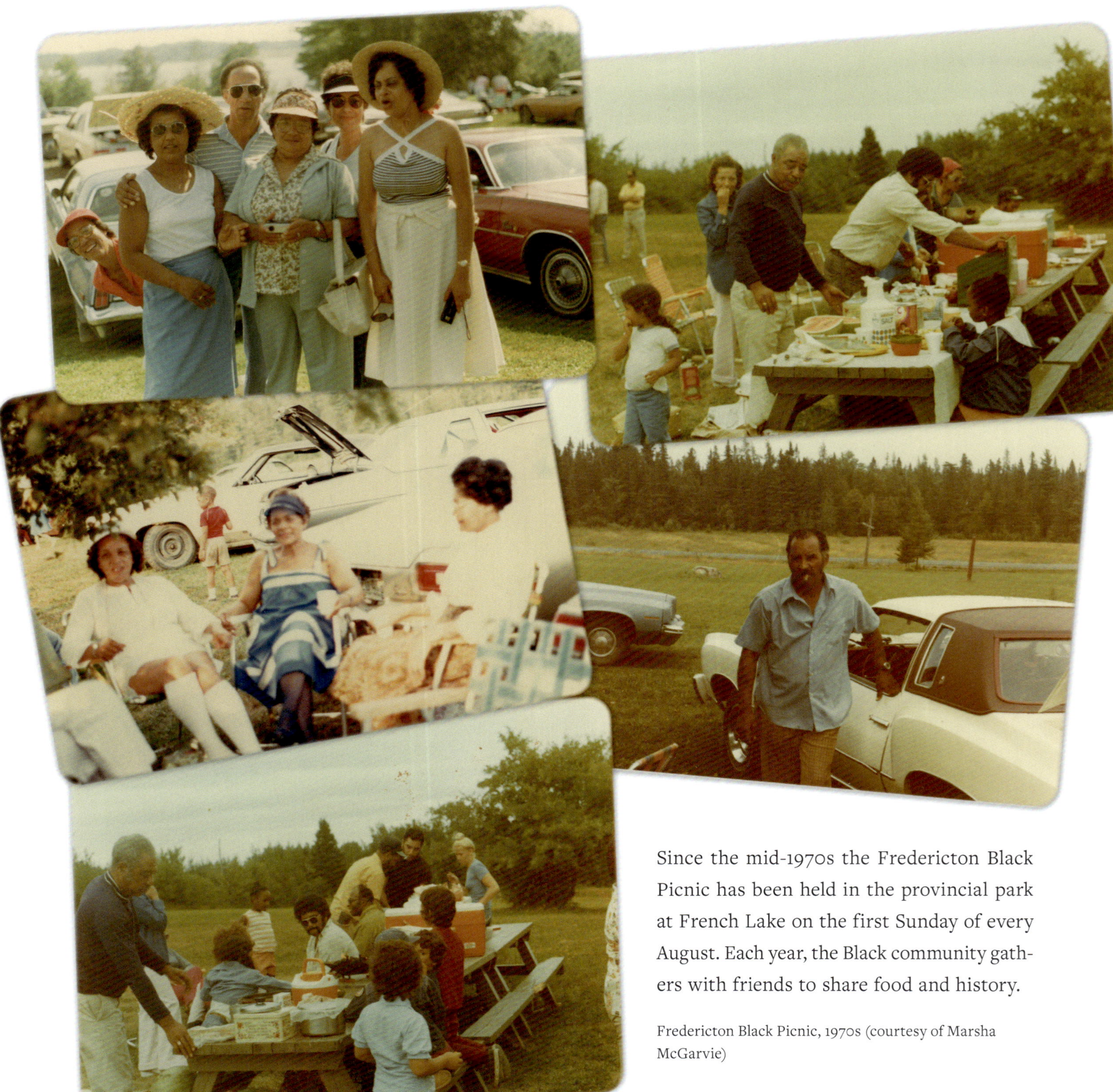

Since the mid-1970s the Fredericton Black Picnic has been held in the provincial park at French Lake on the first Sunday of every August. Each year, the Black community gathers with friends to share food and history.

Fredericton Black Picnic, 1970s (courtesy of Marsha McGarvie)

1970 New Brunswick grade-twelve student Penny Lee Brown refused to read *Huckleberry Finn* in her literature class, claiming it was racist in its depiction of Black people. With the aid of the New Brunswick Human Rights Commission, in particular Frederick Hodges and Joseph Drummond, the book was banned from classrooms across the province.

1972 *The Blacks in New Brunswick*, by W.A. Spray, a professor at St. Thomas University, was published. The book was the first history of Black New Brunswick. Spray recognized Joseph Drummond, Wanda Roche, and Frederick Hodges, three individuals from New Brunswick's Black community, for their contribution to the book.

1974 Frederick Douglas Hodges was elected to the Saint John City Council. He was the first Black person to be elected to public office in the city's history. Hodges had been in the Royal Canadian Air Force, and he also had a long career with the Canadian Pacific Railway. A founding member of the New Brunswick Association for the Advancement of Coloured People, Hodges was also active in the labour movement, serving as the first Black president of the Saint John District Labour Council in the 1960s.

1976 Saint John's David Peters became the first Black nationally certified chef in Atlantic Canada. In the 1960s, Peters had designed and taught the first provincial hospitality course in the province. He later produced and hosted *Afro-vision*, a local Black history TV program, and ran the Iron Duke restaurant, which specialized in Creole cuisine.

Peters is also a cofounder of Provincial Resources of Black Energy (PROBE), the forerunner to the contemporary organization Pride of Race, Unity, Dignity through Education (PRUDE). He remains active in raising awareness of the history of New Brunswick's Black community.

1976 Saint John local Ralph "Tiger" Thomas was inducted into the Canadian Boxing Hall of Fame, the first Black boxer from New Brunswick to achieve this distinction. Thomas had formed the Golden Glove Amateur Boxing Club in 1963, a club that produced several exceptional boxers in the 1970s and '80s. Thomas has since served as president of PRUDE and founded the New Brunswick Black History Society in 2010. He received an honorary doctorate of letters from the University of New Brunswick (Saint John) in 2019 and the Order of New Brunswick in 2021.

1982 Shelley (Peters) Carey became the first Black woman in Canada to join and serve in the Royal Canadian Mounted Police. Born in Saint John, Carey grew up on military bases across Canada while her father served in the army. Carey was posted to Newfoundland for five years, before joining the Canadian Forces and becoming a Military Police officer.

Carey retired from the military in 2008 with the rank of lieutenant colonel. At the time of her retirement, she was the highest-ranking Black person in the Regular Canadian Forces and the highest-ranking Black woman in the history of the Canadian Forces.

On July 10, 2010, Major Peters (ret'd.) and his daughter Lt. Col. Shelley (Peters) Carey (ret'd.) were the guest speakers for the Black Battalion's annual commemorative celebration in Pictou, Nova Scotia. During this event, the RCMP formally recognized Carey for being the first Black woman to join the force.

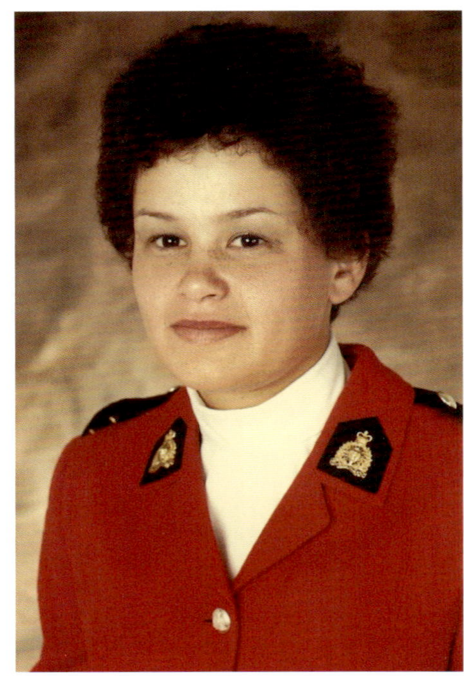

Shelley (Peters) Carey (Courtesy Sgt. Craig M. Smith, M.O.M.)

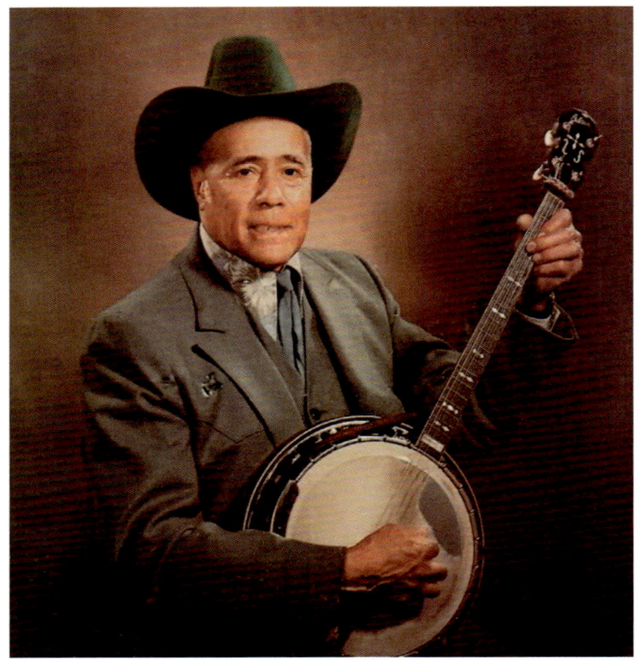

George Hector (Courtesy of Rhoda Williams)

1983 Banjo-playing legend George Hector of New Brunswick was one of the first inductees into the New Brunswick Country Music Hall of Fame.

Born in Gagetown, New Brunswick, Hector took up the banjo at the age of fifteen. He actually made his first banjo himself, but when his father, Lebron Hector, recognized George's love of the instrument he took his son to Fredericton to buy him a proper banjo.

As a member of the Maritime Farmers Barn Dance group, Hector played all over New Brunswick, Nova Scotia, and Maine and appeared on radio and television (including with Don Messer) from the 1930s to the 1960s, while working several day jobs. "I was making $22.50 a week just for driving a car and keeping it shined...not bad for the hungry thirties."

1983 The Fredericton Raceway honoured sixteen old-time harness-racing drivers, including Chester Eatmon, a Black New Brunswicker, who was still racing at the age of seventy-nine. Born in Fredericton, Eatmon was a bricklayer by profession, and harness racing was his hobby. Over a career spanning more than twenty years, Eatmon estimates that he raced in over eight hundred races, memorably telling the *Daily Gleaner*, "If you ever have an accident on the track and are still able to walk, the thing to do is get right back on.... The track is no place for cowardice and if an opportunity opens up, you have to take advantage of it."

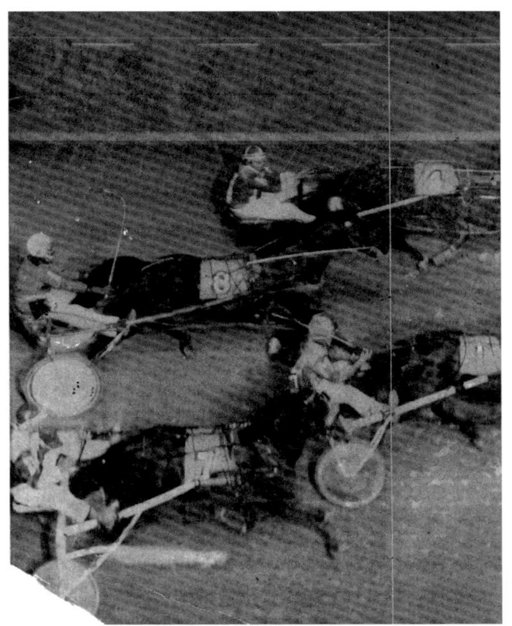

Chester Eatmon racing #8 (Private collection)

1991 Bernard A. Boxill became the first Black person to chair the Harvest Jazz and Blues Festival in Fredericton. He is the son of Carol H. Y. Boxill, the first Black woman to open a law office in Fredericton, who was later appointed to the Privy Council and Canada's Human Rights Tribunal.

2001 Carl White became the first Black deputy mayor of Saint John, serving for three years.

2003 The University of New Brunswick, Saint John, conferred an honorary degree upon Kevin Langford, in recognition of the many years of developing youth within the greater Saint John area. A graduate of Mount Allison University, Langford has created a number of successful children's, youth, and community choirs, several of which have won awards at provincial and national competitions. Langford's choirs have performed at some prestigious events, including a royal visit to Saint John by Prince Charles and Princess Diana in 1983, at the World Curling Championship in 1999, and at the East Coast Music Awards in Saint John.

2010 The New Brunswick Black History Society was founded in Saint John in June, with board members from Moncton, Fredericton, and Saint John.

That same year, Measha Brueggergosman, the descendant of Black Loyalists who came to Nova Scotia and later settled in Fredericton, performed the Olympic Hymn at the opening of the 2010 Vancouver Olympics.

2017 The New Brunswick Black History Society, under the direction of Ralph Thomas, worked with the provincial government to change nine road and place names in New Brunswick that contained racist terms. For instance, Negro Point in Saint John became Hodges Point, in honour of Frederick Hodges, while Negro Lake and Negro Brook in Grand Bay–Westfield became Corankapone Lake (in honour of Richard Corankapone, an earlier Black settler in the area) and Black Loyalist Brook, respectively.

2019 *Rediscovering the Roots of Black New Brunswickers* was launched in February to mark Black History Month. The program highlights Black New Brunswickers who were at the forefront of the fight for equity and justice. The annual program currently has sixty-four posters which hang in the UNB Art Centre each February, as well as accompanying banners that are on display in downtown Fredericton.

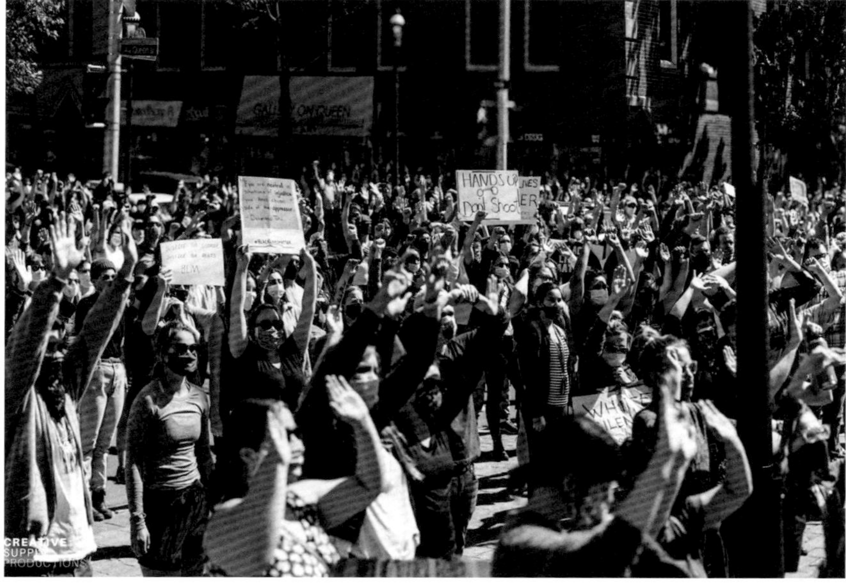

Black Lives Matter march in Fredericton, New Brunswick (Brody LeBlanc Creative Supply Productions)

2020 On May 25, George Floyd, a Black man, was murdered by a White police officer in Minnesota. This very public incident spurred the Black Lives Matter movement across the world. Black Lives Matter Fredericton and Black Lives Matter New Brunswick (based in Saint John) both were formed. The largest peaceful demonstration the City of Fredericton had ever seen was held on June 2, 2020, to honour George Floyd.

2021 The New Brunswick Black History Society's Heritage Room opens in Saint John.

2021 *The Blacks of New Brunswick* was republished, reflecting increasing interest in New Brunswick's Black history. The 2021 edition contains a preface by Thandiwe McCarthy, who spearheaded the republication, and a foreword by Funké Aladejebi, associate professor of history at the University of Toronto. Proceeds from the book's sale fund the creation of bursaries for Black students at St. Thomas University. The republication was a true community event for Black New Brunswickers, with a new cover design by Karrie Nash that incorporated photographs from the Kendall-Marr family collection.

2022 The Women's Auxiliary of the Black Community, Jr., (WABC Jr.) was founded in February and organized their first Black picnic and dance the following July. As WABC Jr. member Naomi Drummond Leslie stated, "We banded together as we knew the next generation had to step up."

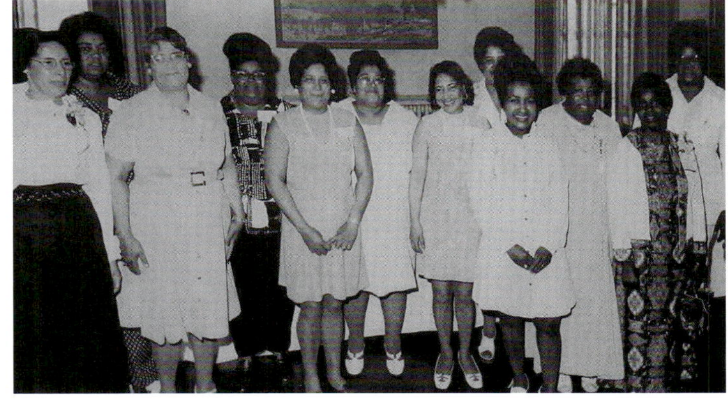

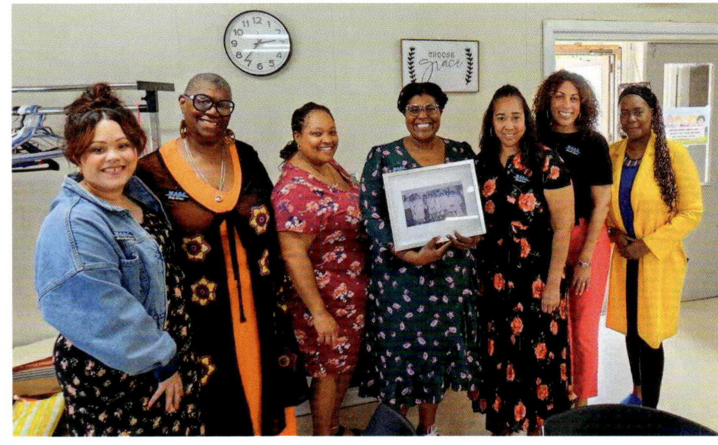

(top to bottom) The original Women's Auxiliary of the Black Community. Left to right: Norma Goree, Verna Drummond, Agnes Roach, Phyllis White, Milita Young, Sandra Hector, Shirley Patterson, Audrey Hodges, Regina Simmons, Josephine Roach, Muriel Dixon (Private collection)

Women's Auxiliary of the Black Community, Jr. Left to right: Anessa Loatman, Holly (Drummond) Giroux, Catrina Loatman, Naomi Drummond Leslie, Kimberly Eatmon, Danielle Bruce, and Jocelyn Smith (Private collection)

2022 Emancipation Day, August 1, was recognized in the New Brunswick legislature, thanks to the hard work of Remembering Each African Cemeteries History (REACH NB, helmed by Mary McCarthy), Black Lives Matter New Brunswick, the New Brunswick African Association, and the New Brunswick Black Artists Alliance. The motion was passed unanimously.

> WHEREAS the British Parliament abolished slavery in the British Empire as of August 1, 1834, by enacting Chapter 73 of the Acts of…William IV, An Act for the Abolition of Slavery Throughout the British Colonies; for promoting the Industry of the manumitted Slaves; and for compensating the Persons hitherto entitled to the Services of such Slaves (U.K.), on August 28, 1833;
>
> WHEREAS slavery existed in British North America prior to its abolition in 1834;
>
> WHEREAS abolitionists and others who struggled against slavery, including those who arrived in Upper and Lower Canada by the Underground Railroad, have historically celebrated August 1 as Emancipation Day;
>
> WHEREAS racist structures and institutional practices have resulted in the inability of Black New Brunswickers to access and enjoy many of the benefits of Canadian society, notably in areas such as education, housing, health, business, the justice system and community development;
>
> WHEREAS Black Lives Matter;
>
> WHEREAS the Government of Canada announced on January 30, 2018, that it would officially recognize the United Nations International Decade for People of African Descent to highlight the important contributions that people of African descent have made to Canadian society, and to provide a platform for confronting anti-Black racism;
>
> BE IT THEREFORE RESOLVED THAT this Legislative Assembly of New Brunswick declare August 1 of every year as Emancipation Day in New Brunswick.

Further Reading

Bell, David. *American Loyalists to New Brunswick*. Formac, 2015.

"Exploring the Lives of Black Loyalists." Black Loyalists in New Brunswick. Atlantic Canada Virtual Archives via UNB Libraries. http://atlanticportal.hil.unb.ca//acva/blackloyalists/en/.

Fawcett, Anne. *Whistling Banjoman: George Hector*. Otnabog Editions, 1999.

Fergusson, Charles Bruce, ed. *Clarkson's Mission to America, 1791–92*. Public Archives of Nova Scotia, 1971.

Little, Peter. *Abraham Beverley Walker: Lawyer, Lecturer, Activist*. New World, 2019.

Manthey, Gwen, Charmaine A. Nelson, Harvey Amani Whitfield, and David Woods. *Edward Bannister: Hidden Blackness | Noir oublié*. Goose Lane Editions and the Owens Art Gallery: 2026.

New Brunswick Black History Society. https://nbblackhistorysociety.org.

Rediscovering the Roots of Black New Brunswickers. Black History Month, exhibitions. UNB Art Centre, accessed April 5, 2026. https://www.unb.ca/artcentre/exhibitions/bhm.html.

Smith, Craig Marshall. *The Journey Continues: An Atlantic Canadian Black Experience*. Black Green and Red Educational Products, 2010.

Spray, W. A. *The Blacks in New Brunswick*. Foreword by Thandiwe McCarthy and preface by Funké Aladejebi. Updated reprint ed. St. Thomas University, 2021. Originally published in 1972 by Brunswick Press.

Walker, James W. St. G. *The Black Loyalists: The Search for a Promised Land in Nova Scotia and Sierra Leone, 1783–1870*. University of Toronto Press, 1976.

Whitfield, Harvey Amani. "Black Loyalists and Black Slaves in Maritime Canada." *History Compass* 5, no. 6 (2007): 1980–97. https://doi.org/10.1111/j.1478-0542.2007.00479.x.

Whitfield, Harvey Amani, ed. *Black Slavery in the Maritimes: A History in Documents*, Broadview Sources. Broadview Press, 2018.

Wilson, Ellen Gibson. *The Loyal Blacks*. Capricorn Books, 1976.

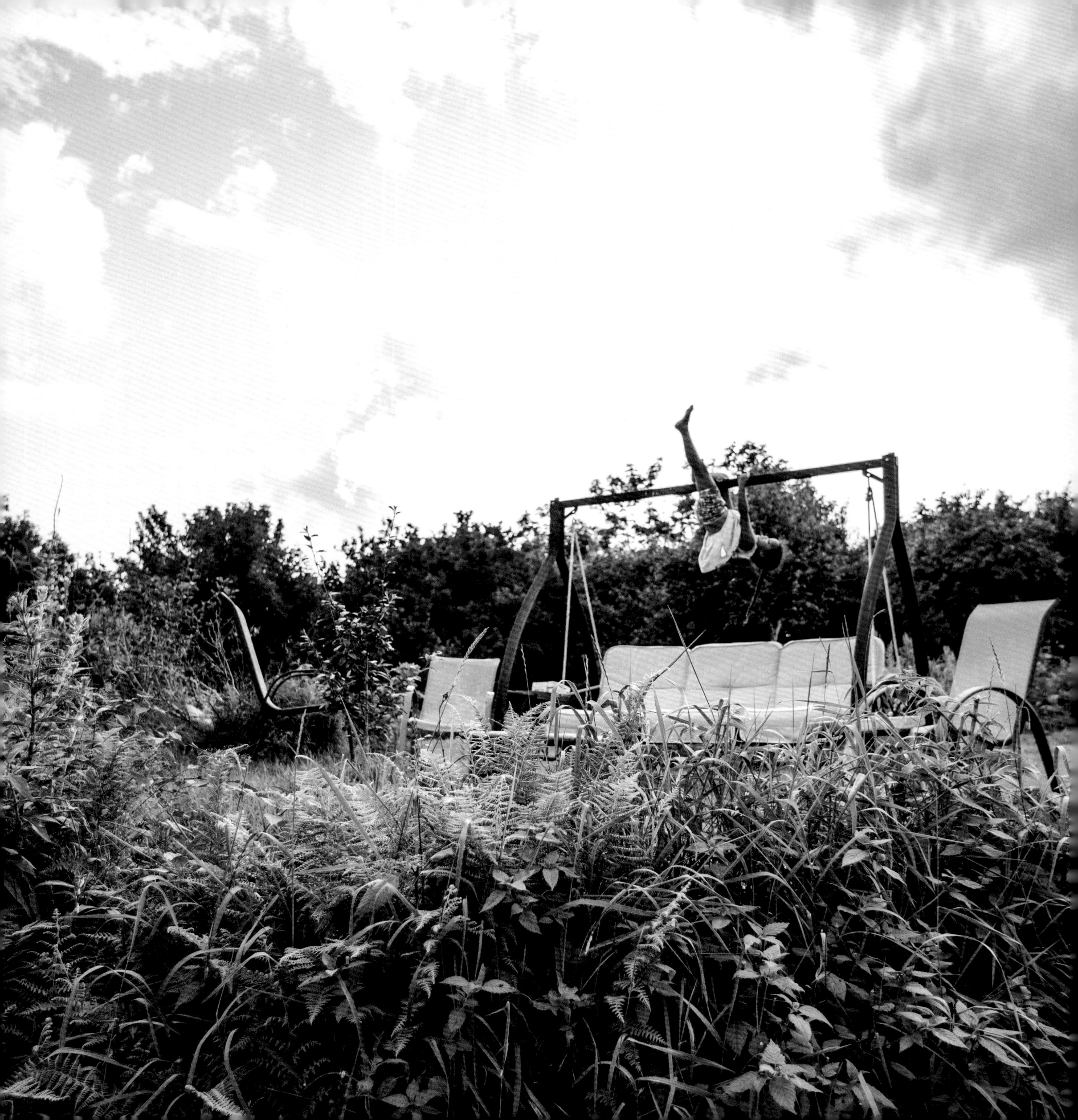

The Fifteen Families

Stewart Tyler Nash
McCarty Peters Mc Intyre
Gendral Talbot Holmes
Haines Hope Shears
Eatmon Mc Intyre Holmes
Hector Richards Nash
Eatmon MacPherson
Edison Howe Lawrence
Dymond Howe Young Roche
Hodges Hector Snead
Skinner Blizzard Halfkenny
Cooke Drummond Leslie
McCarthy Leek Dymond
Johnson

Stewart / Tyler / Nash — Ripples

The street that stopped at their property
Doubled as a driveway
A modest home in Ripples, New Brunswick.
We expected less than a dozen family,
But two-dozen-plus showed up.
The temperature was Caribbean.

The storm smashed against windows
There was just no way
We could snap an outdoor photo.
An' so the family got to work.

Chairs were pulled.
A kitchen table was pushed.
Everything was lifted out of the way.
So that the entire clan could be pictured *together.*

A woman in a wheelchair was asked about mobility.
"Don't worry about me,"
The grandma replied, her eyes gleaming,
"I tell my knees what to do."

Rumours of bad blood evaporated
Under the giggles, grandma hugs
And camera flashes.
As jolting as the lightning of smiles.

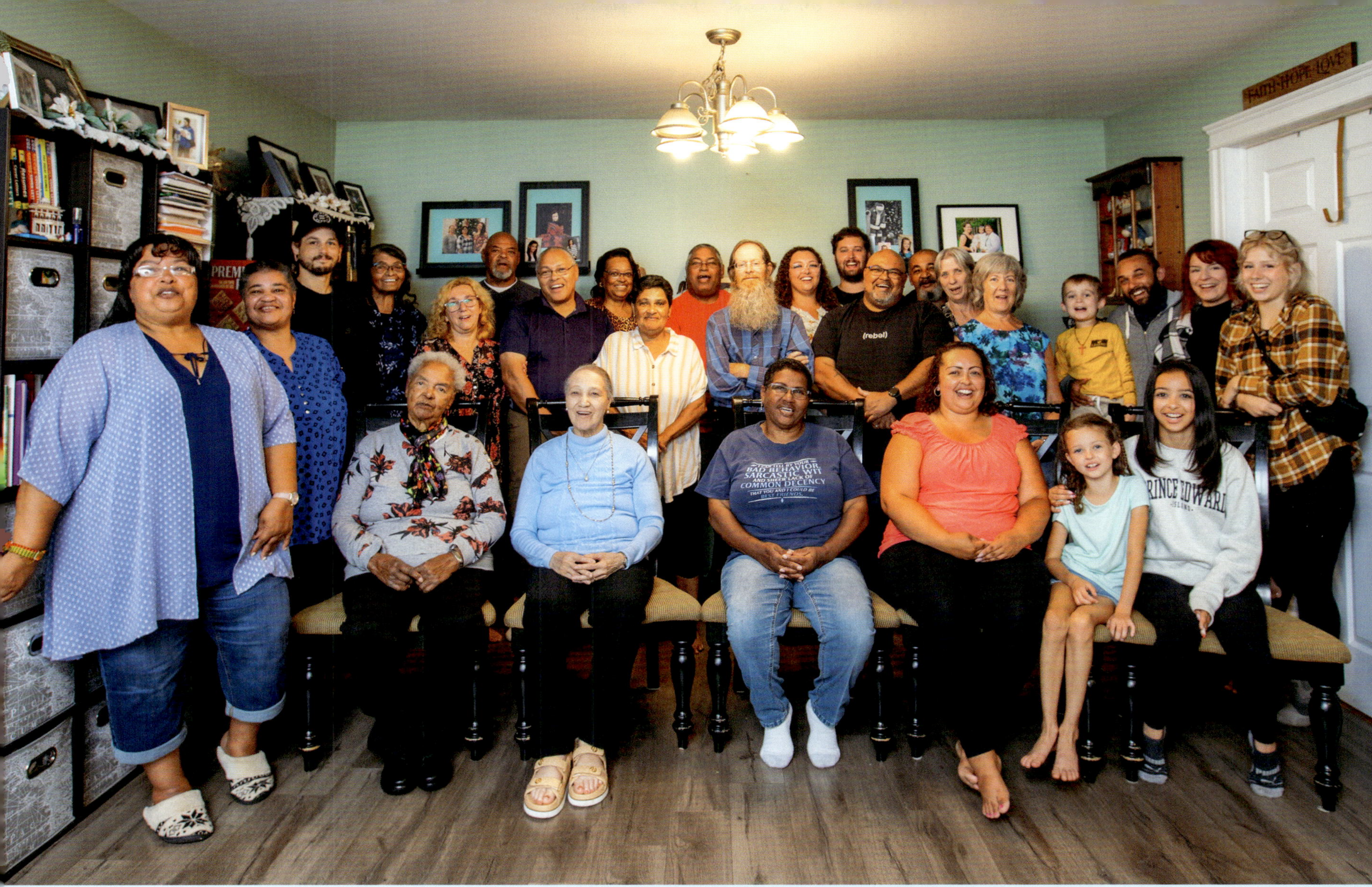

A young girl with a passion for photography
Volunteered her insights and perspectives.
Calling names and making sure that every family member
Could pose, shining before the camera.

While I scanned photos on an old wooden desk
Handmade by a great-grandfather.
The conversations revealed.
No glass ceilings to our heights, only a stone foundation for our floors.

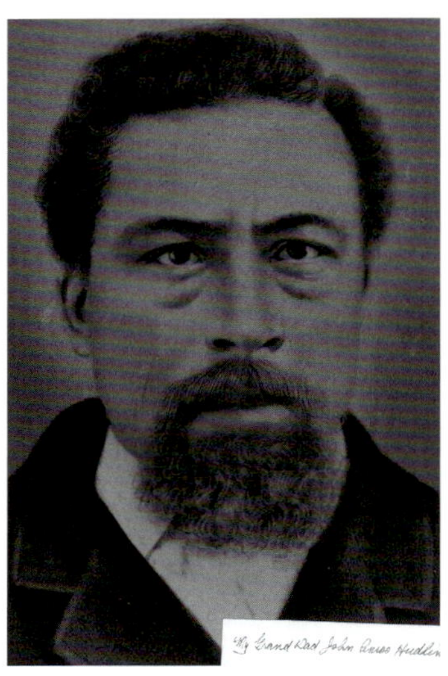

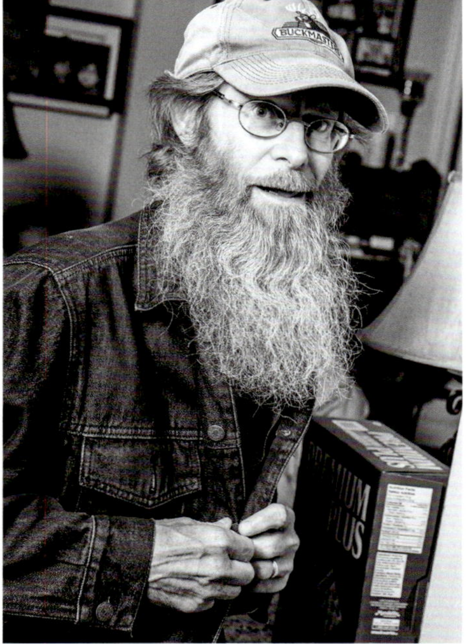

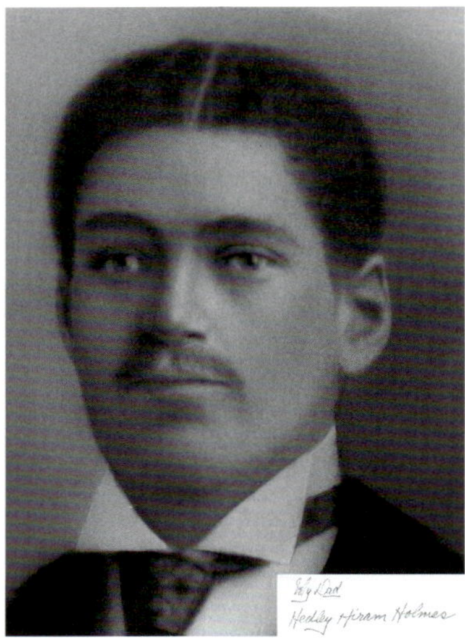

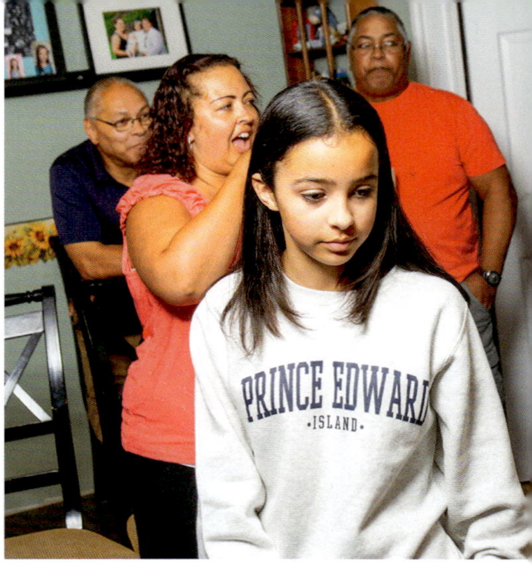

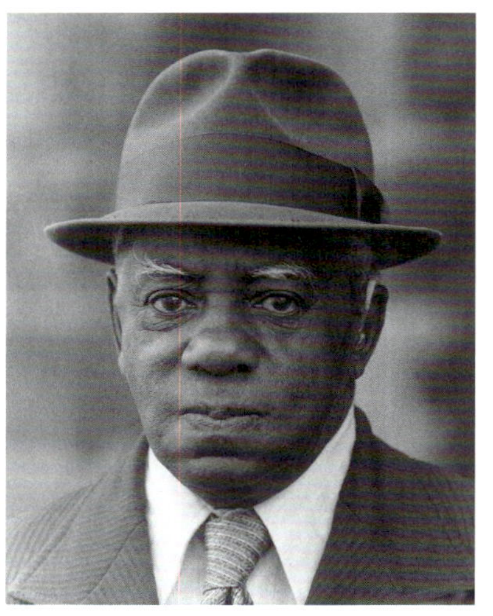

The earliest I have on the Hudlin side is Sarah Hudlin, born in 1798 in Virginia, but no date of death. The earliest I have on the Tyler side of the family is Super Hughes, born in Anguilla, British West Indies, but no dates or anything more.
— Rosemarie Stewart

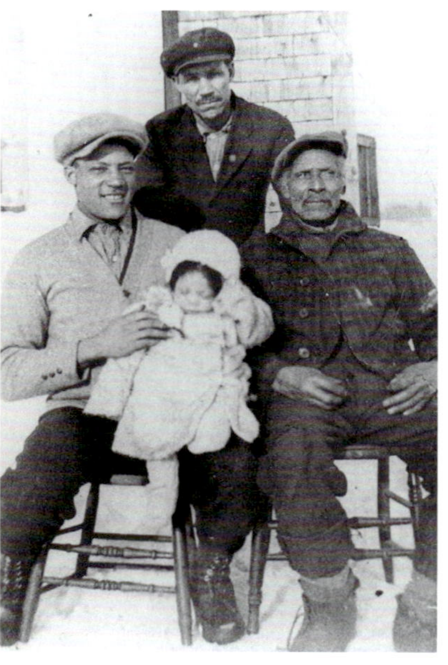

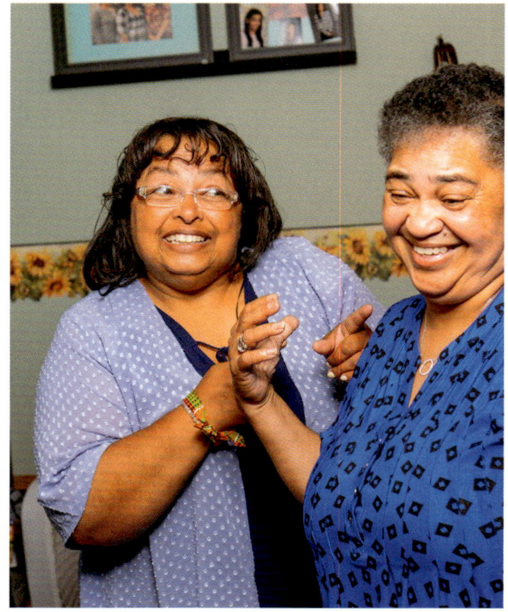

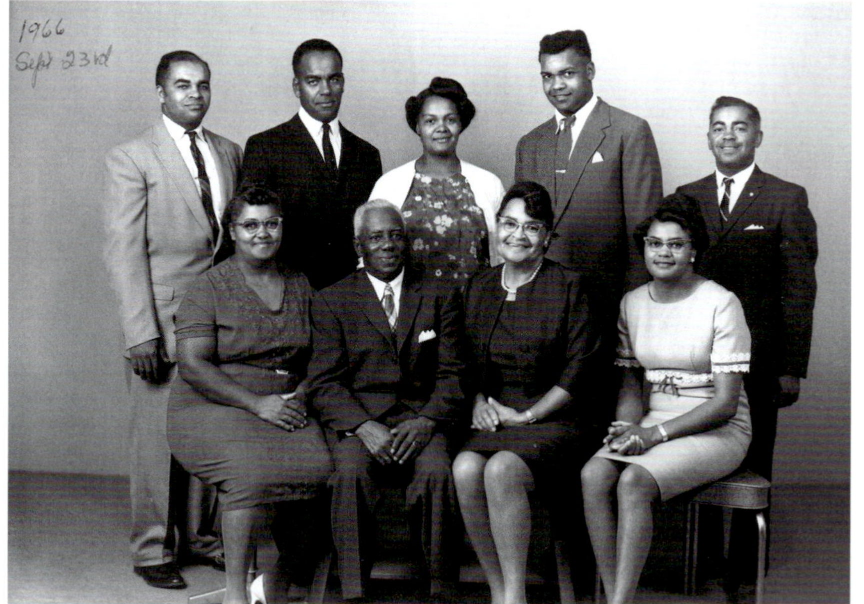

The Stewart family lives in Ripples, New Brunswick, and shares ancestral ties with the Tylers, Nashes, Hudlins, Palmers, and many other Black families in New Brunswick. On the Hudlin side, they've traced their family history back to Sarah Hudlin, an enslaved woman born in 1798 in Virginia. She had three sons, their biological father an unnamed slaveholder. Two of Sarah's sons were able to purchase their freedom, while her third son, Samuel, escaped from slavery: in the mid-1800s, he befriended the captain of a ship that took him to New Brunswick. The government granted him a piece of land in Ripples, off the No. 10 highway between Minto and Fredericton, and he became a farmer.

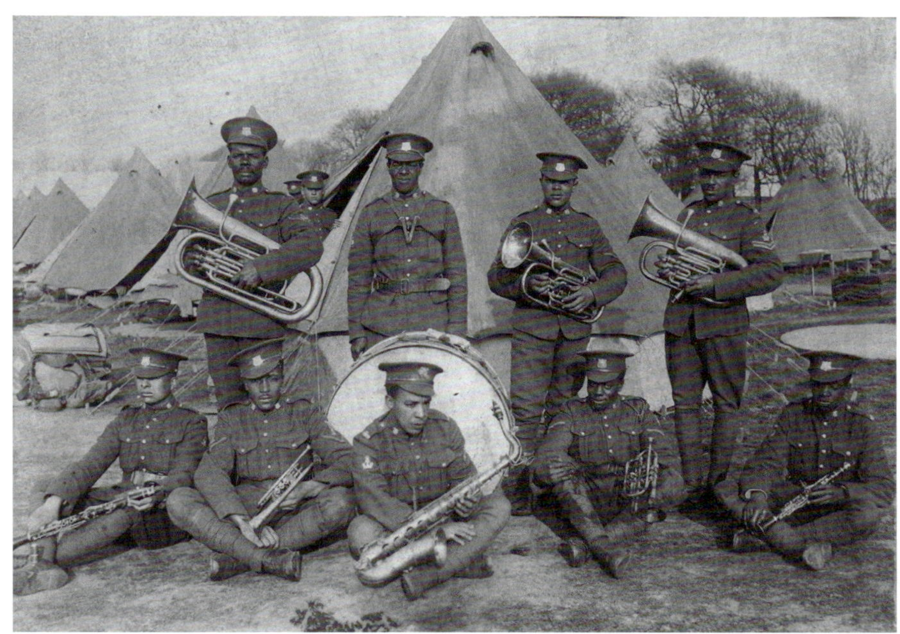

The Tyler side has been traced back to an ancestor named Super Hughes, who was born on the Caribbean island of Anguilla. Some information is missing, but we know the following generation included Thomas Carty, who likely came to New Brunswick; and the generation after that included George Lupee, who was born in New Brunswick in 1825. George's daughter, MaryEaster Lupee McCarty, was Rose Marie Stewart's great-grandmother. MaryEaster was born in Saint John in the 1870s and died in 1961. She married Elizah (or Elijah) Tyler in 1888, and they had at least three children—Charles Elijah, Fannie, and Arthur Seymour, Rose Marie's grandfather, who was born in Saint John on February 22, 1897. Following the death of her first husband, MaryEaster married Clarence W. McCarty in 1904, and they also had several children.

Arthur Seymour Tyler began bugling in his youth, joining the Saint John Brass Band, and later organizing the first Boy Scout Bugle Band in the city of Saint John. In the fall of 1915, a year into the First World War, Seymour,

My grandfather on the Tyler side, A. Seymour Tyler, served in both the First and Second World Wars as a bugler, and he was awarded the Silver Bugle by his regiment in 1939 for twenty-one years of service, along with two blue Service Chevrons and an Efficiency Decoration.
—Rosemarie Stewart

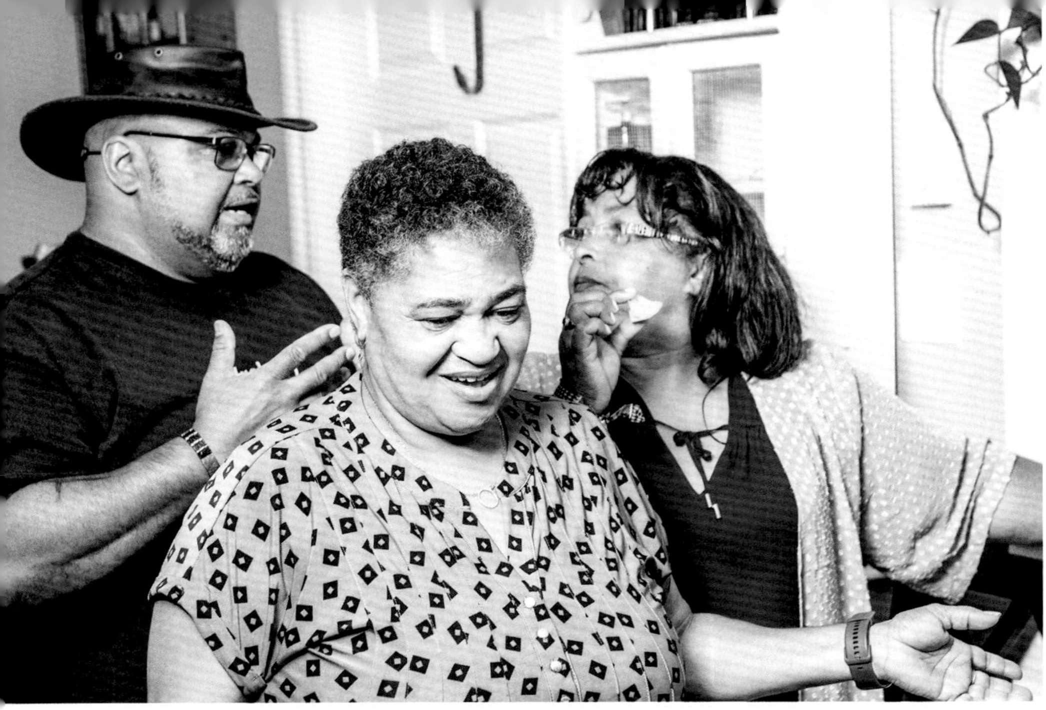

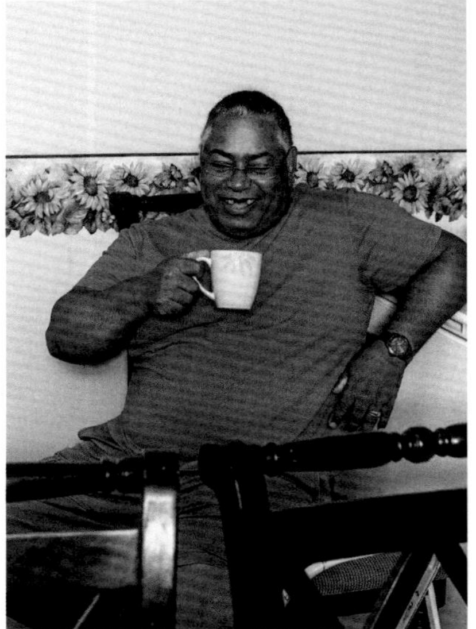

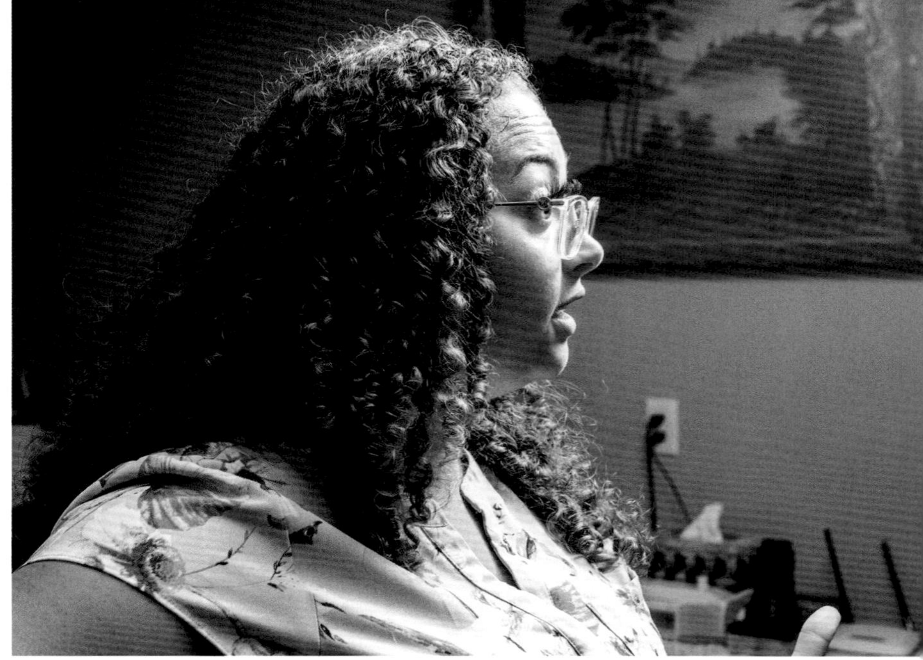

as he was known, along with eighteen others, tried to enlist in the 104th Battalion, CEF (Canadian Expeditionary Force), at Camp Sussex, but they were all rejected because they were Black. A year later, on September 14, Tyler did enlist, this time as one of ten soldiers from the Fredericton area, in Canada's No. 2 Construction Battalion, a segregated unit of the CEF established in 1916. His brothers, Harold McCarty and C. Elijah Tyler, and his cousin, Frederick Lupee, were with him when the No. 2 travelled overseas in March 1917, where they cut, transported, and milled lumber for reinforcing trenches, and Seymour also played in the Battalion Band.

Following his discharge, Seymour Tyler married Lenetta Holmes from Elm Hill, enlisted with the York Regiment militia, and became an award-winning farmer in the Ripples area. At the outbreak of the Second World War, Tyler was mobilized with the Carleton and York Regiment, part of the first contingent to be sent overseas. As the Bugle Sergeant, he led the parade when their ship landed in Scotland. He returned home in 1941, when his leg was broken in seven places during the Battle of Britain.

From 1941 until 1959, he worked as a porter for the Canadian Pacific Railway, after which he retired to his family farm. He died in 1985.

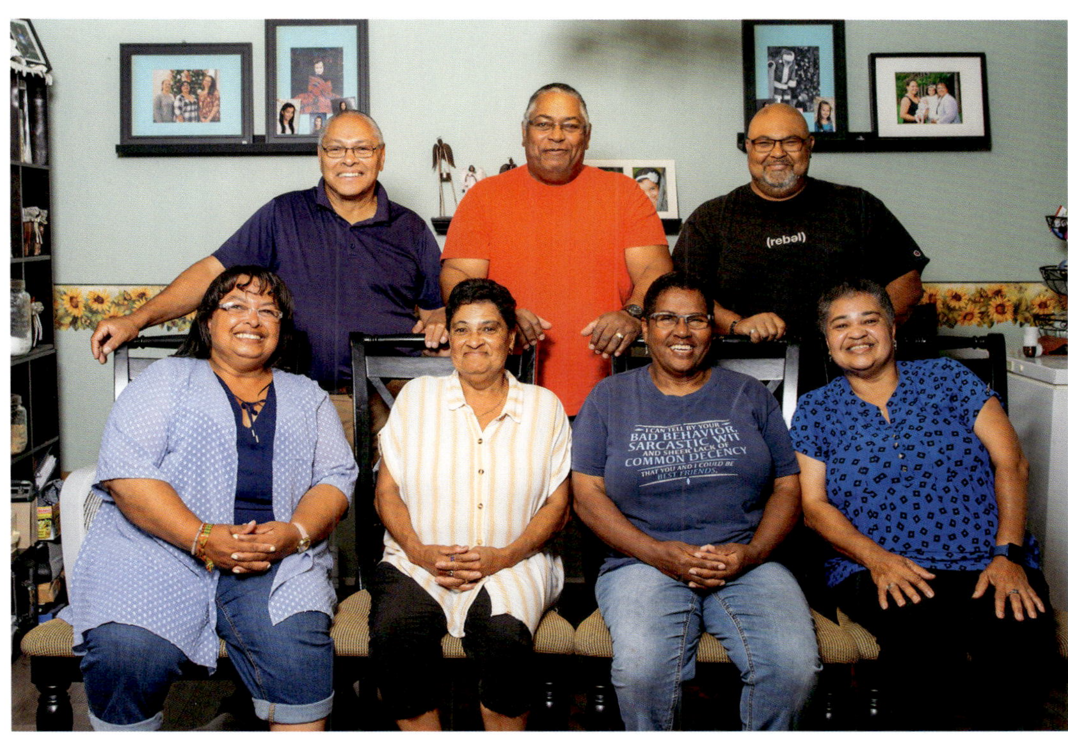
(rebel)
I CAN TELL BY YOUR
BAD BEHAVIOR,
SARCASTIC WIT
AND SHEER LACK OF
COMMON DECENCY
THAT YOU AND I COULD BE
BEST FRIENDS.

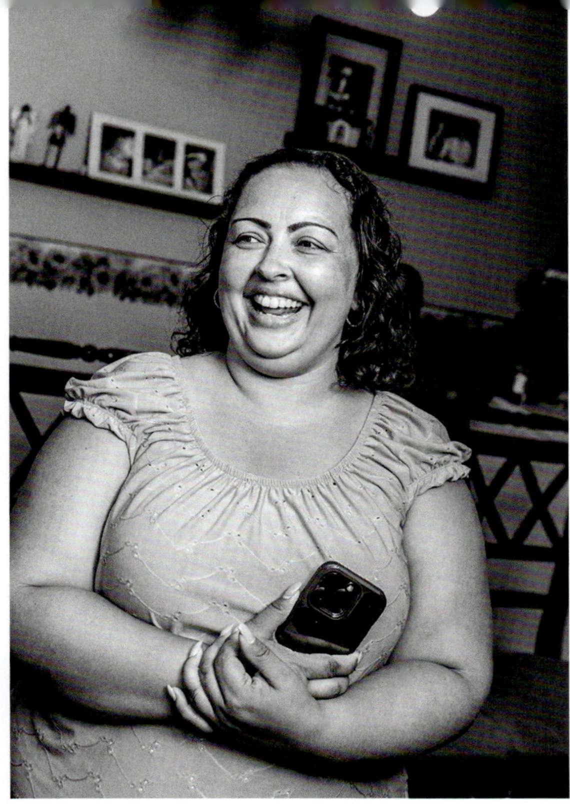

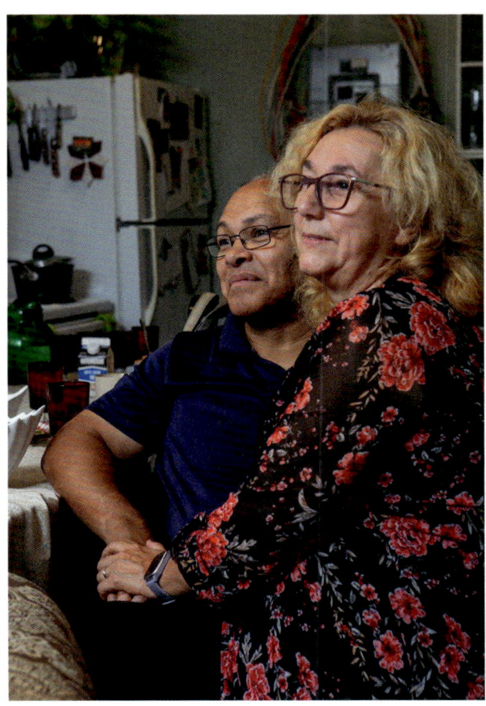

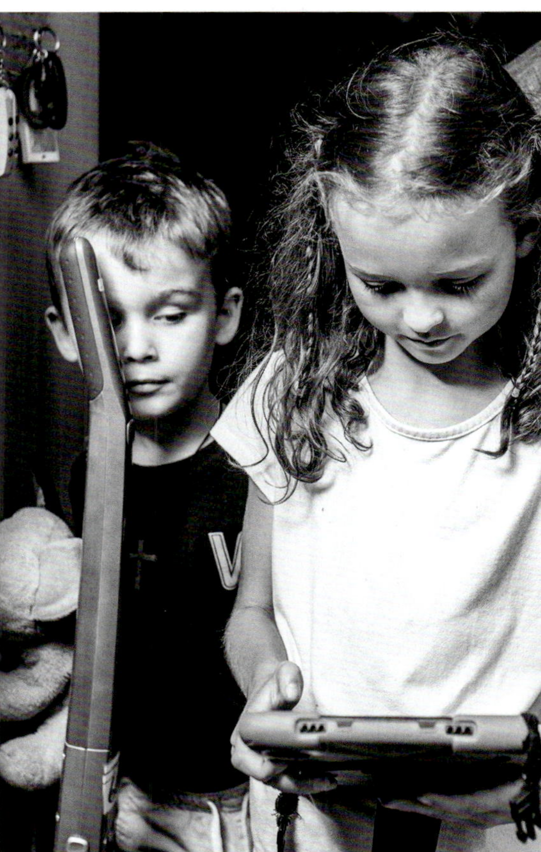

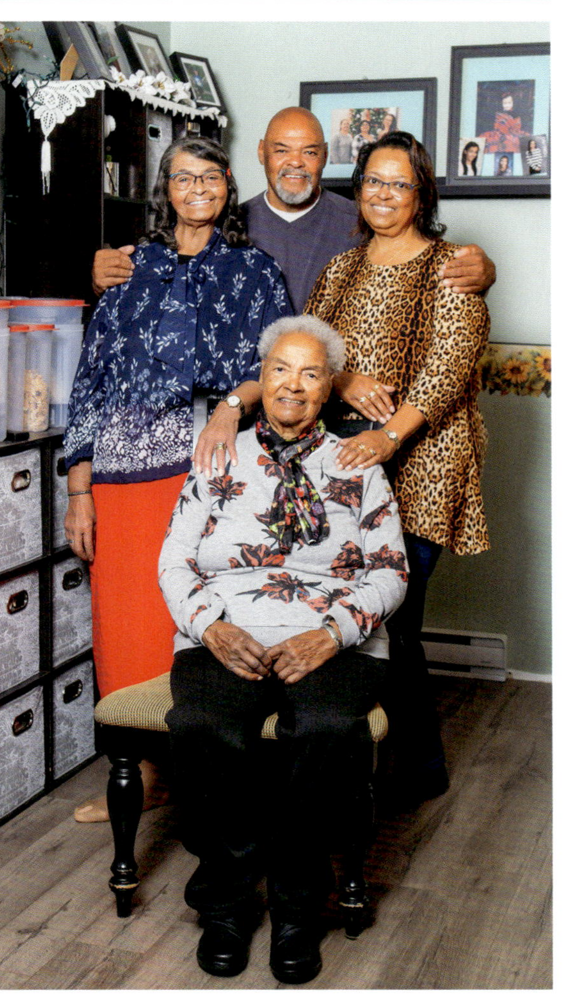

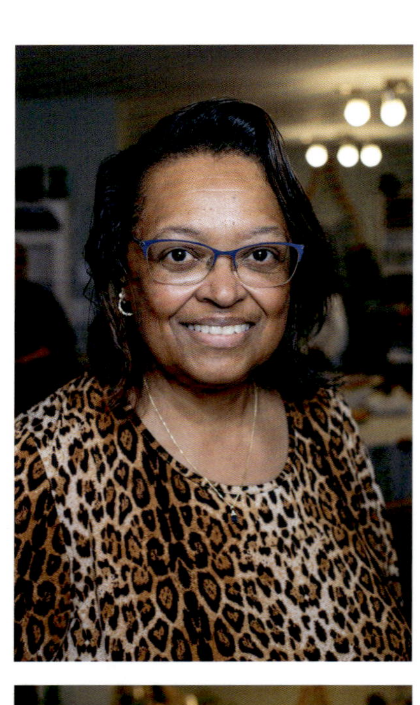

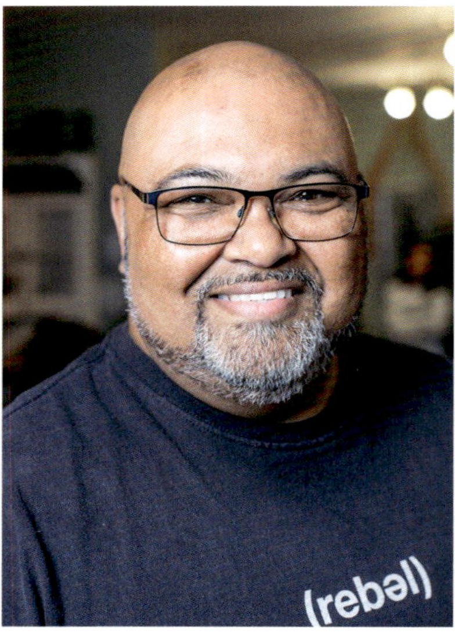

(rebəl)

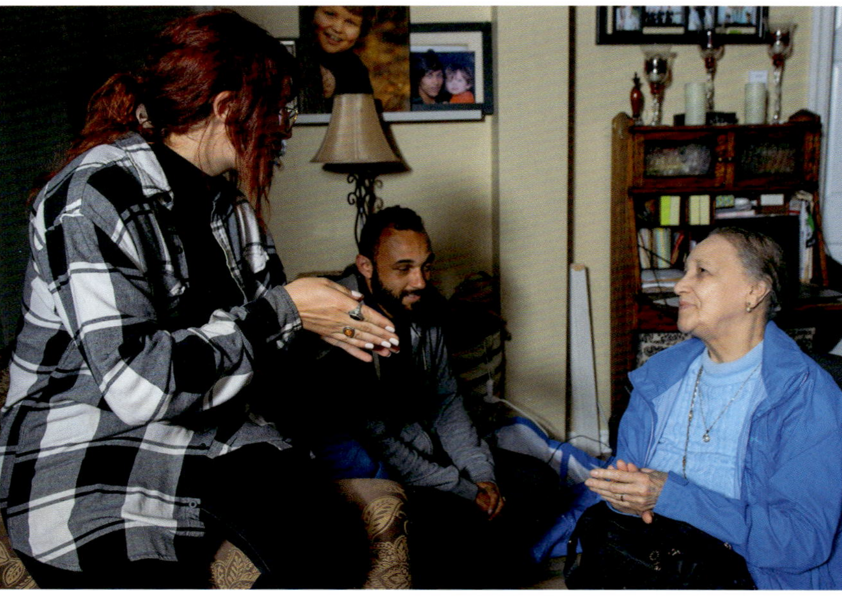

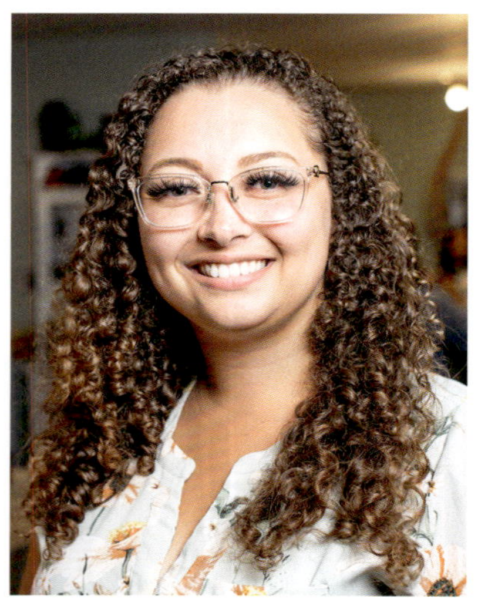

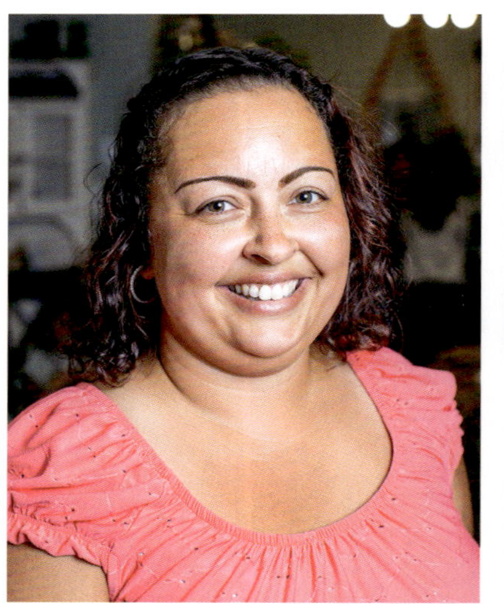

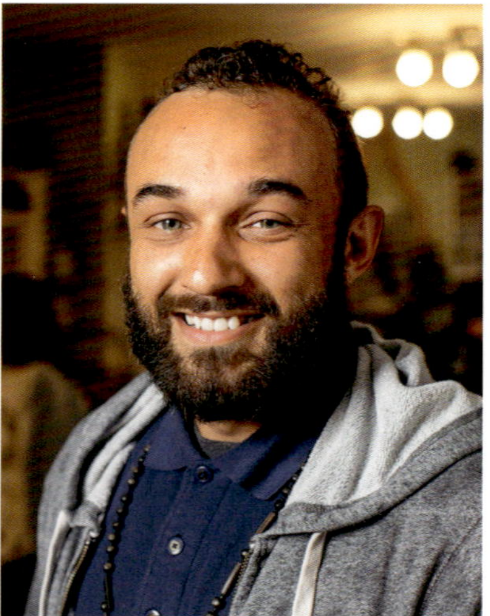

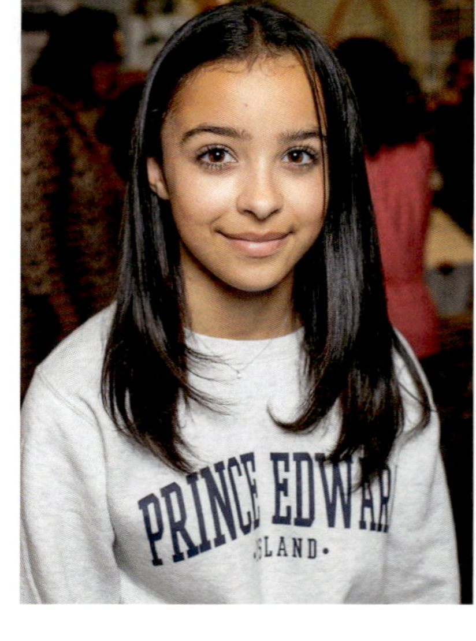

PRINCE EDWAR
SLAND

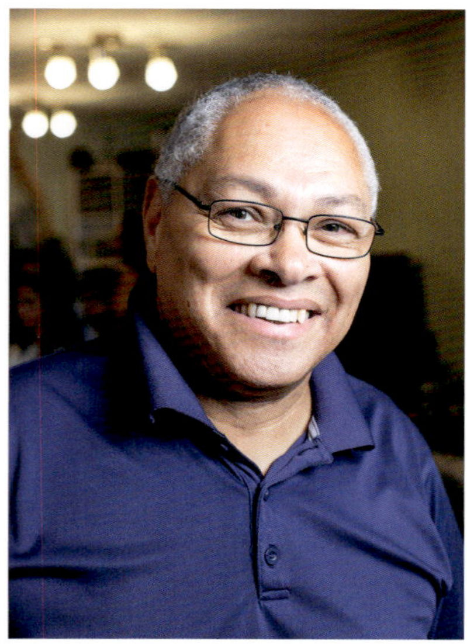

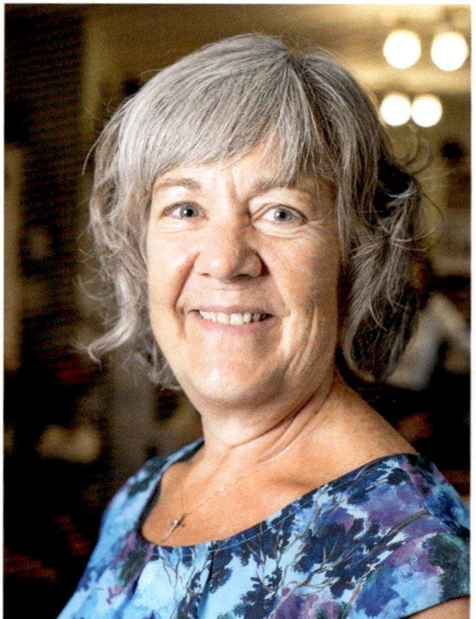

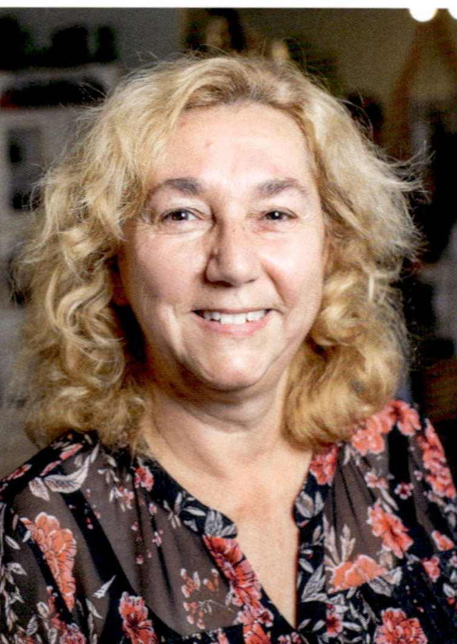

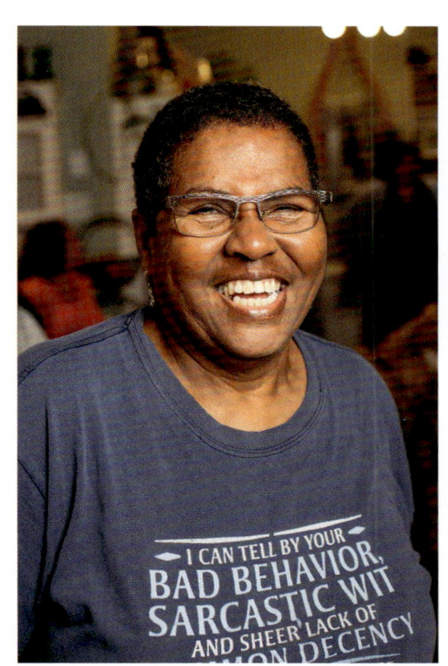
I CAN TELL BY YOUR
BAD BEHAVIOR,
SARCASTIC WIT
AND SHEER LACK OF

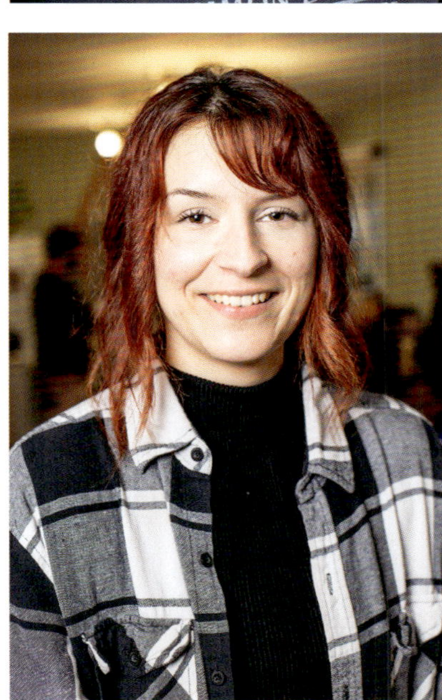

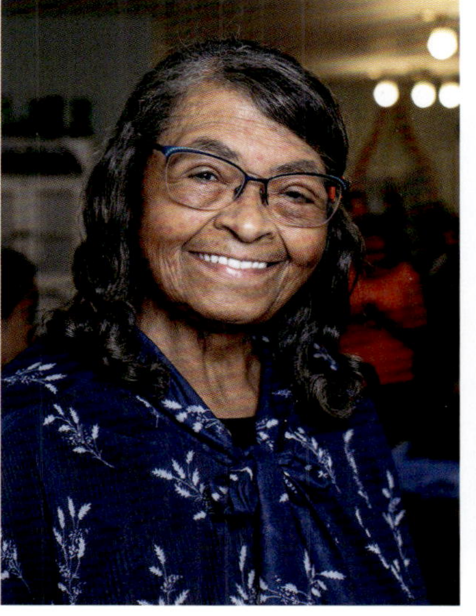

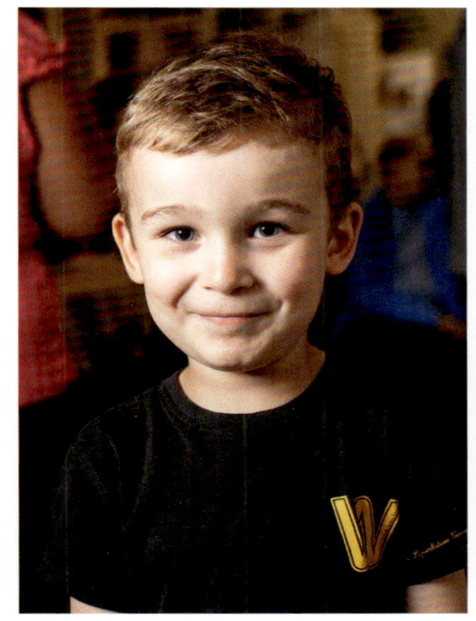

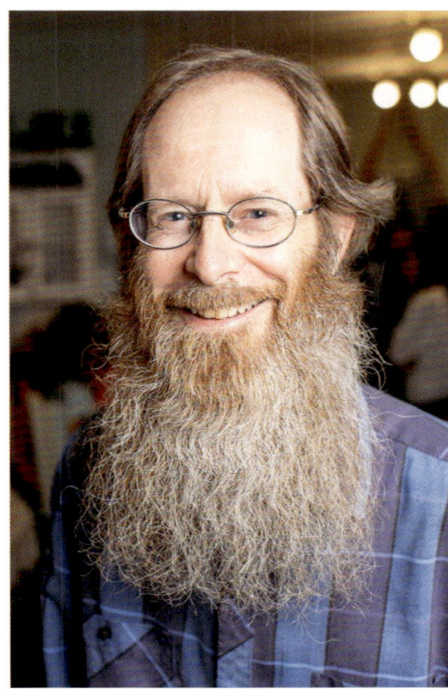

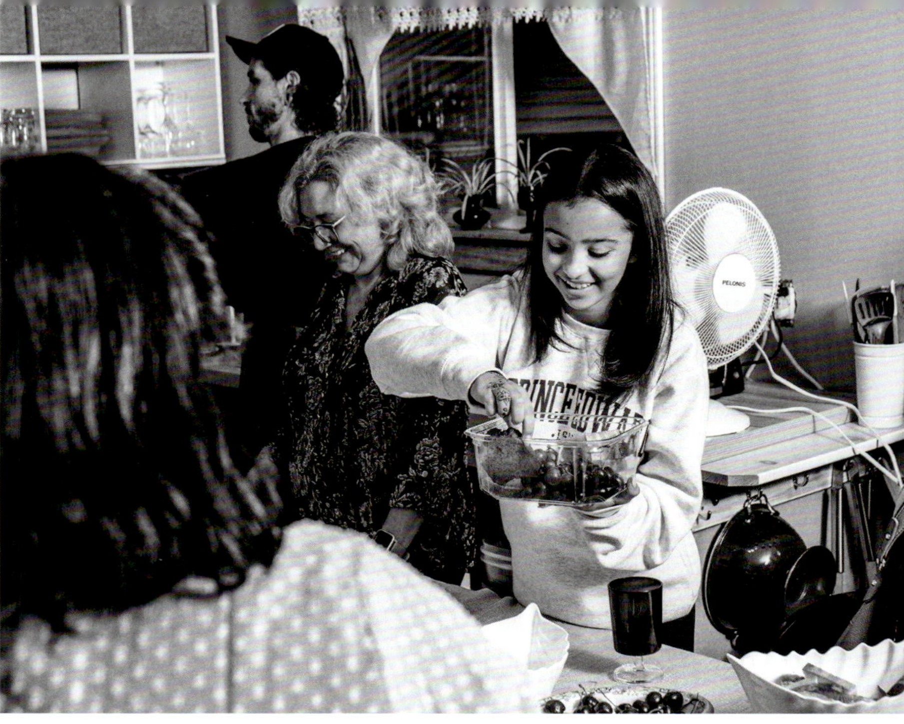

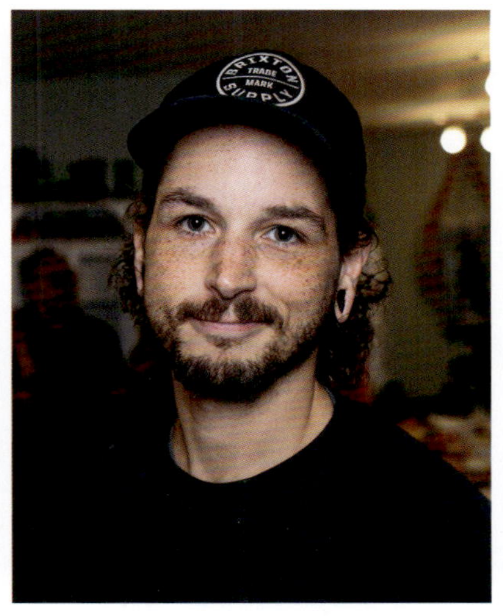
TRADE
MARK

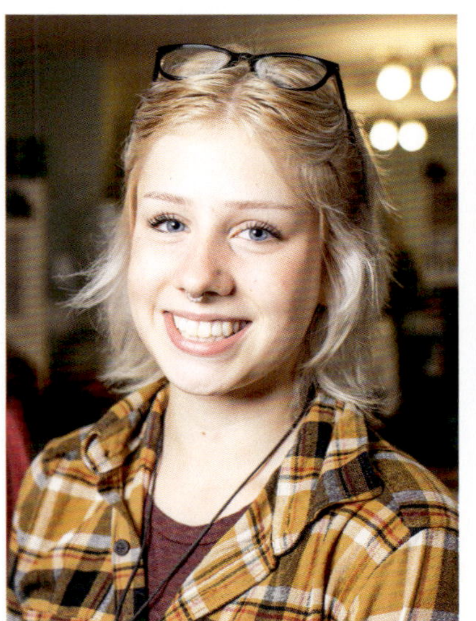

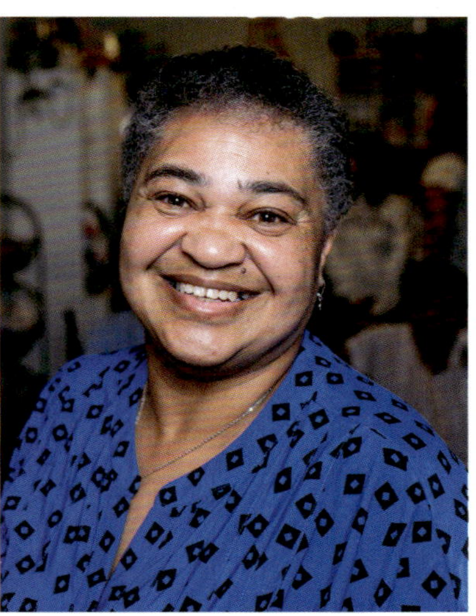

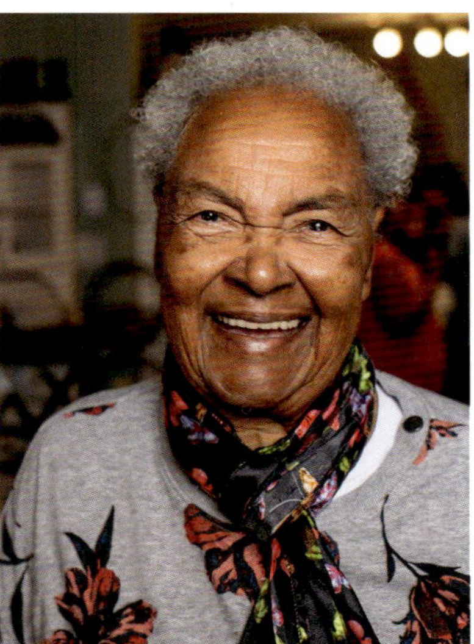

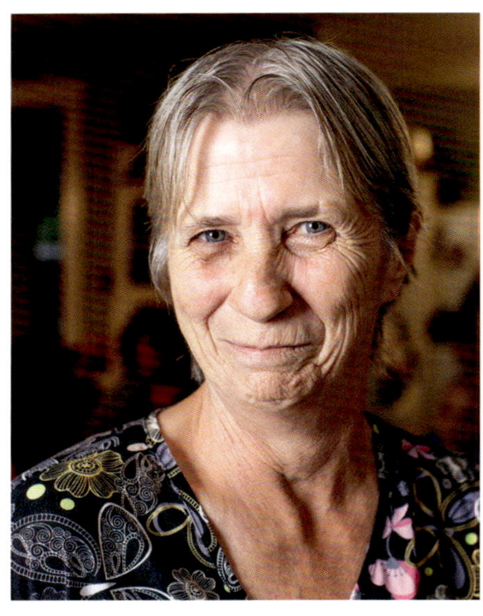

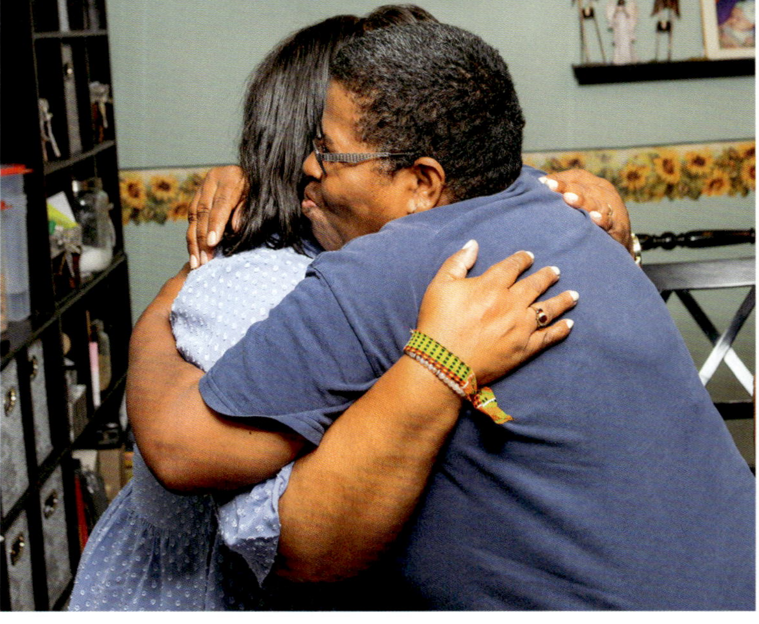

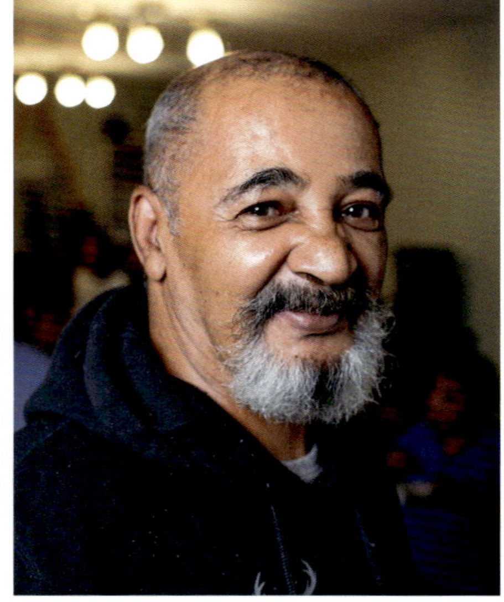

If I had to say what keeps us going as a family, and what has kept us strong for generations, it might be Christianity. That, and the willingness of everybody to be employed.
— Rosemarie Stewart

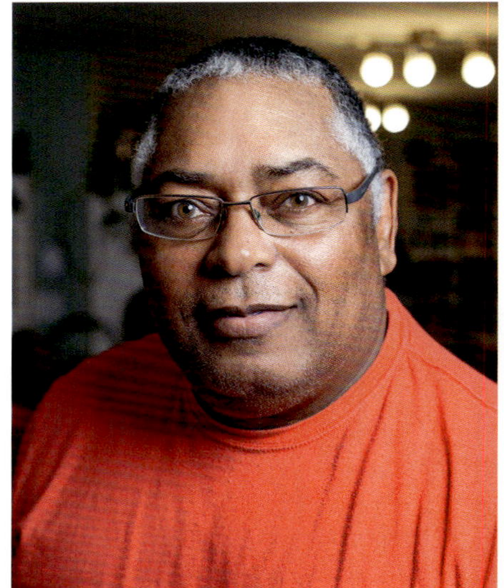

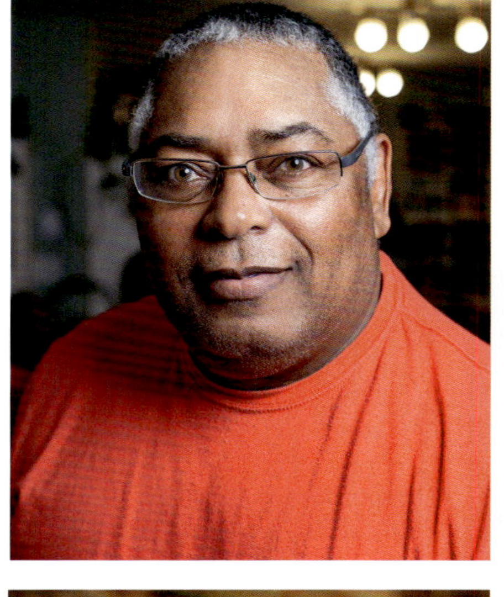

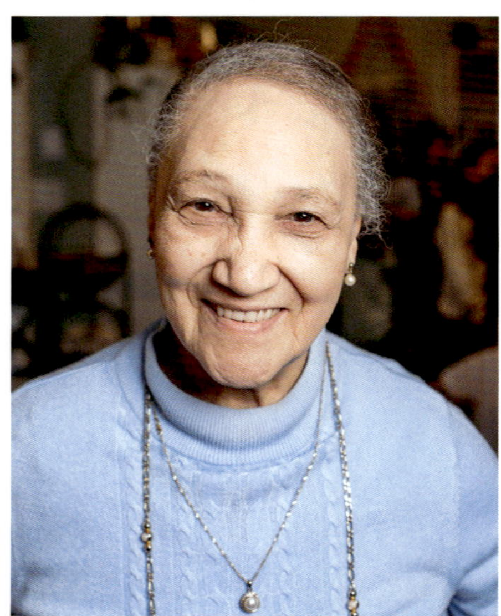

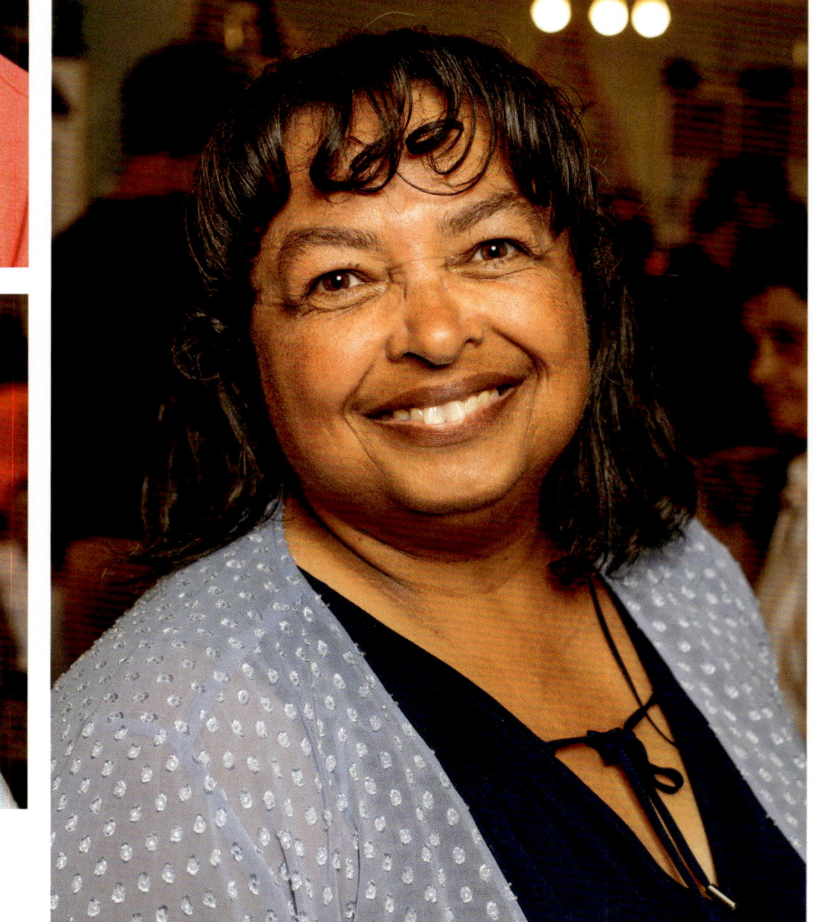

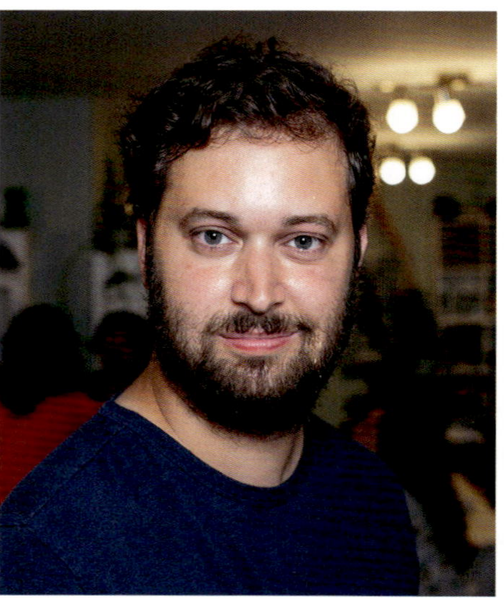

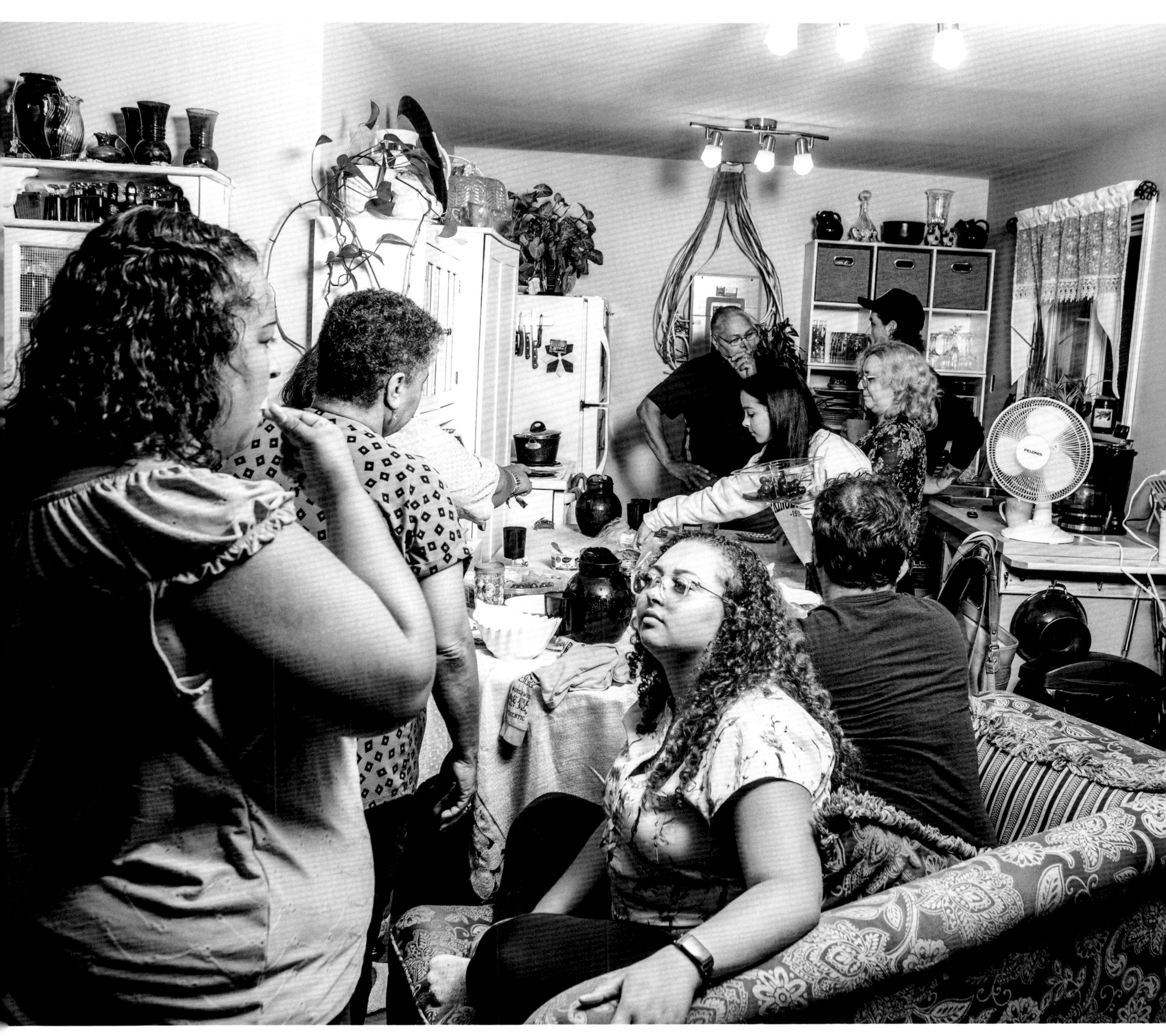
PELONIS

McCarty / Peters — Willow Grove

Many years ago
In the thick New Brunswick forest, down by a lake
Lay eleven acres of land.
Sold cheap as no roads greeted it
Nor did any electricity empower it.
Yet here on this land a speaker powerfully claims things are
"Still DRE."

Today saw a birthday party, that's why
Over a dozen family members navigated the tiny road to here.
A road so narrow that the trees scratched down our cars' sides.
Until we were saluted by the large McCarty flag.

Our host, Rosebud, laughed and told jokes as she introduced everyone.
The site impressed with half a dozen campers and a badminton court.
It took vision, love, and over a hundred pounds of crushed rock.
Yet the McCarty family had built something in the middle of nowhere.

Everything around us was intentional, comforting.
Colourful rocks sprinkled the pathway to the water.
Now, three kids and a dog savoured the breeze-combed lake.
They played on the dock they helped their family build.

The McCarty family purchased their heritage land then invested in
Tractors, chainsaws, trucks, and years of sweat.
To build a sanctuary housing the family feasts and frolics
That matter most.

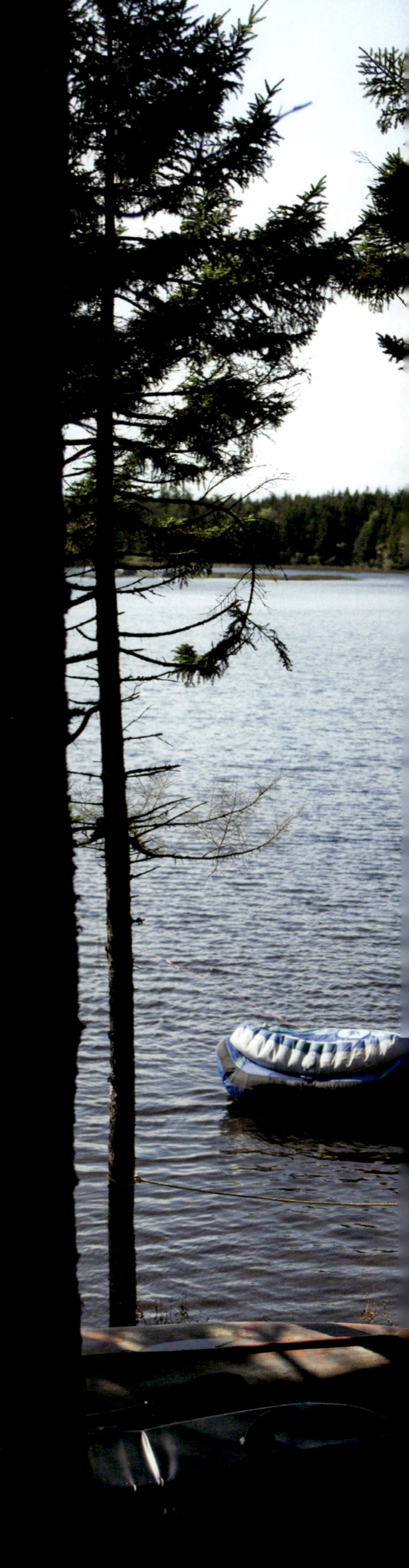

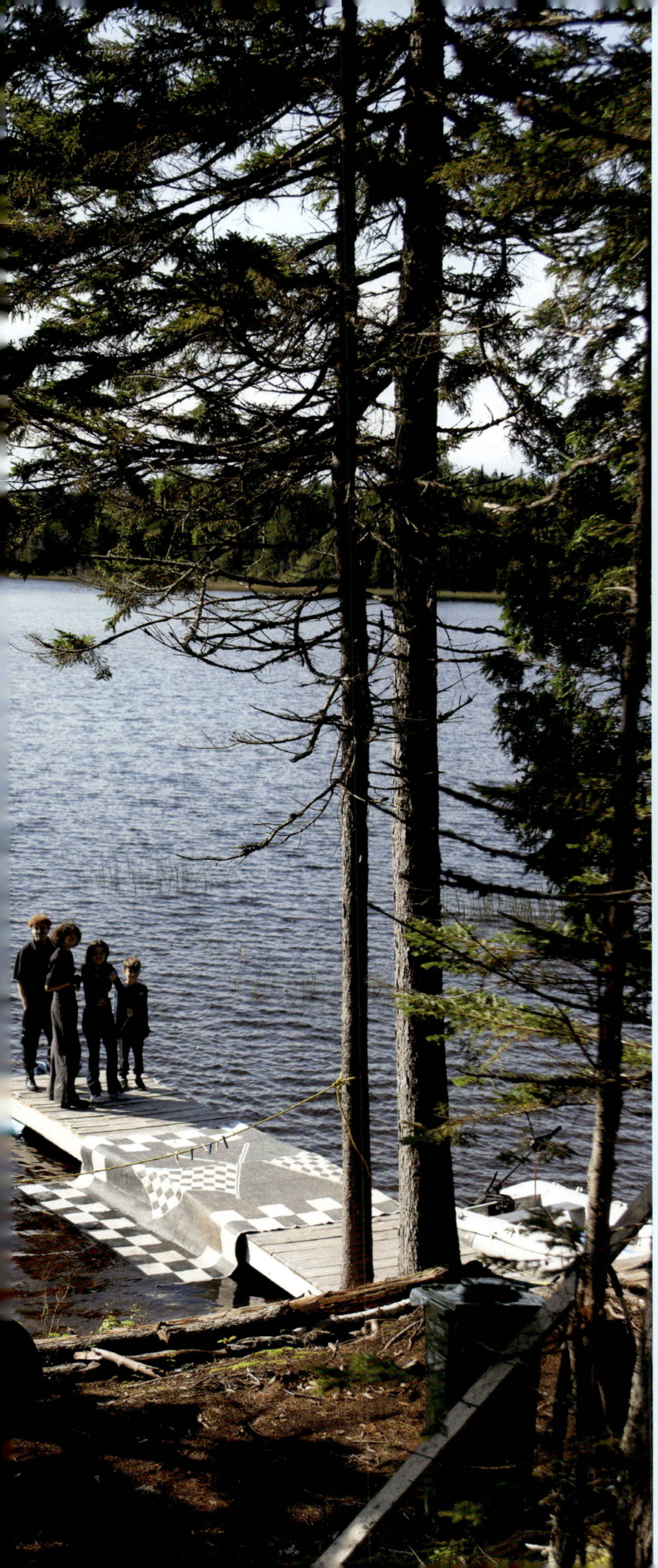

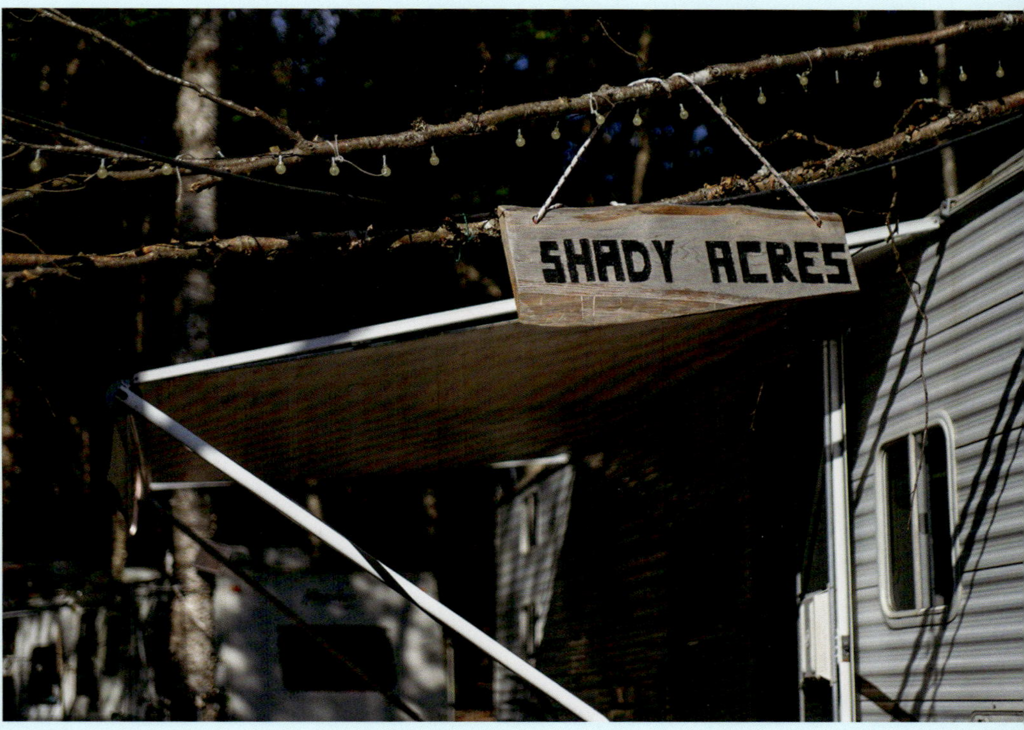

Sometimes history repeats itself, miraculously.
Sometimes those disconnected
Can work their way back
Home.

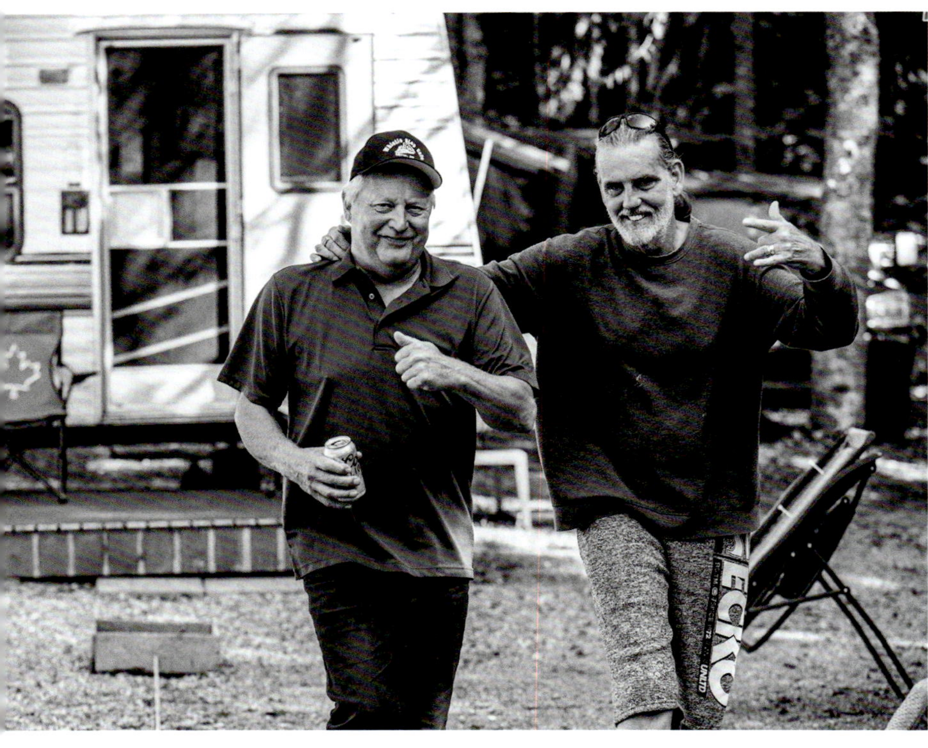

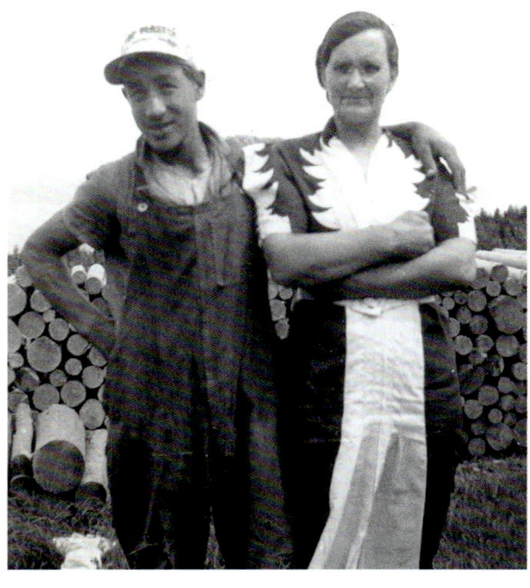

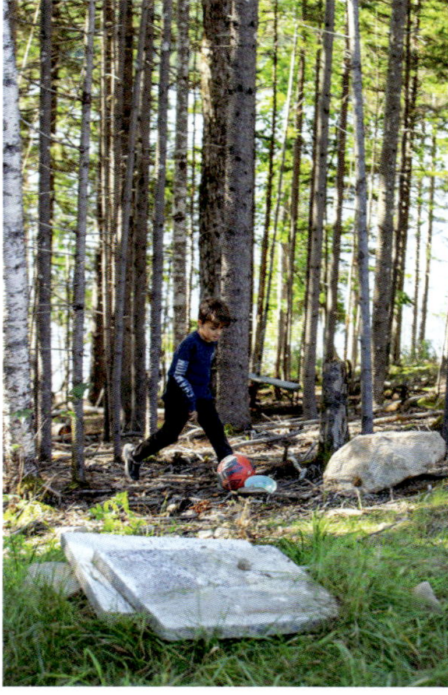

Of eleven children, I was the youngest by a generation. My brothers would visit and help my mother with things like making a bathroom and putting in all the plumbing—amazing. Rumour has it my brother stole the toilet from somewhere in town. Welcome to the '60s.
—Rosebud McCarty

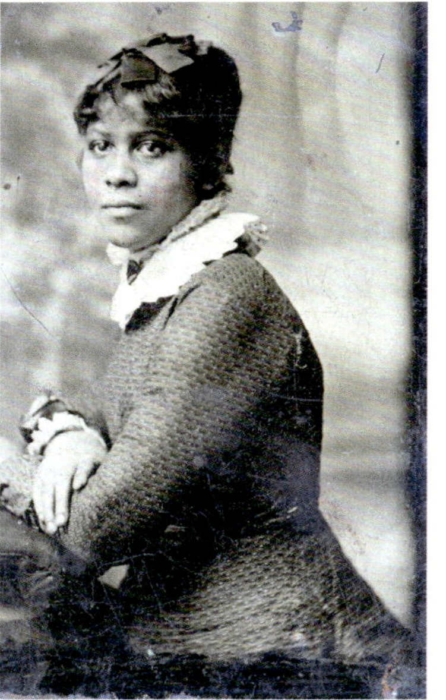

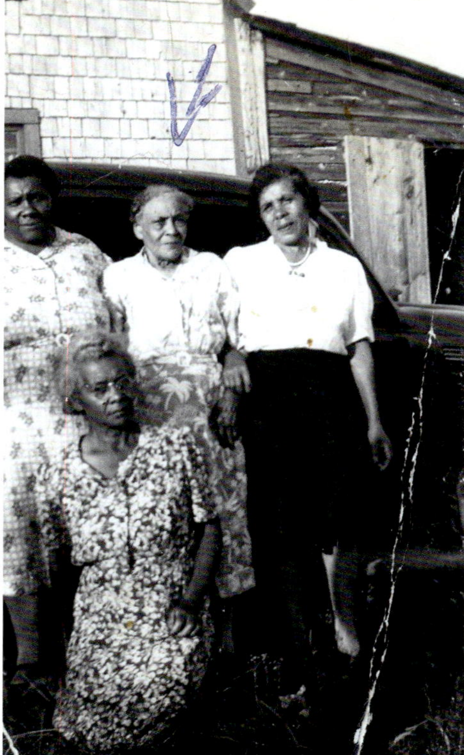

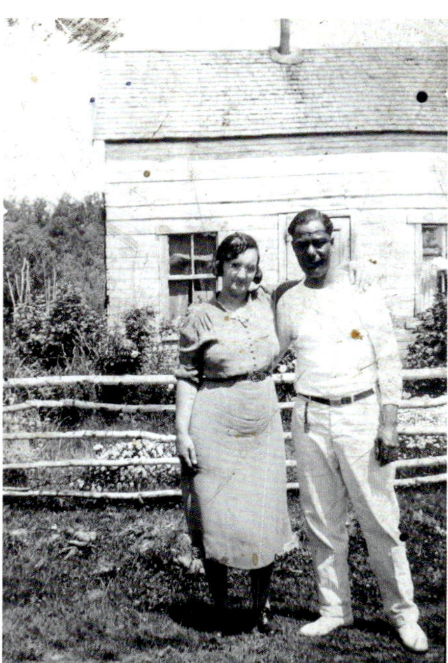

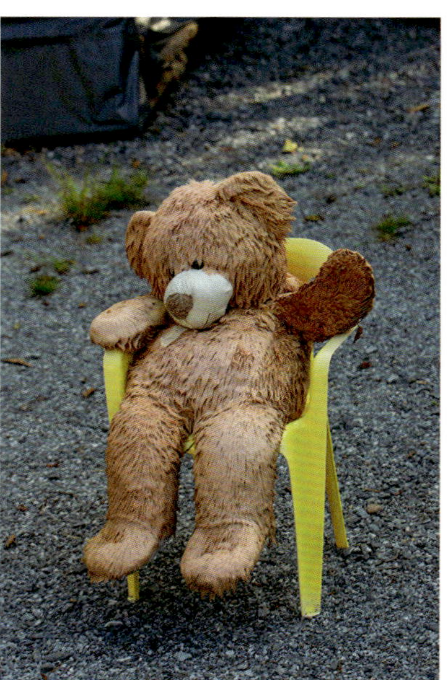

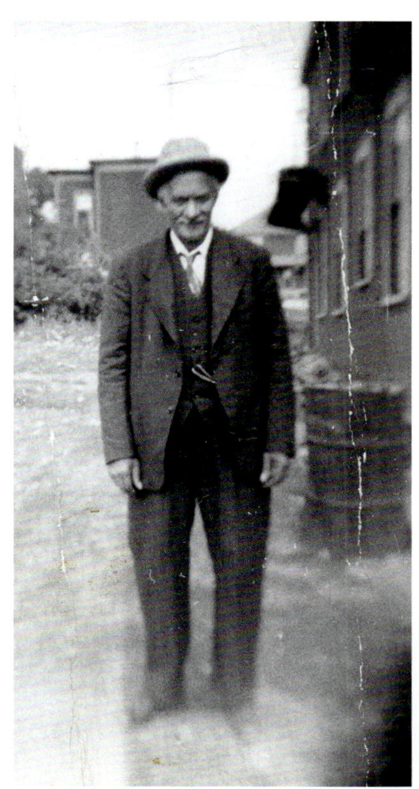

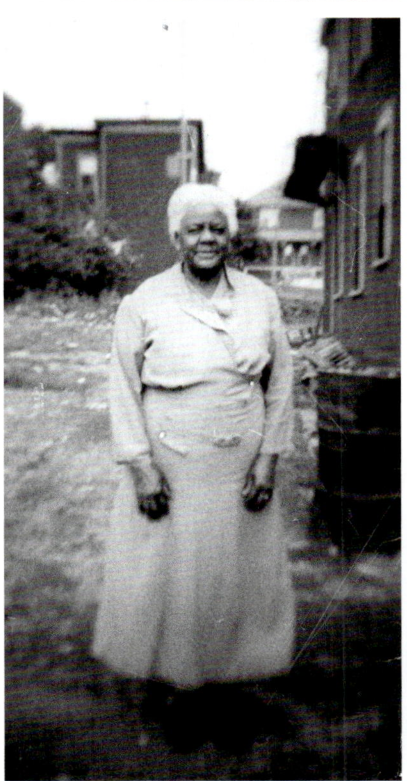

The McCarty family have long been a pillar of the New Brunswick Black community. They date their New Brunswick roots to as early as 1875, when Katherine "Rosebud" McCarty's grandfather Clarence W. McCarty was born in Kingsclear. Rosebud grew up outside Saint John with her mother and her ten siblings, and for decades the family had a designated spot at the well-known Black Picnics at Lily Lake.

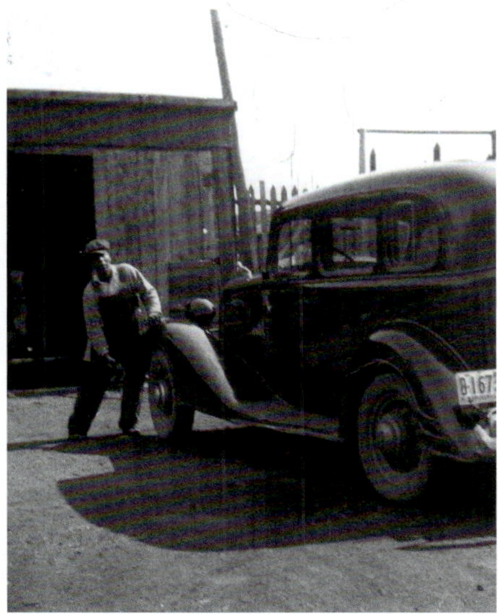

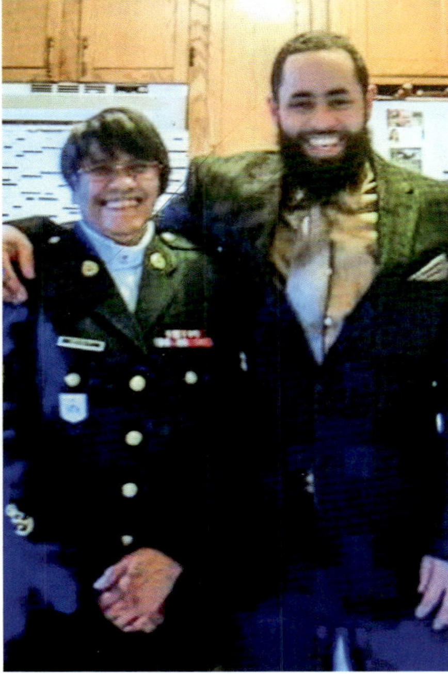

Rosebud's aunt Lila married Ewing Paris, a "strict businessman and a self-employed truck driver with a heart of gold." As her godfather, he gifted Rosebud her first home, in Saint John, where her mother, Katherine Marie McCarty (née Peters), lived until her passing in October 2000. "Her death marked the end of an era."

Multiple generations of the McCartys have served in the Canadian Armed Forces: Rosebud's father, Harold Vincent McCarty, born in 1901, lied about his age to enlist in the First World War in 1916. He returned home to Fredericton in 1919 as a decorated veteran. Though he died in 1957 when she was only eighteen months old, "like father, like daughter," Rosebud lied about her age to enlist in 1973 when she was only seventeen. She served in Afghanistan and the Middle East and retired in 2016.

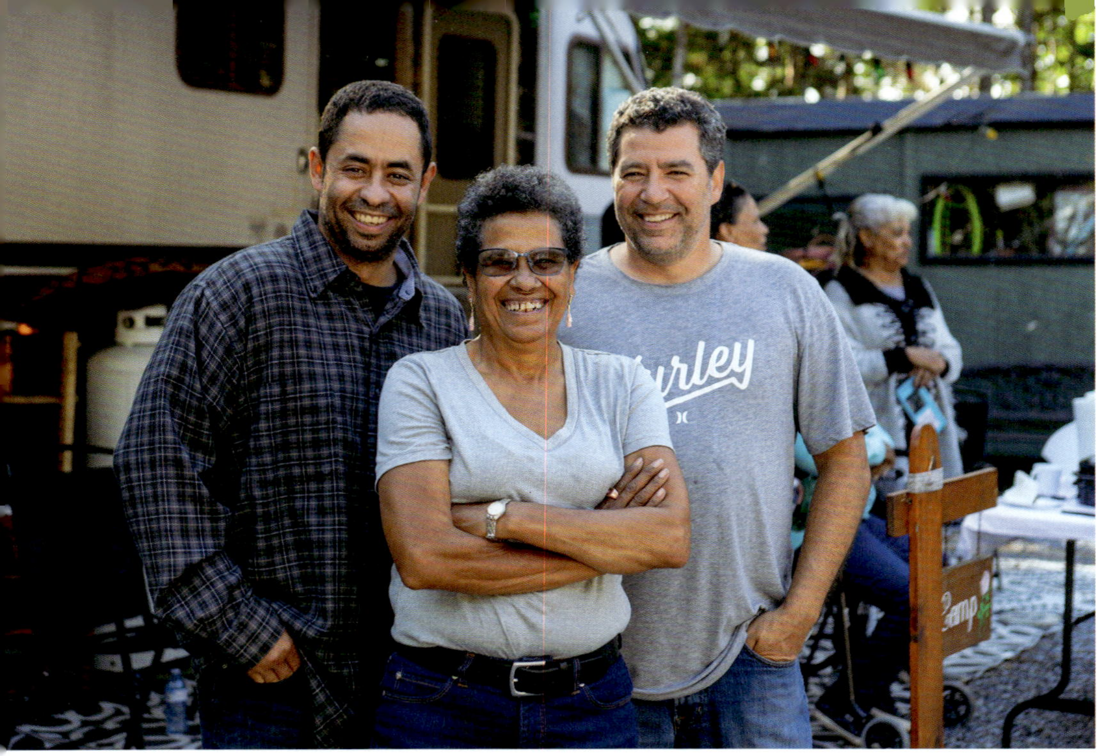

Through research I learned that the land was once granted to Hannah Flood. A few years have passed and I'm still looking for answers. How did so many Blacks lose their granted land in Willow Grove? What happened to the fifty-five acres that surrounded this lake?
—Rosebud McCarty

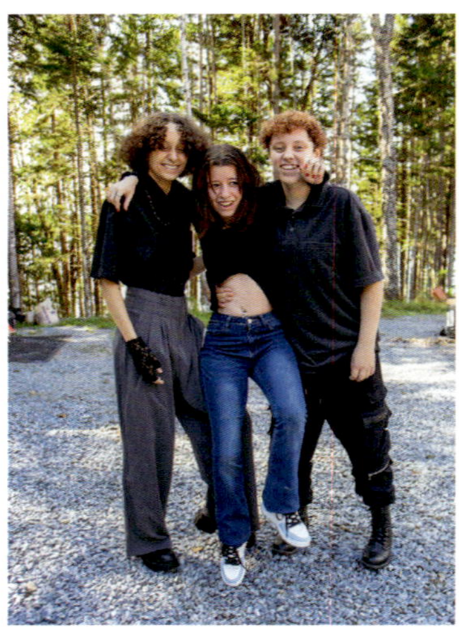

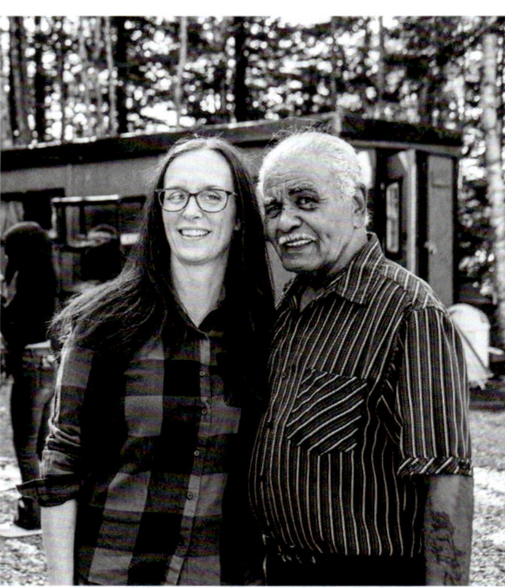

Early in the COVID-19 pandemic, Rosebud bought some land in Willow Grove. Willow Grove was founded by Black refugees and former slaves fleeing the US after the War of 1812. Black settlers received three-year licences to fifty-acre plots of land that were uncleared, rocky, and difficult to farm. Research suggests that the original grant to the McCarty's portion of Willow Grove was licensed to Hannah Flood in 1837.

No longer a family of subsistence farmers, Rosebud and her sons and grandchildren moved to Willow Grove in 2020.

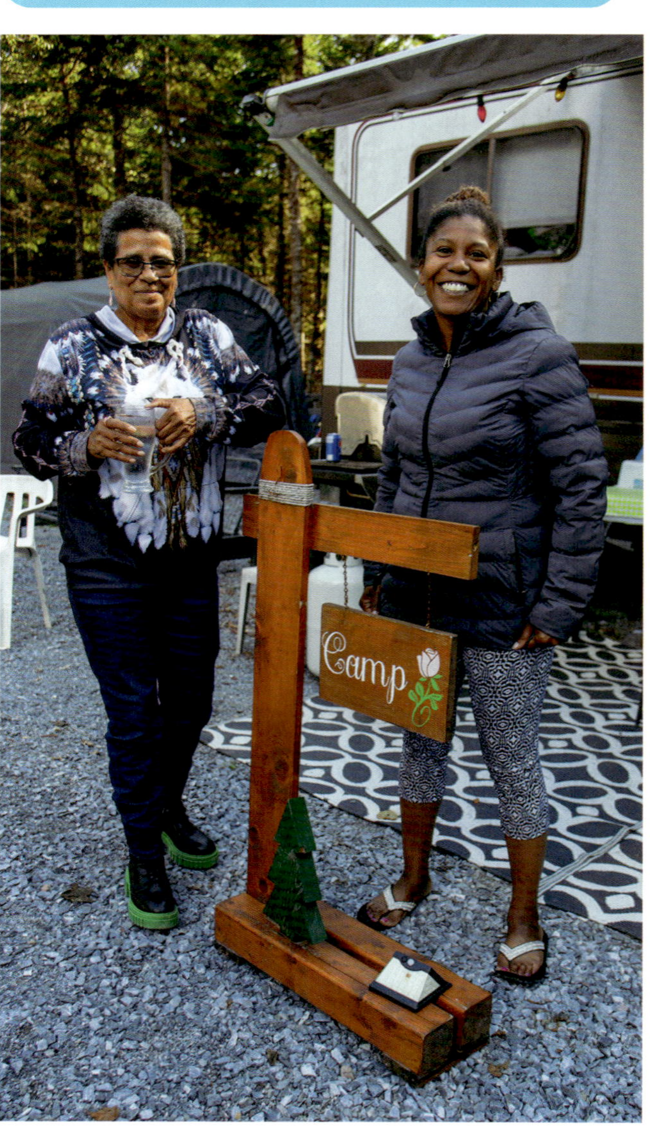

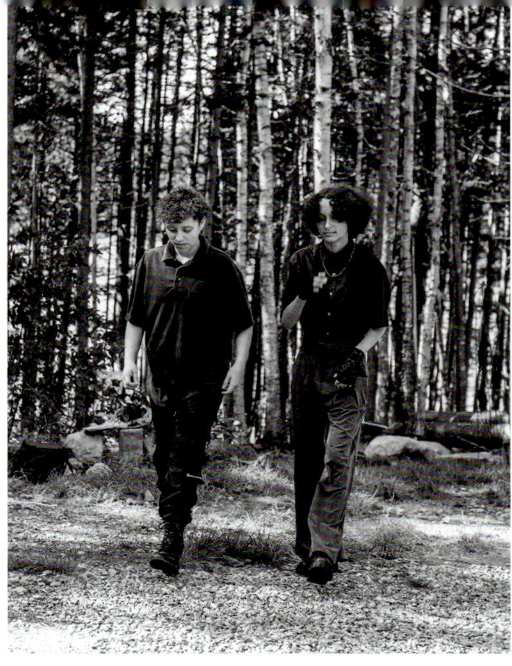

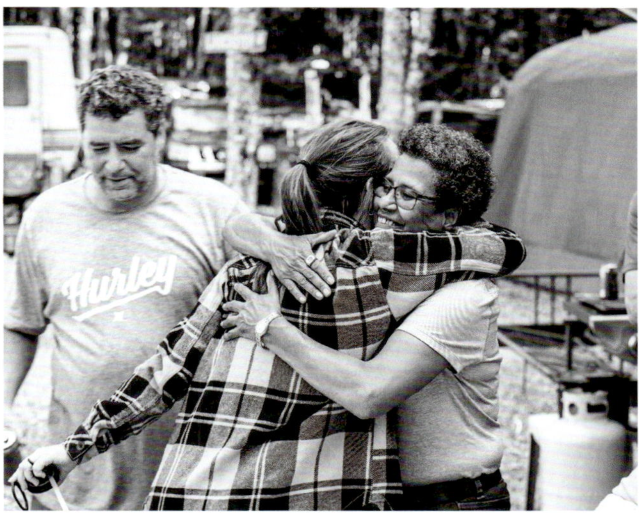

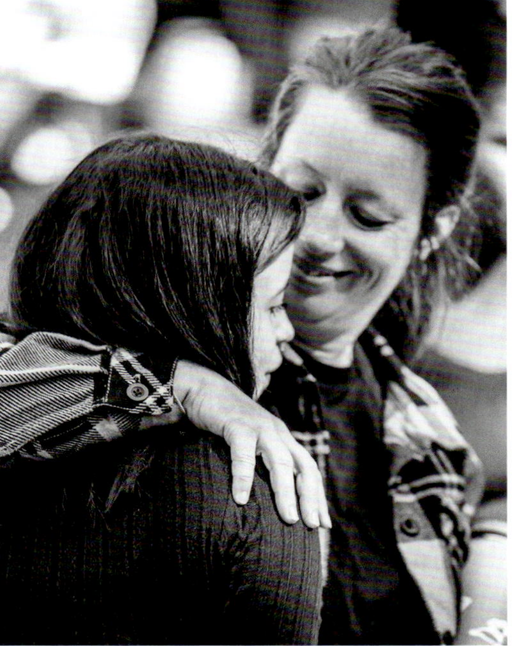

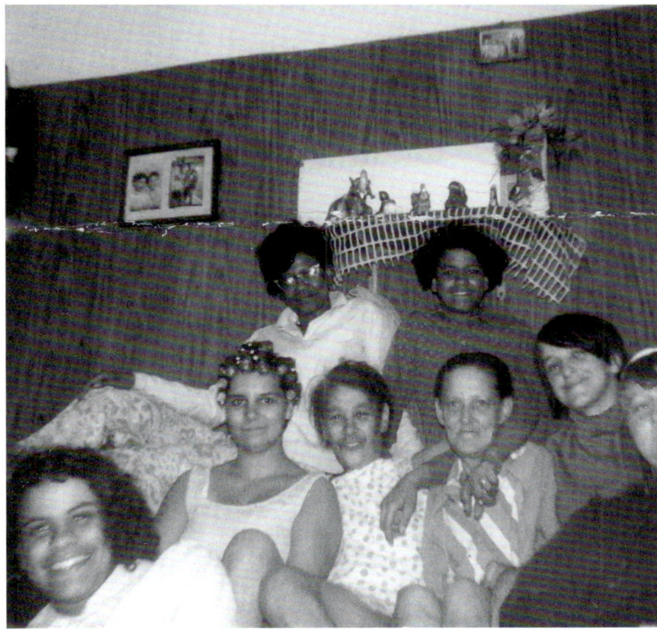

My world changed when I first attended school. The other kids would call me the N-word and laugh when I walked by. Well, I got angry. And I never had that problem again. I'm glad I hit that kid with my science book.
— Rosebud McCarty

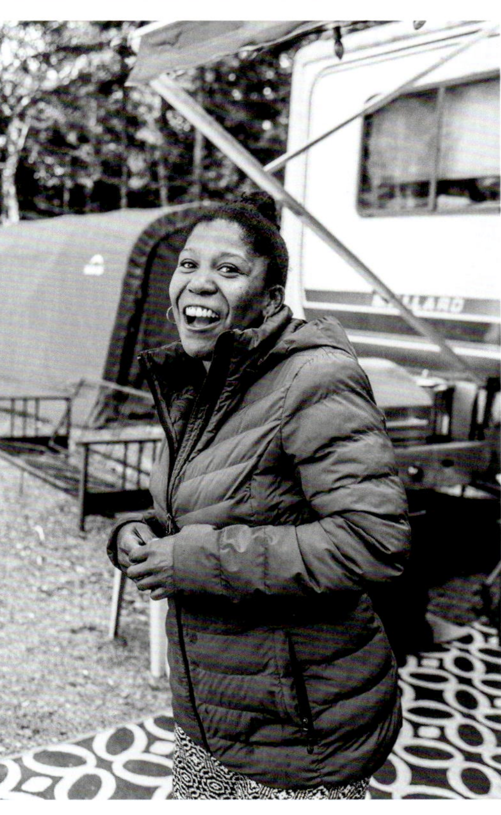

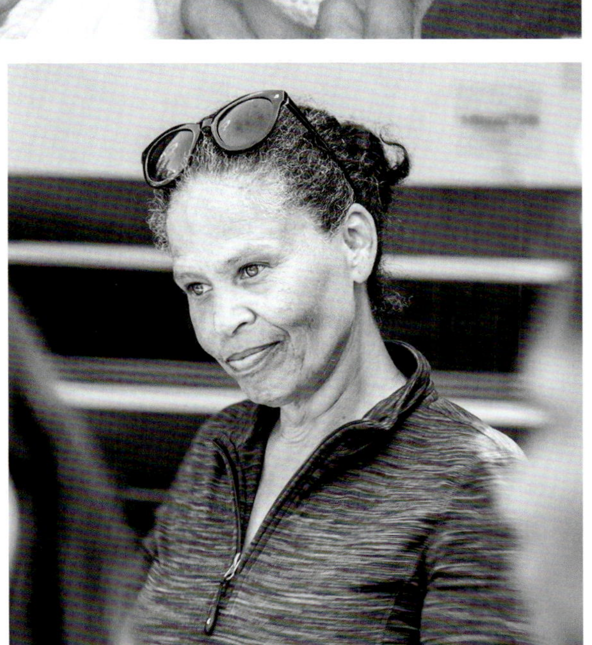

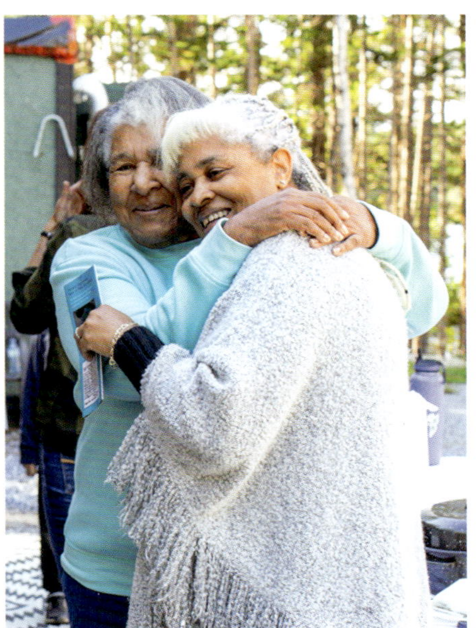

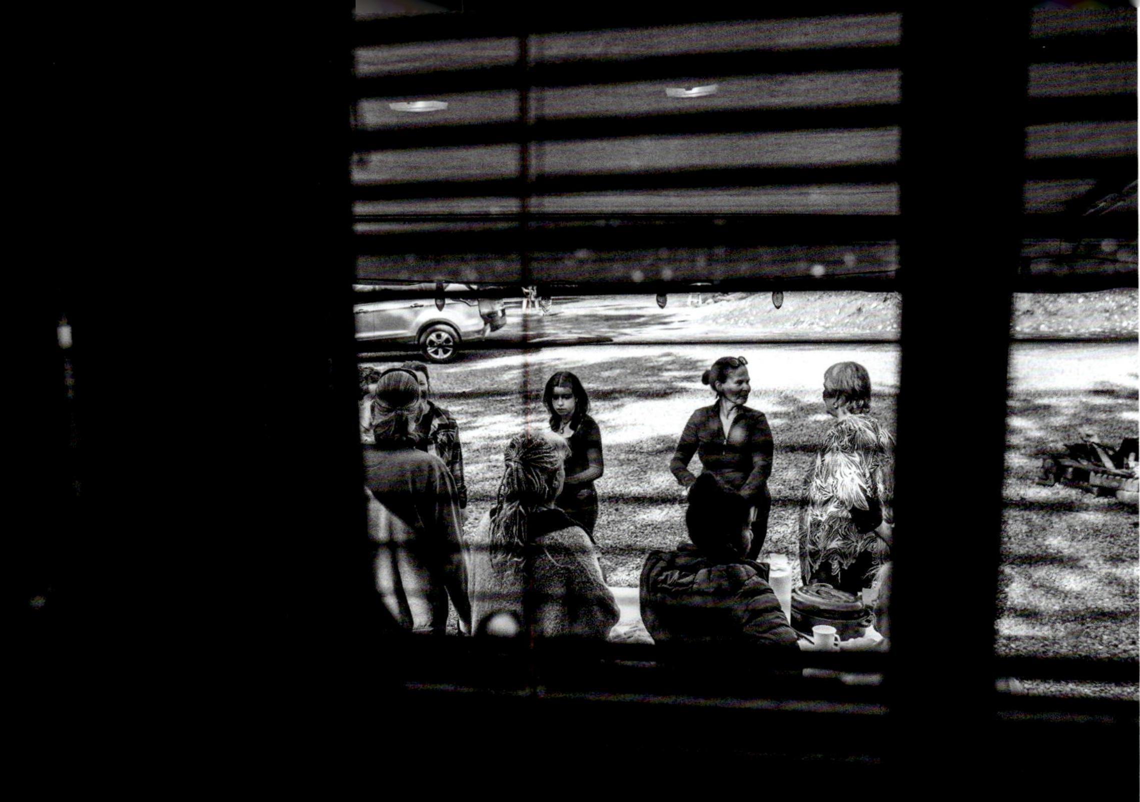

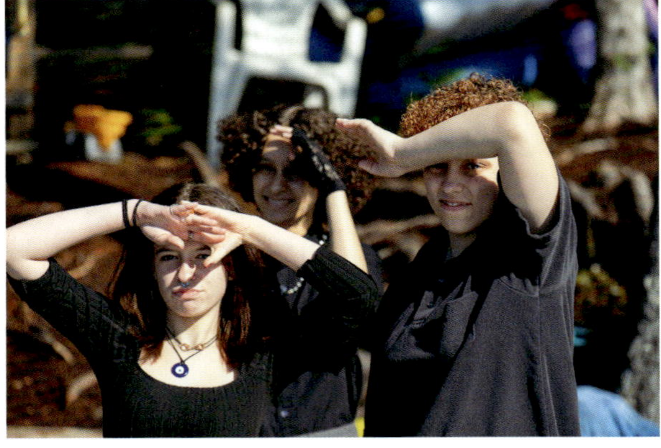

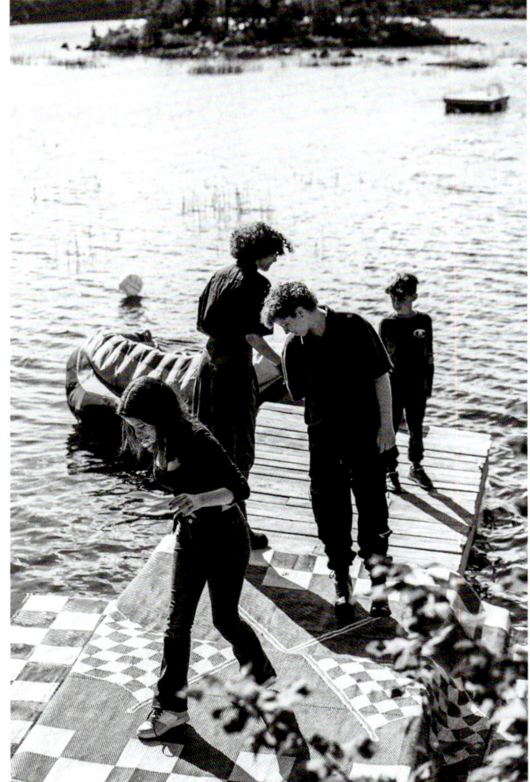

Even though I never really met my father, I followed in his footprints, and when I thought I could not go any longer, I would think of him. This made me strong, helped me dig deep into my soul, and kept me moving forward.
— Rosebud McCarty

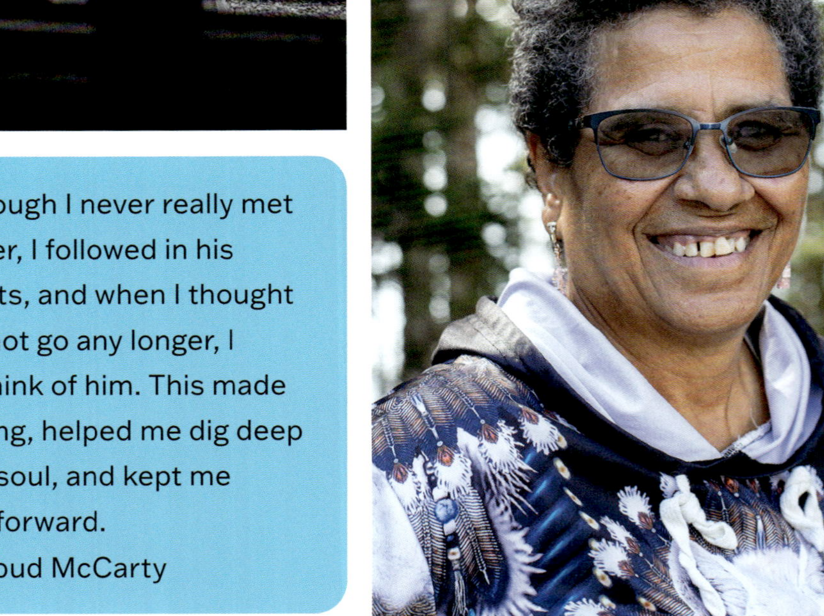

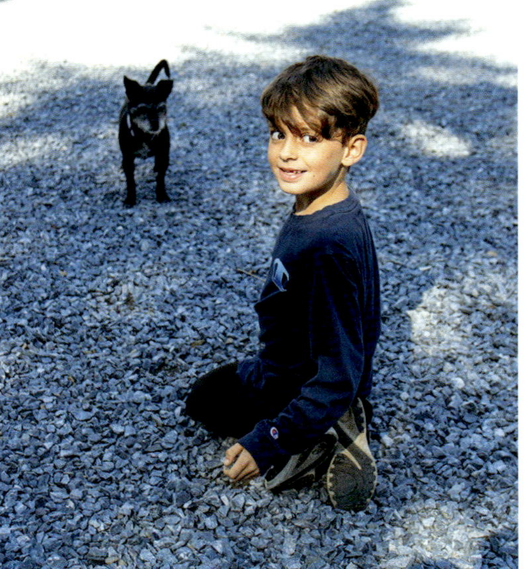

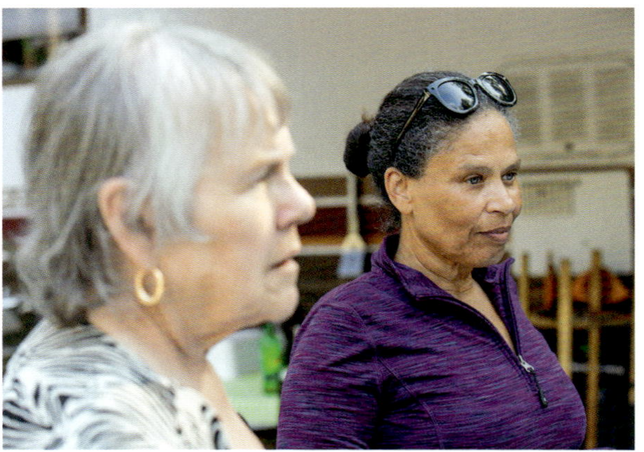

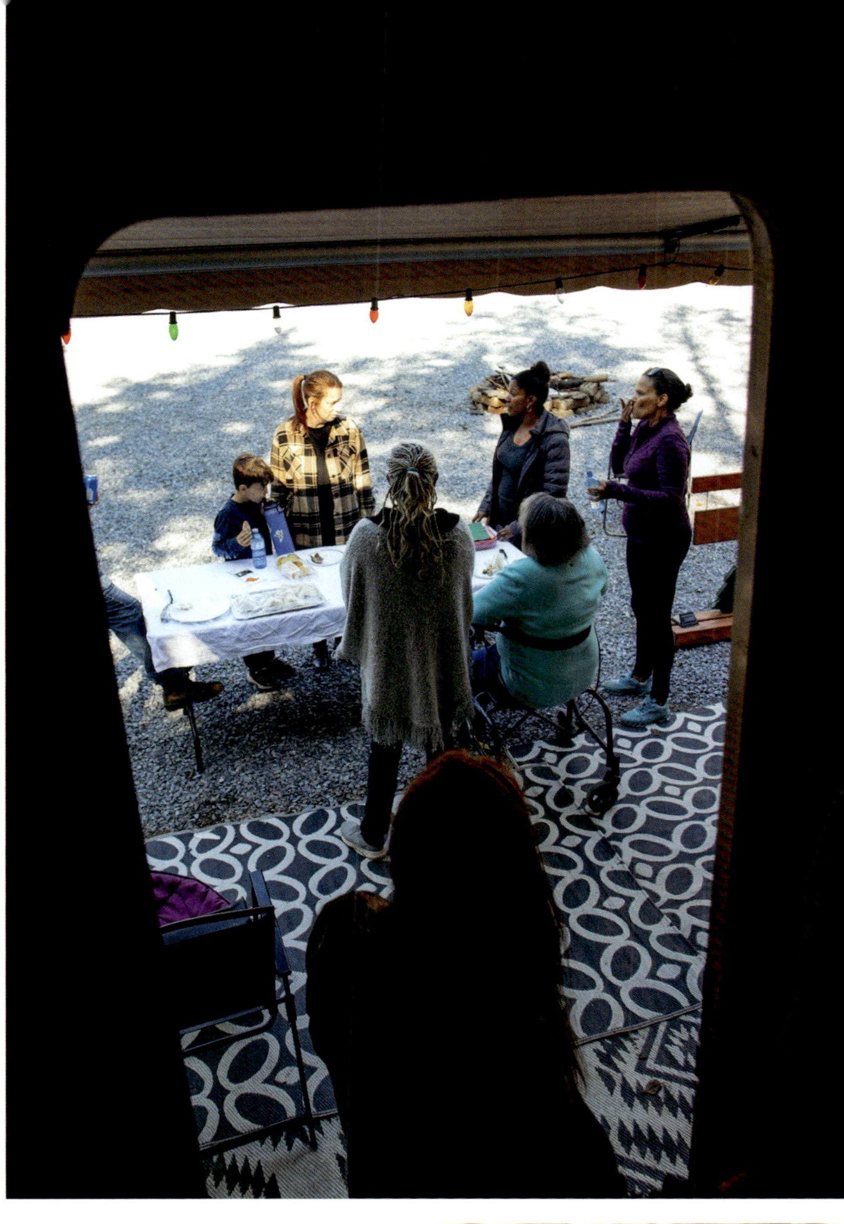
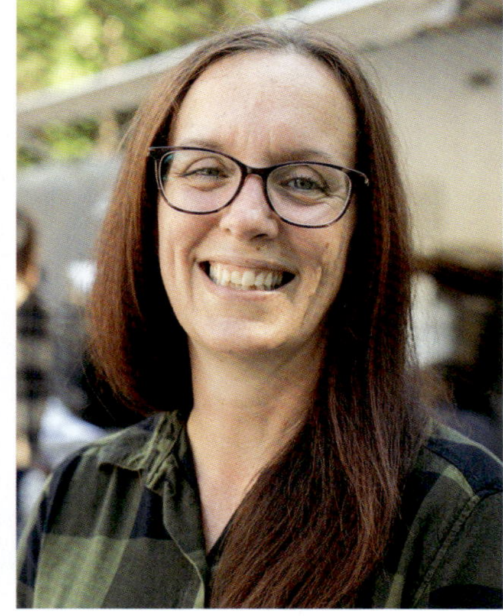
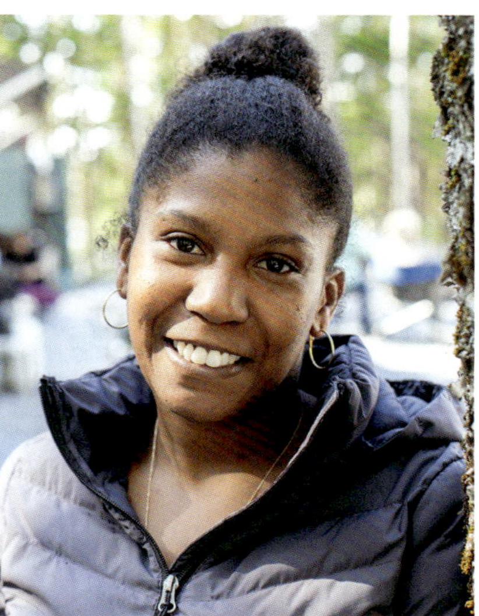
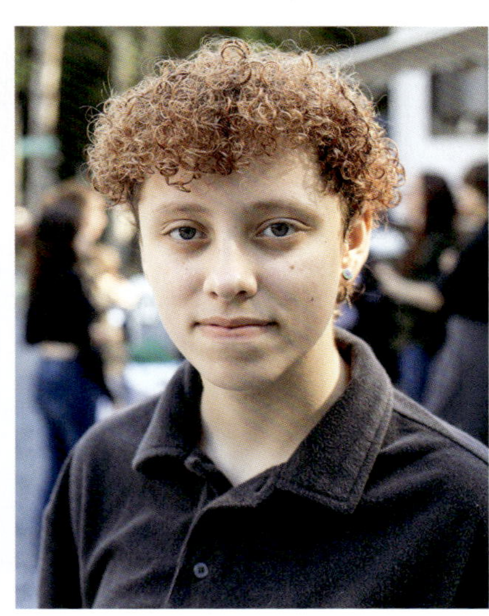
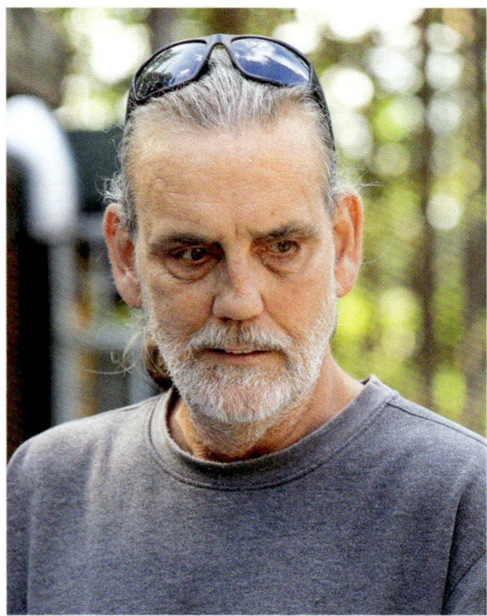
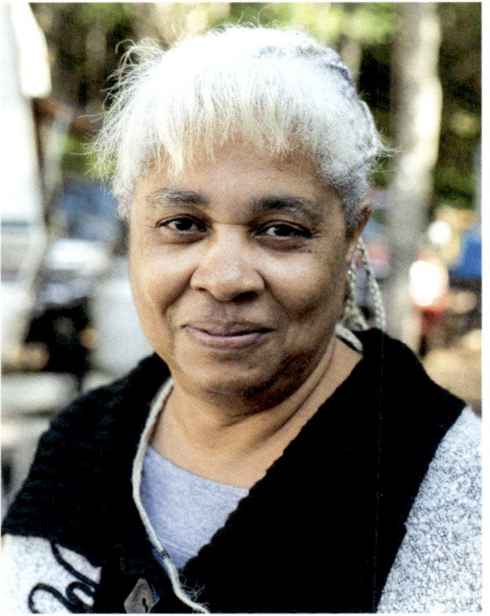
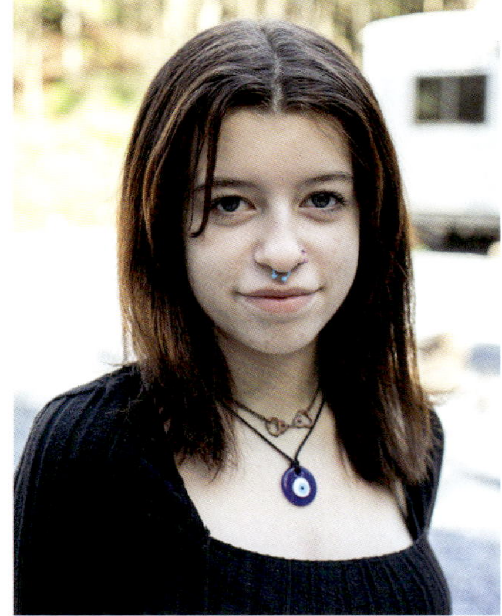
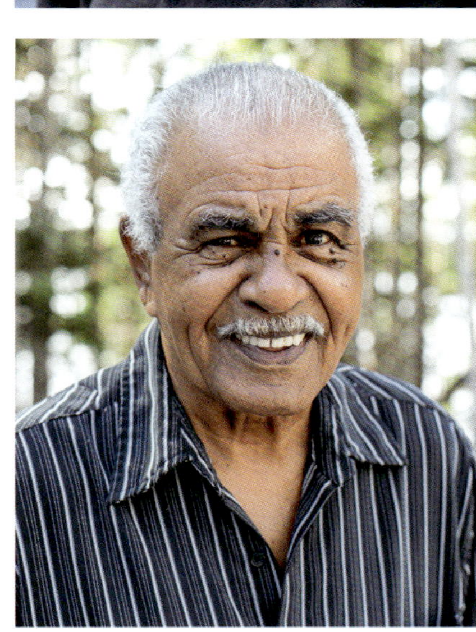

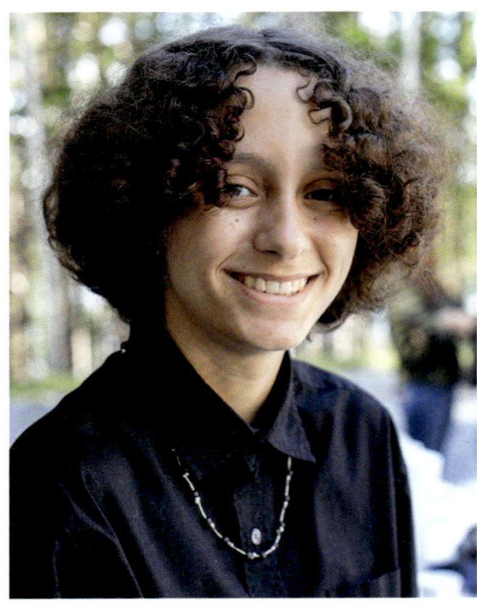
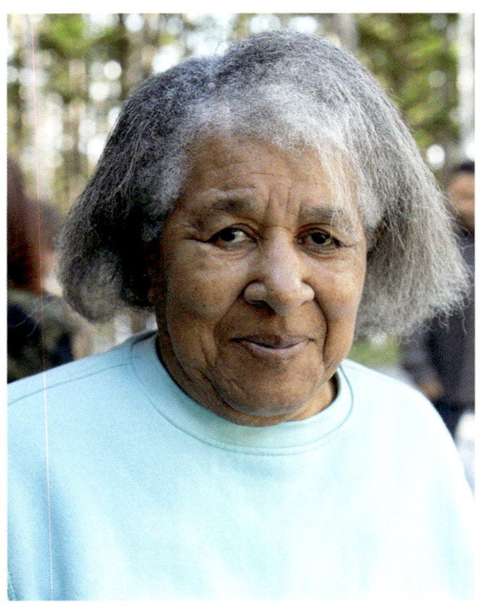
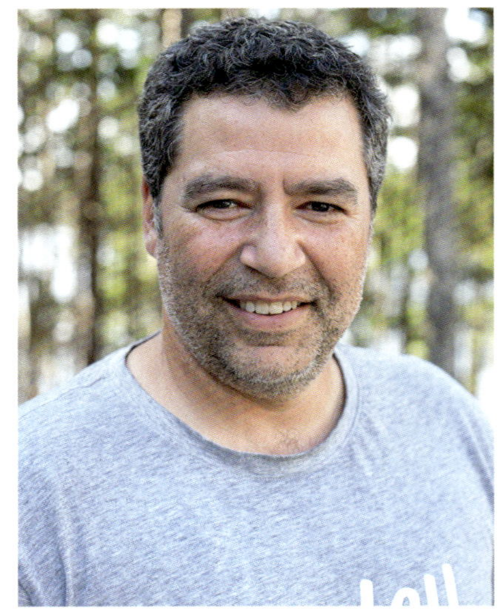
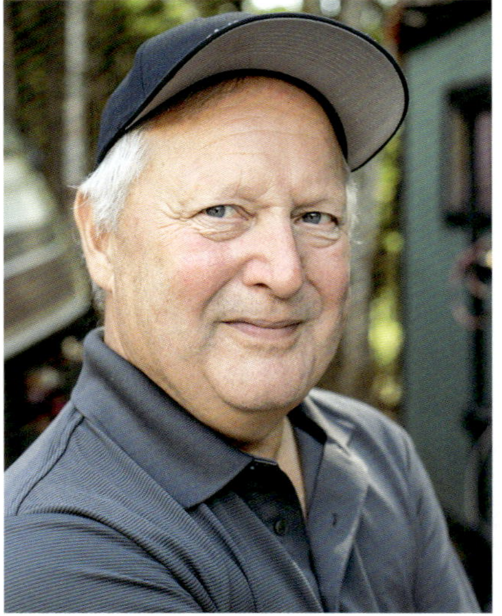
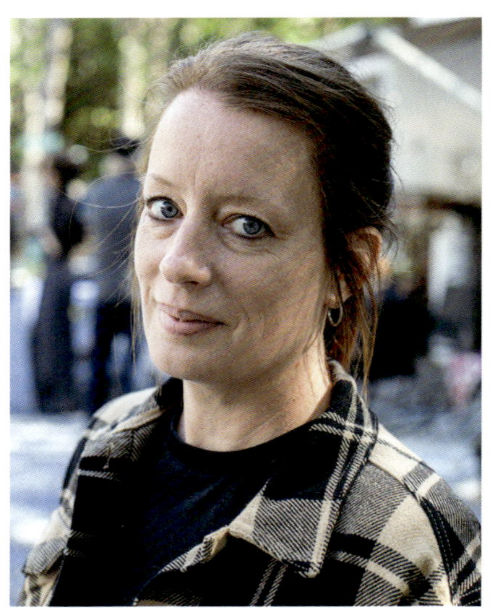
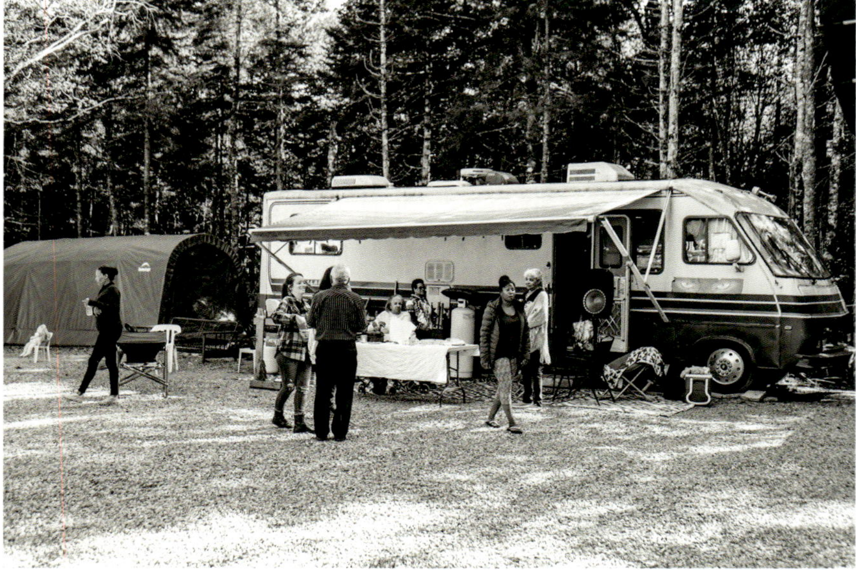
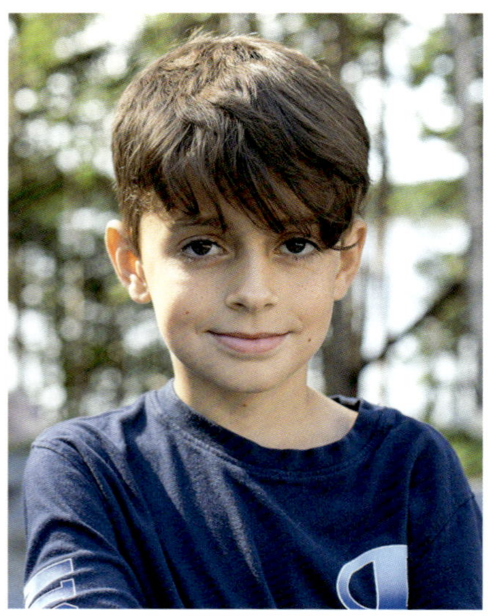
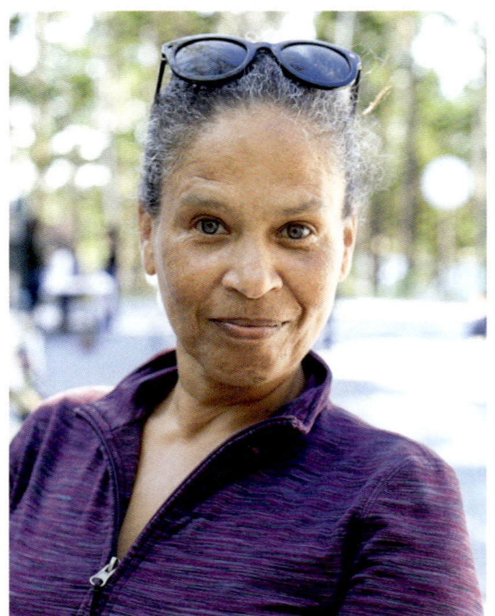

As a child, I lived on a dead end called the Proud Road, with only three families on it at the time. We had no indoor plumbing, and the nearest corner store was two and a half miles away. There was no car, money was not part of the conversation, no city transit.... But as my mother always said, "You have two feet and a heartbeat."
—Rosebud McCarty

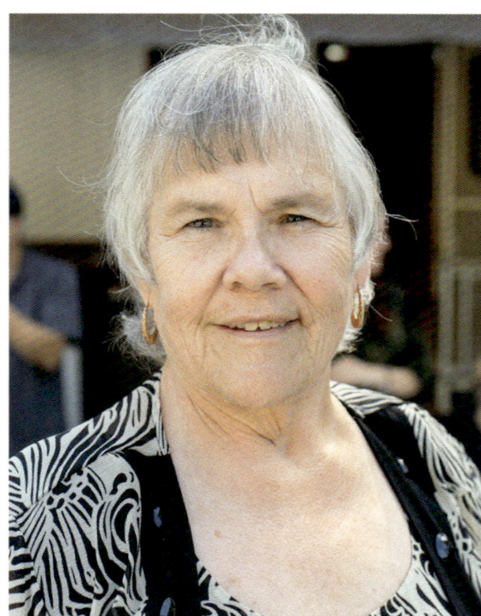

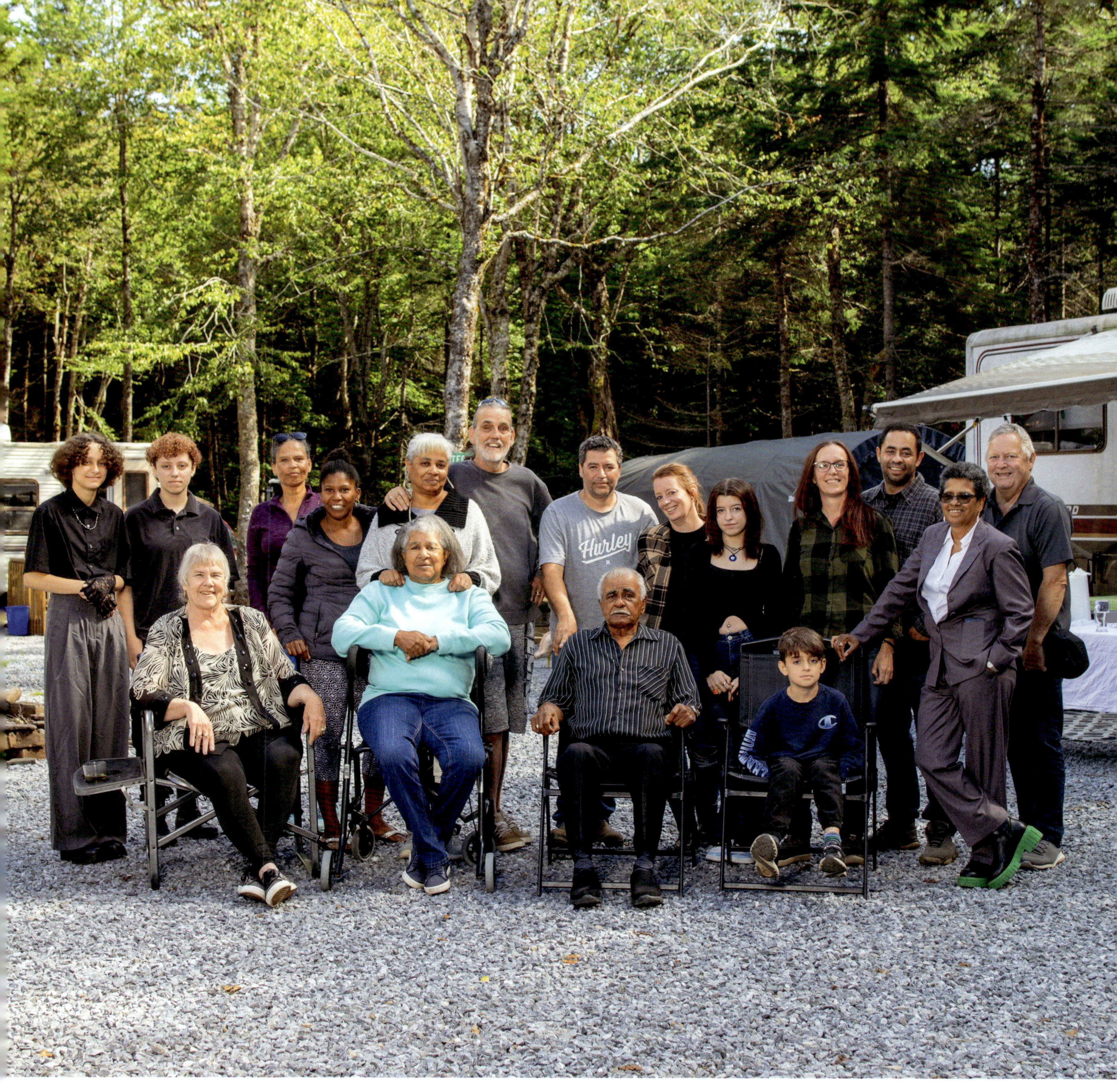
Hurley

Mc Intyre / Gendral — Elm Hill and Gagetown

North of Elm Hill, New Brunswick
A Black community nearly as old as Africville.
There is the Orchard View Long Term Care Home,
Where the Mc Intyre photo shoot took place.

Unity is what will heal our community.

The staff were delighted to do all they could
To grant us a feeling of home.
Reminding us that history
Is eventually where all our elders live.

Unity is what will teach our community.

Inside one room stood Gerald and his aunt Audry.
A woman in her nineties with care-giving eyes.
"God only favours the love in your heart."
A quote to frame the acclaimed gathering.

Unity is what will free our community.

Gerald built steel poles and plaques in Elm Hill
To project Black history to every onlooker.
So that any visitor to this once-thriving settlement
Could see the ancestral vision.

Unity is what will safeguard our history.

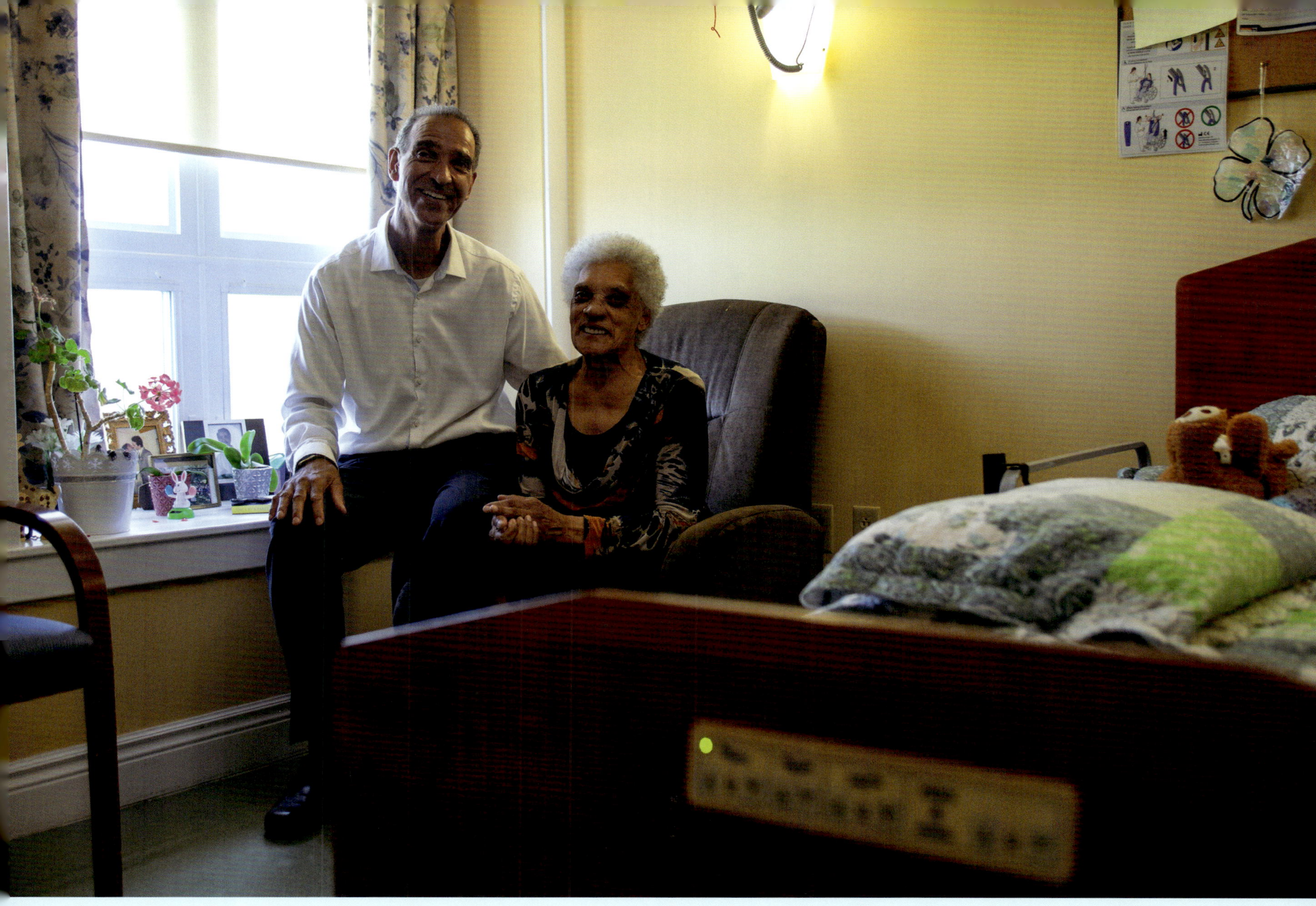

As I sat in the bathroom, next to the toilet,
Scanning documents, thus augmenting history.
I smiled, reflecting on past lives and passed-down passions.
Across the room Audrey watched, and she was smiling, too.

Family history says that four Mc Intyre brothers decided to jump ship in a wooden barrel and swam to the shores of an area known today as Grand Lake. Like other Black community members of the Grand Lake area, they were offered grants of land in Elm Hill and decided to relocate.
— Gerald Mc Intyre

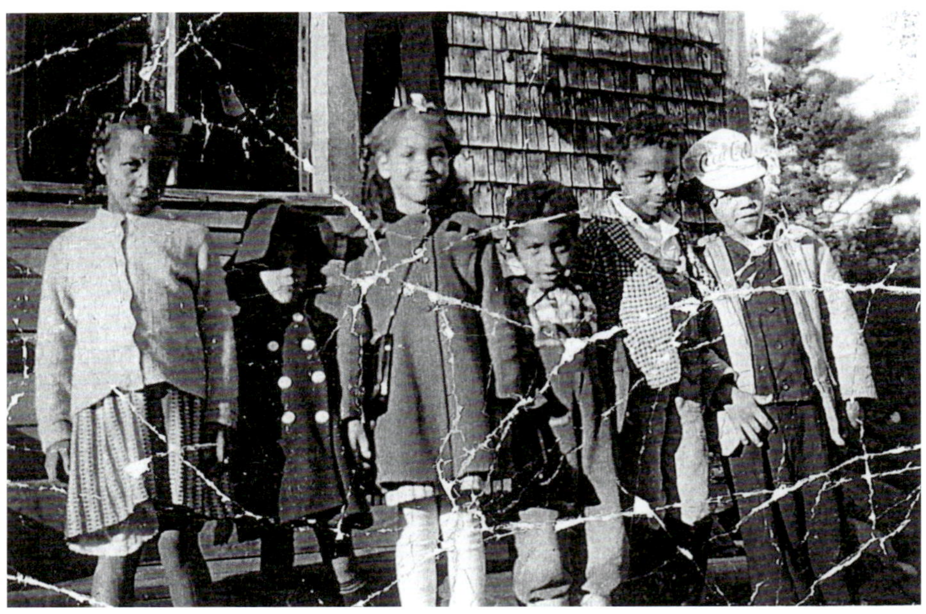

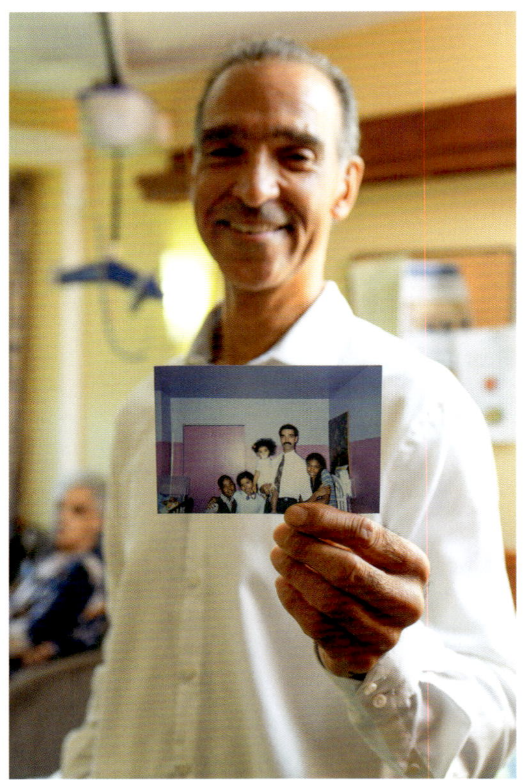

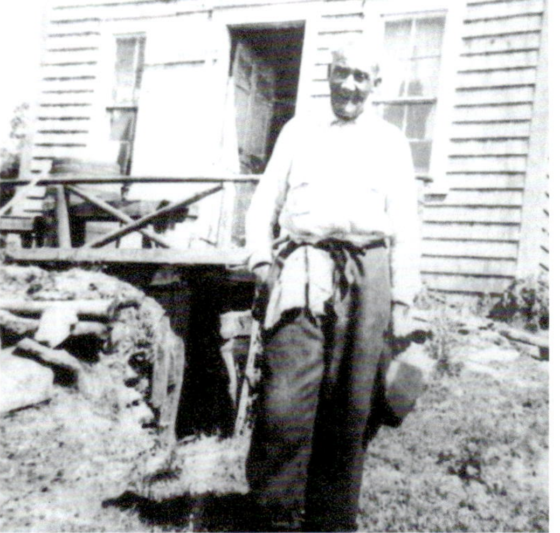

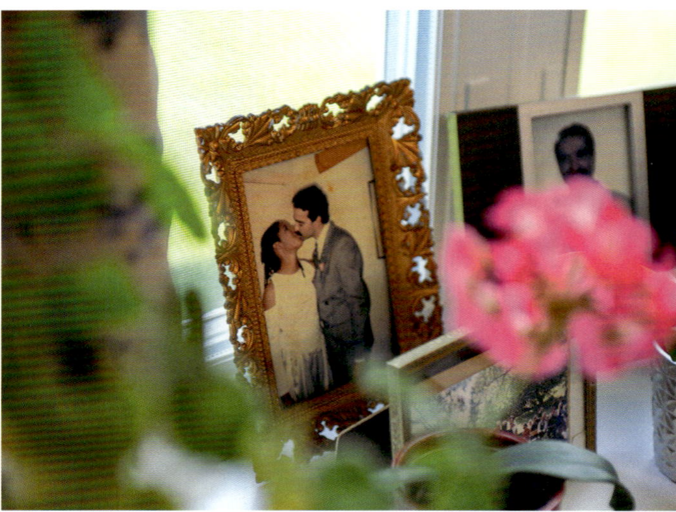

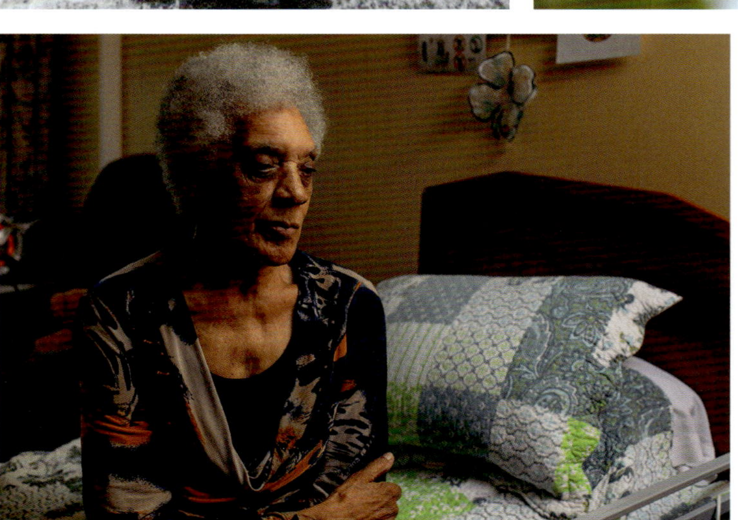

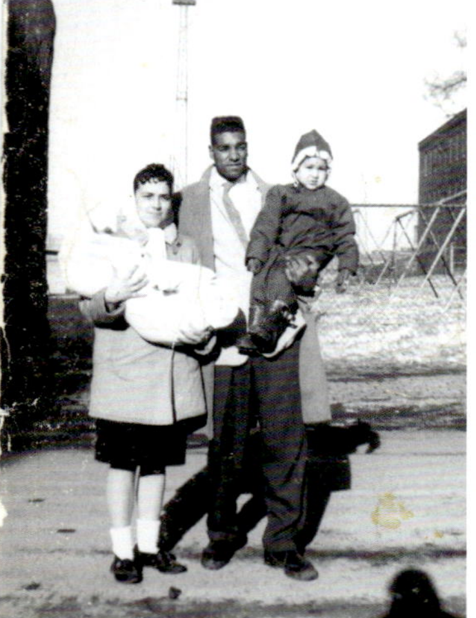

Despite popular belief, the first Afrocentric individuals to arrive in the Americas were not slaves, but explorers in the 1500s, followed by indentured servants in the early to mid-1600s. Gerald Mc Intyre, who is an activist for anti-racism and social justice, as well as a family genealogist, can trace his family back to the early 1600s.

The first African Canadians to settle in Elm Hill originated from the US, as free escaped slaves and loyalists. The Mc Intyres helped to develop and grow the beautiful village of Elm Hill and the Elm Hill community, when it was originally settled in 1806, with approximately 240 people, two churches, a store, and a post office.

Gerald's great-great-grandfather was a cook who arrived on a ship from Jamaica. In 1853 he had a daughter named Adelia Gendral. Adelia was born near the lower Queenstown Quarry, but eventually moved and settled in the Elm Hill Community, where she opened her own store. She married John Mc Intyre, who was tall and slender and apparently quite handsome, with curly hair and light skin. They had daughters and many sons, including one in 1891 named Elbridge Blair Mc Intyre.

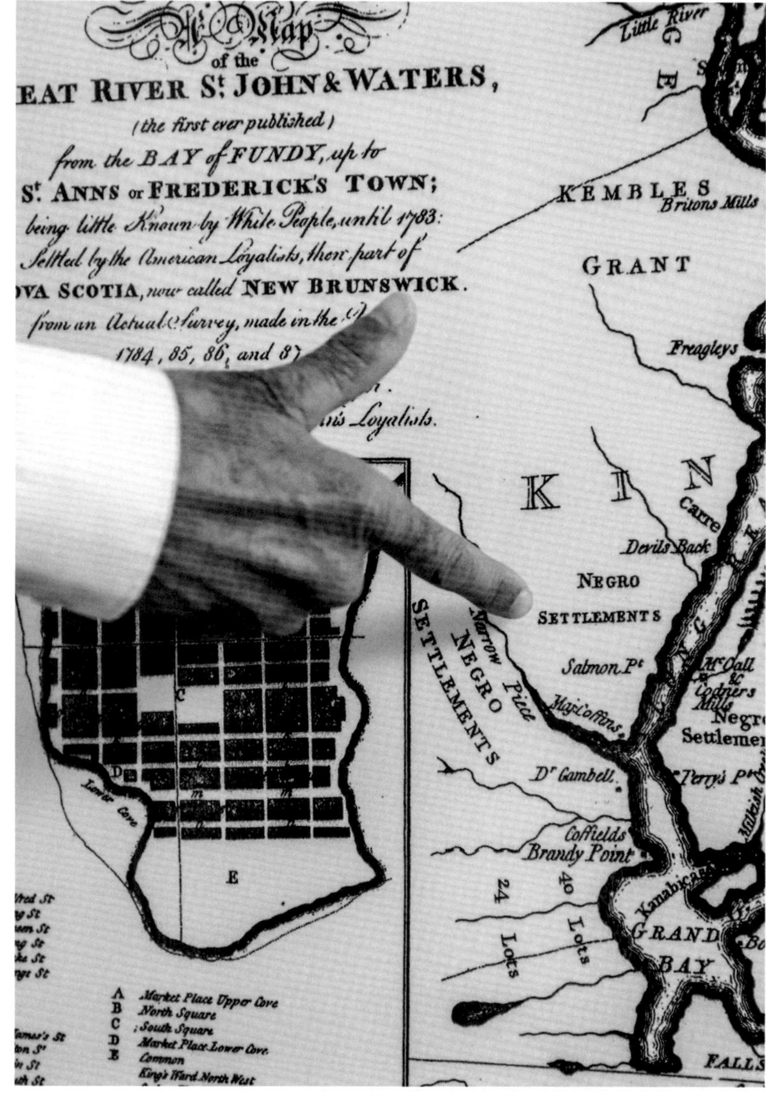

Elbridge married Mary Elizabeth II in 1931, and they had four children: John Leonard, Audrey Leona, Alvin Willard, and finally Gerald Freeman. In the early 1960s Gerald moved to Montreal to find work, because farming in Elm Hill was dying. He there met Gisele Grazulise, and they had a child and named him Gerald Hudson Mc Intyre. Gerald Jr. returned to New Brunswick, purchased land in Elm Hill, was married, and had many children of his own.

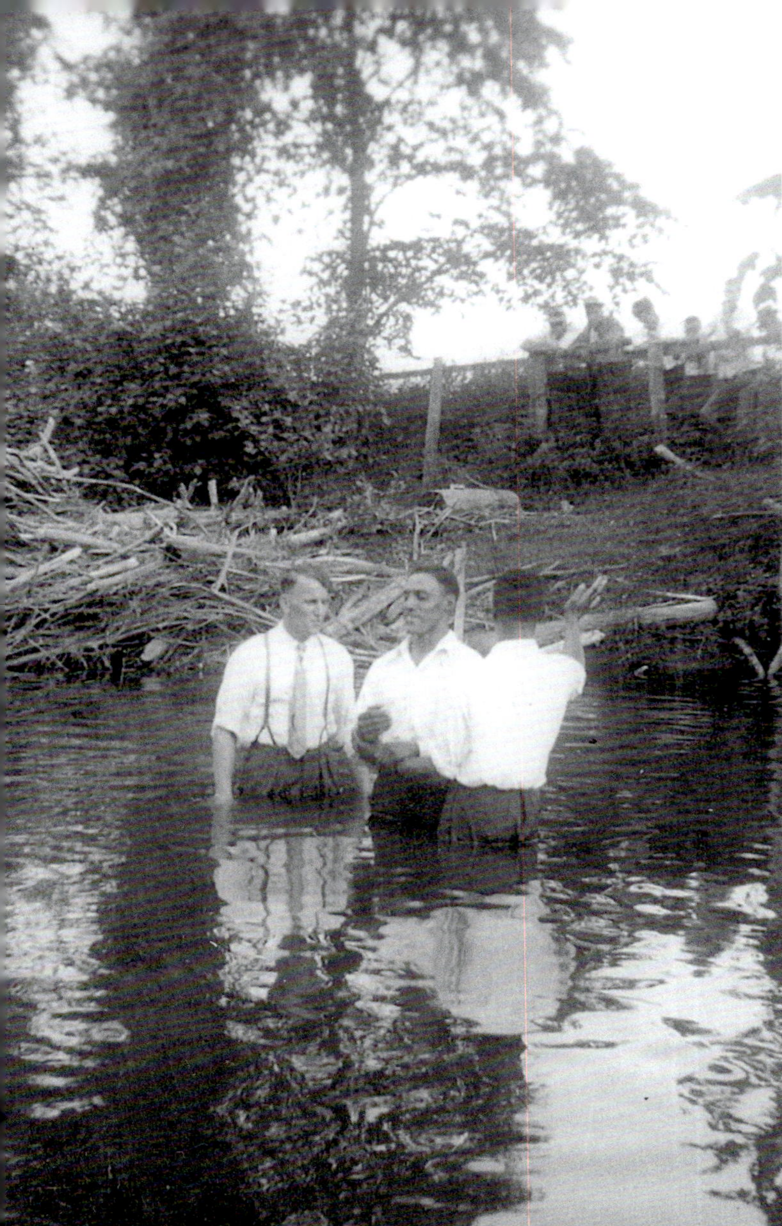

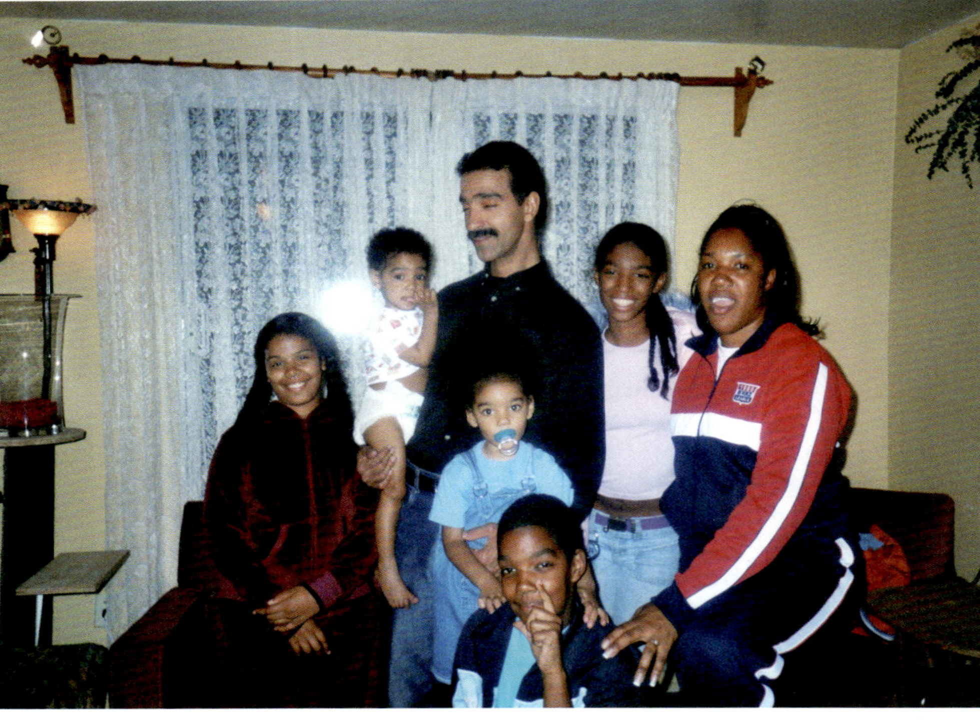

My great-grandparents Adelia and John often travelled on the ferry boat, which was one of the ways people got around back then. On one of those trips, some White women were flirting with John and ignoring Adelia, who was dark skinned. Until John exclaimed, to their surprise, that Adelia was his wife.

—Gerald Mc Intyre

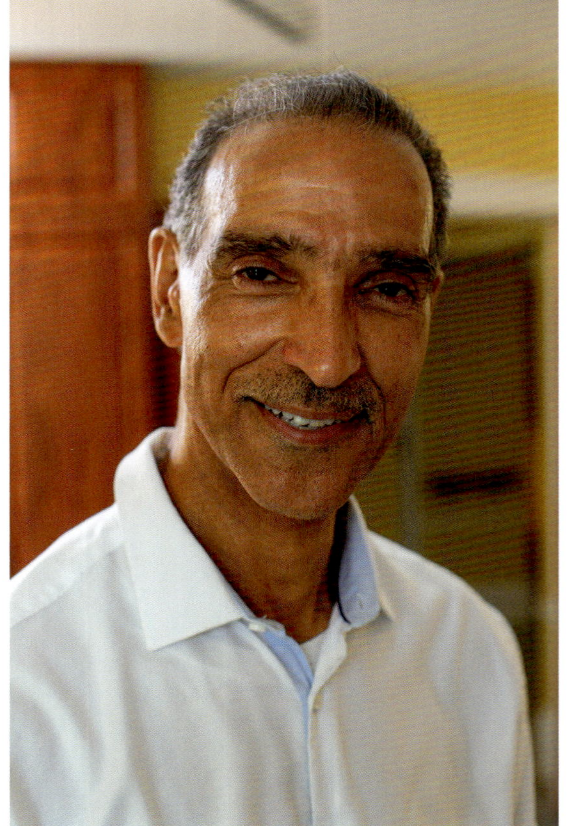

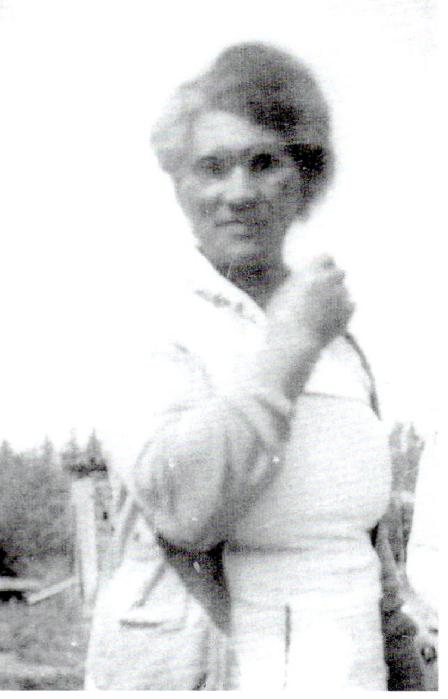

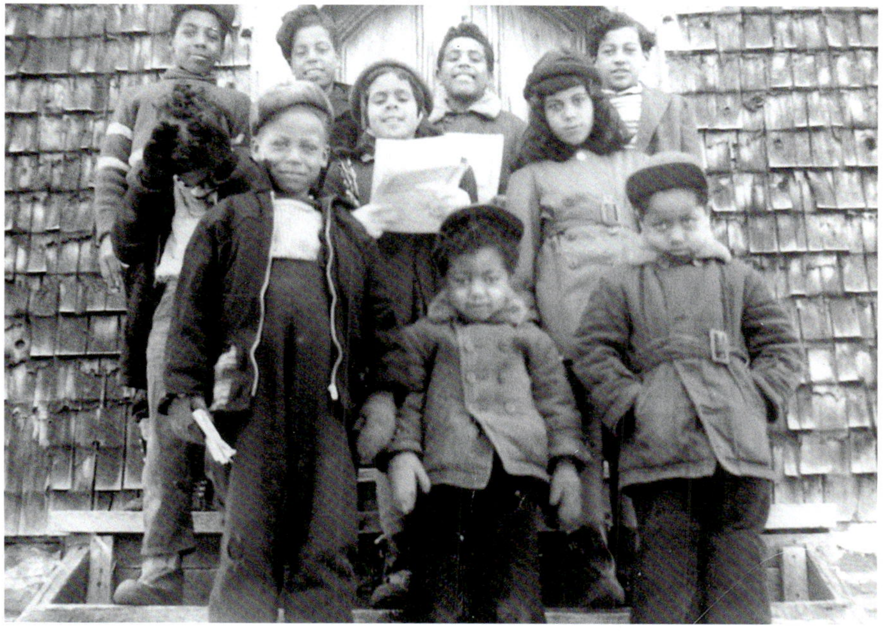

On another branch of the family tree, my grandmother Mary's grandparents were Deborah Ann Cameron and the one we all call Grand-Daddy Bill, who was also a Mc Intyre. They were married in 1860. As the story goes, Deborah's brother did not approve of their marital union, because Deborah was a White woman. He sent slave catchers from the United States to capture him, but Grand-Daddy Bill escaped, found his way back to freedom via the Underground Railroad, and was reunited with his wife. Mary Elizabeth Mc Intyre, their daughter, was my great-grandmother.
— Gerald Mc Intyre

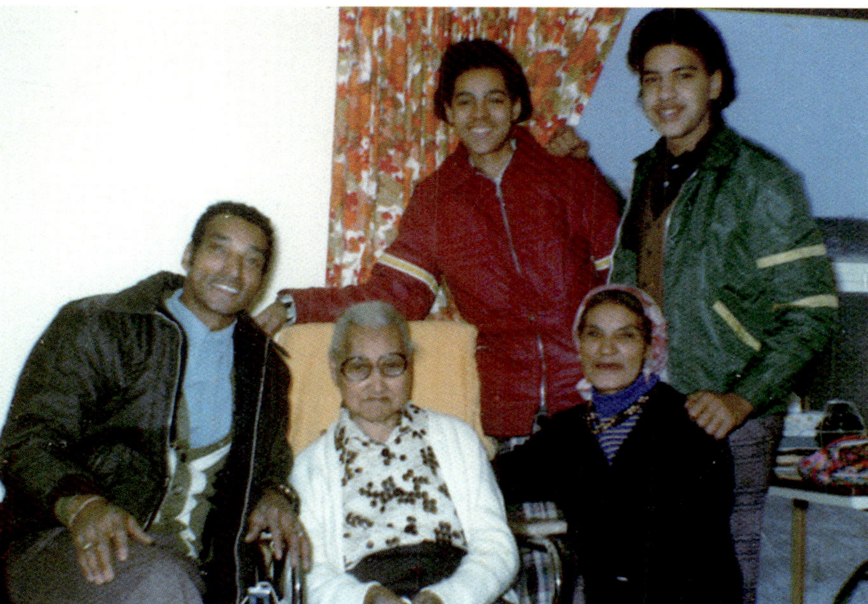

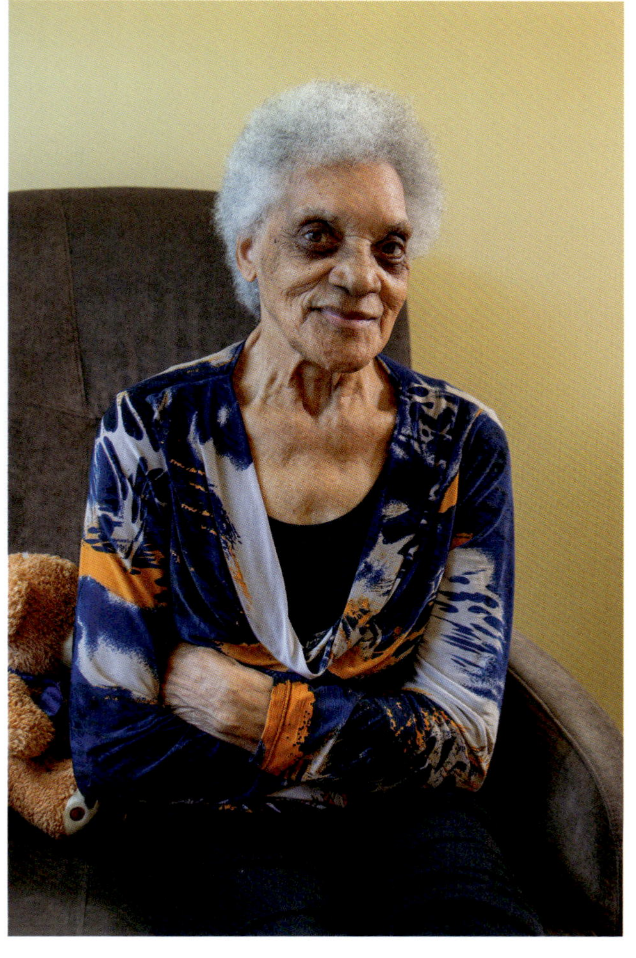

Talbot / Holmes / Haines — Riverview

Riverview, Moncton, New Brunswick
Gary and I blazed through a blizzard.
Saw cars pitch into the ditch dividing the highway.
But kept our eyes on the photo-shoot prize.

Once we arrived, we toured the Talbot home.
Downstairs was the largest personal library
I've ever seen: tomes on Black leaders—Marcus, Martin, Malcolm, Mandela.
An' the other room boasted more instruments than an orchestra.

Then at the kitchen table.
Talking history, scanning photos—black and white.
When suddenly, the neighborhood and home plunged into darkness.
The only light? Gary's battery-powered studio lamp.

A bang upon the door revealed
That even a city-wide power outage
Won't stop pizza from being baked and brought.
And so our photographic fun continued non-stop.

Since I couldn't scan photos anymore,
I played my part as the high-tech kitchen lamp,
Using my smartphone's flashlight
To help folks choose between pizzas—pepperoni or deluxe.

One family member refused to leave their room
Promised he'd never let a camera steal his soul.
But after an hour of hearing his family's laughter,
He barged in, deciding to add his mug to the precious canvas.

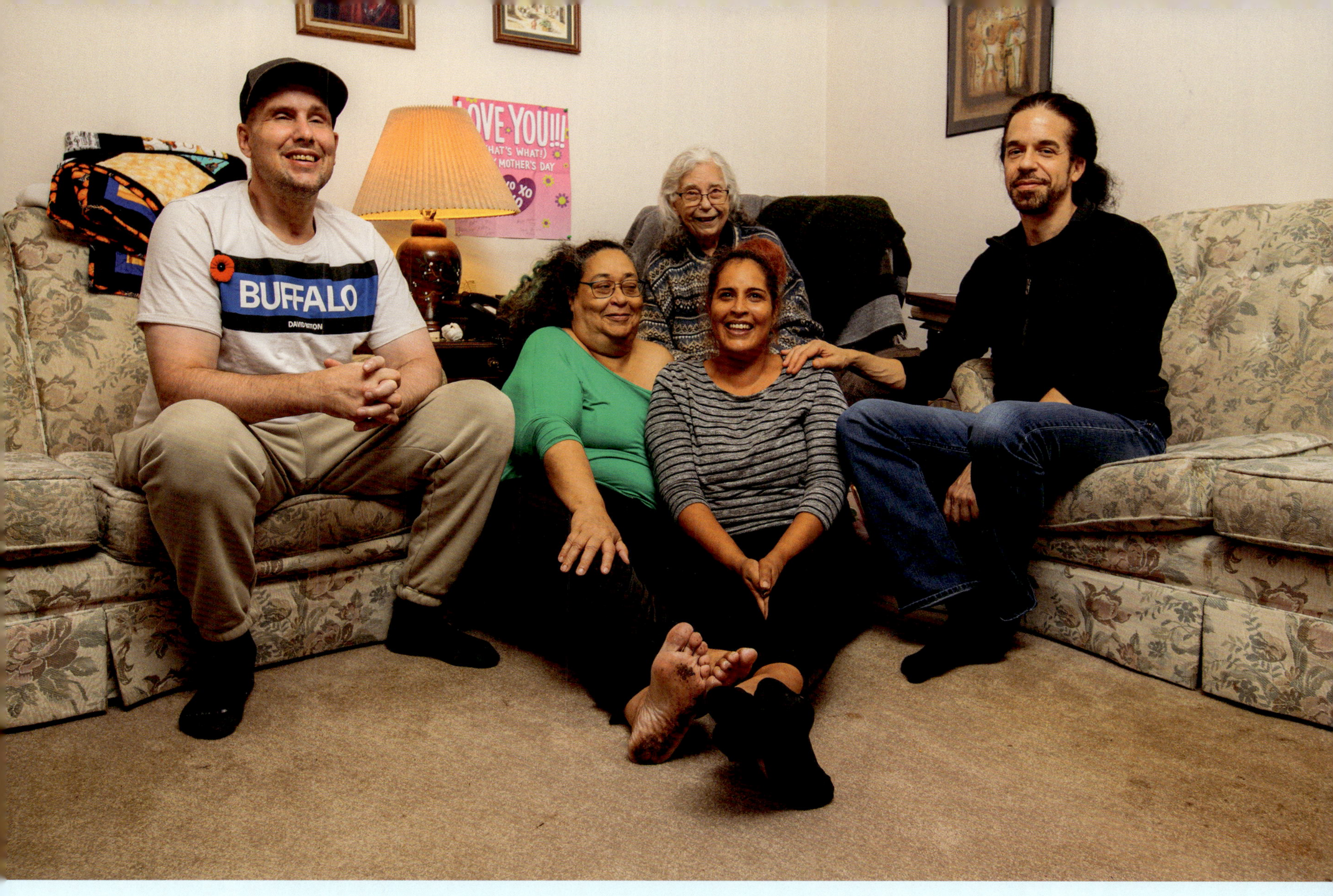

Creeping our way home was as coffin dark as the photo shoot.
The highway a black vista of unbroken snow
While a truck blazed, slowly, the track ahead
Like a pioneer breaking ground for roots.

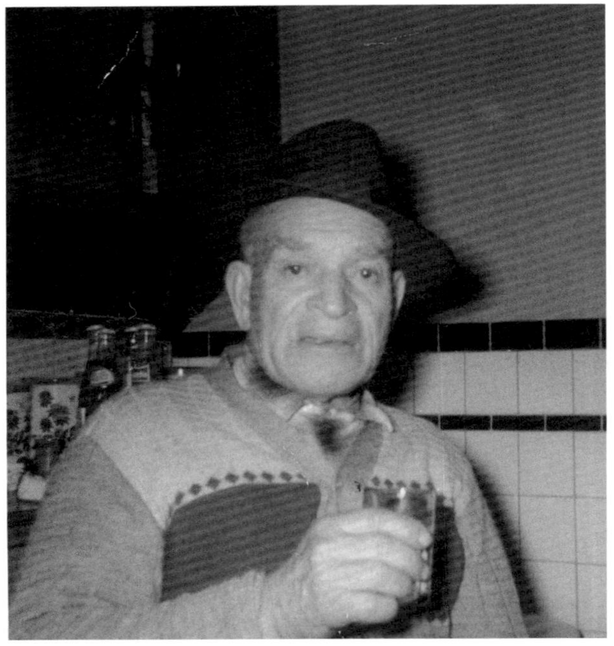

During his youth, my father would travel between Elm Hill and Saint John by steamboat. I always imagine my father and his siblings sitting on the side of the boat chewing on a piece of hay, relaxing in splendour and awe.

My father was so proud of his heritage, of his ancestors and his descendants. He taught the importance of knowing where you come from, where you are at, and where you are going from there.

— Christine Talbot

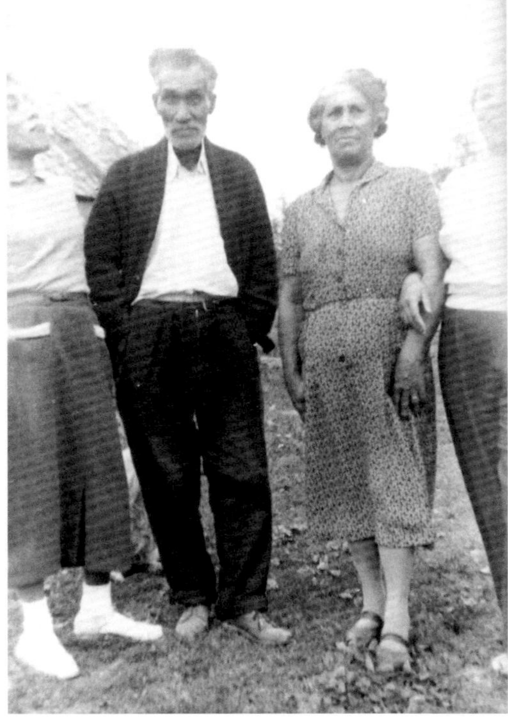

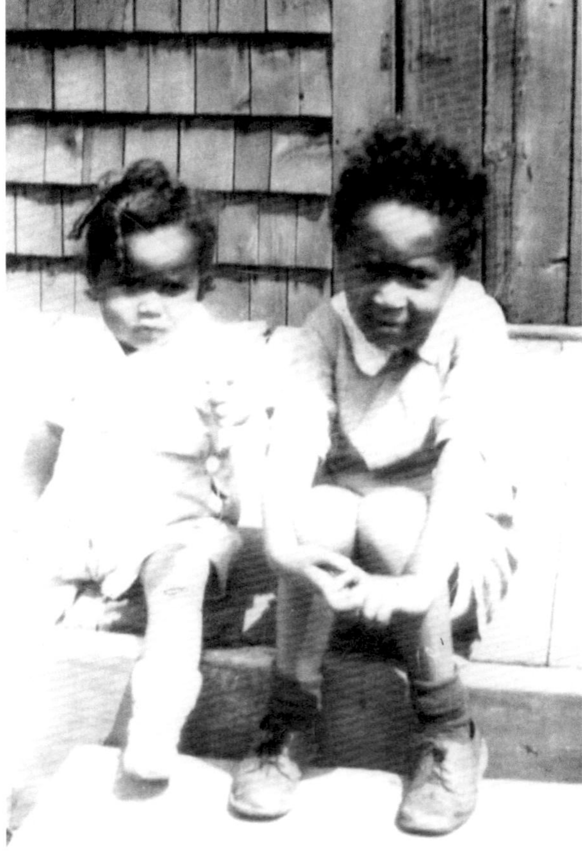

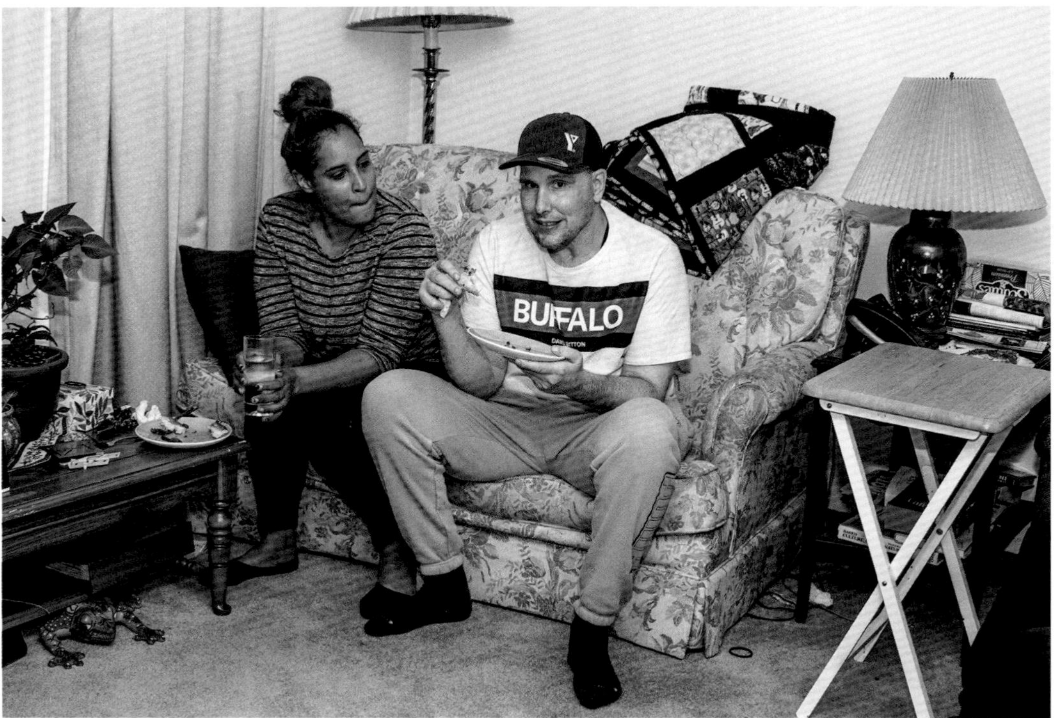

Christine Talbot can date her family back to 1776, and to the 1806 settlement of Elm Hill, New Brunswick. She describes Elm Hill's pastoral beauty. "Imagine skating parties on Lake Otnabog. Imagine rich farmland, full hunting grounds, plentiful fishing, and people owning cattle, chickens, and pigs. Imagine a long-standing picnic tradition where family and friends gathered to share food, stories, enjoying music and dancing. Imagine hard-working men and women who took pride in themselves and worked hard to better their lives and the lives of their children. There are still many residents of Elm Hill who carry on these practices today." The Talbots have ties to the Holmes, Haines, Nash, Hudlin, and Mc Intyre families.

Christine's great-great-grandmother was Hannah Holmes, the daughter of Patrick Holmes and Martha Bree Holmes of Saint John, where Hannah was born in 1856. Hannah bought property in Elm Hill, and she married Major Eatman of Elm Hill in 1877. Among their children was Olive Eatman, who was born in 1893. Olive married James Holmes, and they lived on Hannah's Hill as a young married couple. Their first of four children, Ruby Christina Holmes, was Christine's grandmother, born in 1911.

> Hannah died in 1932 the day before my father was born. Olive and two of her sisters, Gladys and Dulcie, often said I looked like Hannah, which made me feel closer to her.
>
> Hannah's land is still loved and cherished today. Hannah's Hill still has an apple tree that was present before my father's birth. It stands strong and we bask under its branches every summer. That tree is our resilience and strength.
>
> — Christine Talbot

Tragedy struck in 1918 during the Spanish flu pandemic. After James travelled to the village of Gagetown to fetch a doctor for others that were sick, he fell ill and died, and Olive Eatman Holmes became a widow. When she remarried, to Ed "Boss" Haines, they moved down the road to his property and continued to grow as a family. Olive's brother, Uncle Mann, also lived on the property.

Meanwhile, Olive's daughter Ruby married William Arthur Talbot in 1930, and Christine's father, James Arthur "Skip" Talbot, was born to them in Truro, Nova Scotia, on July 16, 1932, after which he grew up in Saint John. Skip was the first Black Canadian to hold the position of radio operator / flight service specialist for Transport Canada and also the first Black Canadian to hold a bilingual position as a maintenance supervisor in communications while stationed in Sept-Îles, Quebec. He and Christine's mother, Patricia, married in 1955 and went on to have six children. Skip was committed to anti-racism, equality, and a cross-cultural understanding of social-justice causes as he worked to achieve equality for minorities with organizations that ranged from the RCMP to PRUDE. He was also known to host the Elm Hill Annual Black Picnic.

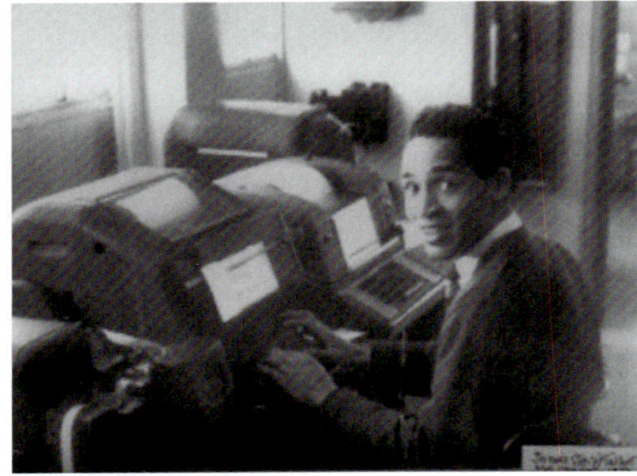

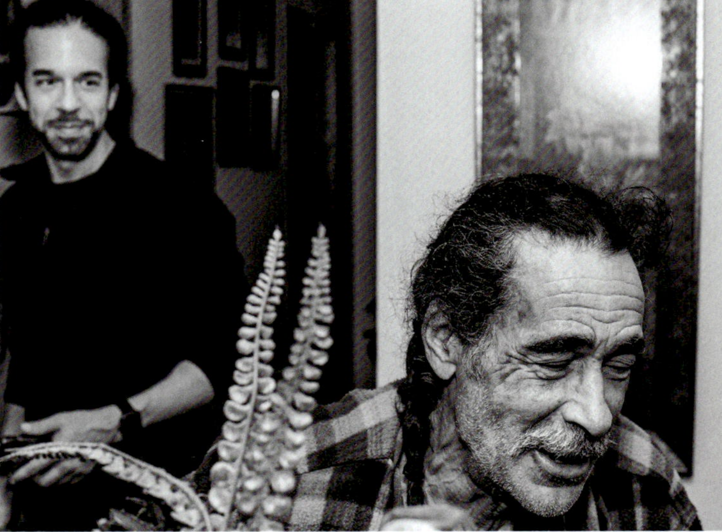

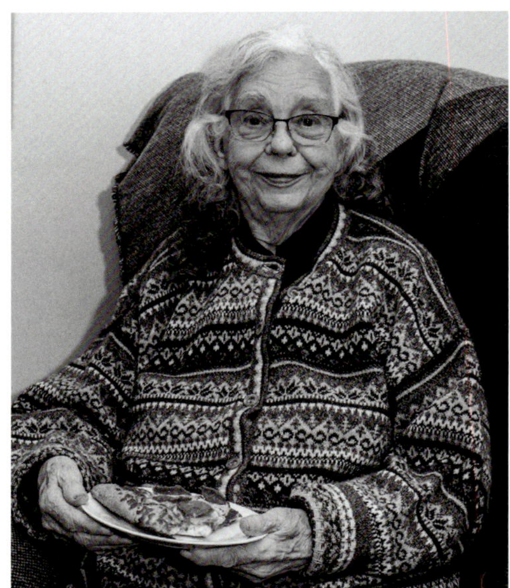

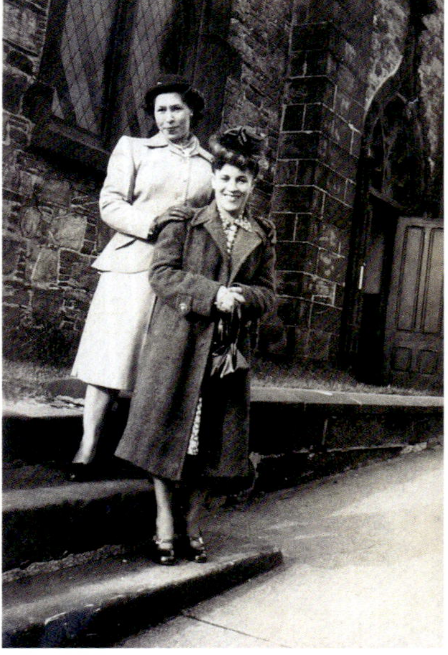

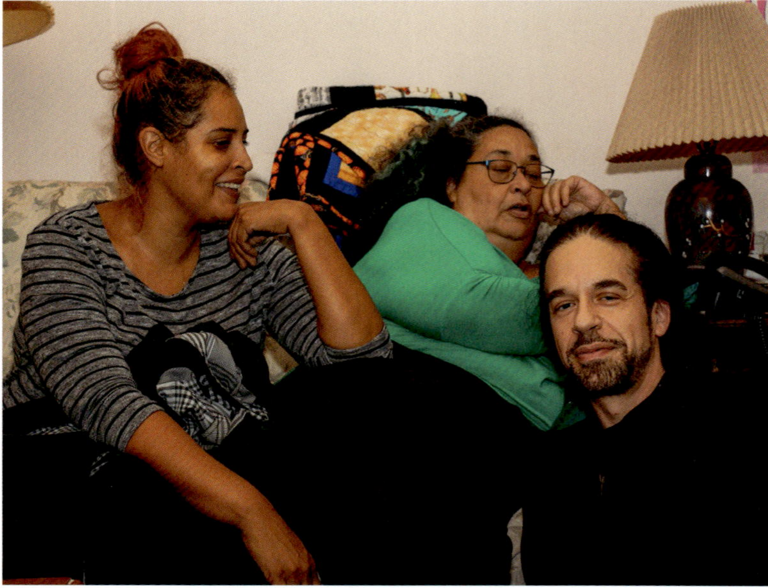

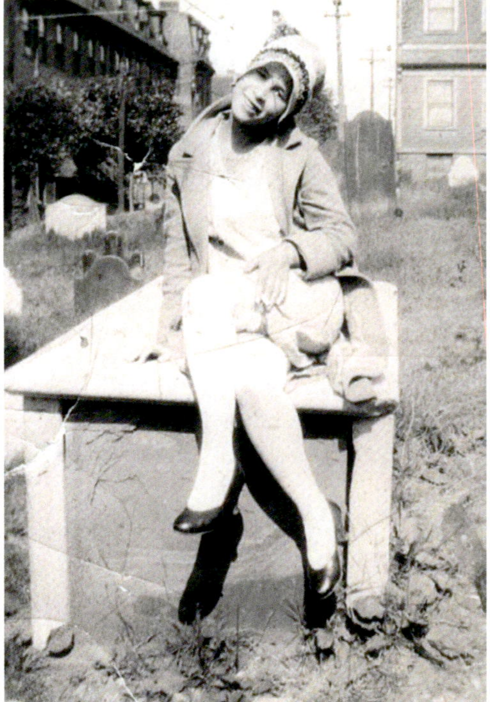

Family can be complicated, but it cannot be denied. Holmeses are part of the history of Elm Hill, of New Brunswick, and of Canada. We are here to stay.
—Christine Talbot

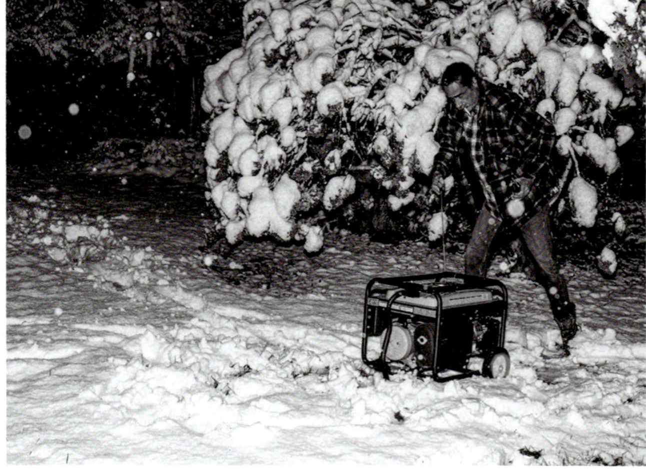

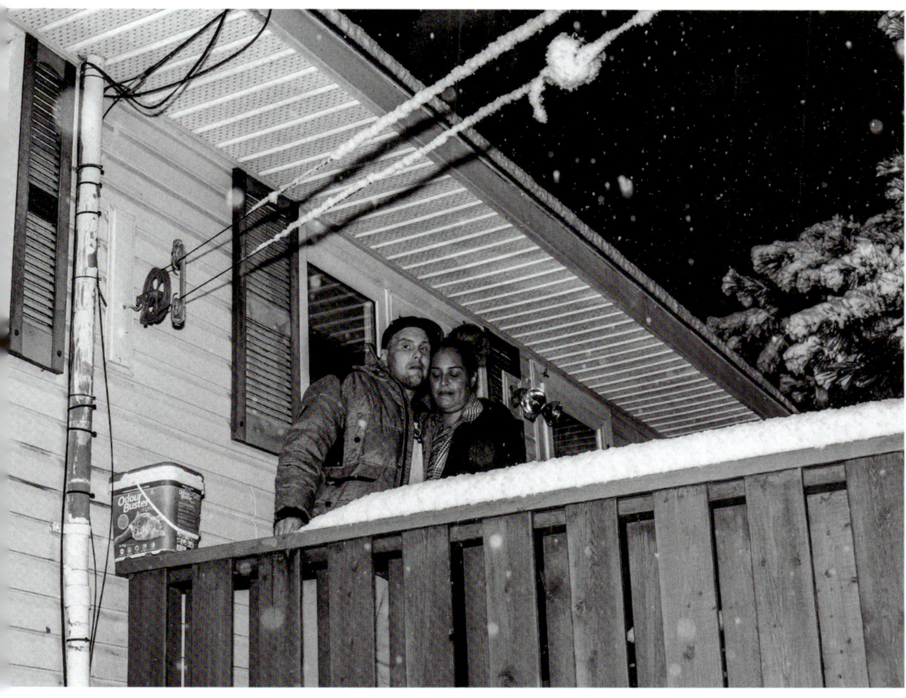

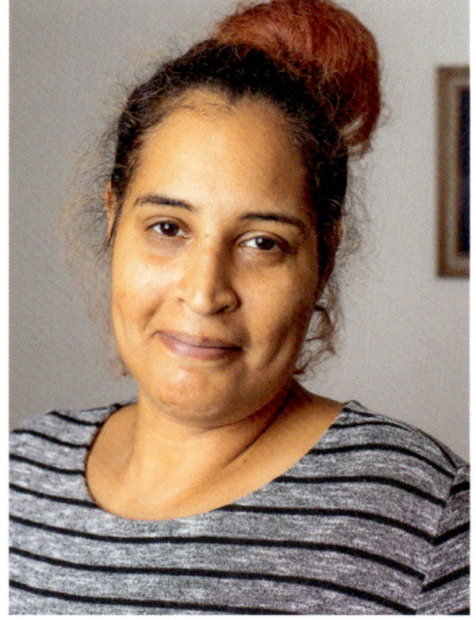

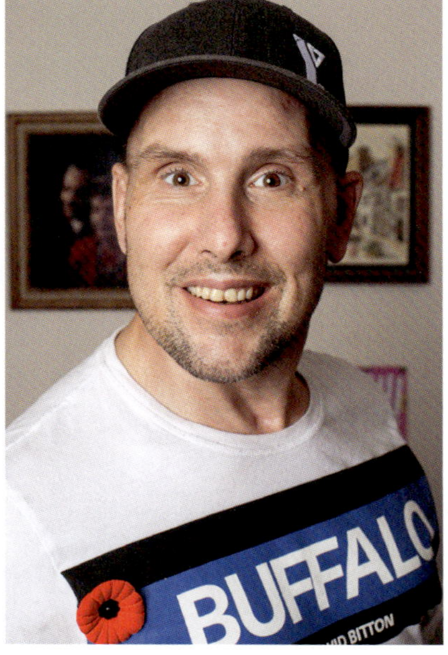

Hannah's Hill keeps me grounded. It brings me peace. When I look to the left or the right I feel the ancestors speaking and letting us know that they are there, holding us up. The descendants of Hannah Holmes have carried on building families and homes, some developing careers and some, like me, dreaming of returning to the land.
—Christine Talbot

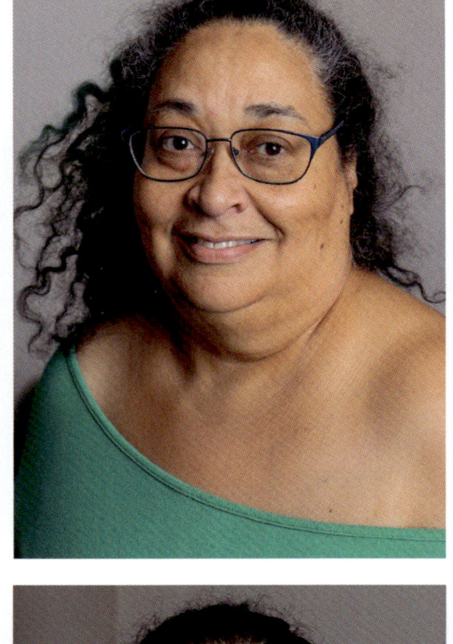

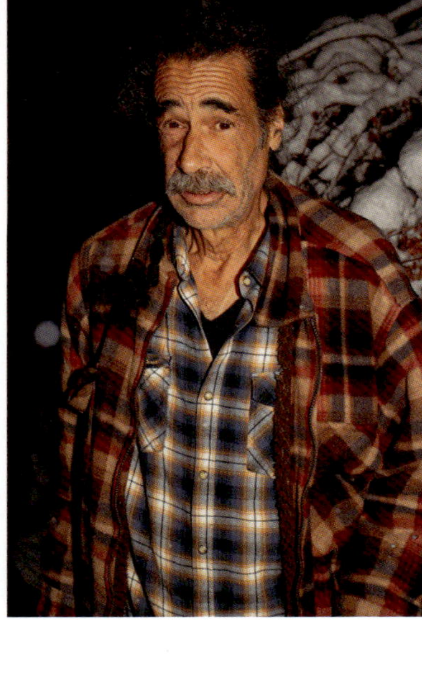

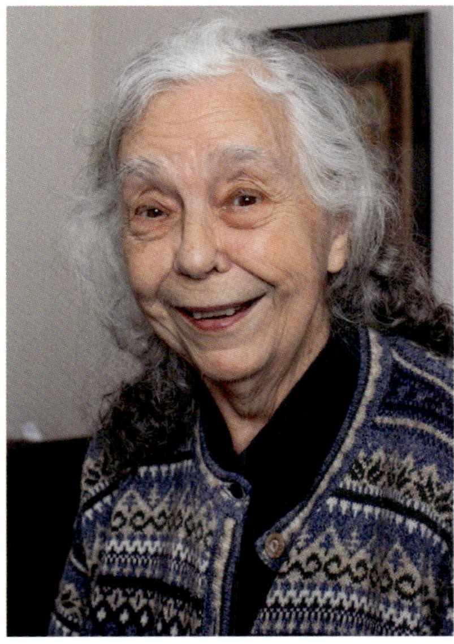

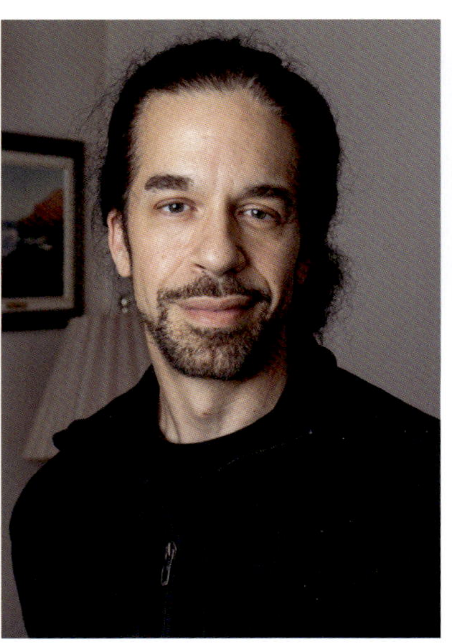

Hope / Shears / Eatmon / Mc Intyre — Saint John

In the middle of Saint John
Sits a home positioned next to a large maple tree.
Planted on the property by a strong hand
Many decades ago.

When the city demanded a highway
That would drive right through his land.
He sold nothing. Instead,
He made the city carve steps up to his property.

See, Nathan Hope is used to bending steel.
Laboured decades in Irving factories.
He is a builder whose soul lights up
When he gets down to work, magic with his hands.

Community was a love he learned young.
His mother had twenty brothers and sisters
And every aunt, uncle, and cousin
Forged the family values that made his backbone iron.

This is a family that fixes anything that breaks.
Making sure everything and everyone
Works as best they can:
For what else is a heart but endless support?

It's a family with a name
Like steel beams in a suspension bridge.
A name that brings us and the world what we need:
Hope.

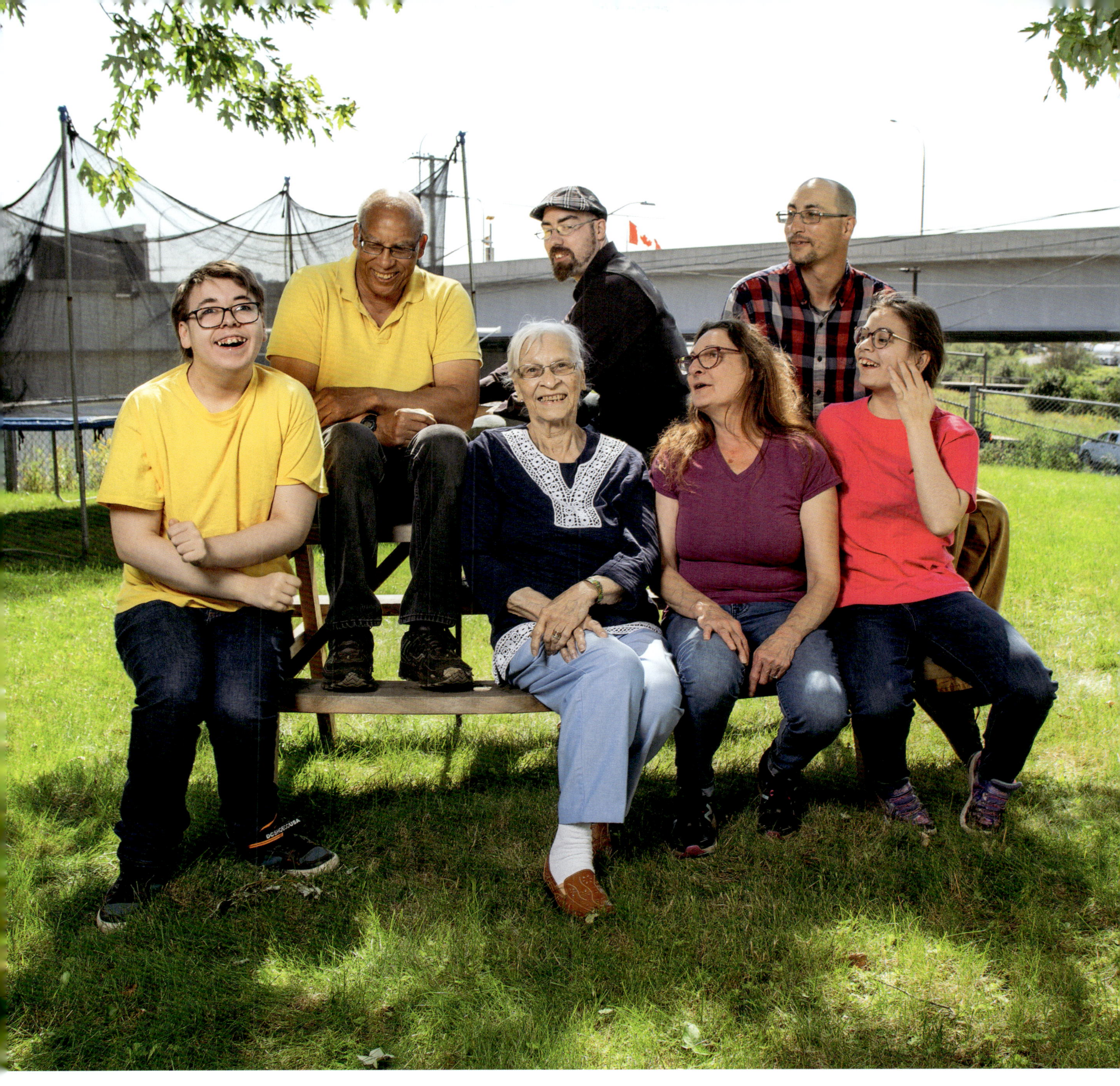

Hope / Shears / Eatmon / Mc Intyre — Saint John

My mother was raised on the Range Road in Willow Grove. Her father, J. Wilfred Shears, had twenty-one children over the course of two marriages. My mother was born twentieth of twenty-one brothers and sisters. My parents, Randolph and Vona, met, married, and resided in Saint John and raised their nine children Teala, Randolph (Zane), Nathan (me), Tennyson, Robert, Vona, Morgan, Anita, and Kirkland.

—Nathan Hope

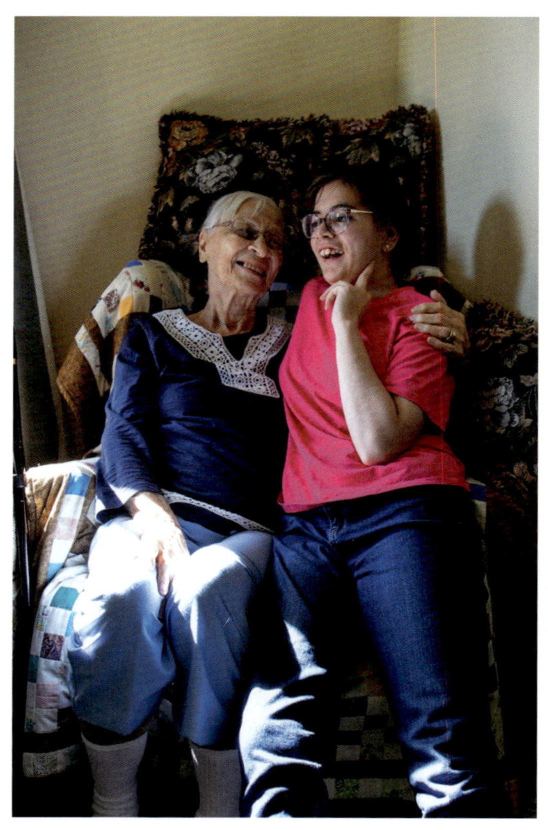

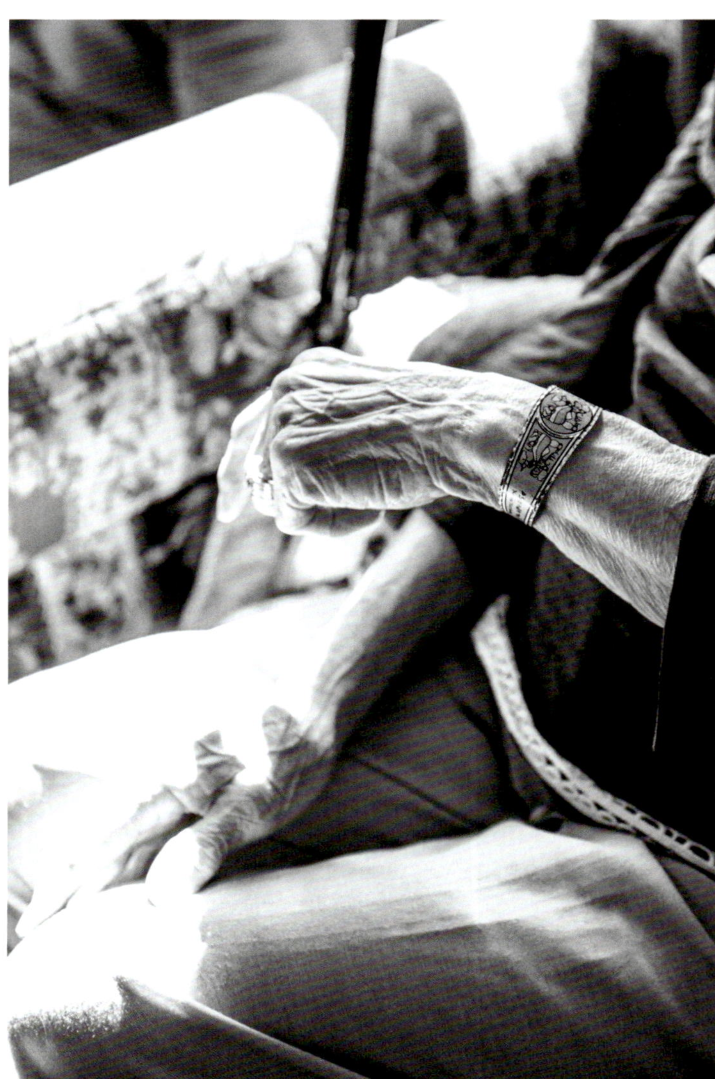

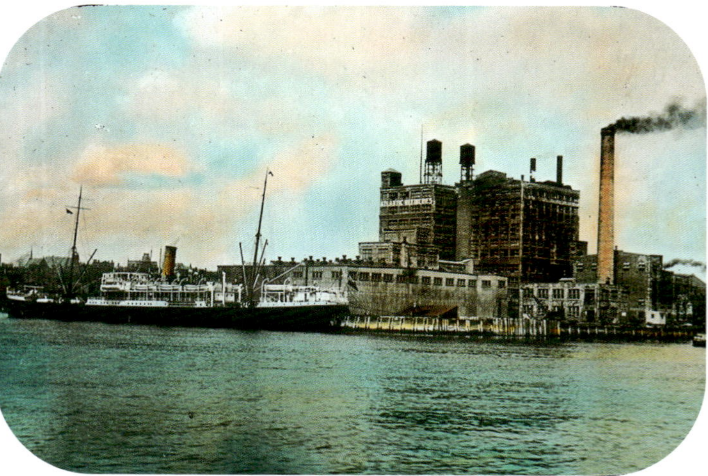

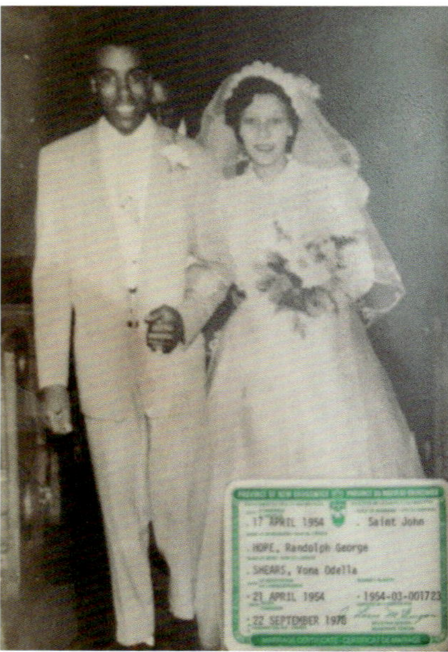

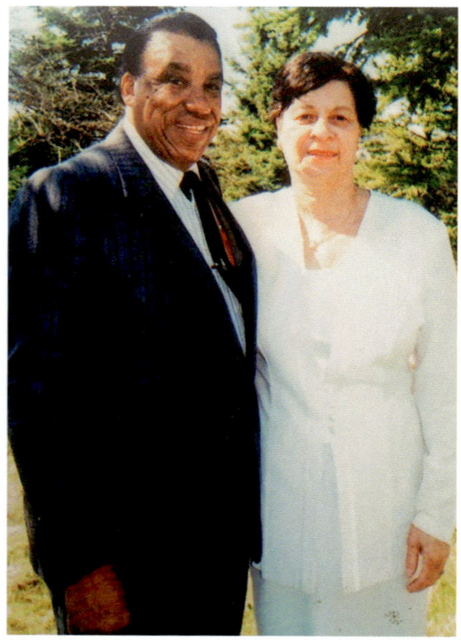

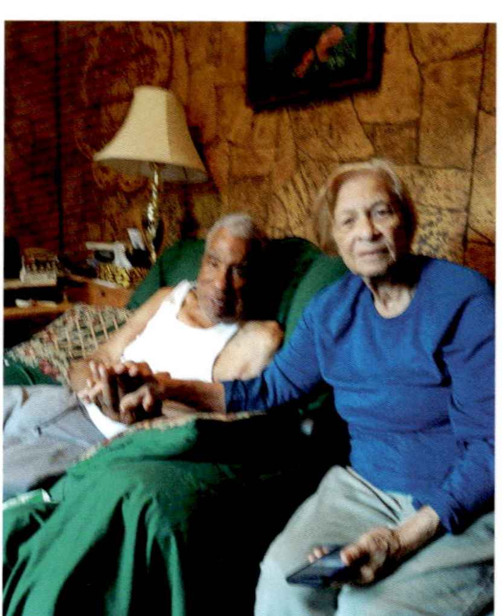

The generations of Hopes that are alive today have strong connections to Elm Hill. They date their roots back to the 1640s under the Mc Intyre line: Nathan Hope's paternal grandmother was Edith Mc Intyre, the sister of Mary Elizabeth Mc Intyre I, and his paternal great-grandfather was Lemuel Mc Intyre.

Nathan's father, Randolph George Hope, was born in Saint John in 1928 to parents Edith (née Mc Intyre) and George Hope. There were seven children who survived to adulthood: Annie, Mary, Hazel, Ruth, Bruce, Randolph, and Grace (half-sister); and a son, Andrew, who died young when he was hit by a train.

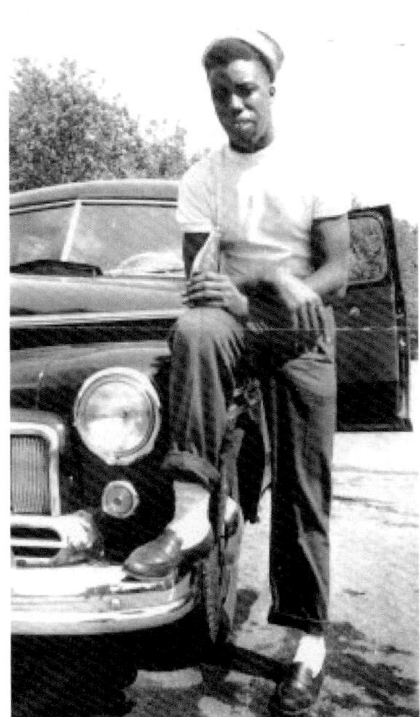

When Randolph was fourteen, he left his job at a sugar refinery and served in the Canadian Merchant Navy during the Second World War. Randolph was later denied pension benefits from the federal government, and in 1998 he and three other Merchant Navy veterans embarked on a hunger strike to petition the government of Canada for the compensation they deserved. They won their case, and in 2000, veterans began to receive reparations. In 2021 Randolph recorded an interview for the Memory Project, an initiative of Historica Canada that arranges for veterans to share their stories. He died in 2022 after sixty-eight years of marriage to Nathan's mother, Vona Odella Hope (née Shears).

Nathan Randall Hope and his wife Patricia Eileen Hope (née Ward) met and married in Saint John. Their children are Kayol, Destin, Natouri, and Sarah James. Nathan and Patricia are also raising two of their grandkids, Joshua and Melissa Hope. They have property in Elm Hill and love going there because "it's just a beautiful place. It ties us to our roots, relatives, and friends."

The Hopes also have connections to Willow Grove along the Shears line: in 1830, Wilfred Shears was born at Big Hole Reserve, Northumberland County. His son Simon Shears was born in 1853, and Simon's son, Joseph Wilfred Shears, who went by "Wilfred," was born at Case Settlement, Kings County, in either 1874 or 1876. Wilfred had two marriages, to Rosella Eatmon and later to Lavinia Christine Mc Intyre. Joseph had twelve children with Rosella, and nine with Lavinia, of whom Nathan Hope's mother, Vona Odella, was the eighth born. Wilfred died in 1941, one of the last people to be buried at the Black Settlement Burial Ground at Willow Grove. His wife Lavinia lived until 1977 and was buried at Ocean View Memorial Gardens cemetery in East Saint John.

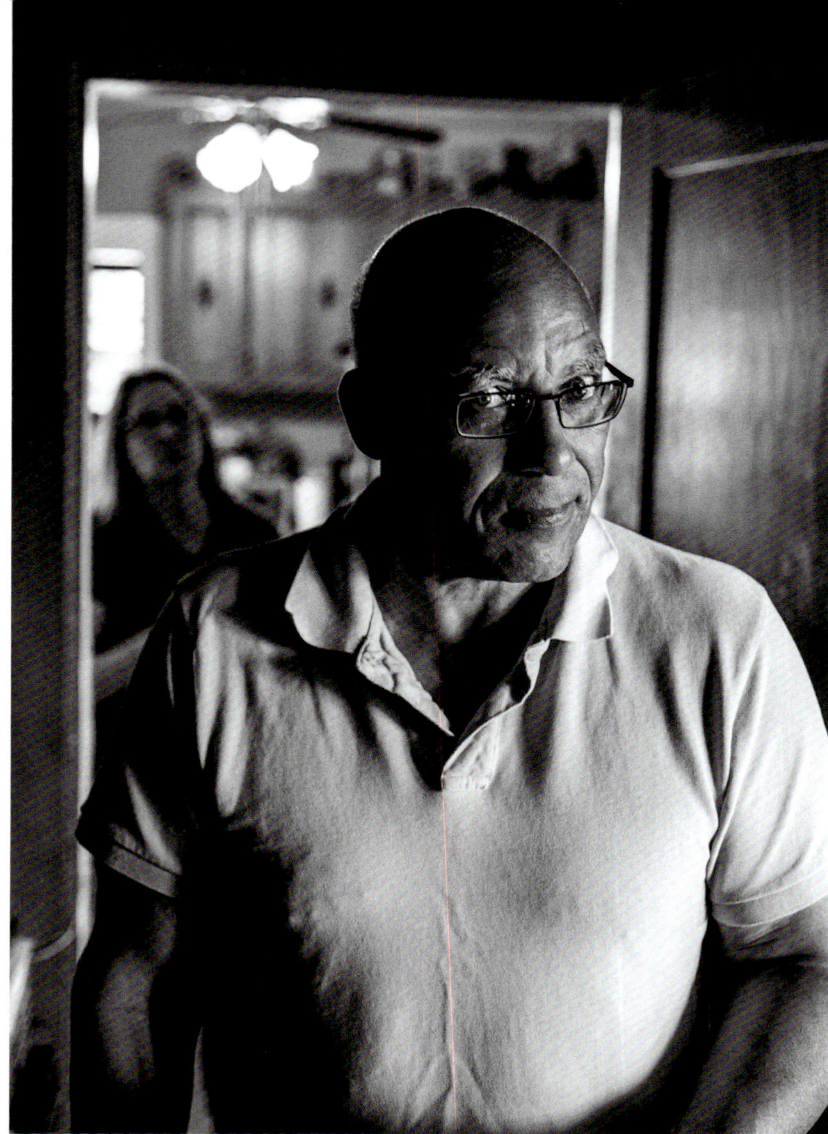

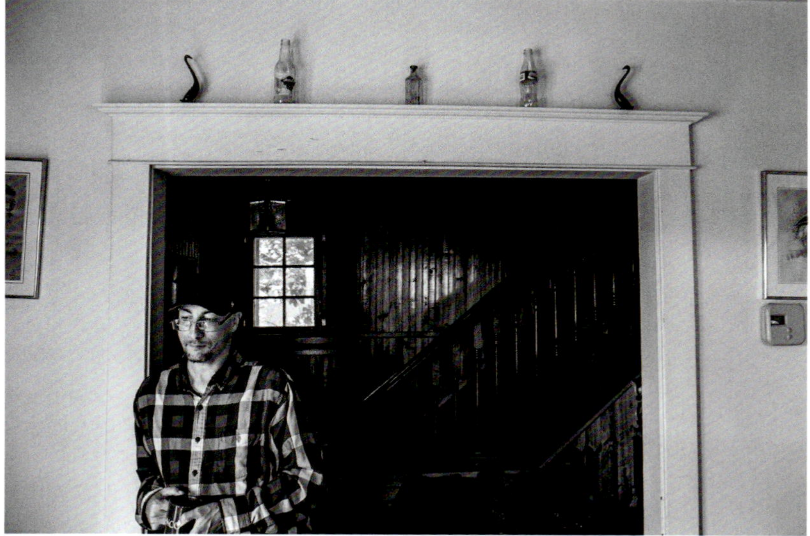

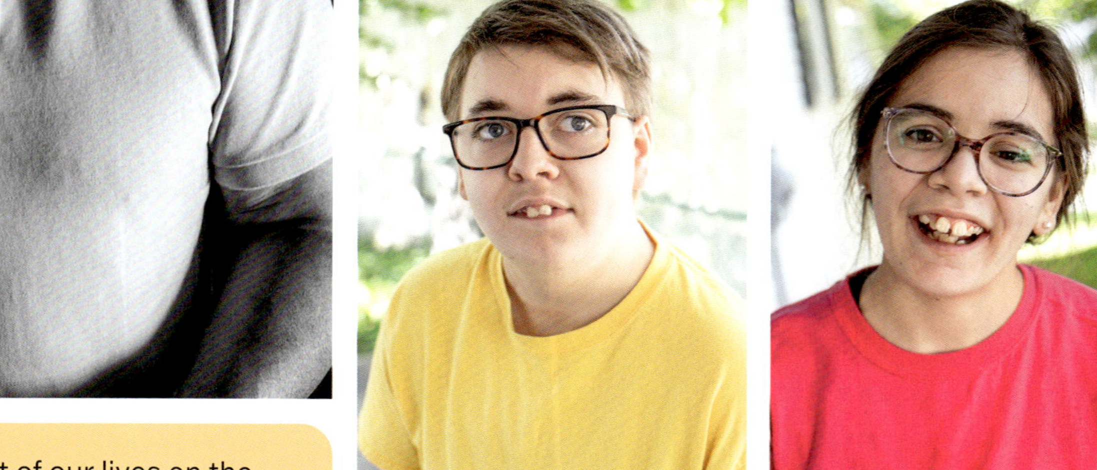

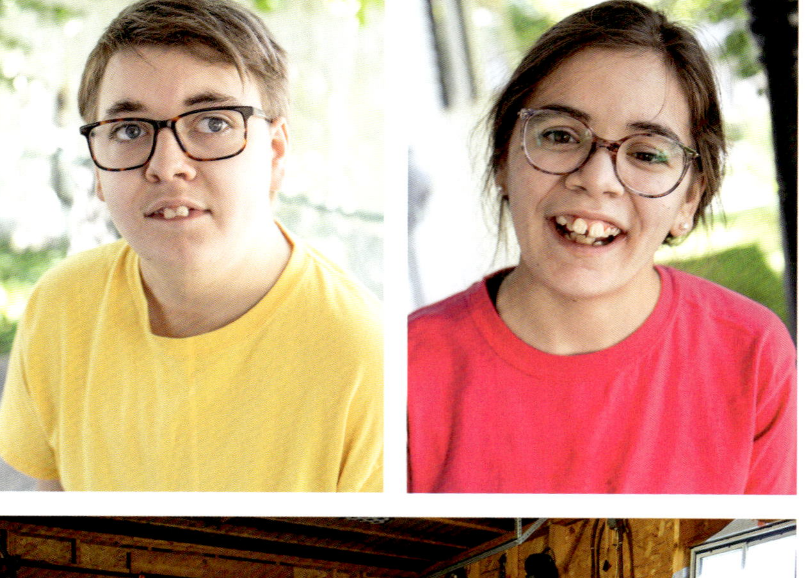

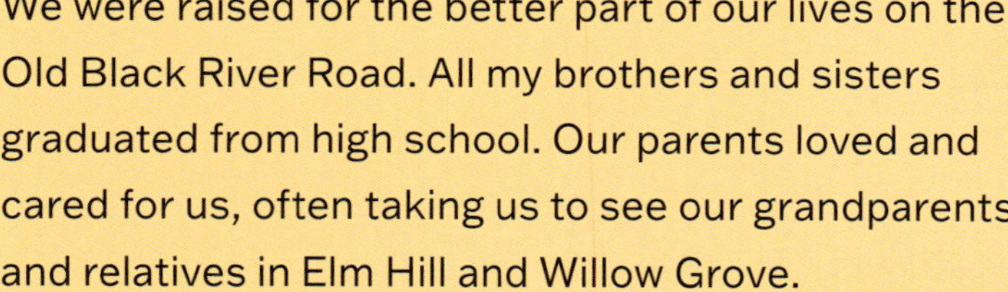

We were raised for the better part of our lives on the Old Black River Road. All my brothers and sisters graduated from high school. Our parents loved and cared for us, often taking us to see our grandparents and relatives in Elm Hill and Willow Grove.
— Nathan Hope

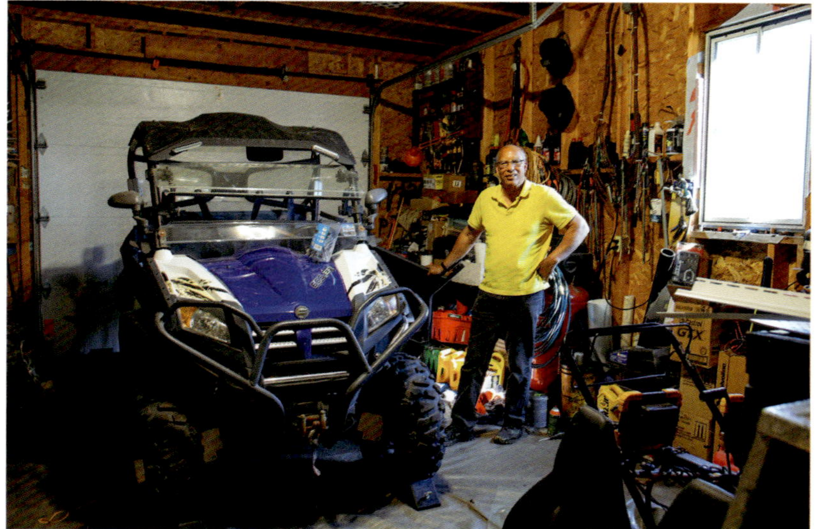

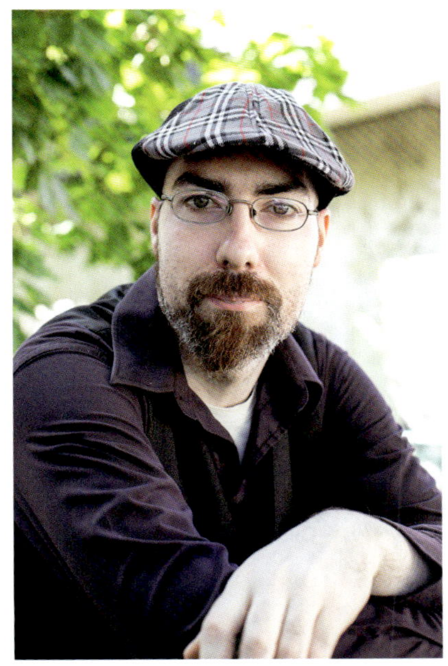

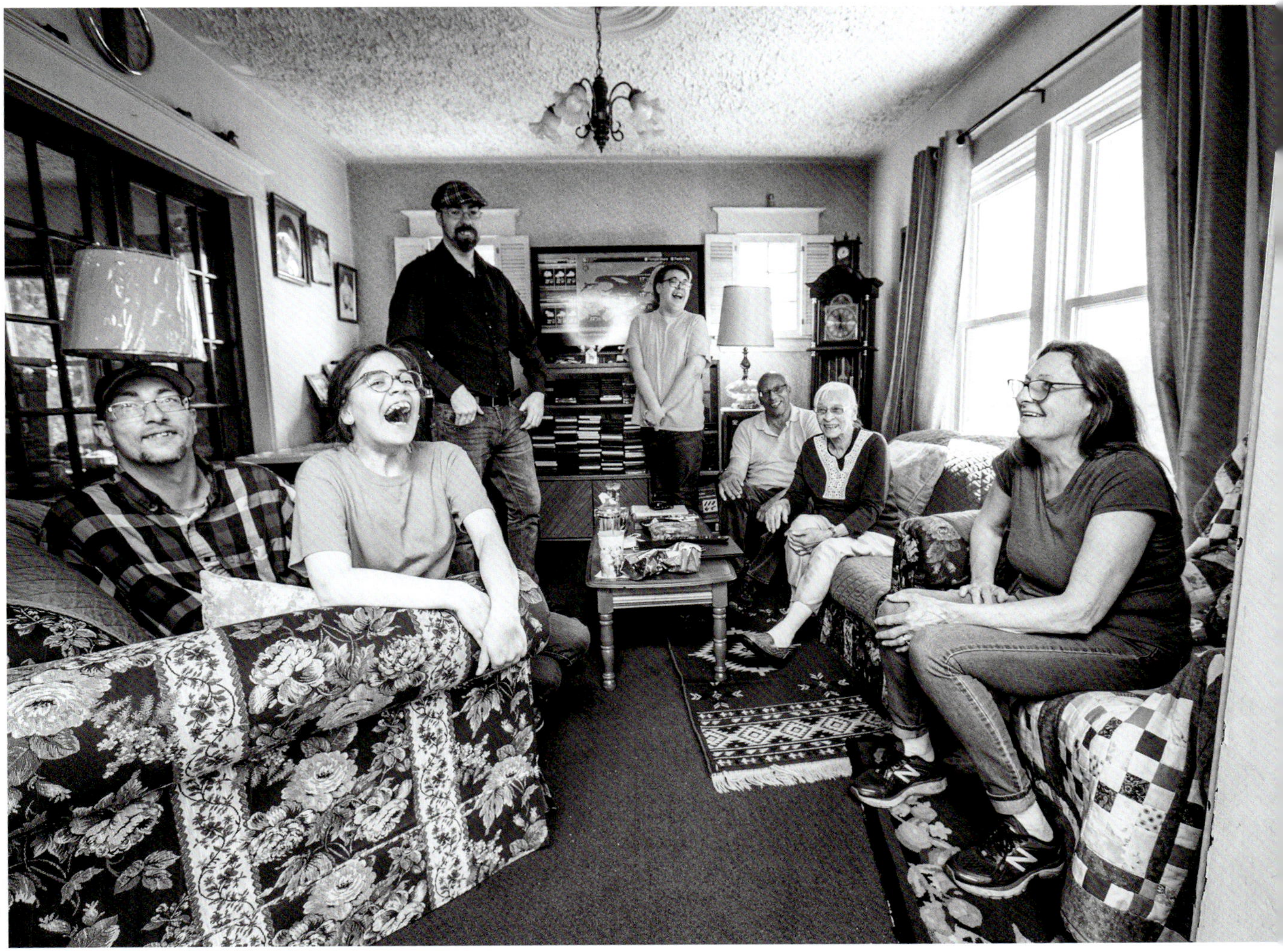

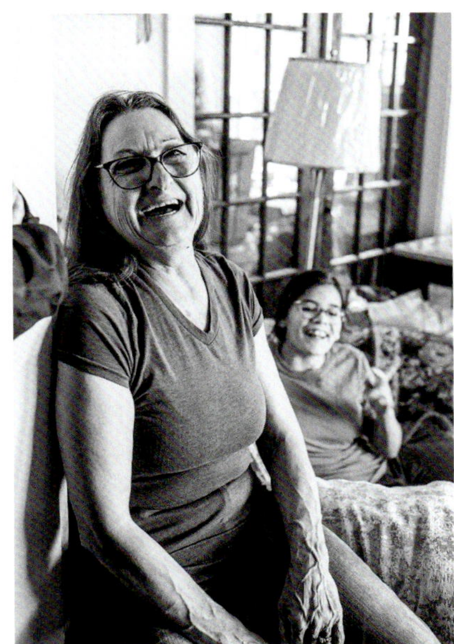

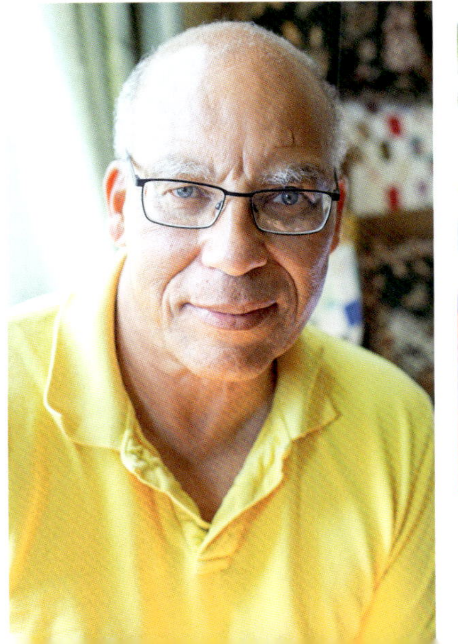

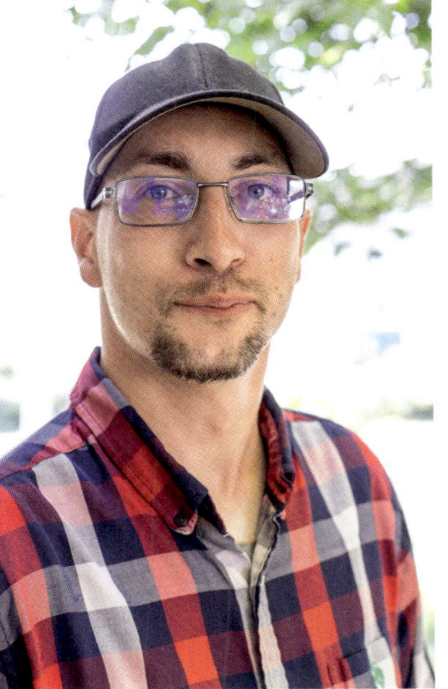

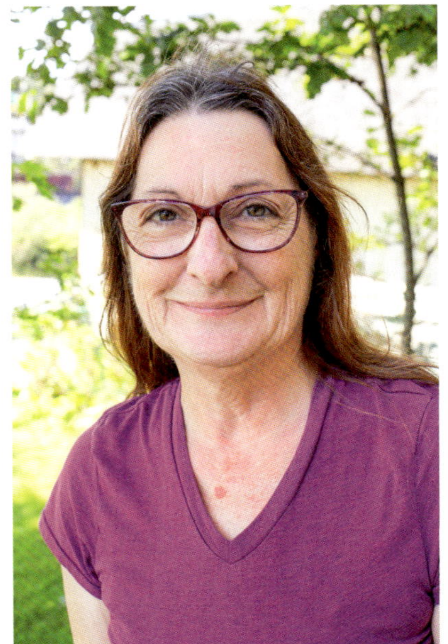

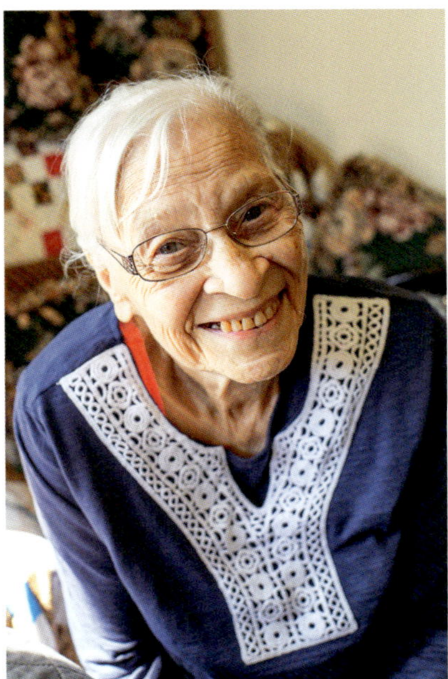

Holmes / Hector / Richards — Saint John

This family's as old as Saint John.
But drifted out west.
All was well
Until unthinkable tragedy happened.

To awake from this nightmare of grief
The clan moved back east, to their roots.
To reassemble orchards and vineyards
To reject graveyards.

After the welcoming intros, the warm courtesies
I smile and announce,
"Gary Weekes is the best photographer in Canada
And today he works for you!"

Soon every face finds its smiles for the camera,
While photos of the lost are held high.
Those who have passed, never pass from us —
Are imperfectly preserved in the family photo album.

The event has every generation generating laughs
And I'm once again reminded
How much families need these moments
To last—and never be forgotten.

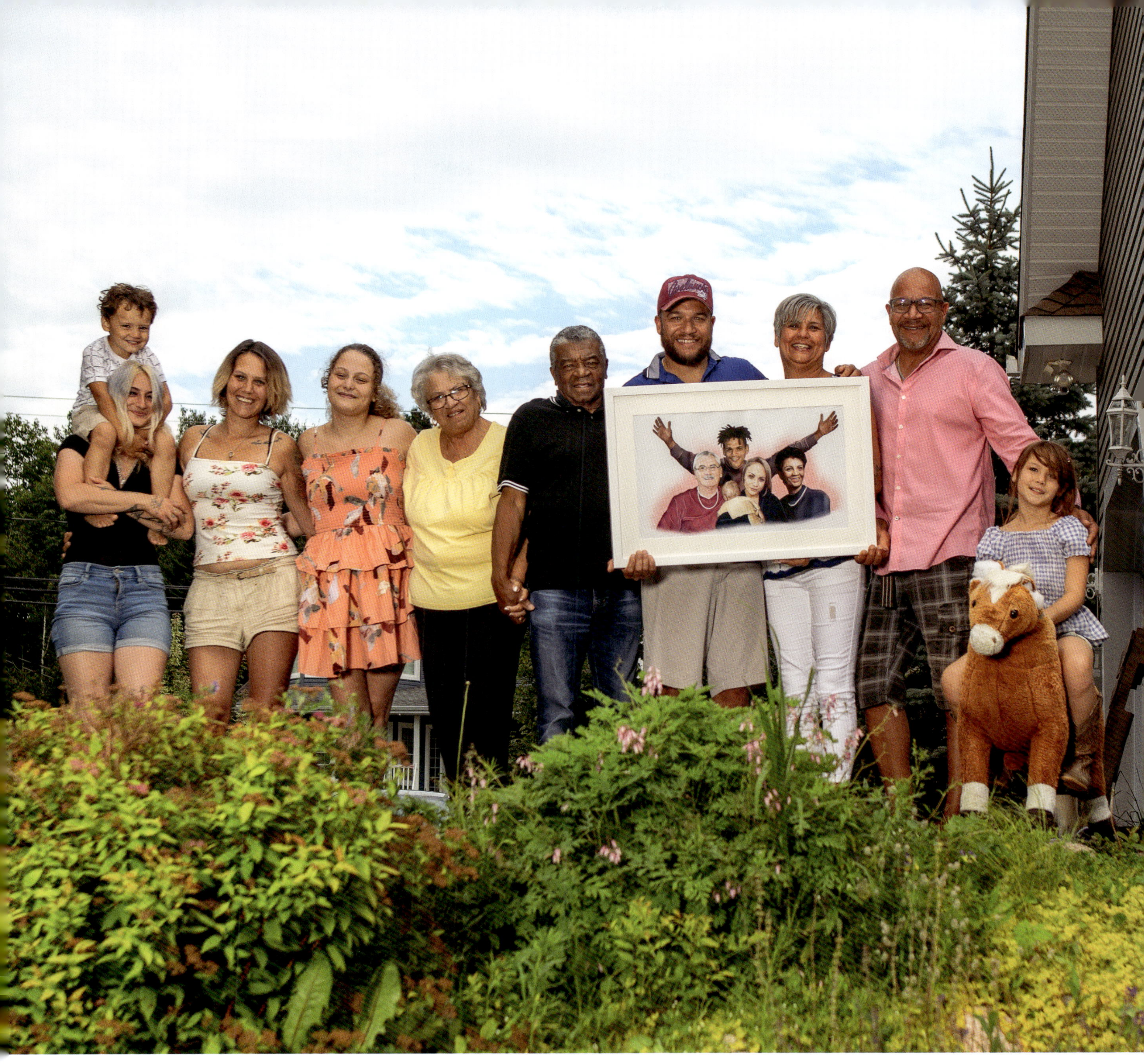

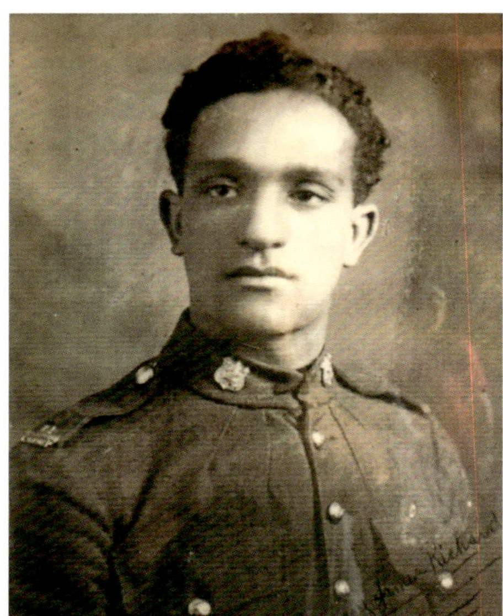

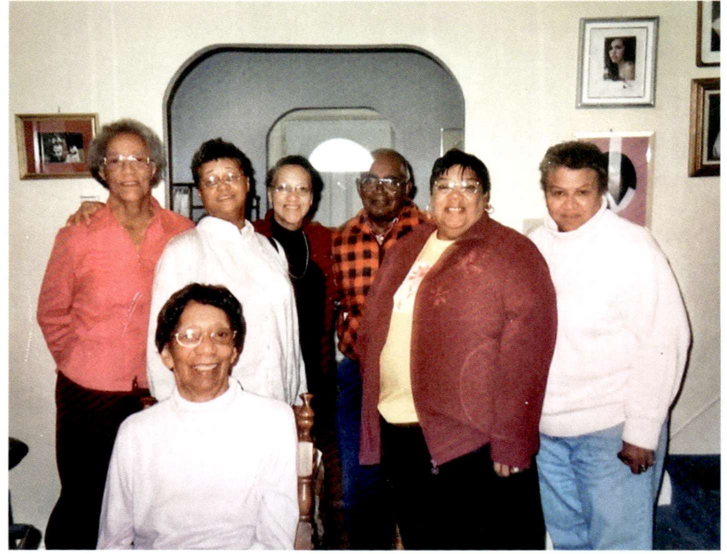

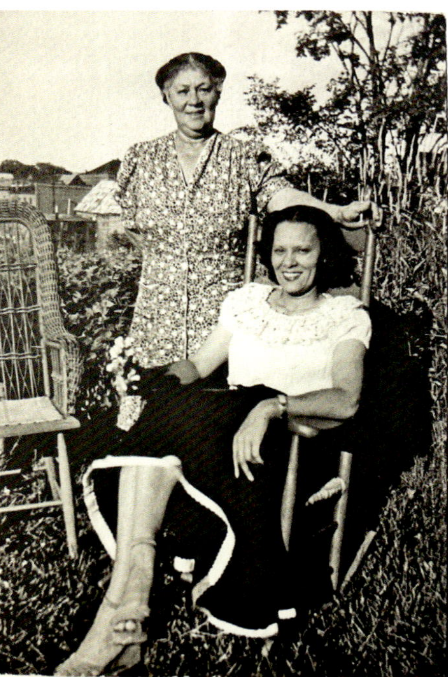

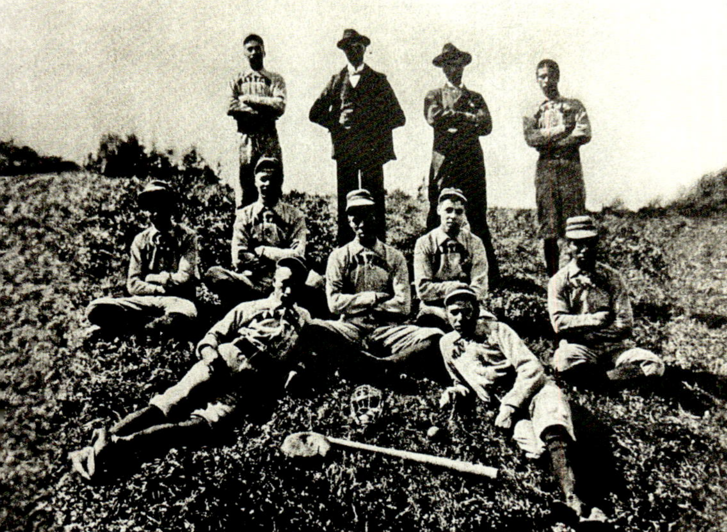

Keeping a good name and education have held true for me and helped me go very far in my professional life. I will always honour my ancestors, and I truly hope future Hectors, Holmeses, and Richardses continue our family journey of loving, caring, giving, and making a positive impact.
— Tim Holmes

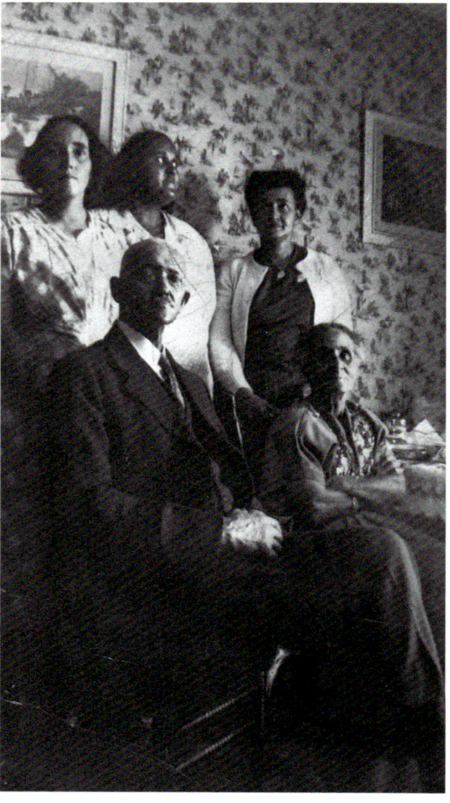

(PANB P498-052)

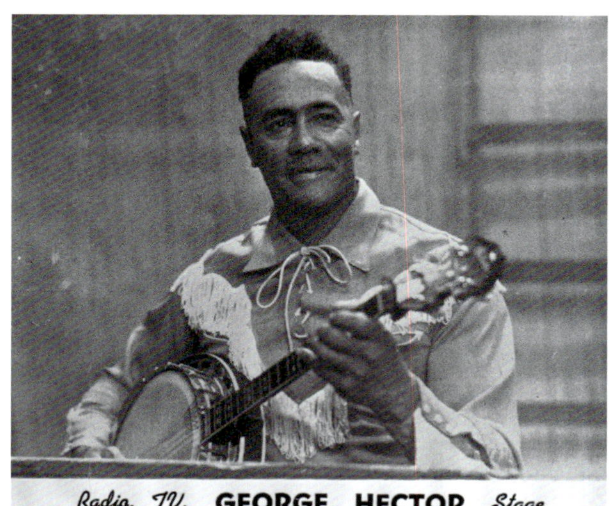

George Hector, ca. 1950–70 (PANB P498-9w)

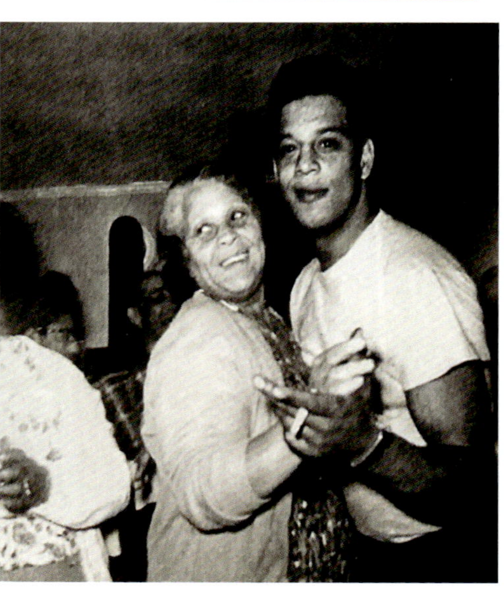

The Hector family were trailblazers as far back as the early 1780s, when they immigrated with other Black Empire Loyalists from the American colonies to Canada. In 1792, Izzy Hector, a distant aunt of Tim Holmes, was among almost 1,200 other Nova Scotians that set sail from Halifax for Sierra Leone, Africa, where they founded the city of Freetown. But many Hectors chose to stay, moving instead into New Brunswick, and in the late 1800s, they were well known around the sports fields of Saint John.

The Holmes and Hector families are now also connected to the Richardses through Tim's wife, Julie. Julie's grandfather Percy Richards was a First World War veteran who served with the No. 2 Construction Battalion. Other members of the Hector and Holmes families may have fought in both world wars; Tim's grandfather Holmes was a Second World War veteran.

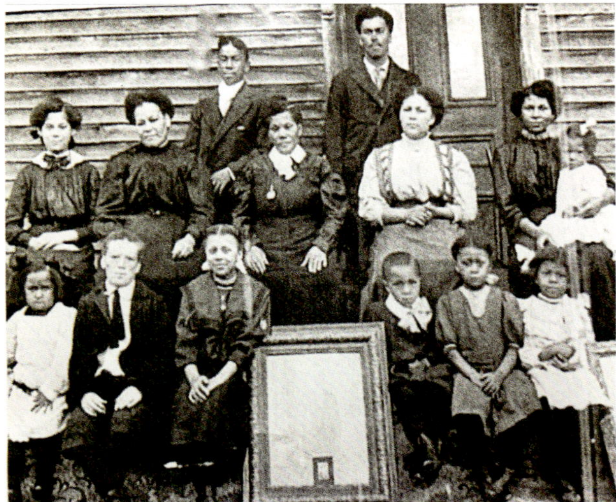

Tim Holmes's grandfather on the Hector side, Gordon W. Hector, worked at the Atlantic Sugar Refineries in Saint John before marrying Thelma, Tim's grandmother. The next generation included Tim's mother Sandra, who counted among her siblings Tim's aunt Constance.

Dr. Constance Timberlake was born in Saint John in 1930. As a young woman, she moved to the United States to become a teacher, then went on to get a PhD and became a professor at Syracuse University and commissioner of education at Syracuse, New York. She was a civil rights leader, a human rights advocate, and an advisor to two presidential administrations.

> My ancestors worked hard to give us a name that was "Good." The good Lord knows when it came to my education my mother, Sandra Hector Holmes, made sure this was a priority.
> —Tim Holmes

Constance fully embodied the two messages that have been passed down through the generations of the Holmes-Hector family: "Keep a good name and get your education! Two things nobody in this world can take from you and will take you far!"

Another notable relative of Tim's was his cousin George Hector, who was widely known as the Whistling Banjoman. He played at local fairs and square dances for decades. He released his only album in 1982, when he was seventy-one, and was one of the first inductees into the New Brunswick Country Music Hall of Fame when it was founded in 1983.

I spent every second weekend with my Holmes grandparents, and conversations with my grandfather were always full of wisdom. He wouldn't give me answers, just asked questions, then left me to think and come to my own conclusions. What a great way to learn! And my grandmother Holmes had the kindest of hearts but would not take crap from anyone. Know your worth but always be kind!
—Tim Holmes

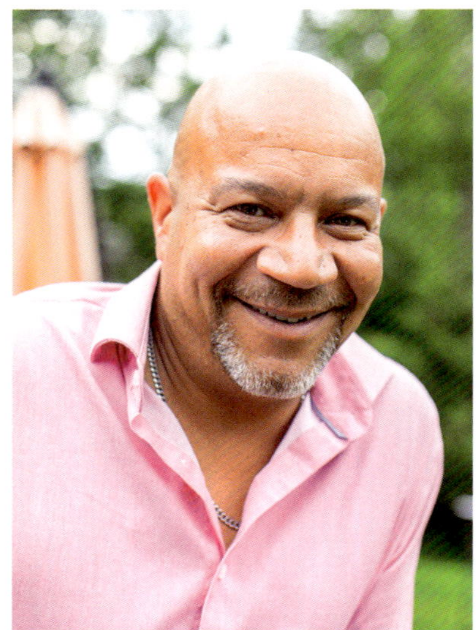

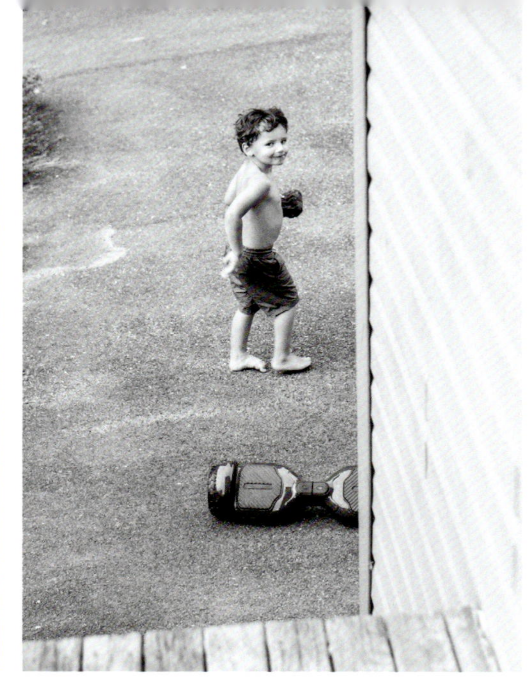

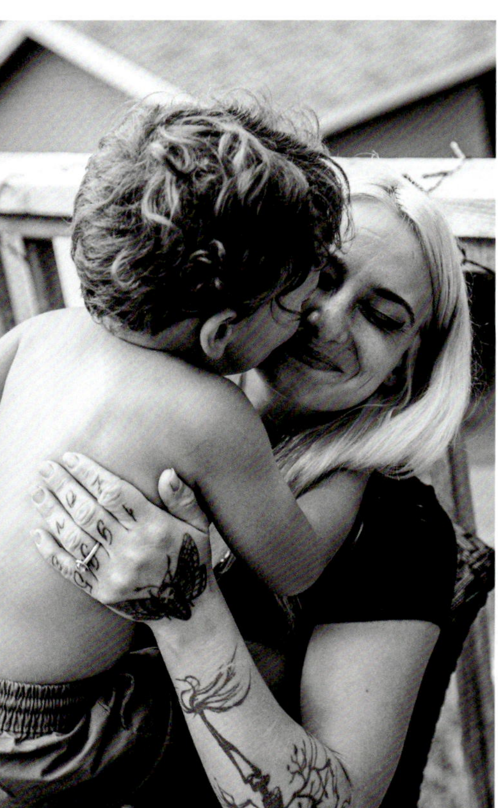

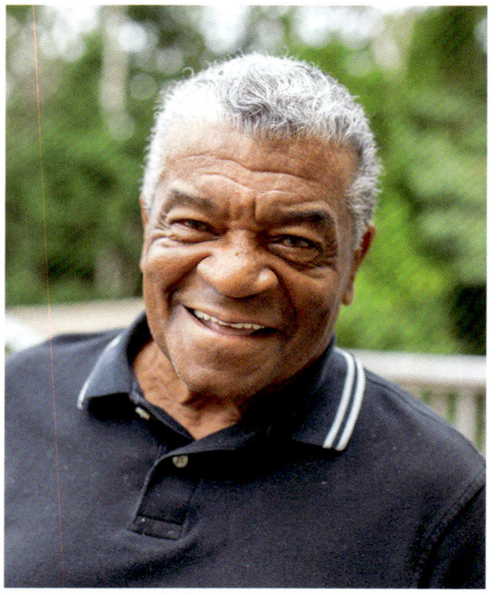

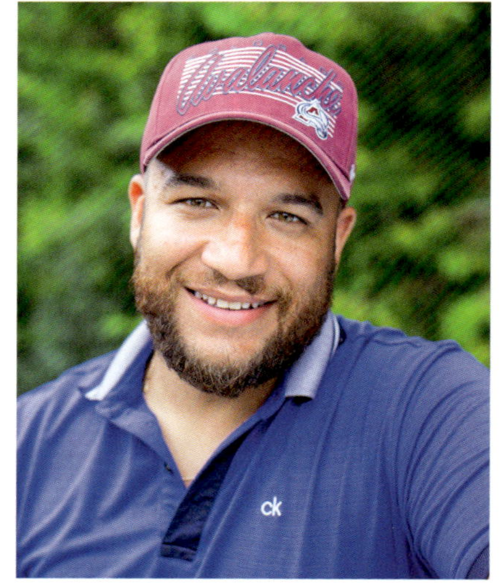

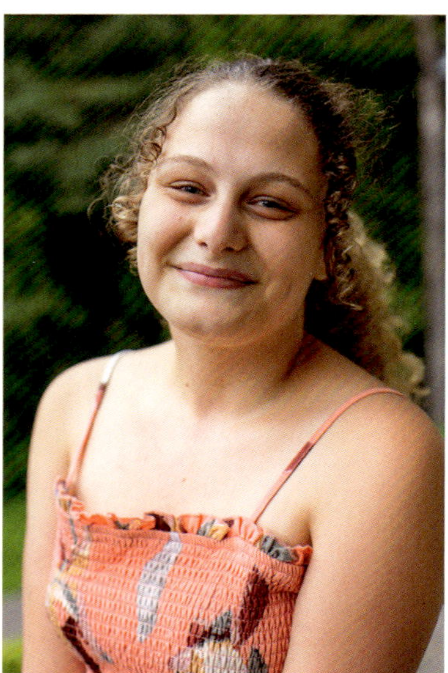

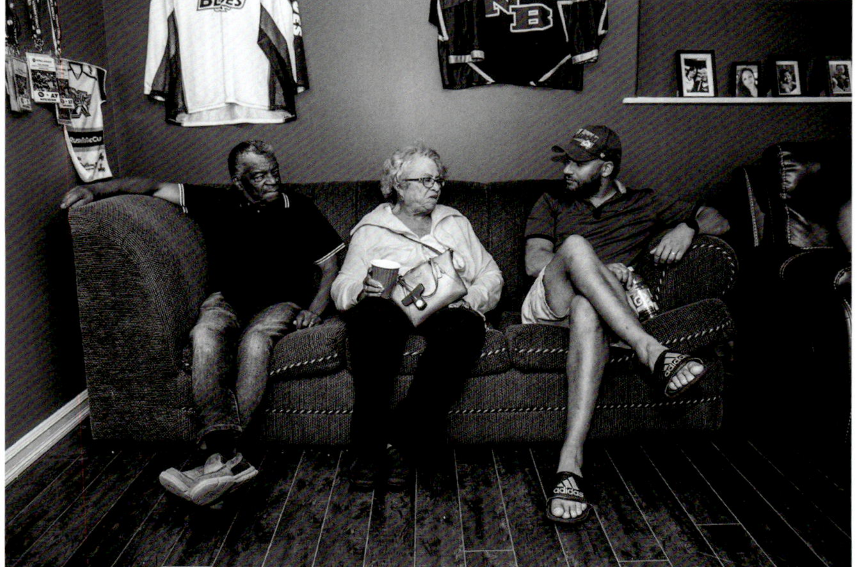

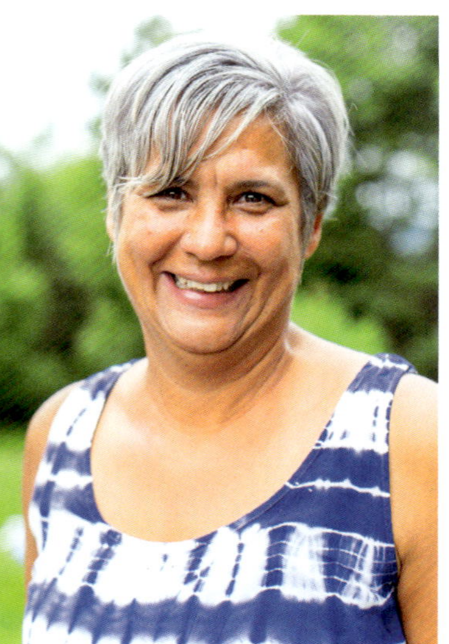

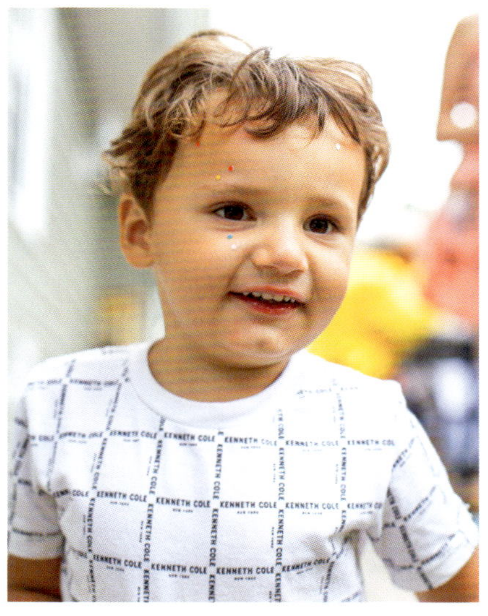

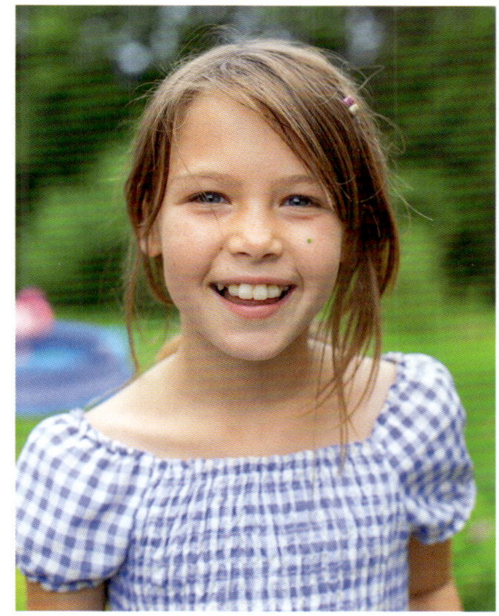

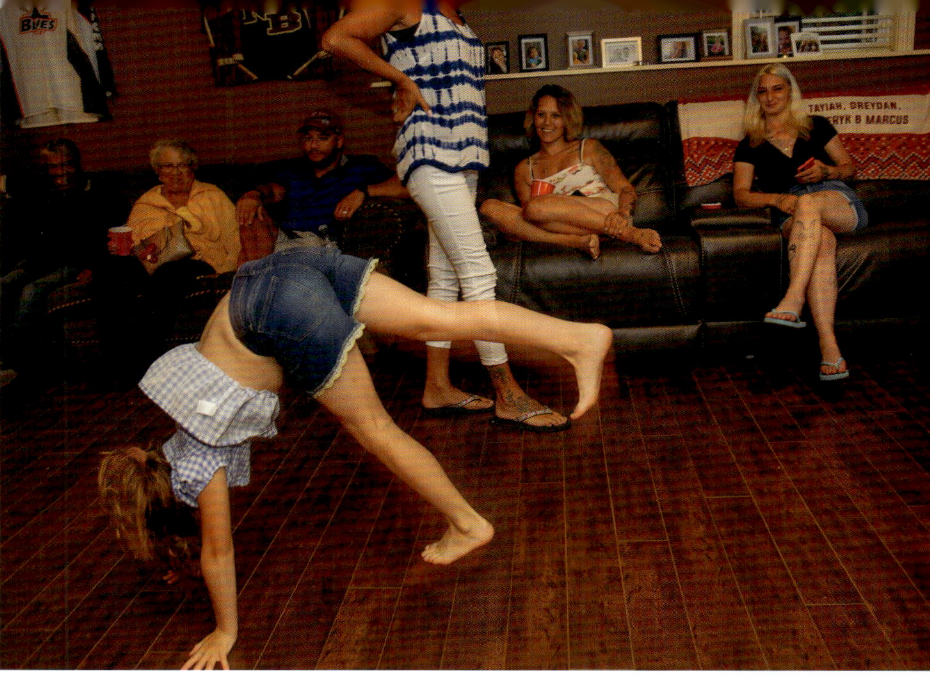

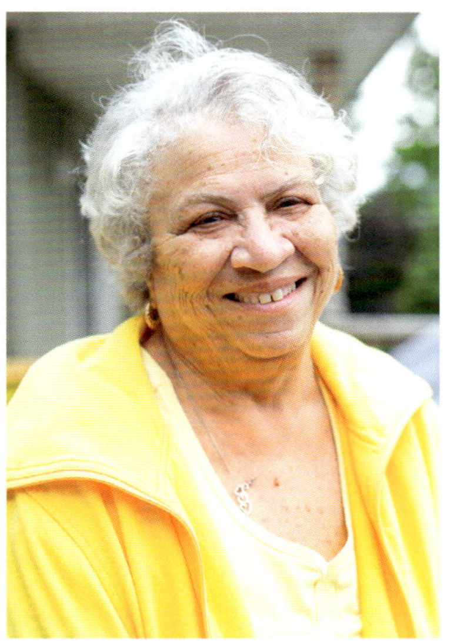

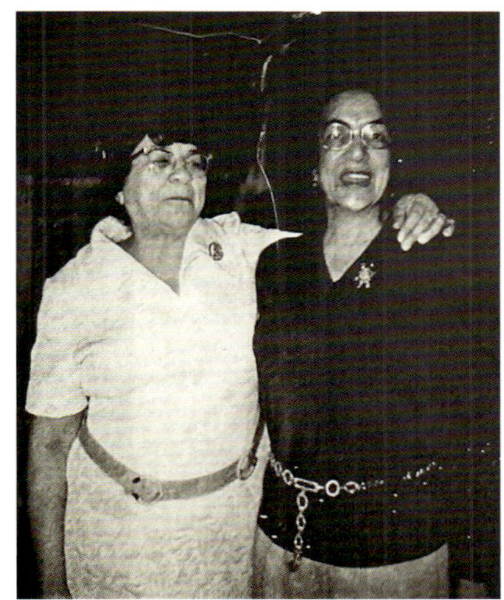

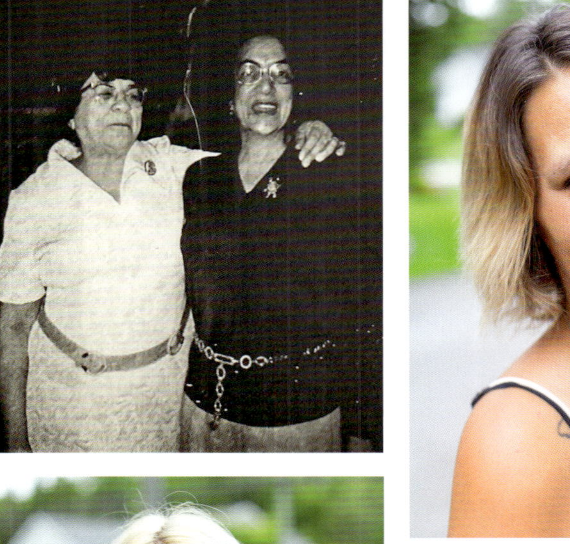

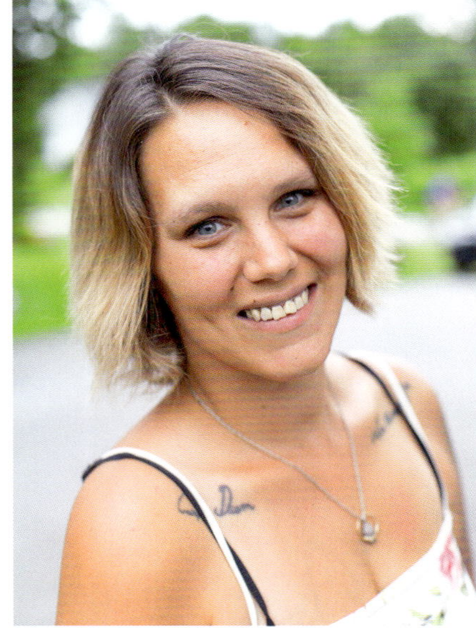

My grandmother Hector took care of me as a toddler, and everything was centered around family. I still can feel her warmth and the electricity from her hugs. As a young boy I heard the stories of my grandfather Hector who worked at the sugar refinery and would do the work of many men to allow his coworkers time to have lunch. This act of caring for others stuck in keeping a good name.
—Tim Holmes

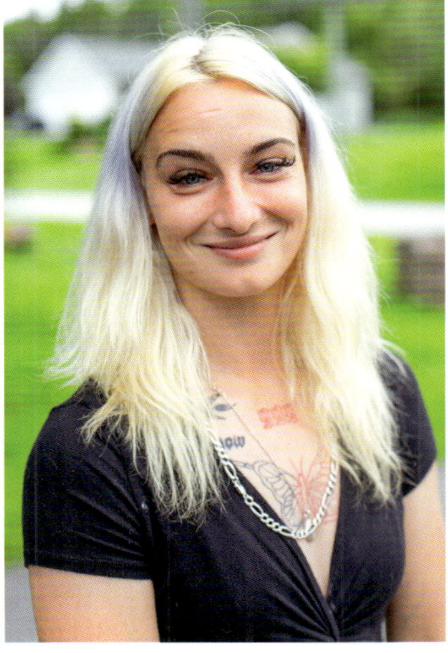

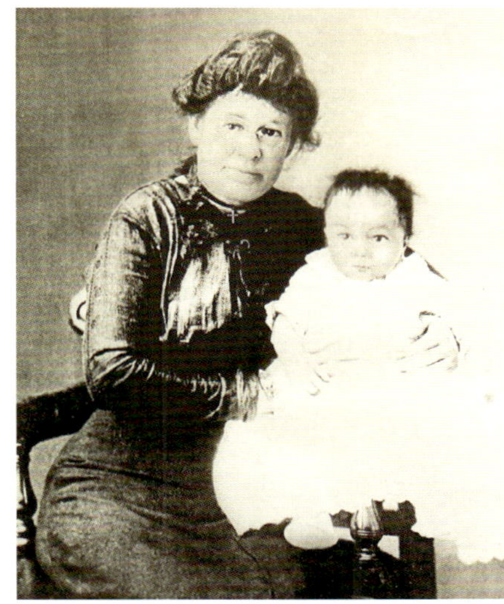

Nash / Eatmon — Fredericton

It was a cold noon in Fredericton
As we pulled into the long driveway
Of the Nash residence.
"Let's get this show on the road," our host said.

Family from Nova Scotia dropped by,
Innocent of the photoshoot.
But every family member that stopped by
Got a hero's welcome, even the project crew.

A table chequered with family photos caused
Everyone to draw closer, to connect.
Between smiles everyone paused
To feel the healing when surrounded by loved ones.

We decided to gather the clan outdoors.
An' even with ice underfoot and freezing winds
The Nash family's warmth
Shined through the cold, to the camera.

A family member was to pick up coffee and donuts
The double cream an' sugar got the loudest welcome
The only unwelcome sight was my wallet.
Exiled back to pocket.

Even as I scan documents from another room.
I find myself chuckling at the jokes I overhear.
It has become such a familiar sound.
That of shared heritage gracefully flipping frowns.

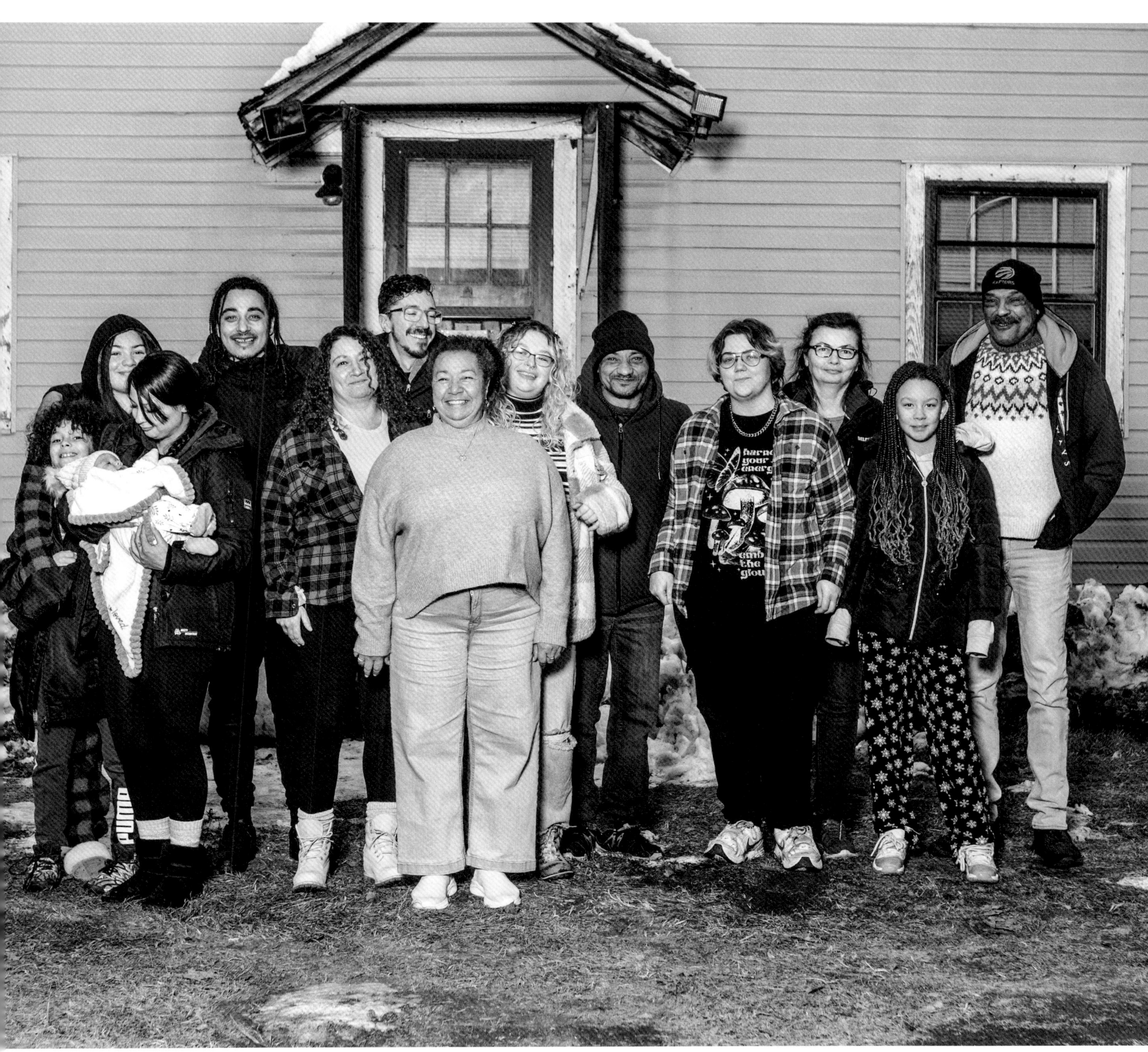
PUMA

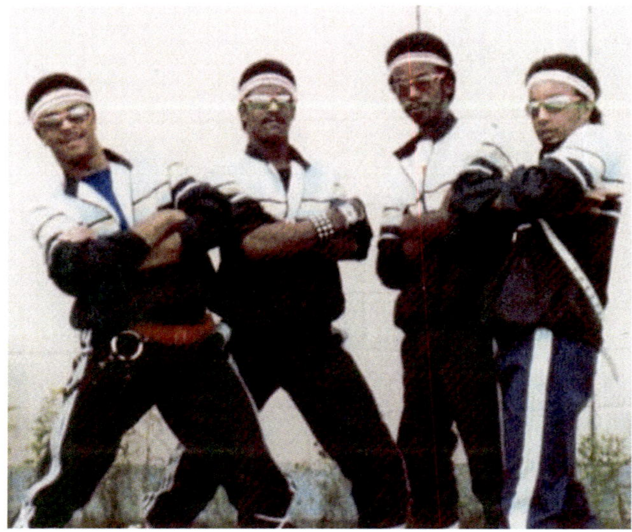

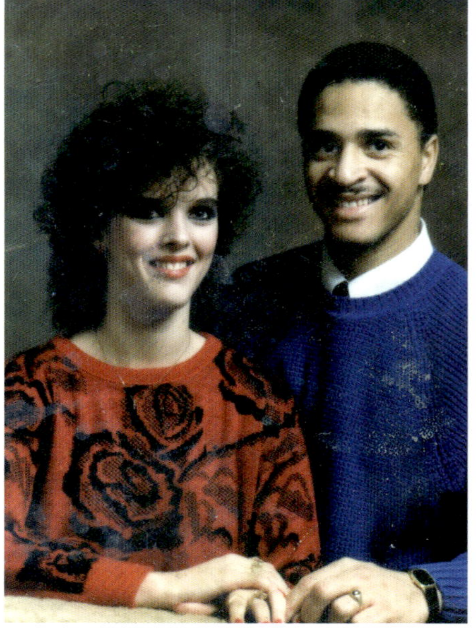

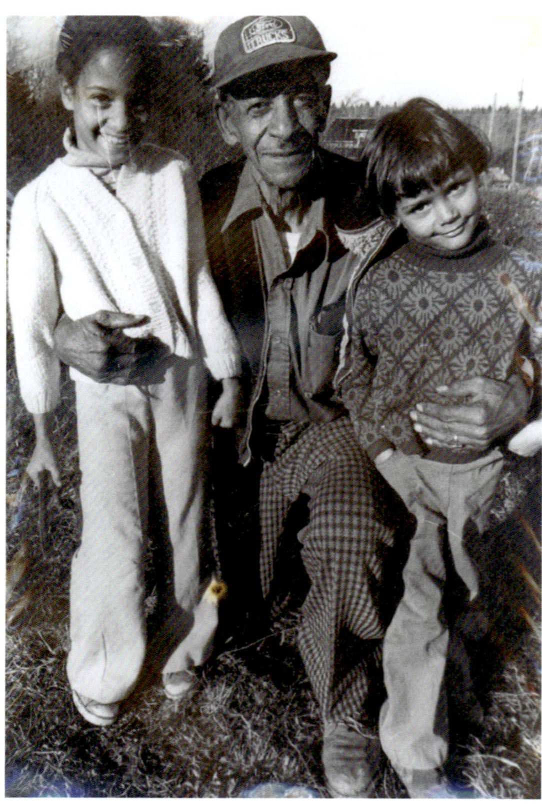

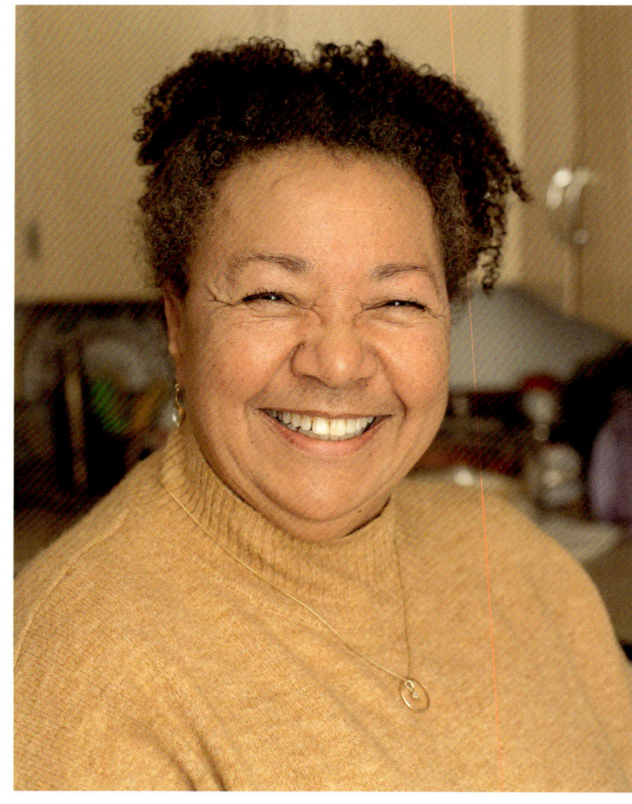

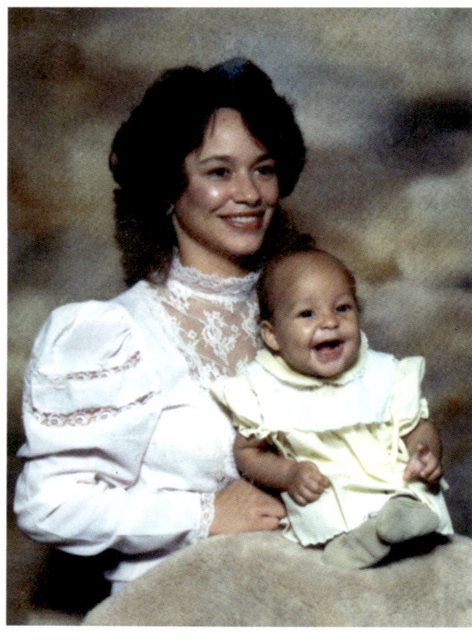

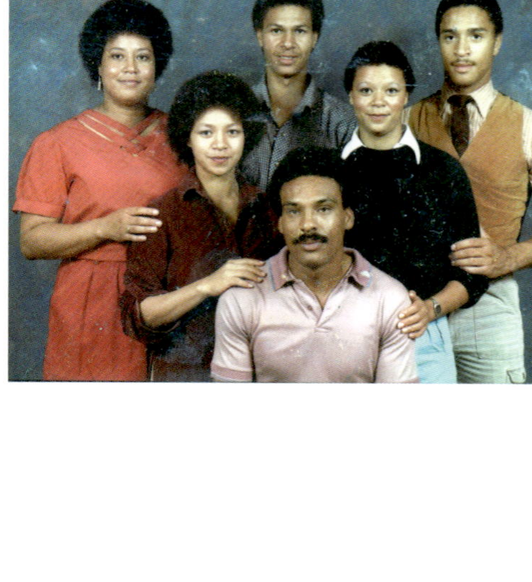

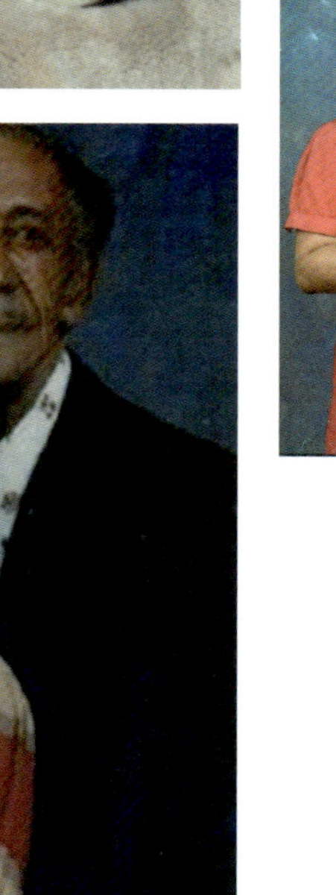

The Nash family is a quiet, independent, hardworking family that originally lived off the land on the outskirts of Fredericton. Debbie Nash is unable to trace her family back much past her parents, Elizabeth "Bessie" Eatmon (née Nash) and Chester Adolphus Eatmon, but she has been told that her father's grandmother was named Deborah and her mother's grandmother was called Jane: "I never met grandparents, aunts, or uncles and must say I was jealous and felt ripped off—I missed out being spoiled stinky by a nanna and poppa." It seems likely that Chester's mother was Rosella Mc Intyre, daughter of Deborah Ann Cameron and William Mc Intyre.

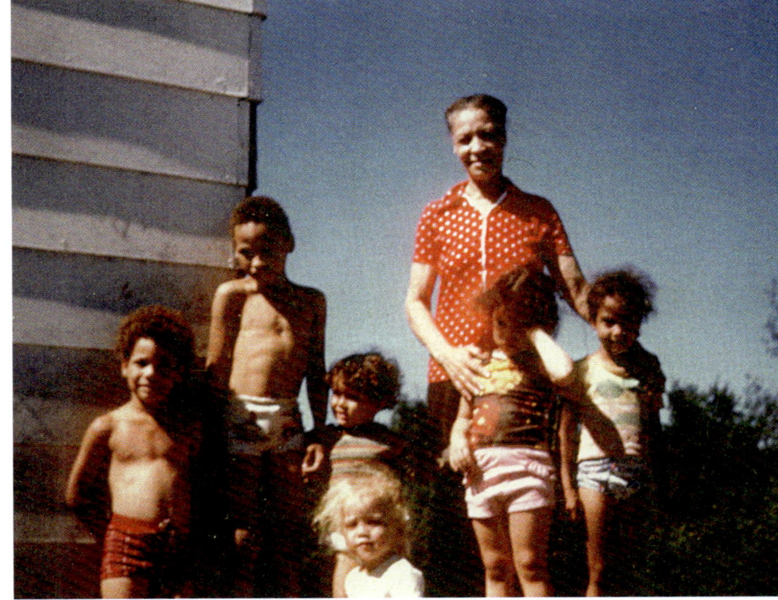

Bessie Nash, Debbie's mother, was born in Marysville, New Brunswick, in 1927, and was the middle child of five. All four of her siblings died before they were fifty-five, from illnesses and accidents. Her family "felt no need for schoolin'" and needed all hands working on the farm, where she grew up. "A kindred spirit, a simple, kind country soul," Bessie went to work for a White woman when she was fourteen: "The only extra was work on Wednesday evenings—for the ladies' bridge night."

After Bessie married Chester Eatmon, who was born in 1904 in Elm Hill, they had seven children, including Debbie. Chester, a harness racer, was often absent, and Debbie and her siblings were mainly raised by their mother, who imparted to them a strong work ethic—"Do the best, whatever you do"—that allowed little room for complaining: "You have to remember there is always someone else worse off than you." Both parents have now passed, and Debbie's sister Maggie and her baby brother Allan are also gone. The five remaining children are scattered between New Brunswick and Ontario. Debbie still lives in the Fredericton area and has four grown children of her own, who she did her best to raise in the same way.

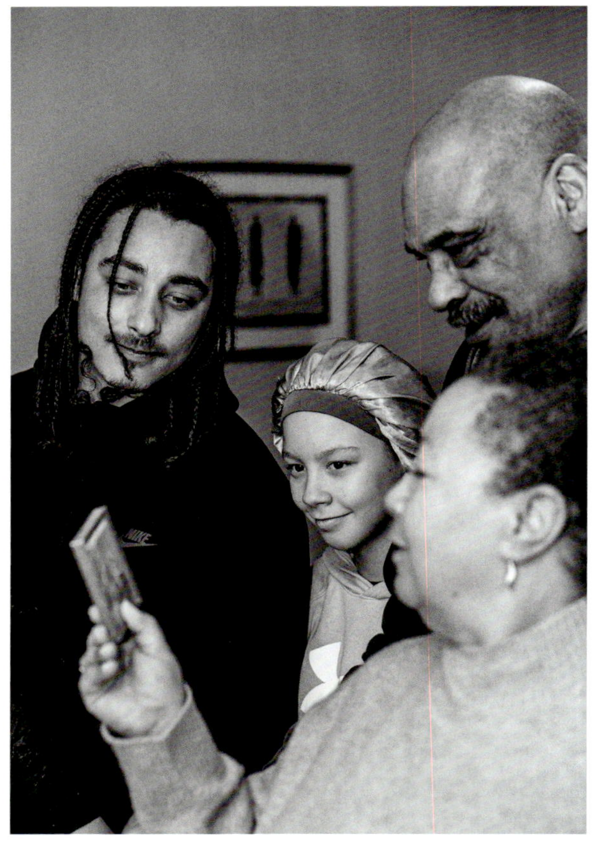

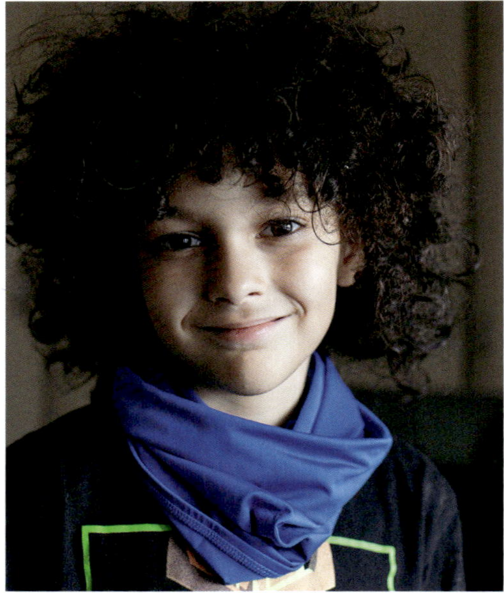

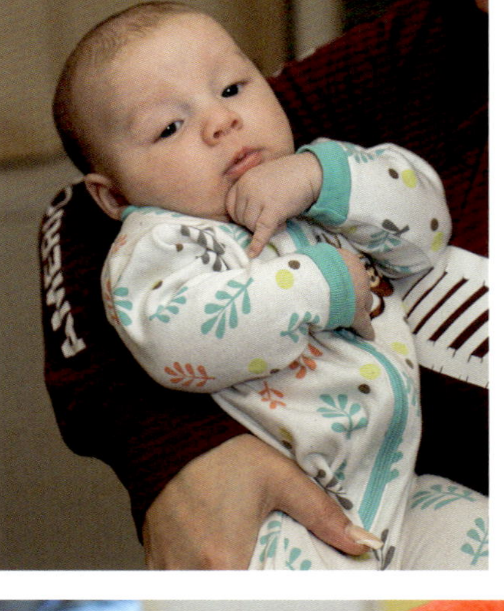

I didn't even realize that we were poor until I entered school, where it was made abundantly and harshly clear: I was poor and Black! Kids can be cruel in their ignorant truth when in their youth.
— Debbie Nash

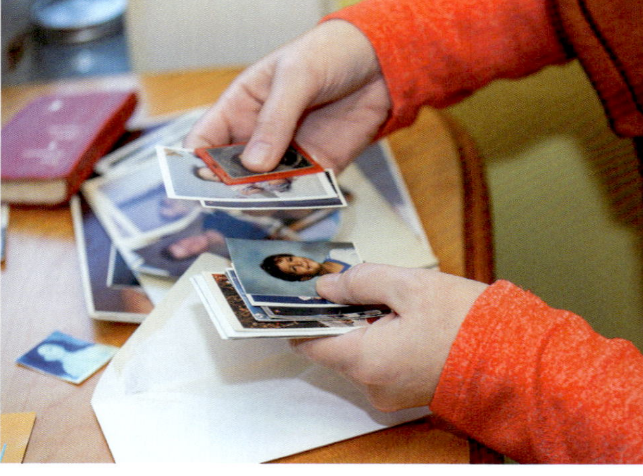

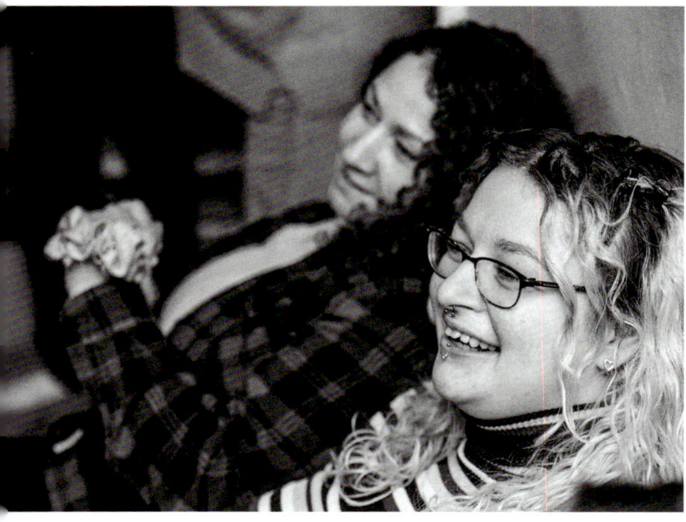

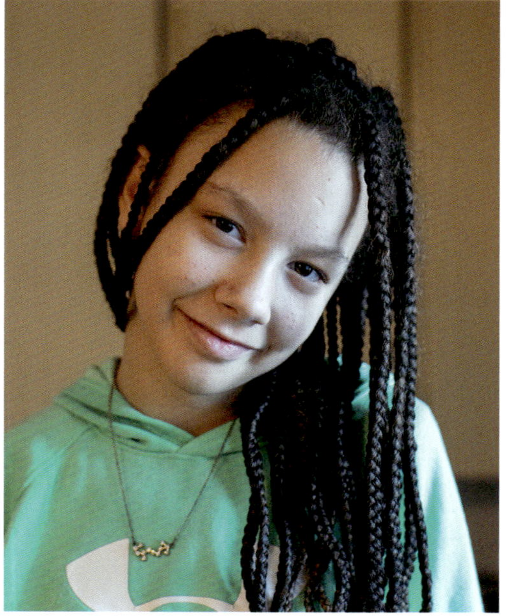

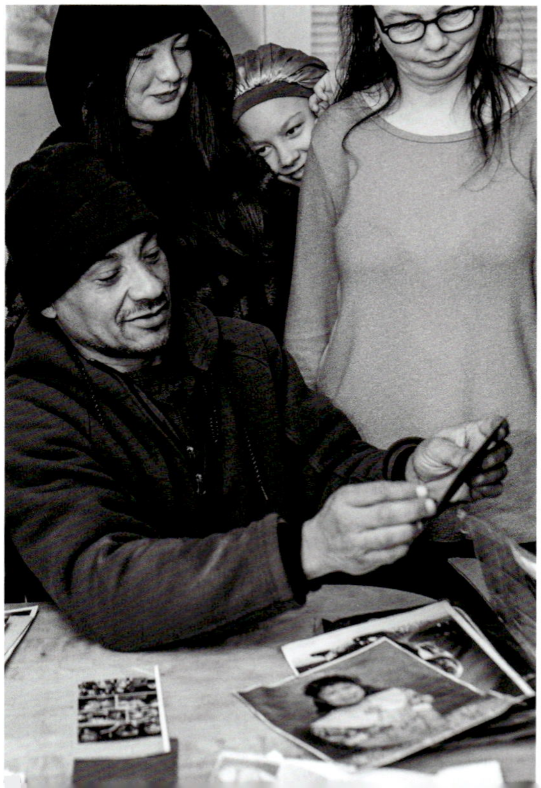

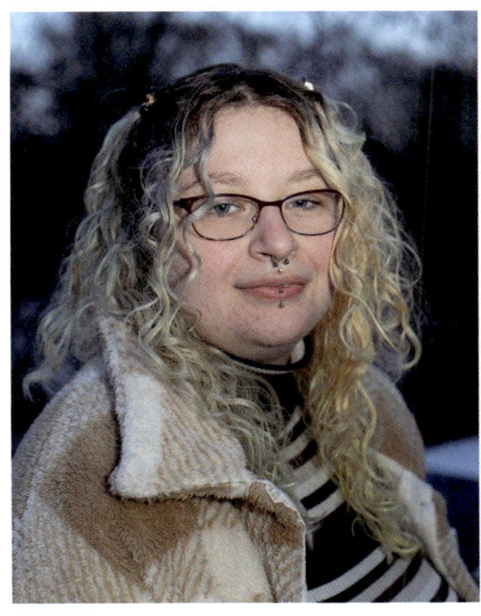

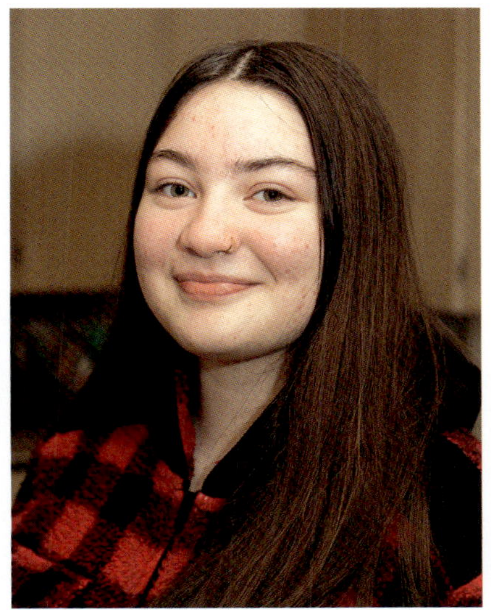

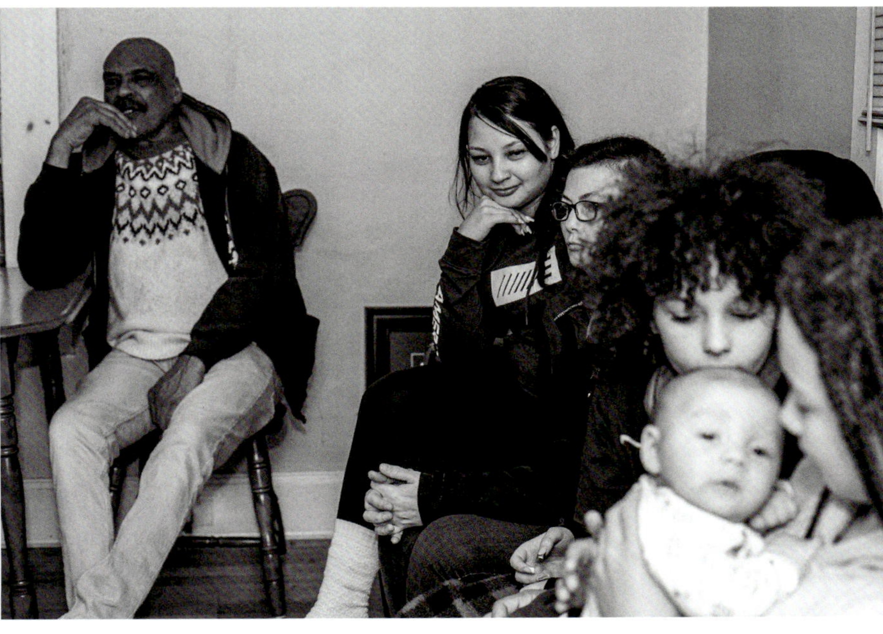

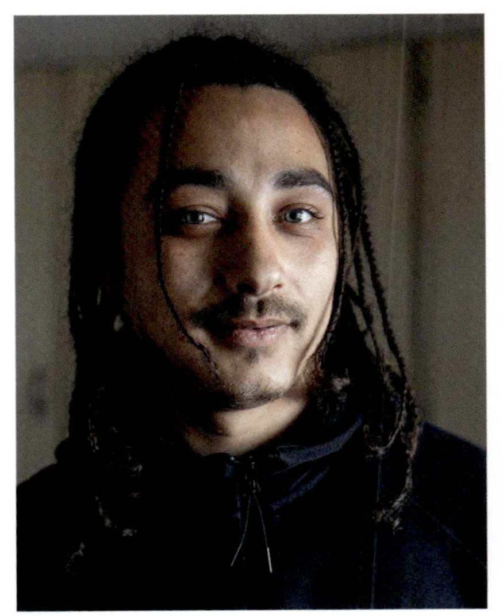

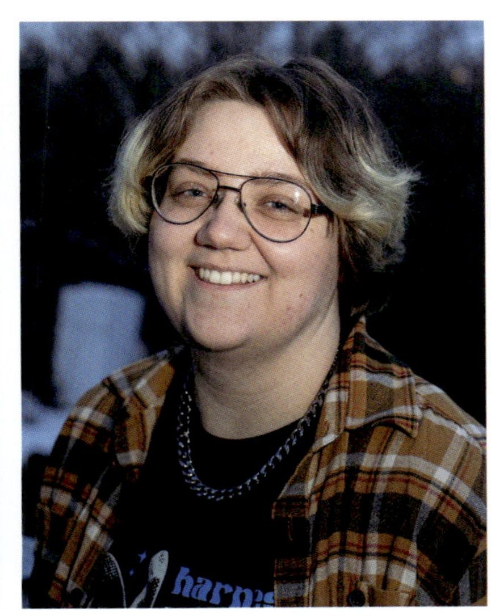

On the many nights my dad wasn't home, I cherished the time I spent with my mother. Mama mending clothes and treating herself to humbug candies. Me, curled up on her bed, listening to fantastic stories about her childhood: "Did you know sulfur and molasses were used to cure picking your nose — which meant you had worms?" She covered her mouth to laugh, self-conscious of her dental plates. I said, Mama you're allowed to laugh, even if you snort, which made her laugh more. Her laugh always did my heart good.
— Debbie Nash

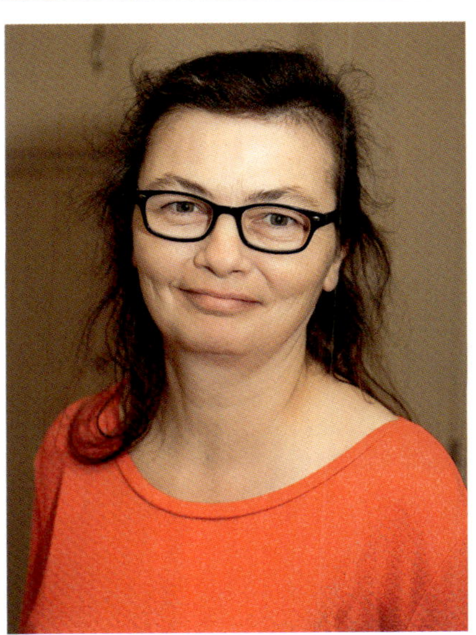

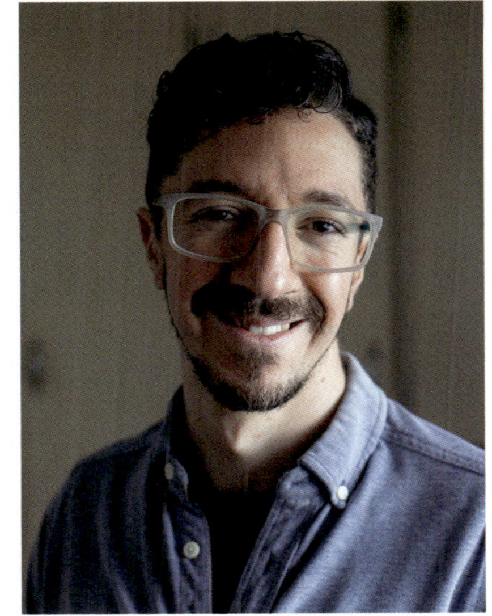

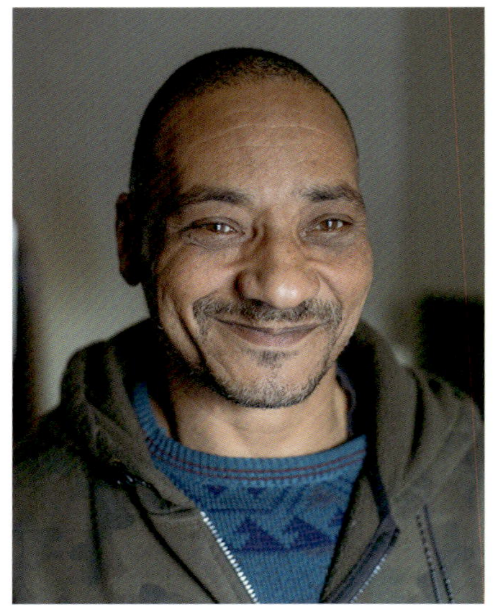

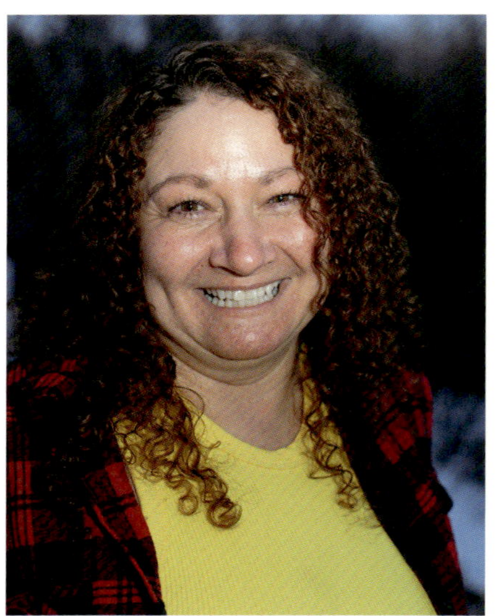

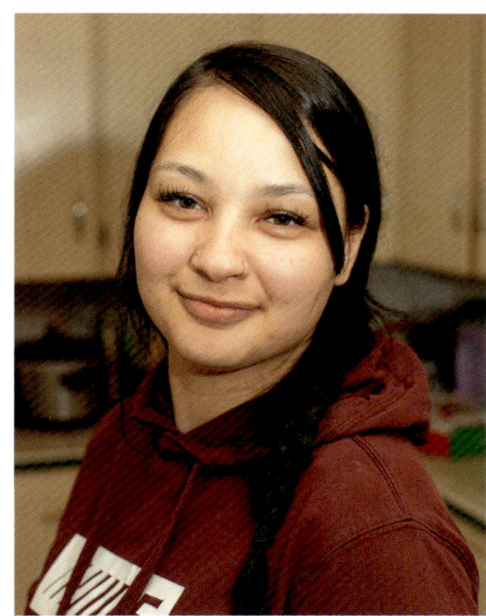

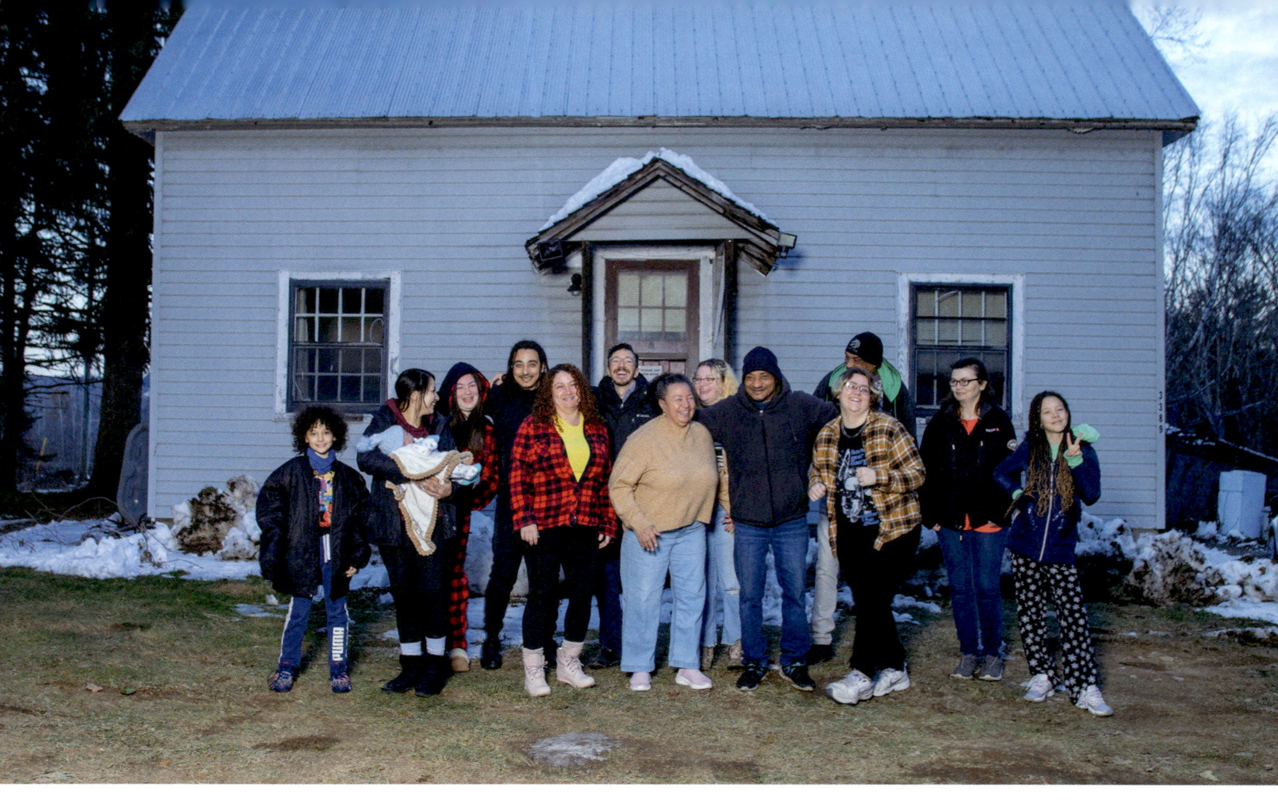

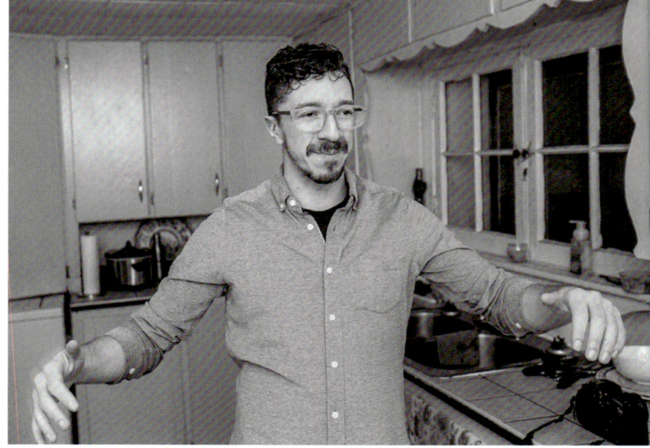

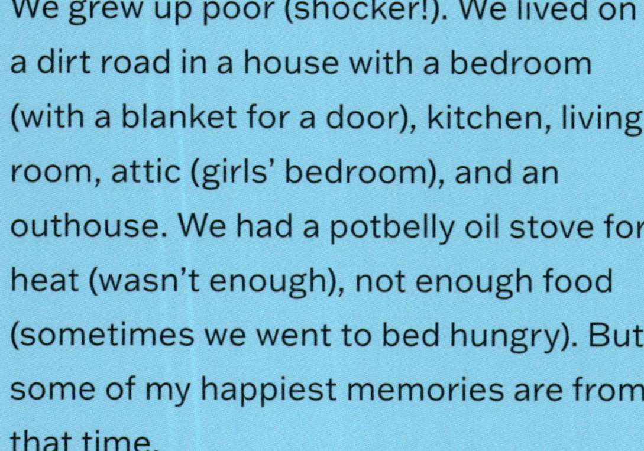

We grew up poor (shocker!). We lived on a dirt road in a house with a bedroom (with a blanket for a door), kitchen, living room, attic (girls' bedroom), and an outhouse. We had a potbelly oil stove for heat (wasn't enough), not enough food (sometimes we went to bed hungry). But some of my happiest memories are from that time.

— Debbie Nash

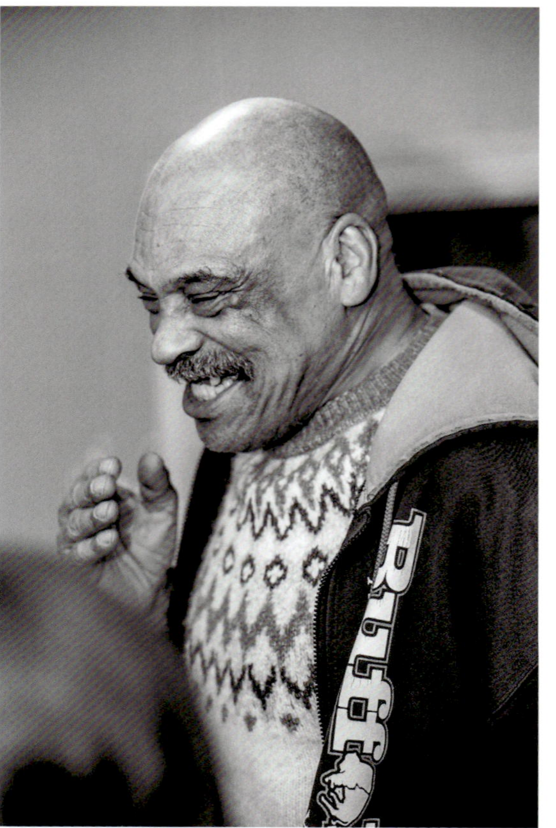

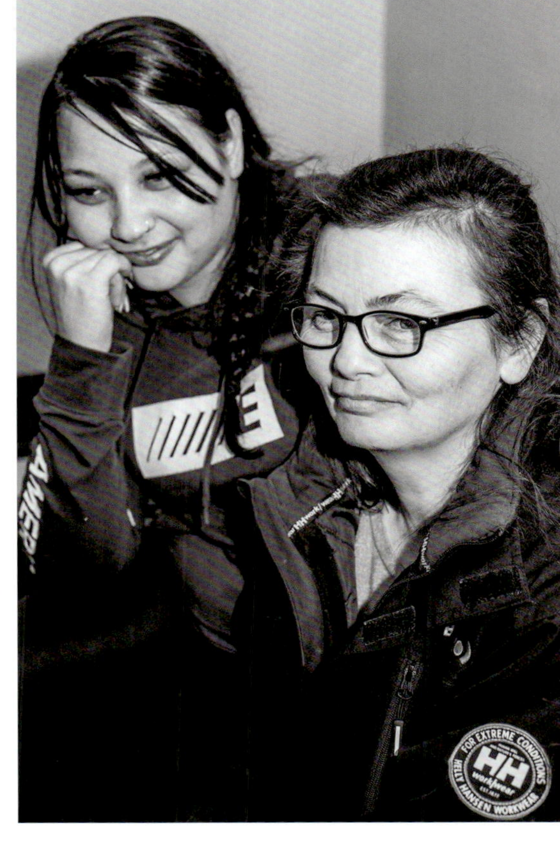
FOR EXTREME CONDITIONS
HH
workwear
HELLY HANSEN WORKWEAR

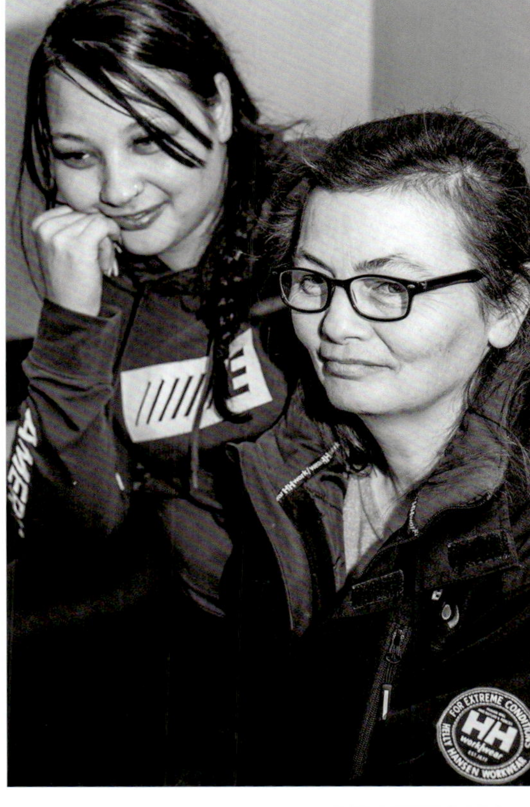

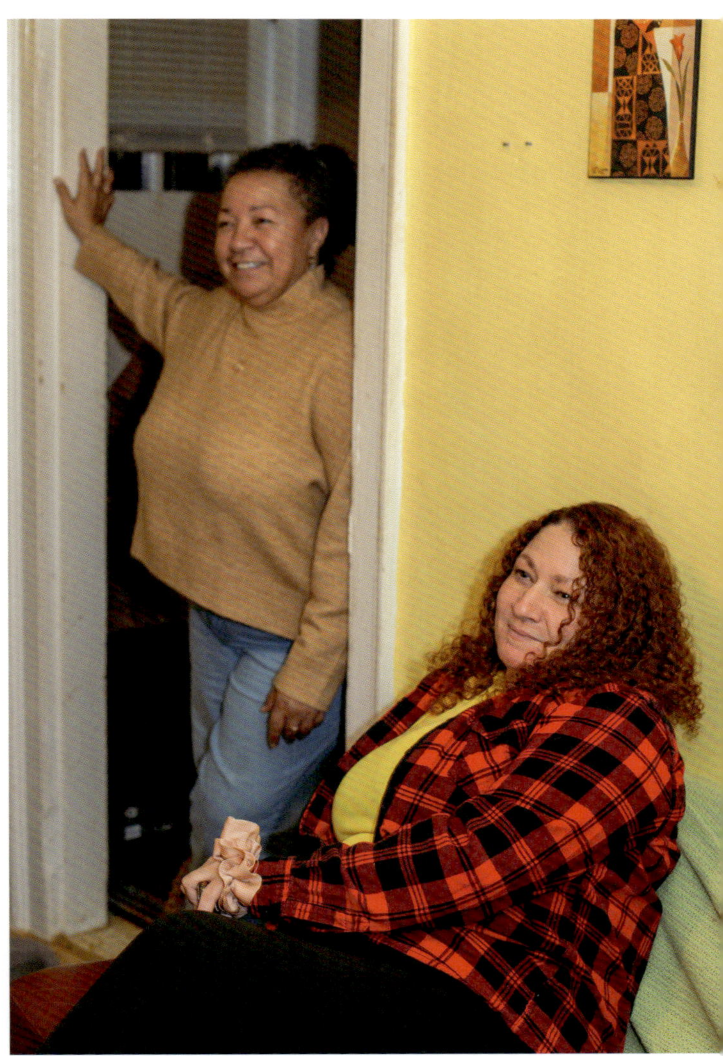

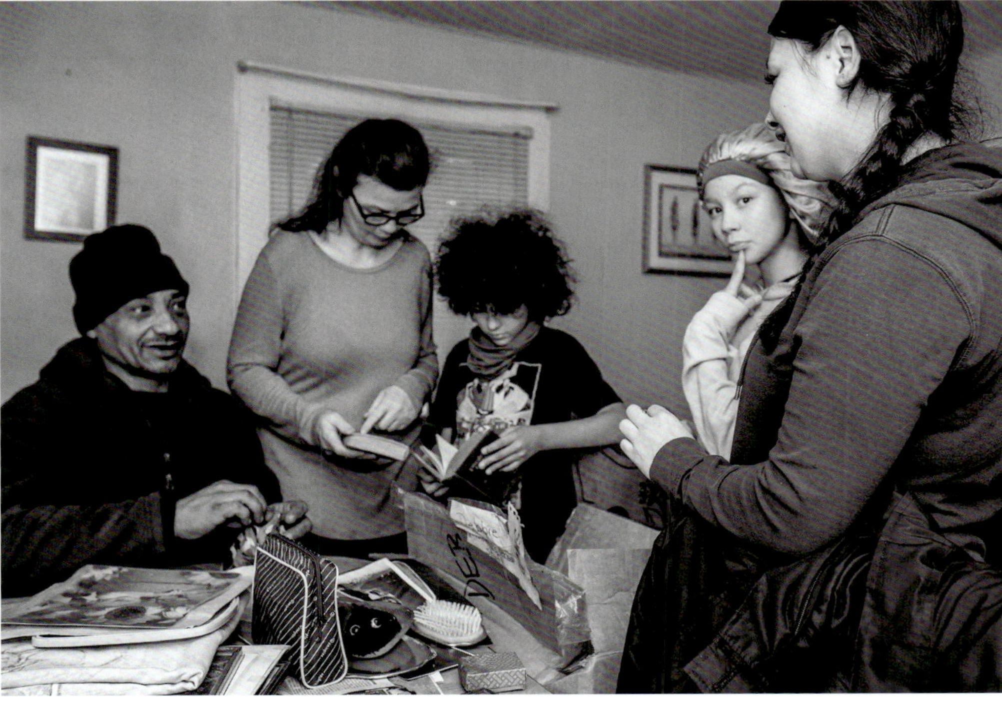

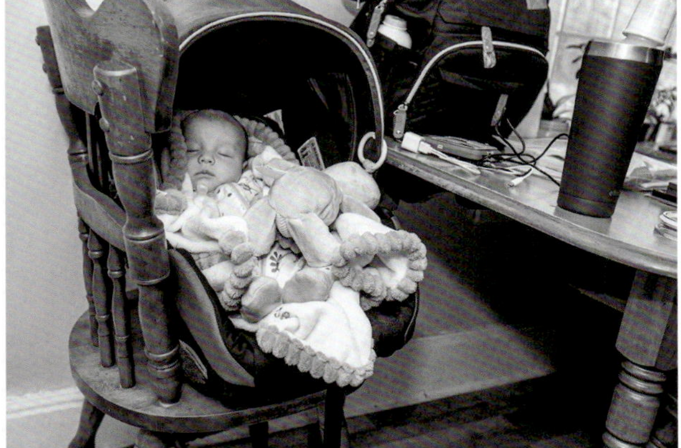

It tickles me when I see a trait in a child of mine that reminds me of Mama, that I managed to instill. What more could a parent want than to see it going down the bloodline? We live in and by our present, future, and past, no matter where life takes us. We were — and are mostly still — poor and obscure but strong, resilient, and robust, and we are still a family, and we are still here.
— Debbie Nash

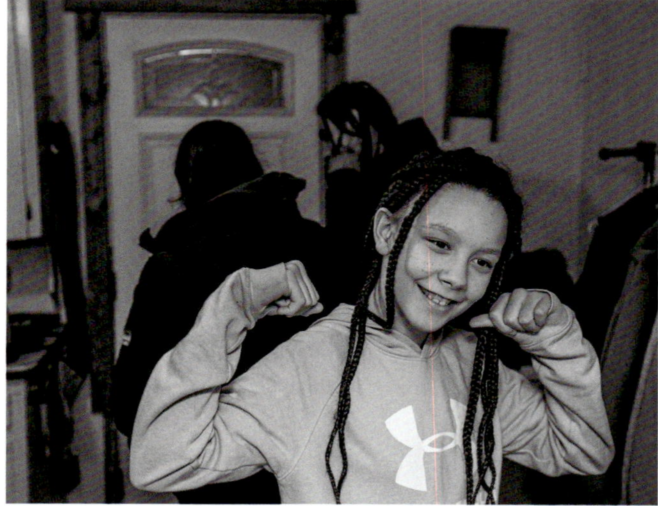

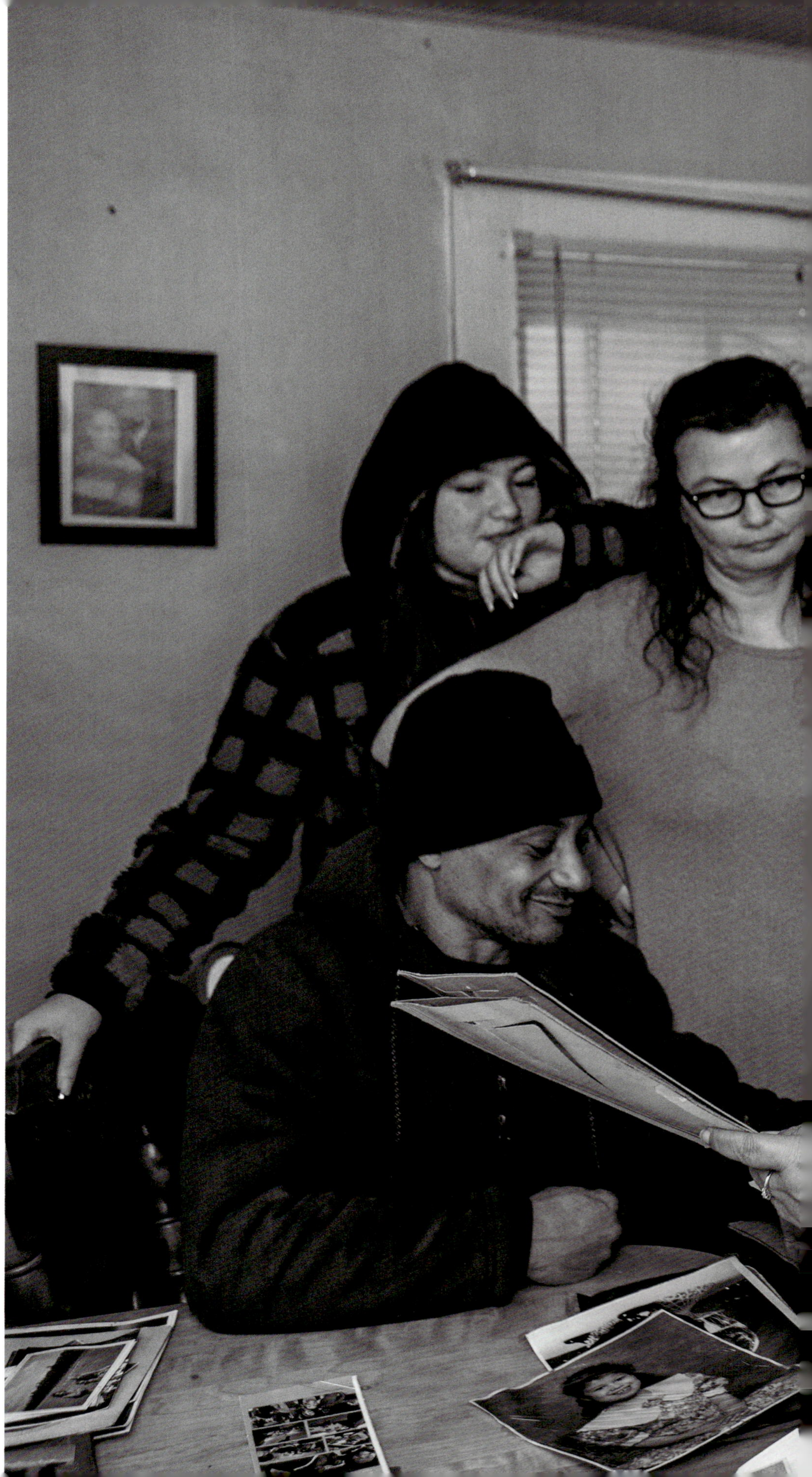

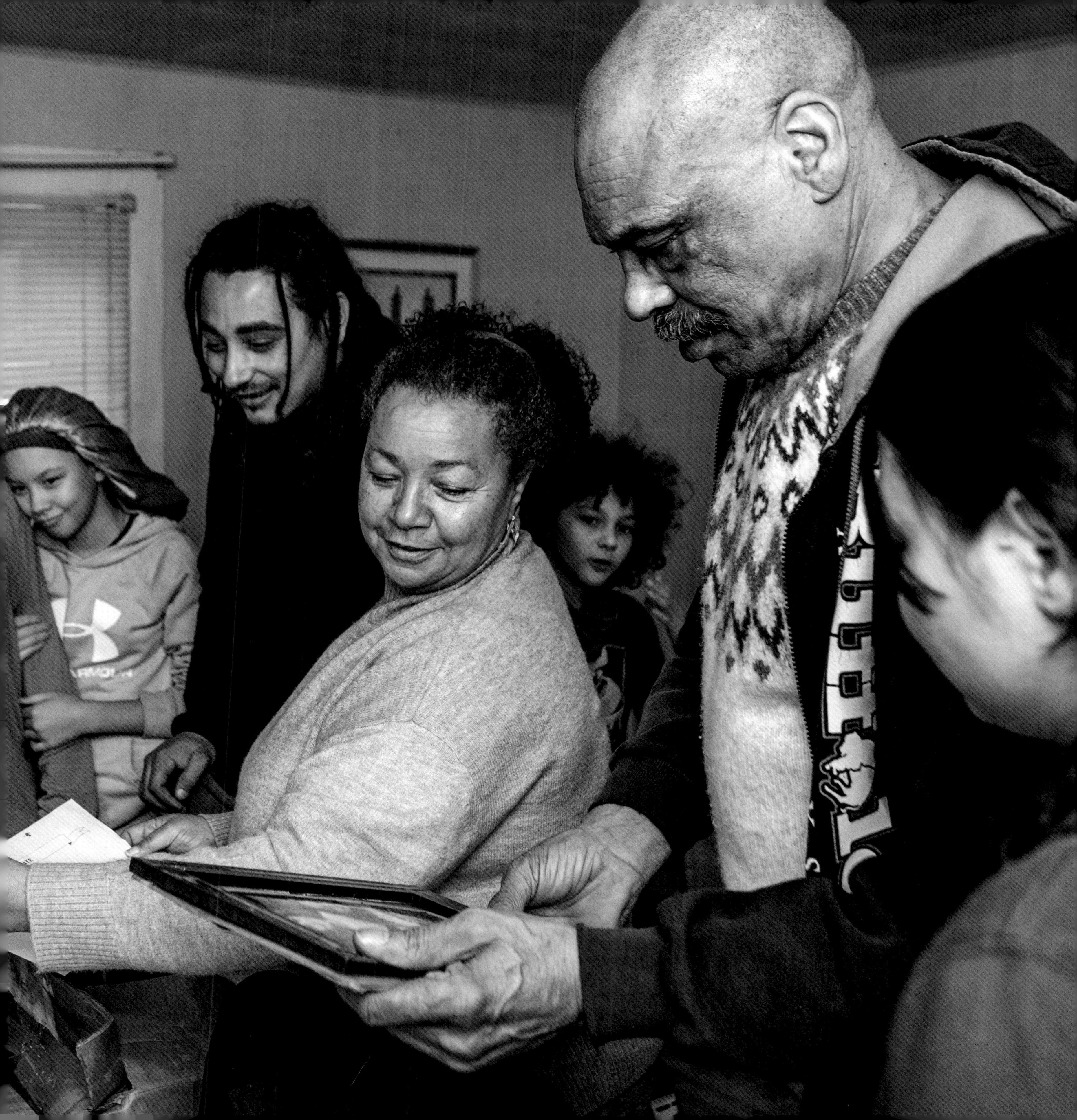

MacPherson / Edison — Kingston Peninsula

In the Kingston Peninsula
A ferry ride away.
Is found a family that knows its heritage.
But not its history.

It felt like we'd escaped to a tropical island.
The large pond on the property wiggles
As rocks and laughter skip across its girth.
This is clearly a lineage that knows its worth.

As the two parents and four children guide our tour
Pointing out edible flowers, prescribing certain herbs for tea.
We realize that every one of them is barefoot.
"Tender footed" they jokingly dub our guarded soles.

The Barn is wondrously a classroom.
A whiteboard speaks to the day's lessons.
The thick blue marker reminding the children
Of the links between being rooted and navigating their ancestral paths.

There is as much greenery inside the home as outside.
On the kitchen ceiling the alphabet, planets, and zodiac signs
Are burned into the rafters.
Bowls of fresh fruit garnish corners, but candy is invisible.

The four children desire chalk and blackboard,
Dream to move their grounded community forward.
Find their strength in the solid earth
And their smiles in the shining sun.

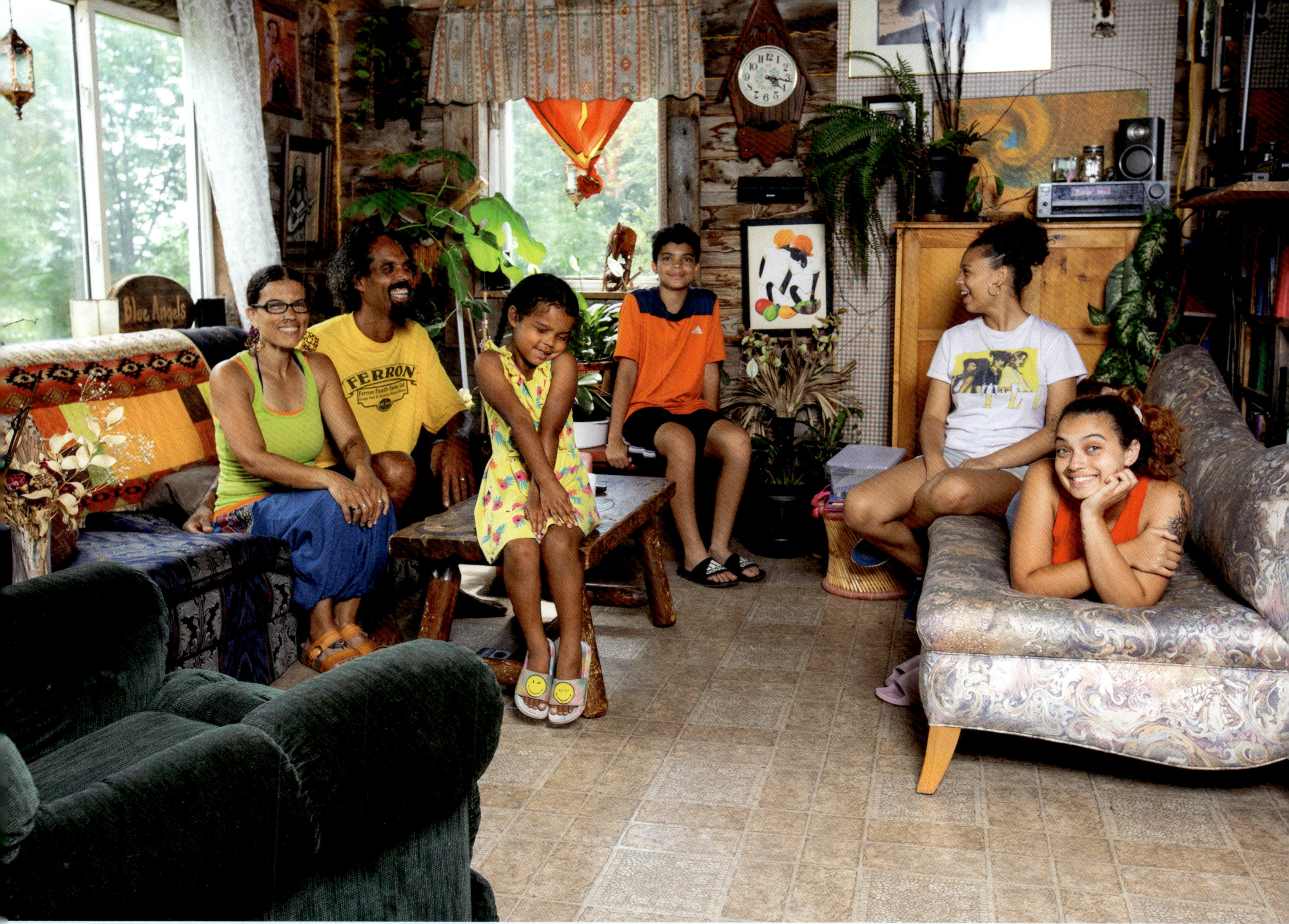

A family anchored in Acadie,
Armed with a curriculum
That connects them to white waves
And green woods.

A family determined to engineer utopia.
Just as the Black pioneers imagined they could.

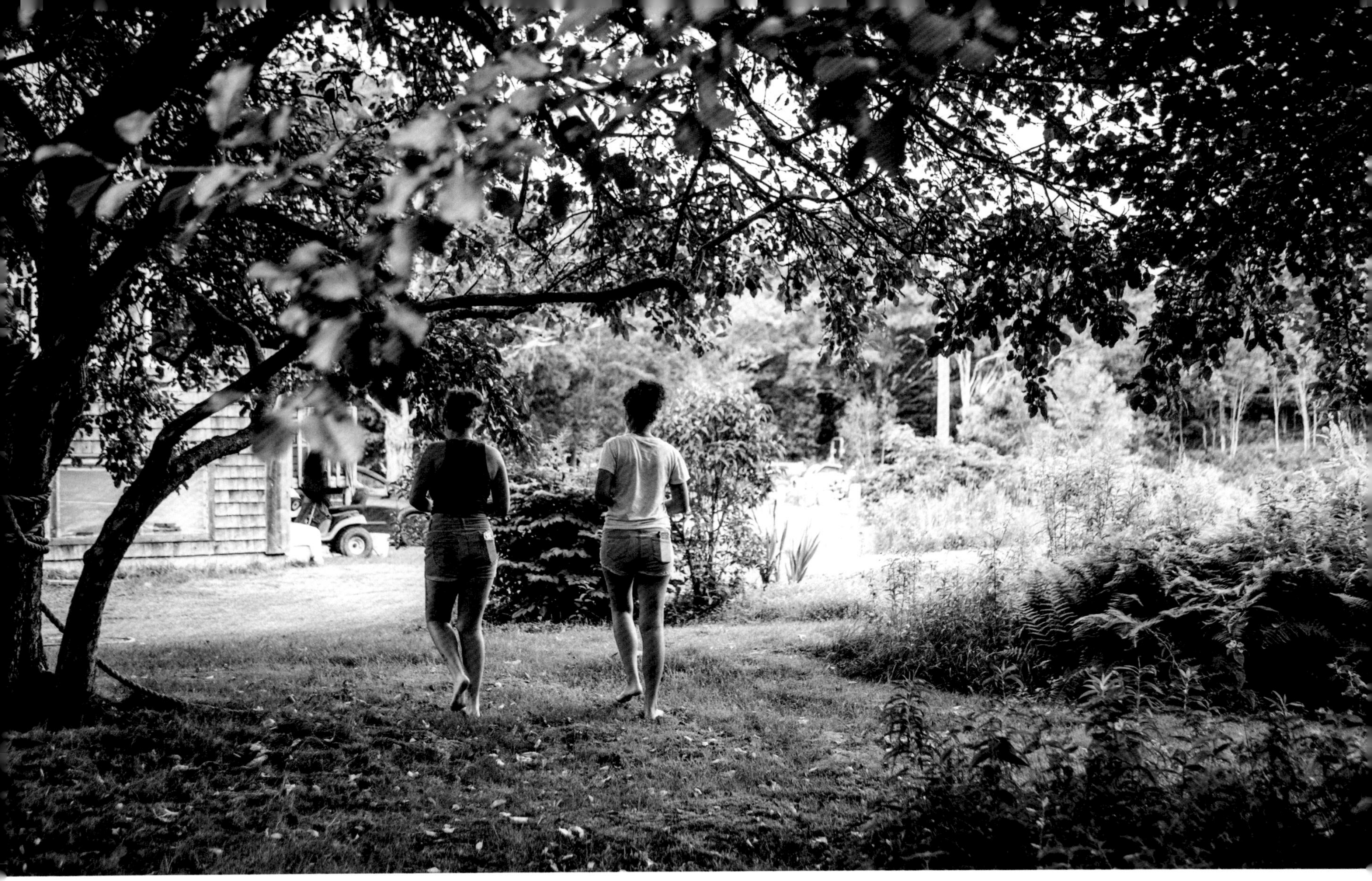

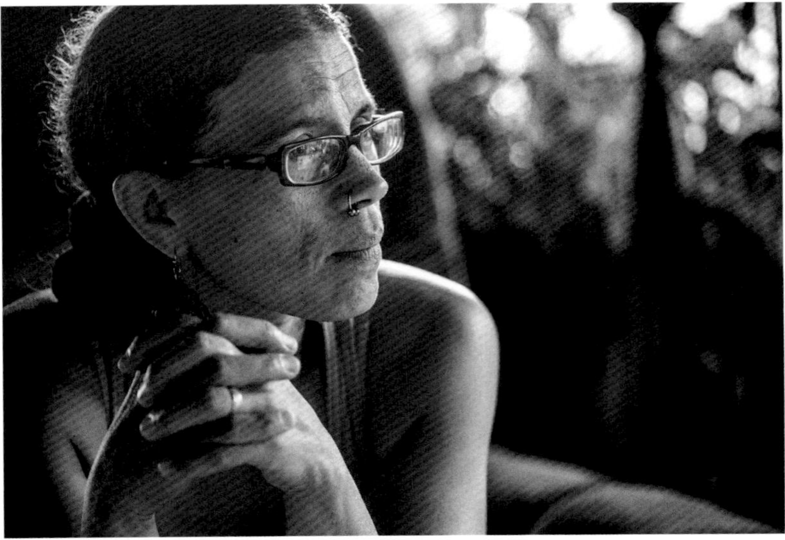

It was court proceedings, Katimavik, social inclusion, volunteering, immigration, protests, Sisters of Charity, water rights, the Council of Canadians, spirit of the four winds, school and business presentations. It was grassroots action, research, and development. It was snowstorms, Black History Months, Elizabeth Weir, King's Square, council-chambers podium, and preaching our evangel.
—Tanya MacPherson

Bubba MacPherson was adopted, and Tanya MacPherson was raised by her grandparents. Tanya MacPherson can trace her family tree back along a line of Shears, who were among the original settlers of Willow Grove in the late 1700s. Tanya's grandparents were Charles and Ella (née Shears) Edison. Her late father, whose name was Ronald Arthur Edison, had six biological children, including her, and Tanya was able to connect with them in 2024.

Tanya and Bubba both grew up in Saint John and were mentored by strong Black influences. Among their heroes are the early developers of PRUDE back in the 1990s.

They now live on the Kingston Peninsula and are raising their four children close to the earth, in harmony with the land. By example, they teach their children four basic lessons and have witnessed them all take hold:

1. Apologising to plants
2. Mitigating for each other
3. Reading at bedtime and creating a life of books
4. Serving in and engaging with their community

A grassroots family, Tanya and Bubba run a small holistic-agriculture business and are often called on to do public presentations at schools and businesses about Black history. The MacPhersons demonstrate that an Afrocentric Black family, proud of their roots, can have success without trying to scale the economic staircase.

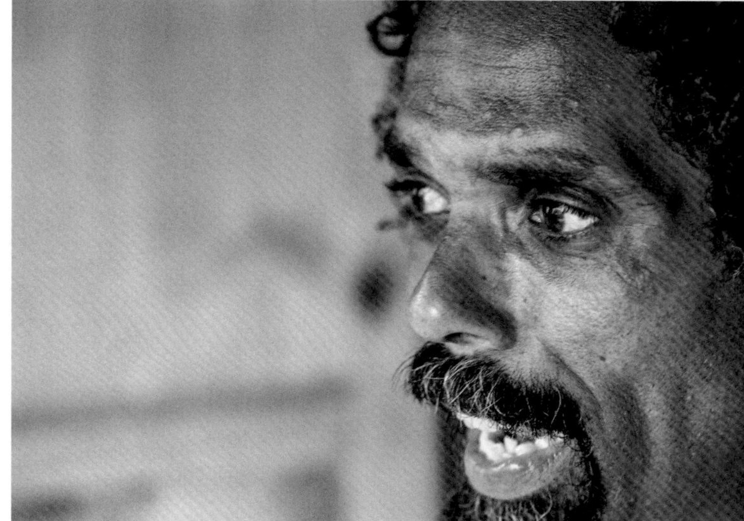

The unfolding began as a request for legal assistance at the Black organization PRUDE. There, as I exited the elevator, was Tanya, glowing in service, organization, and grassroots action, with brains, strength, tenacity, and great beauty with great modesty.
— Bubba MacPherson

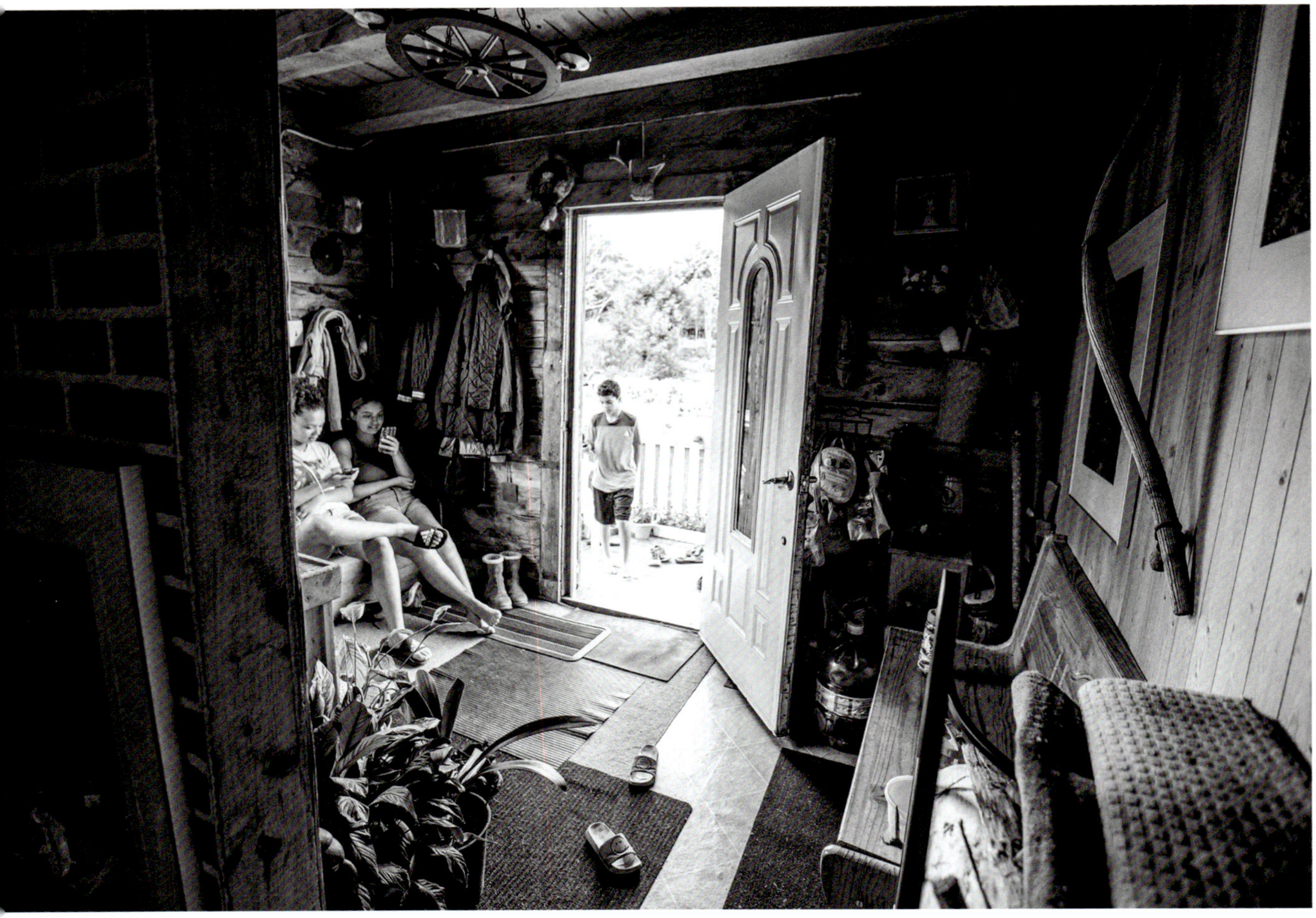

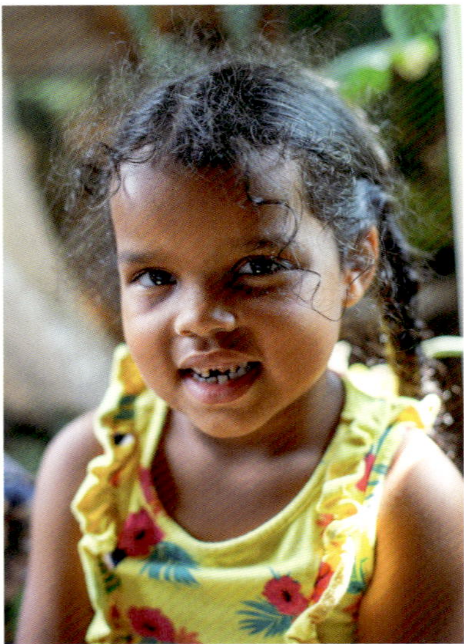

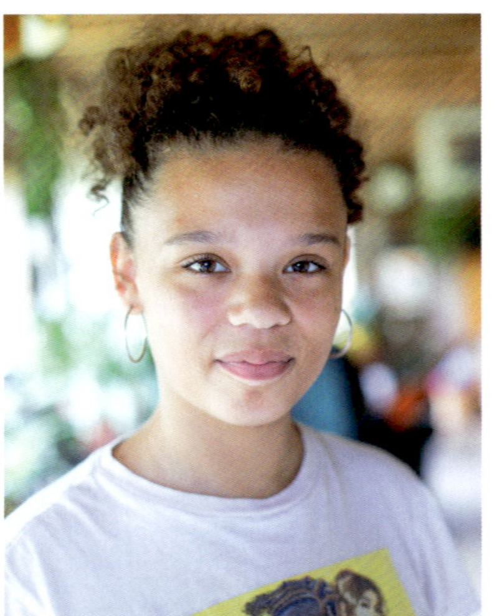

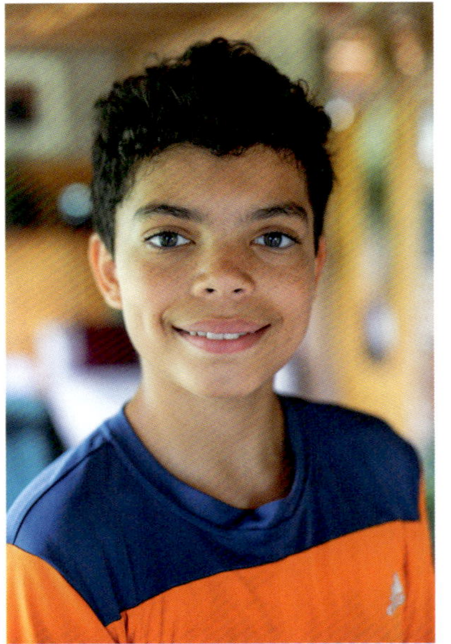

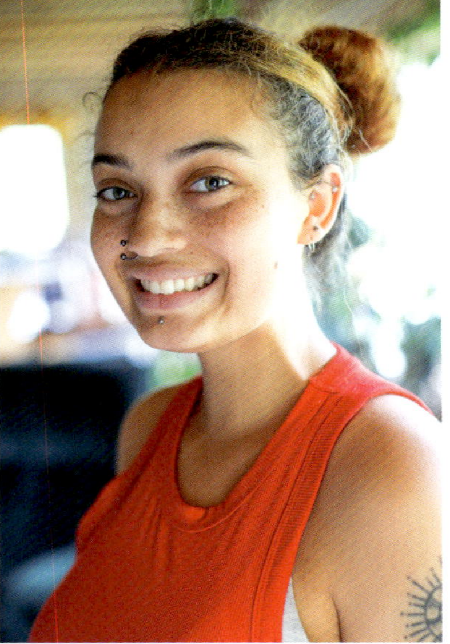

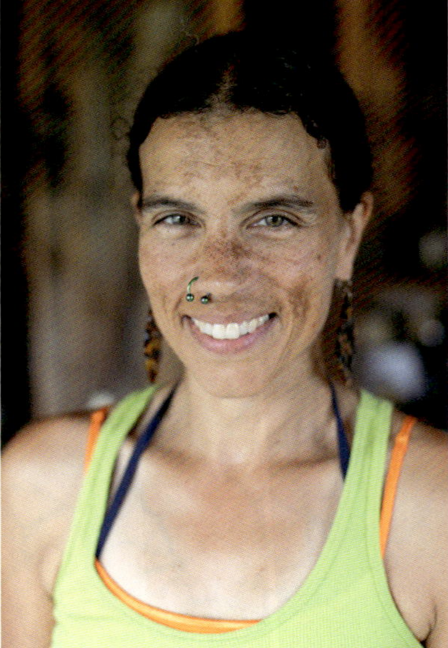

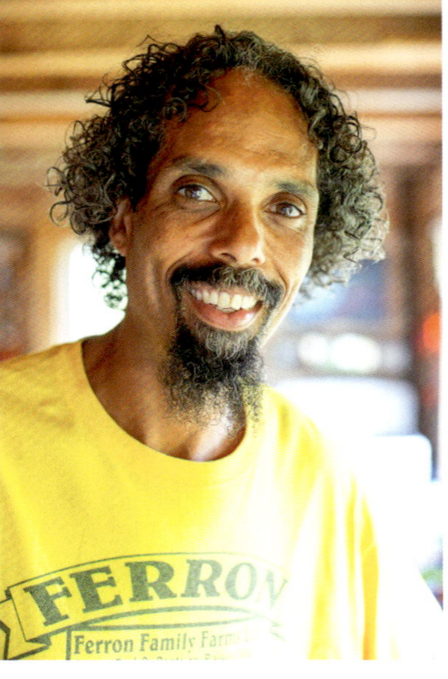
FERRON
Ferron Family

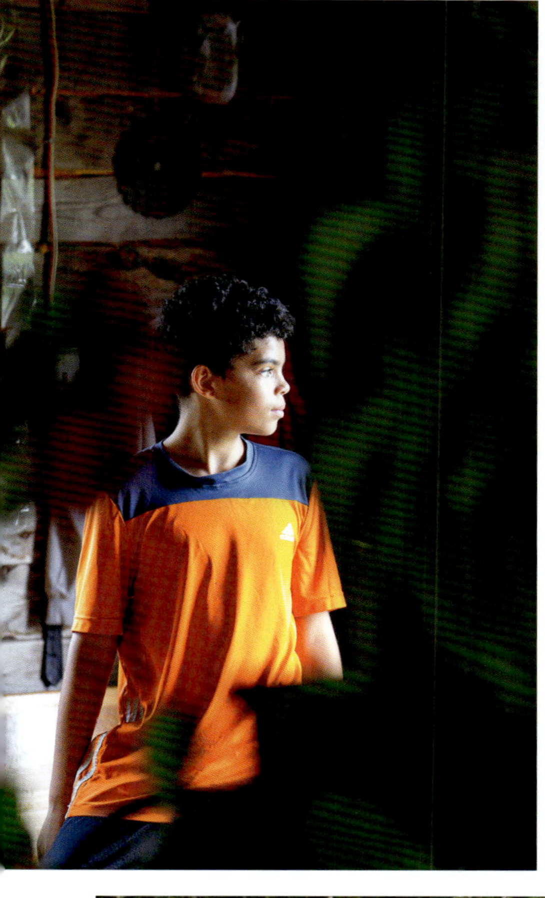

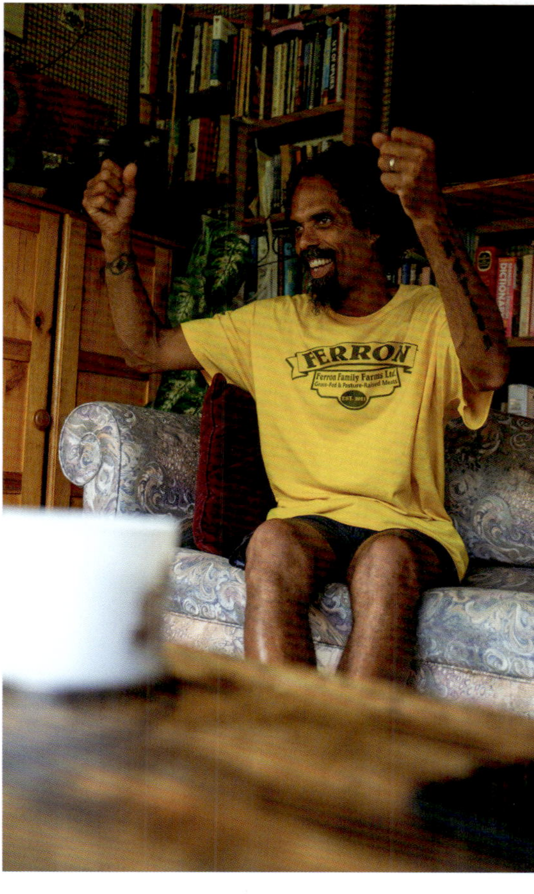

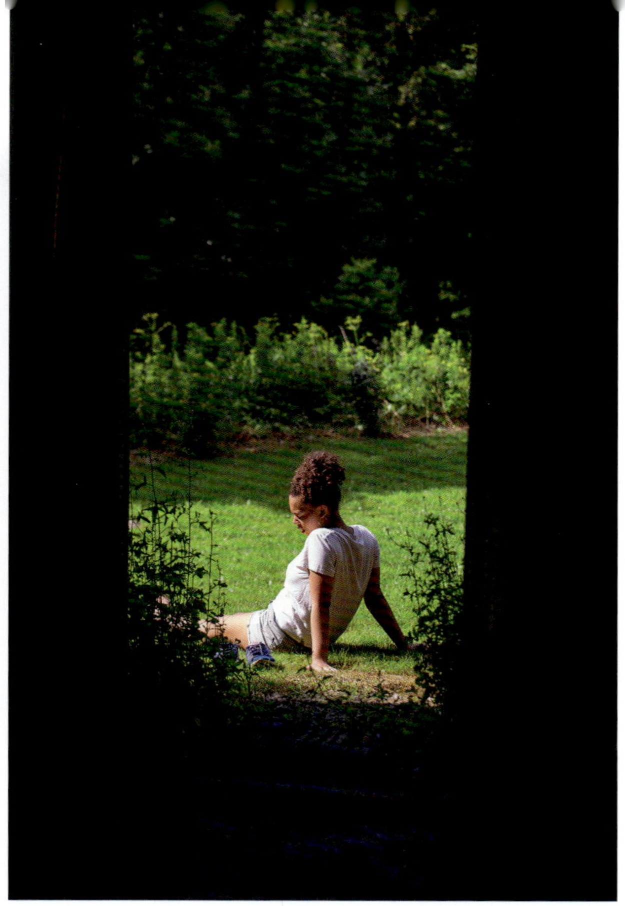

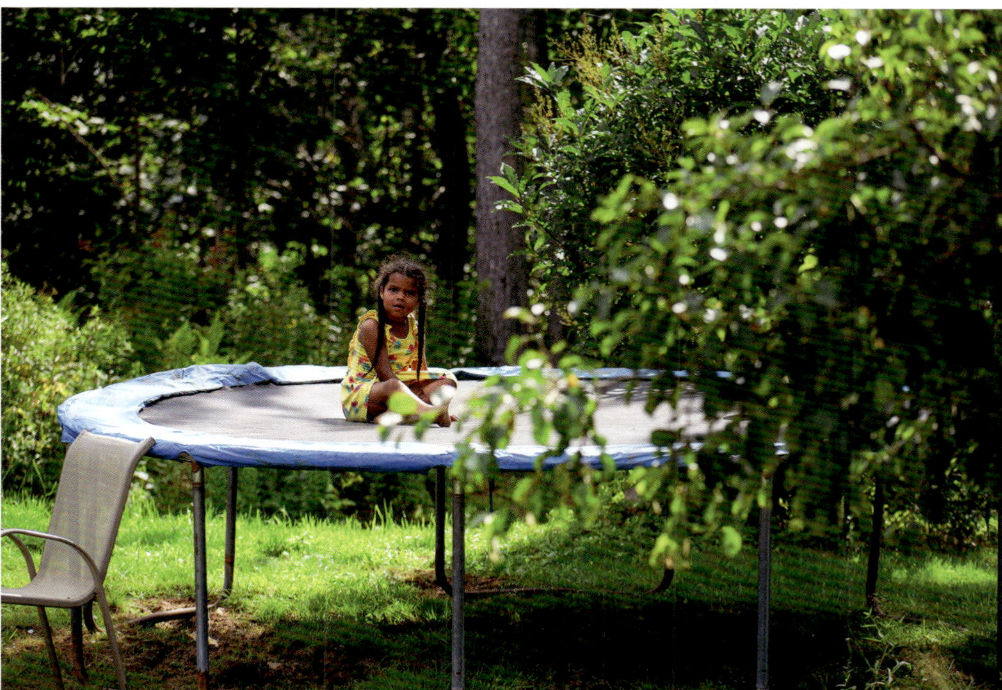

Our love grew into children: four children, thirteen-year spread. We would print off name meanings during the day and pillow-talk them at night. The children's name process is one of our fondest memories and proudest moments. They all possess understanding we didn't have:

Amina Takota
Mahailya Irie
Solomon Ezekiel
Nyah Taraji Ma-at

— Tanya MacPherson

Howe / Lawrence — Fredericton

In Fredericton we walked into the Howe home.
This was a mature generation
Who refused to let history hide them.
Instead, they summoned history from personal archives—to make it live.

The walls of the home? A bold art gallery.
Our African heritage showcased proudly.
This family was well prepared to do the work of recall.
Every piece of furniture transformed for our visit.

The dining room table was covered in memories
Photos on tin and yellowed newspapers.
Clippings of family accomplishments
Dating back to the early 1800s.

A woman finds a photo of her younger self.
The smile is the same.
The eyes have just as much life
As the moment the historic photo was taken.

A man asked for “Whiskey with only a splash of Coke”
Then grinned and said
“Actually, just show it the bottle.”
The laughter was sweeter than the slices of chocolate cake.

Sweeter still is the intoxicating memory
Of a moment of wit
That says,
Survival is our happy ending.

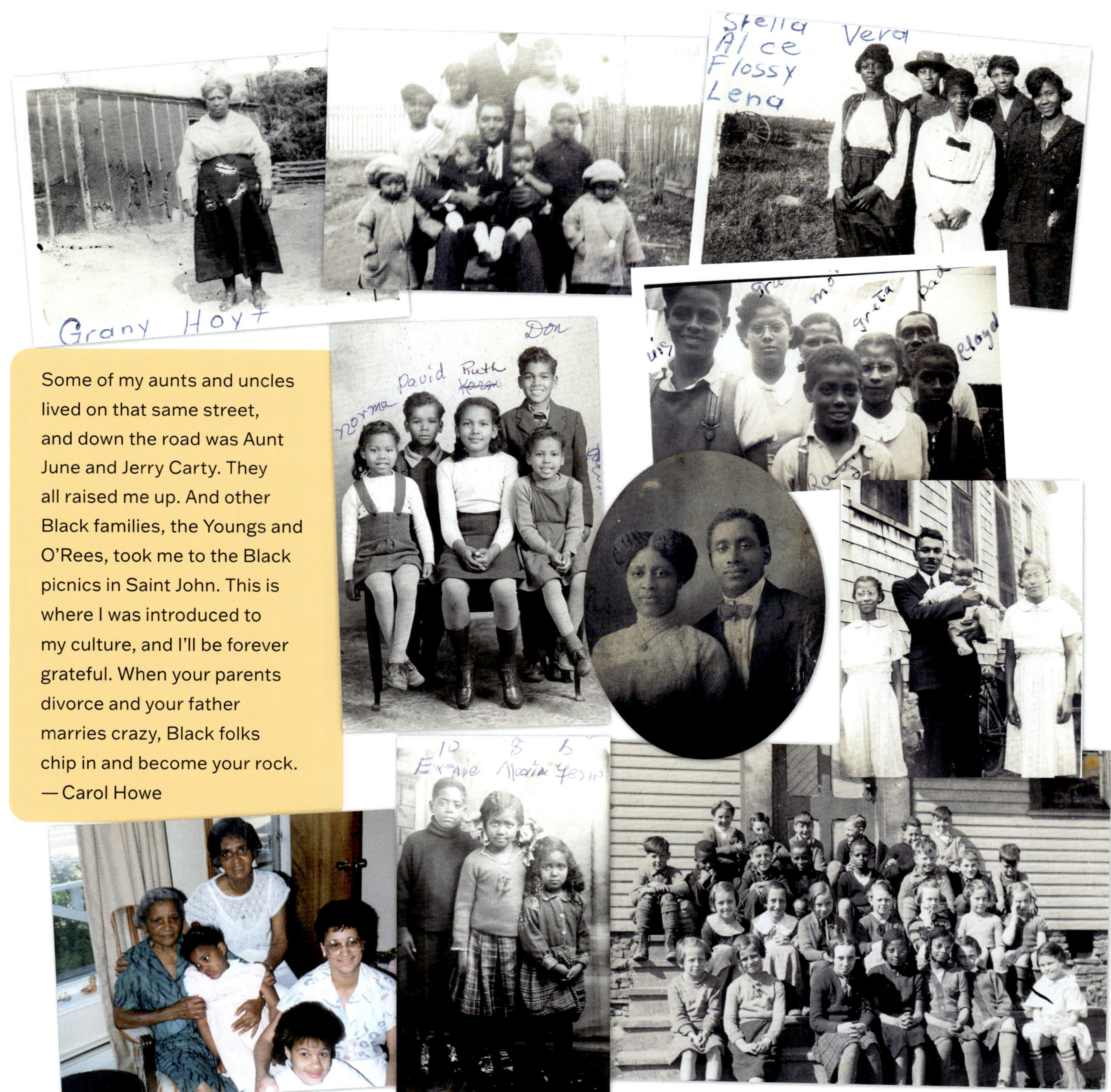

Some of my aunts and uncles lived on that same street, and down the road was Aunt June and Jerry Carty. They all raised me up. And other Black families, the Youngs and O'Rees, took me to the Black picnics in Saint John. This is where I was introduced to my culture, and I'll be forever grateful. When your parents divorce and your father marries crazy, Black folks chip in and become your rock.
—Carol Howe

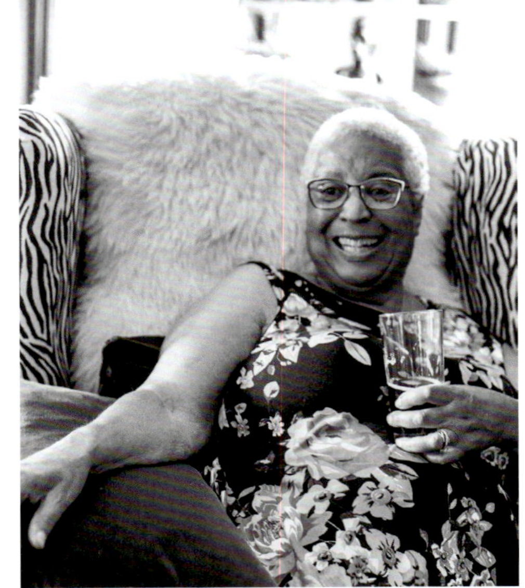

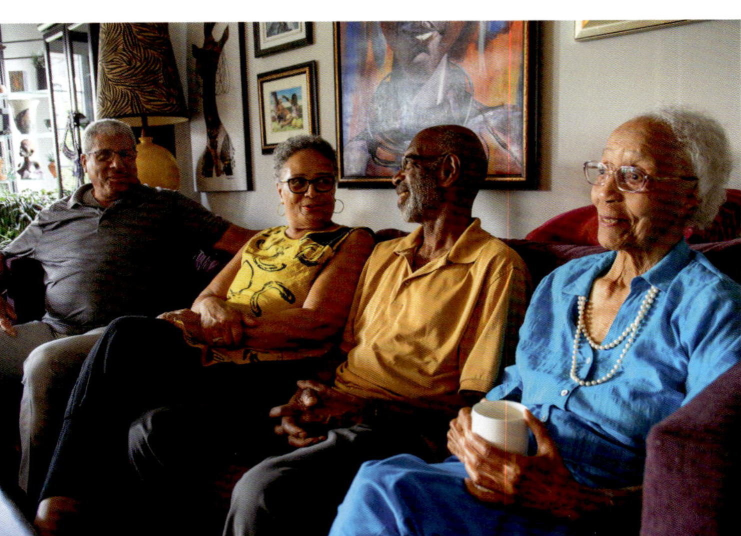

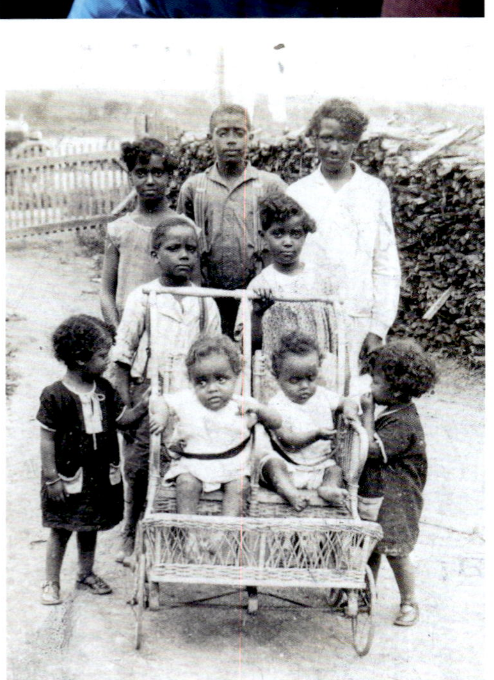

I grew up in Ontario, but ever since I can remember, I spent the whole summer in Fredericton. I can remember crossing the old bridge and going up the hill to Highland Ave. with such excitement. We would stay with my father's parents, Ernie and Stella Howe. My grandfather had the first dog kennels, and they would bark when we drove into the yard. My grandfather was a rich storyteller and loved his wife Stella fiercely!
— Carol Howe

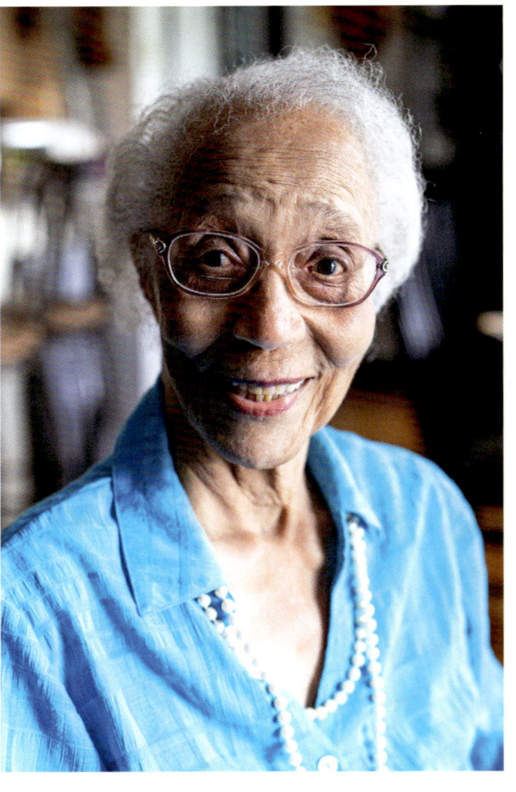

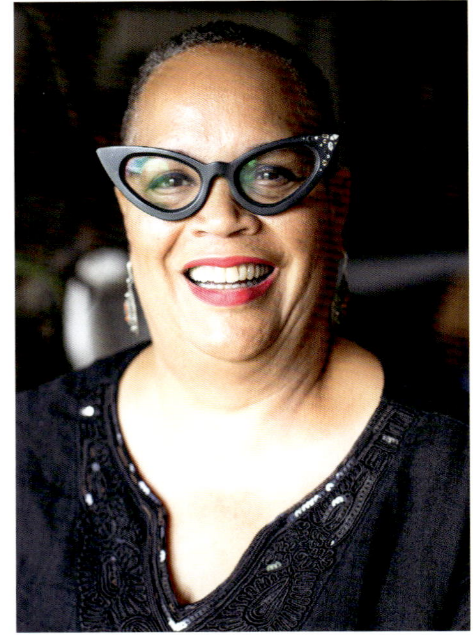

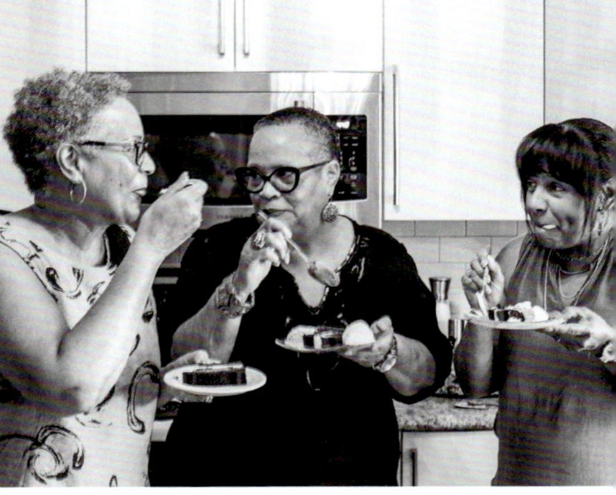

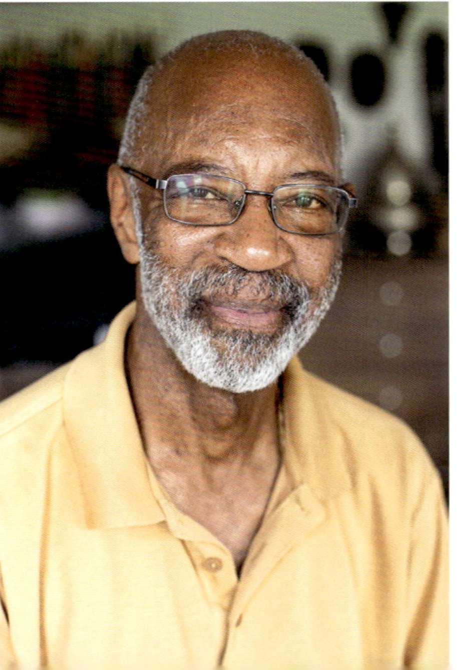

The Howes can trace their family back at least four generations in Atlantic Canada, and they also have connections with the Dymond family and the Skinner-Blizzards. Carol Howe's paternal grandmother, Stella, was a Hudlin-St. Louis. Her great-grandfather was from St. Lucia and may have a connection to the Stewart-Tyler family, who also trace their roots back to Sarah Hudlin. The Hudlins have their own rich history of running from the South and arriving in Canada in a barrel.

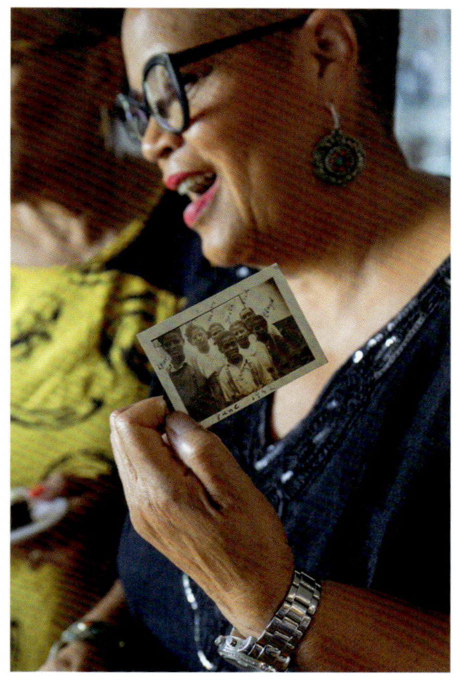

Carol Howe's grandfather Ernest Howe had the first dog kennels in Fredericton. His son Carl Howe, Carol's uncle, was a track star in his youth and became Fredericton's first Black city councillor, in 1971.

On the Lawrence branch of the family, Carol's maternal grandparents, Woodford Smith Lawrence and Emma Augusta Lawrence had, among other children, two sets of twins: Grace (Carol's mother) and Greta were born in 1926, and Lloyd and Louis were born in 1927. Carol remembers her grandmother as "my favourite person. I had a special bond with her," noting that her grandmother was responsible for preserving much of the family history. "When you're young you think you'll remember everything, but her memory was exceptional. All the old pictures and clippings are because of her."

Louis became a professional boxer in 1950, winning the Canadian middleweight championship at York Arena in Fredericton in 1955. He was inducted into the Canadian Boxing Hall of Fame in 1988; the Fredericton Wall of Fame in 2002; and, posthumously, the New Brunswick Sports Hall of Fame in 2024. Carol recalls that Louis retired from boxing "because the Mob was trying to tell him what to do. You don't tell Louis Lawrence what to do." After leaving the ring, Louis was employed by Canadian Pacific Railway and Via Rail and retired after thirty-eight years of service.

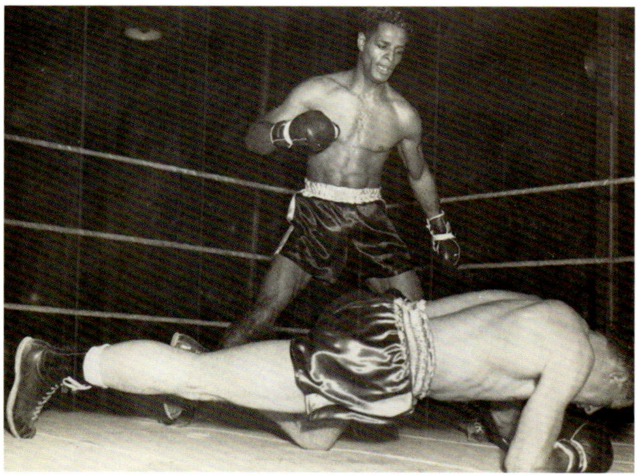

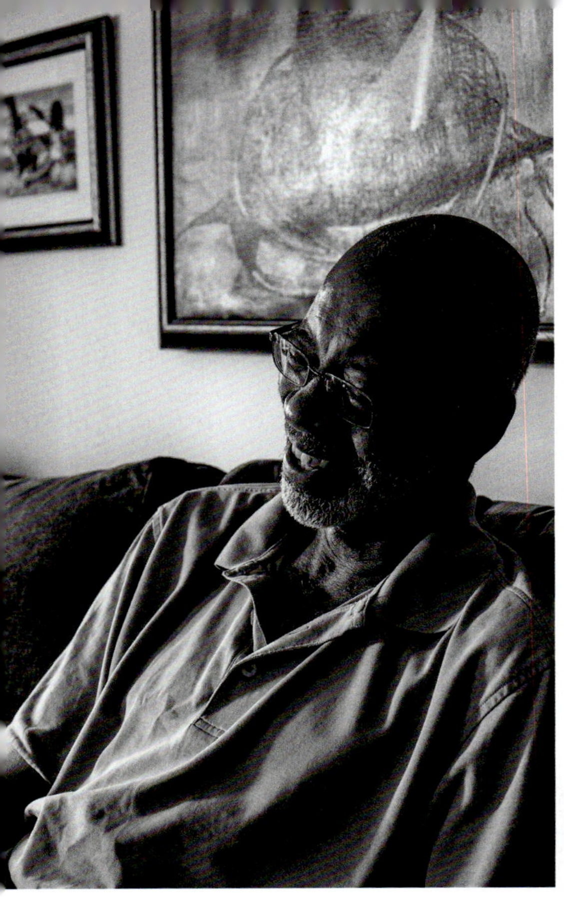

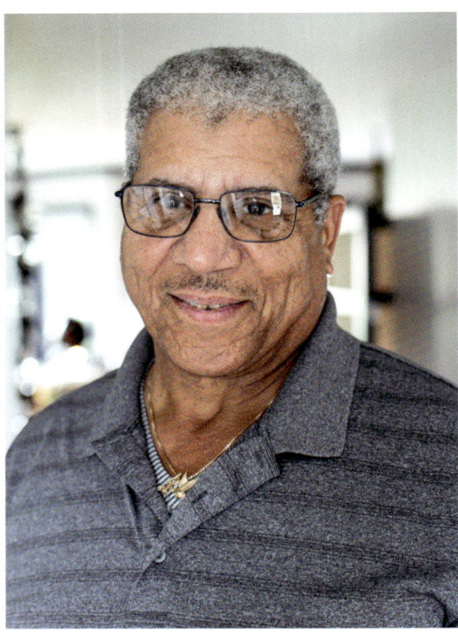

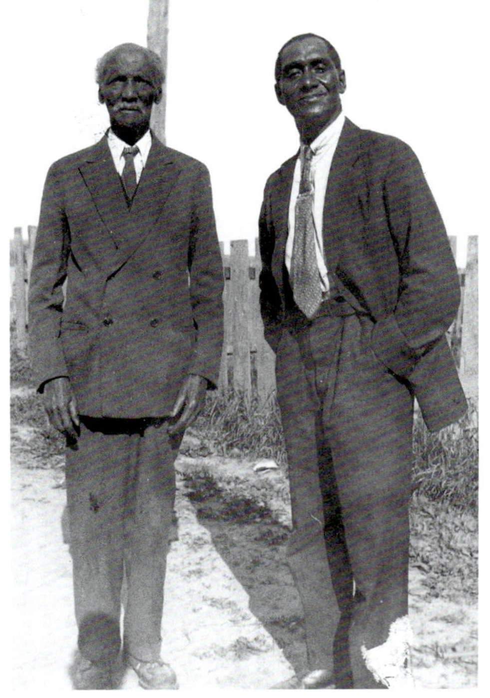

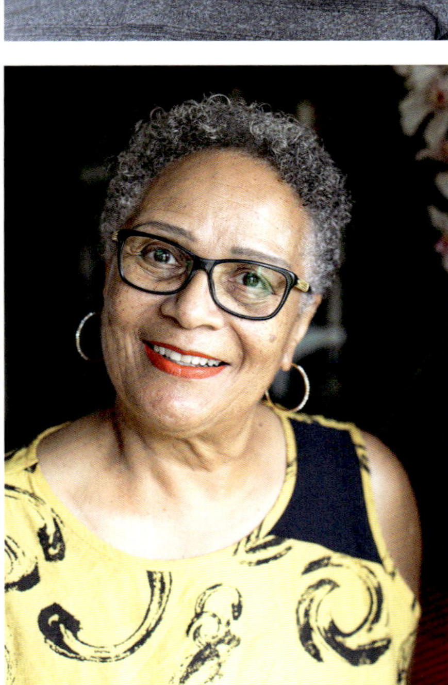

The Howe men were in World Wars I and II and my great-uncle Percy was an excellent shooter. Uncle Percy taught my father how to shoot. He took my dad to the apple orchard in Springhill and told him to shoot an apple out of the tree. My dad did and Uncle Percy said, "No, you shoot it through the stem!" He was a sniper in the war and rarely missed a shot.
— Carol Howe

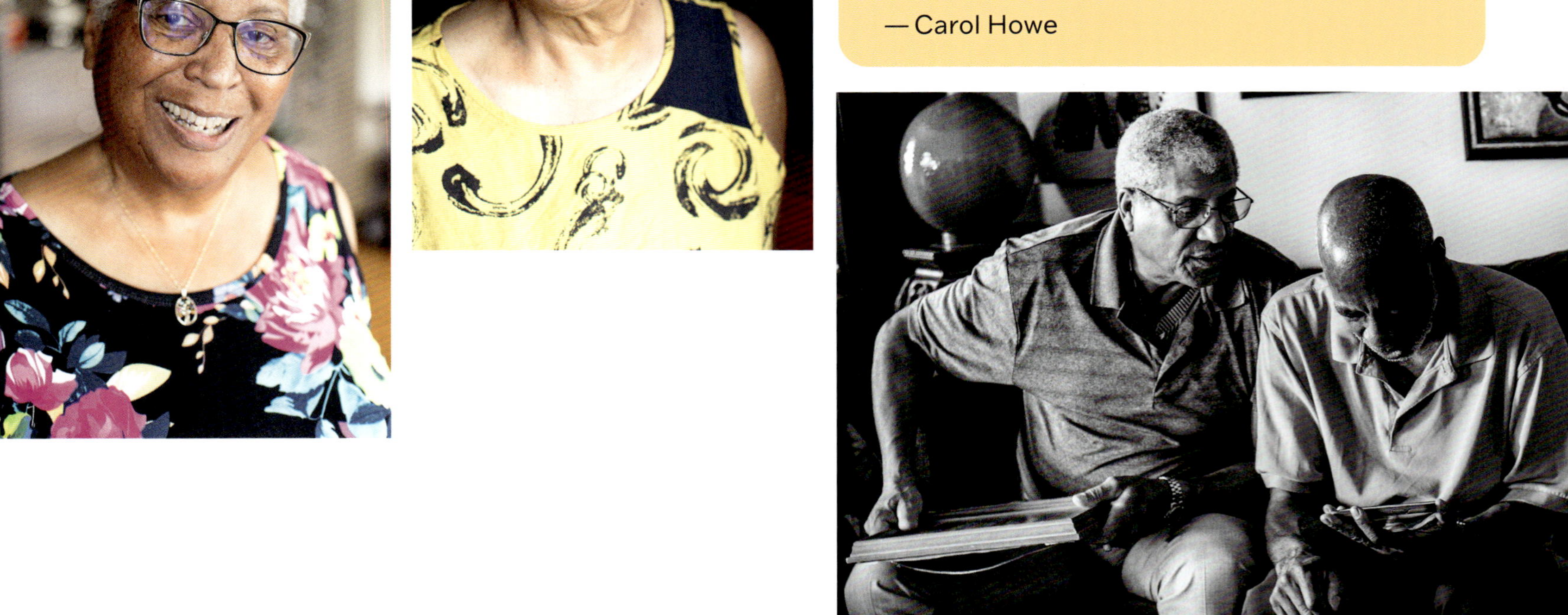

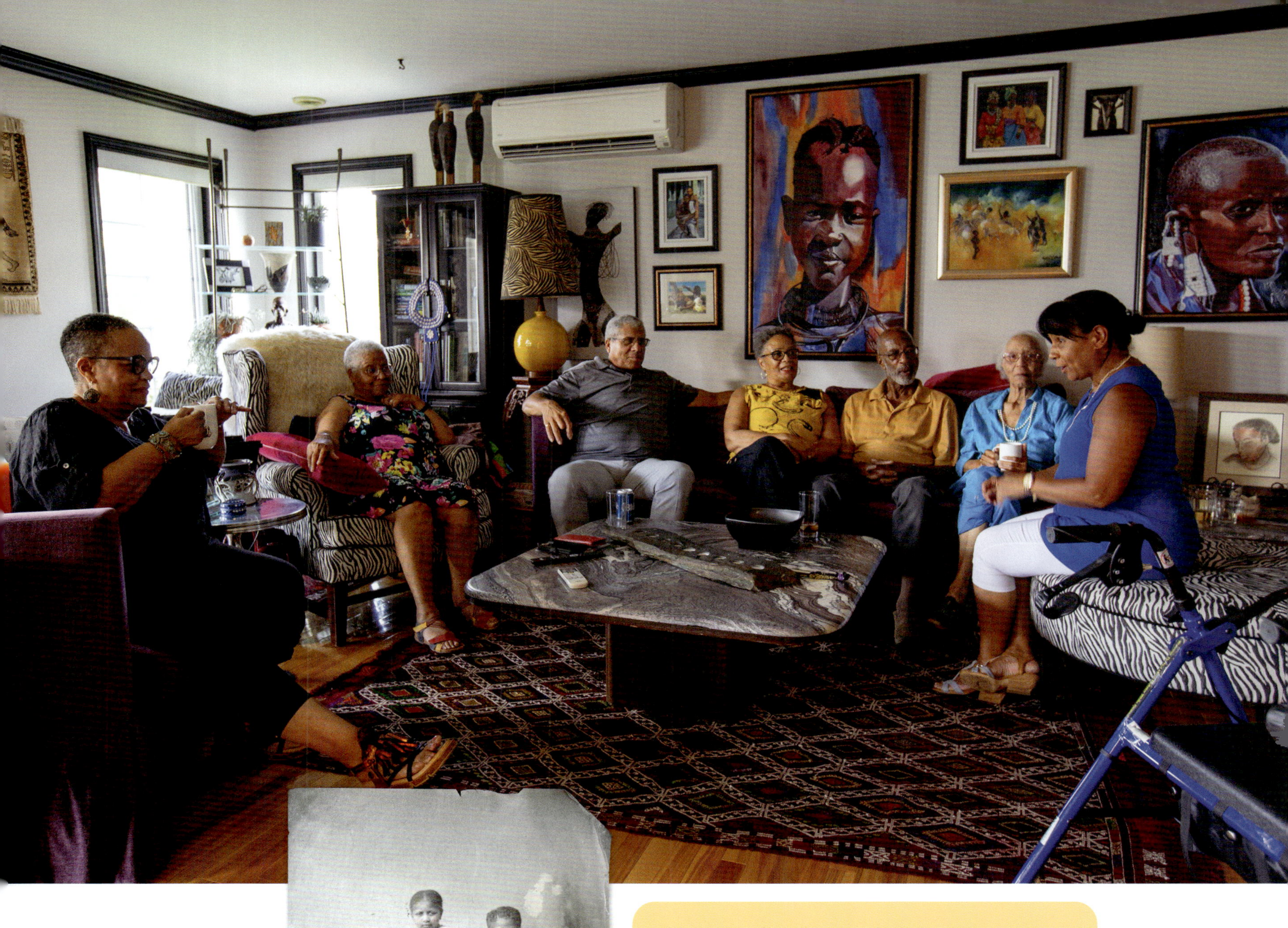

My whole family attended church every Sunday, and we'd have dinner after, and it was an event. We would all sit for hours to listen to family history and other stories. My childhood was full of love, and I felt safe and cherished in that house. It was a magical place, and I learned the power of family.
— Carol Howe

Dymond / Howe — Fredericton

In Fredericton, New Brunswick
We met
The wild family.
Their hands wafting cards, smokes, and hard drinks.
Every handshake felt like clenching stone,
every hug was like clasping solid oak.
As if life's pressures had forged all out of iron.
Except their eyes. Such soft eyes.
Every pair of pupils projected a beautiful, moving picture.
I couldn't escape their compassion.
This was a family that made their own way.
Their own way.
"Ain't nothing harder than Dymonds!"
The rainstorm that day couldn't stop four generations.
From preserving this celebration.
"Ain't nothing harder than Dymonds!"
They screamed between camera flashes.
Watching it all, I was forced to agree.
For there are few things as tough
Few things as sharp
And so few things as beautiful
As Dymonds.

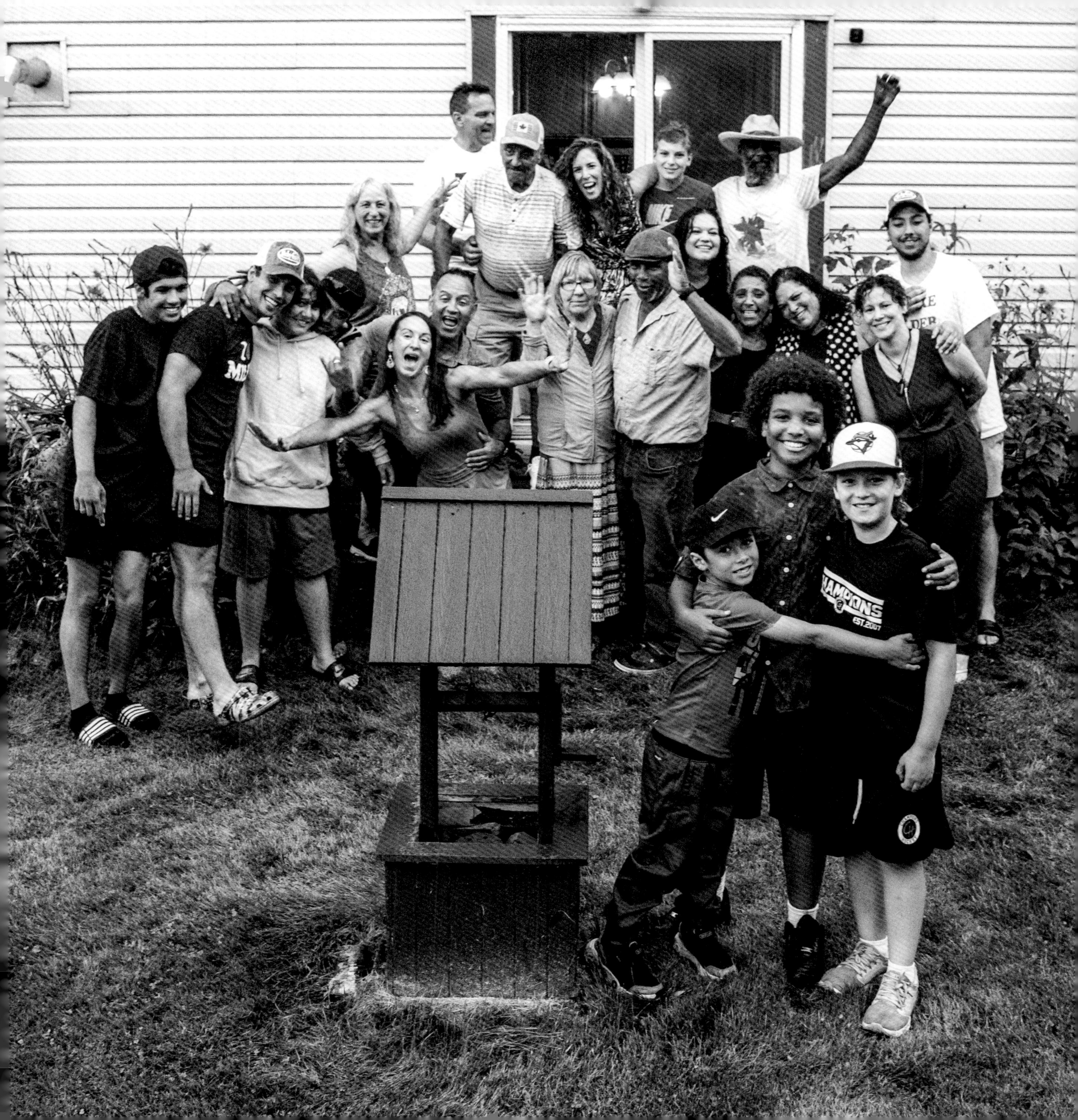

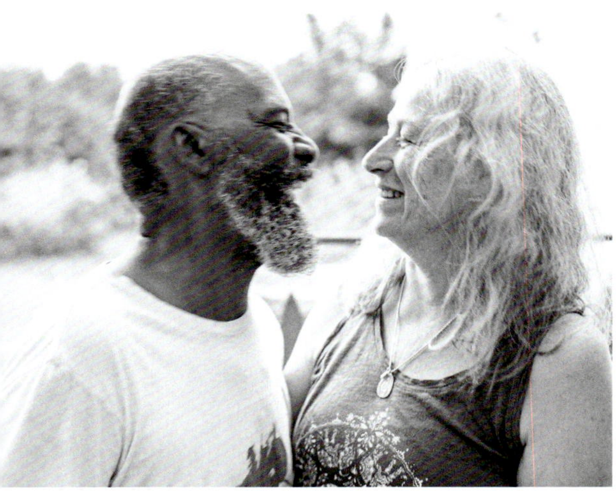

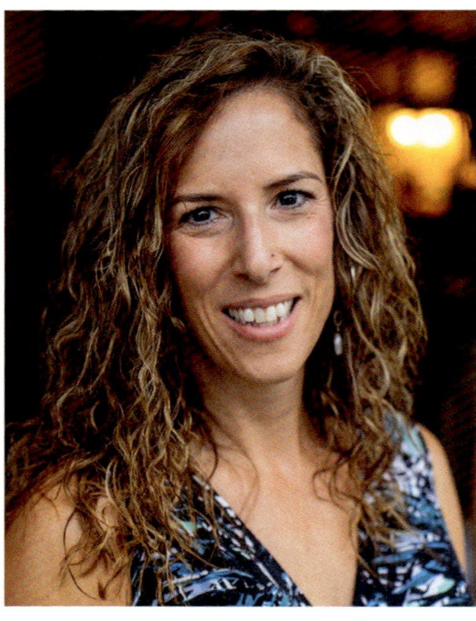

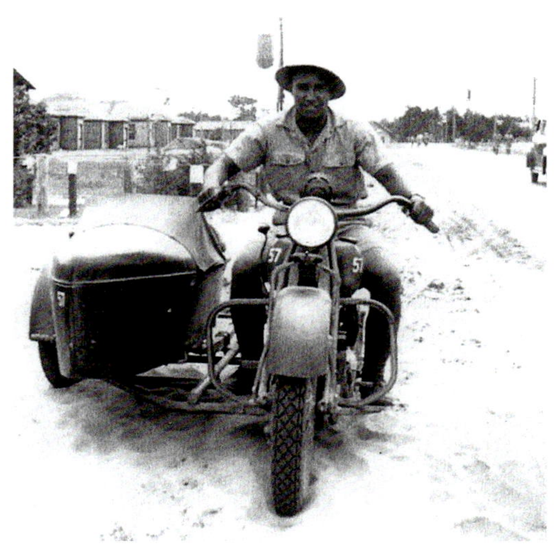

When I think of the generations of our family, one common thread has woven us together since long before I was born: love. Regardless of age or gender or whose place we are at, it feels like home when we're together, when we're around our family, our roots, our ancestors, our environment, and our history.
— Lenisha Dymond

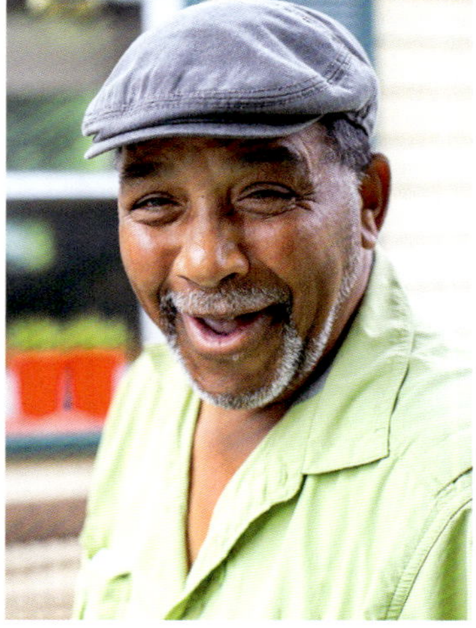

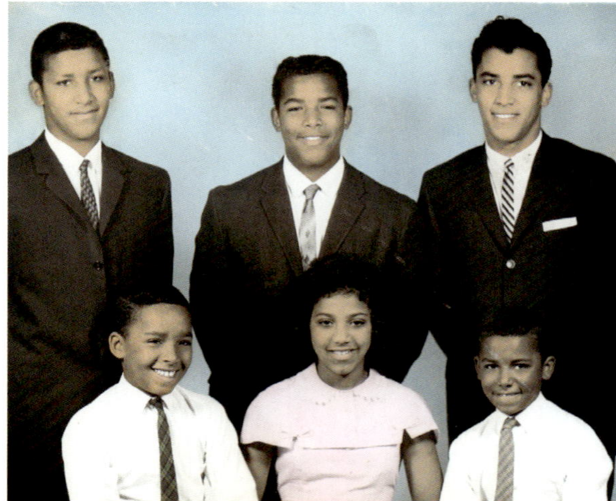

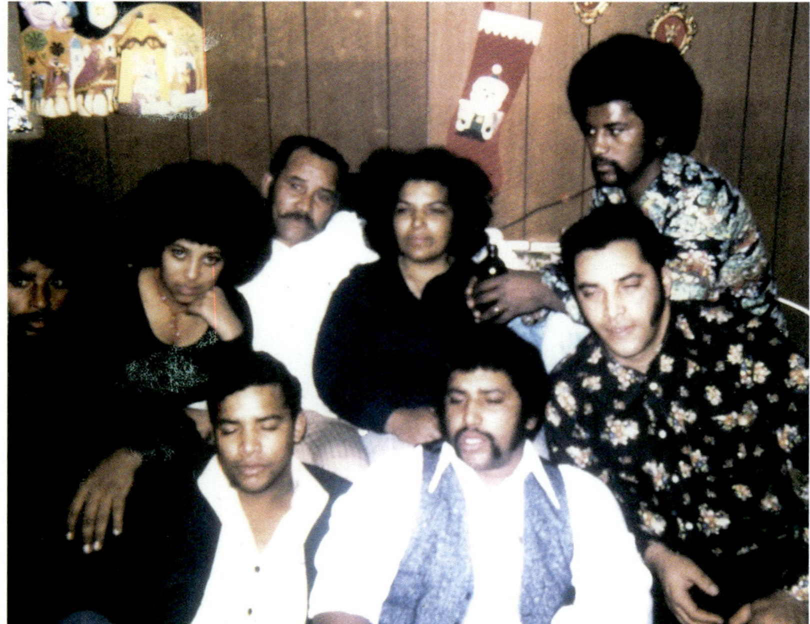

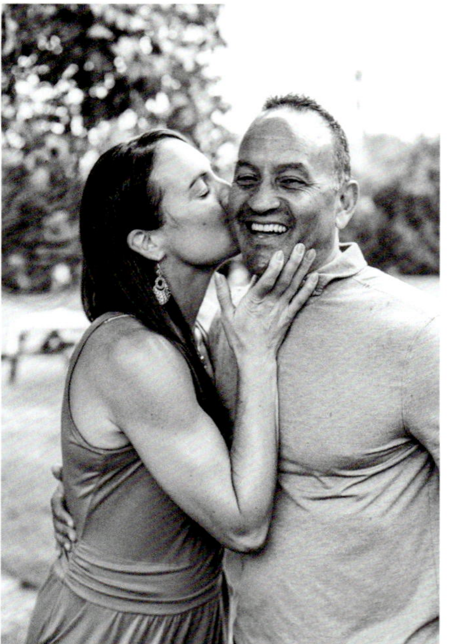

The Dymonds have a proud and strong family legacy. They are the descendants of Florence Howe Dymond and Charles W. Dymond, grandparents to Lenisha Dymond, who lived in Woodstock in the early years of their marriage. From photographs and the associated memories and stories, Lenisha knows that her great-grandparents were Myles and Ada Rae Dymond, and Myles's mother was Frances-Ann Kendall Dymond; and from another picture she knows that her Nanny Florence's parents were Amy and Percy Howe.

Stories of how the Dymond family name came to mean what it does today have been passed down through the generations. War-time stories; family stories of love and sadness; memories of births, weddings, funerals, family Christmases, and the Annual Black Picnic in Geary, NB, all provide snapshots of the lives of each family member in a given period of time. These experiences have built the Dymonds into the fierce and impressive family they are now.

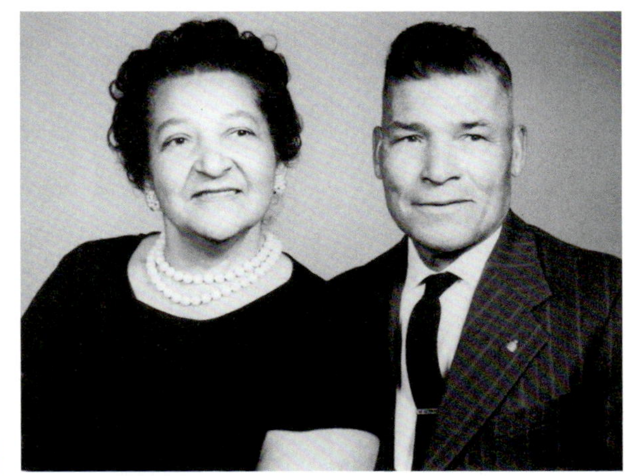

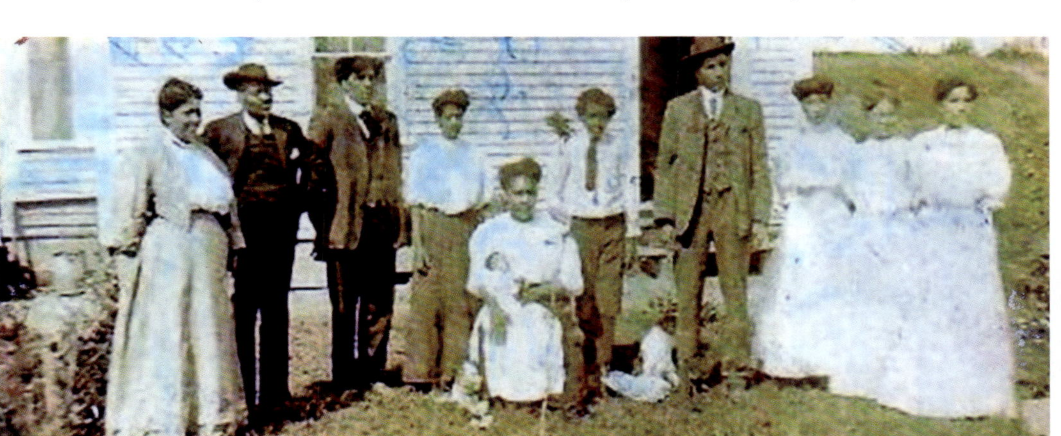

Our parents knew each other as children and grew up together with their cousins, just like my cousins and I have, where we are all more like brothers and sisters and best friends. Our parents would visit their families in Woodstock almost every weekend, and my grandfather would take them out for lunch or dinner at the nearby food stand, and that tradition continues.
—Lenisha Dymond

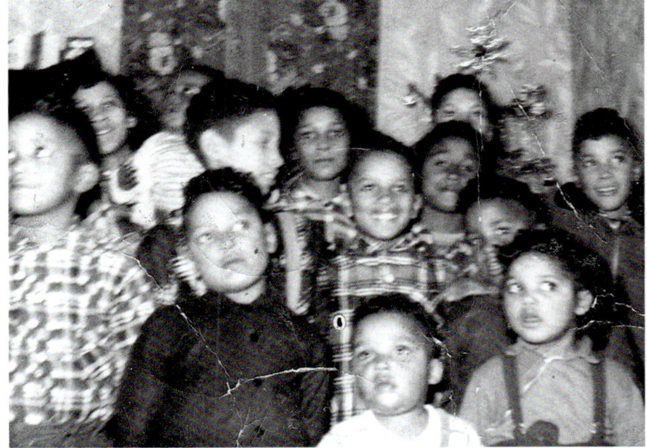

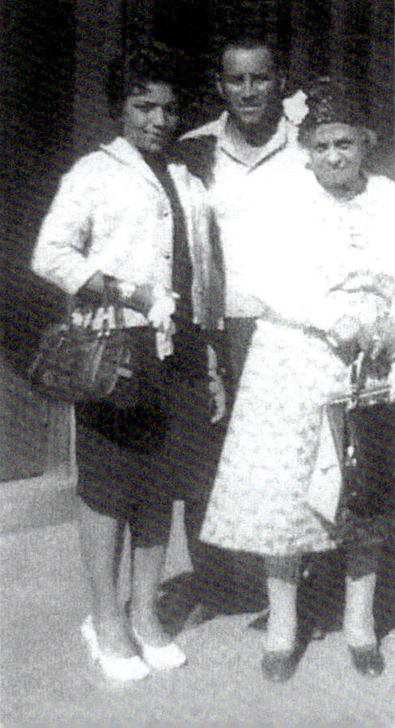

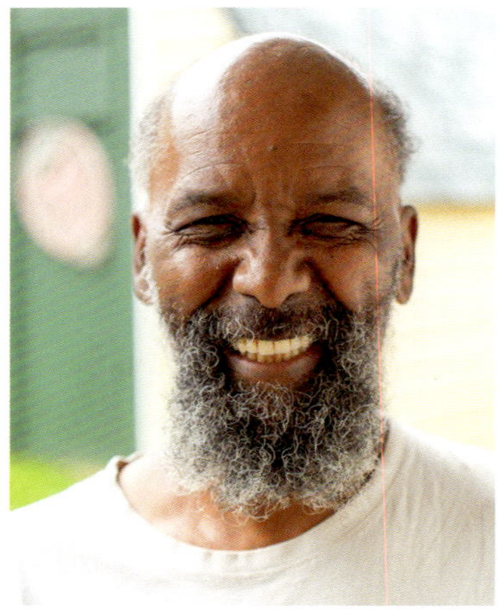

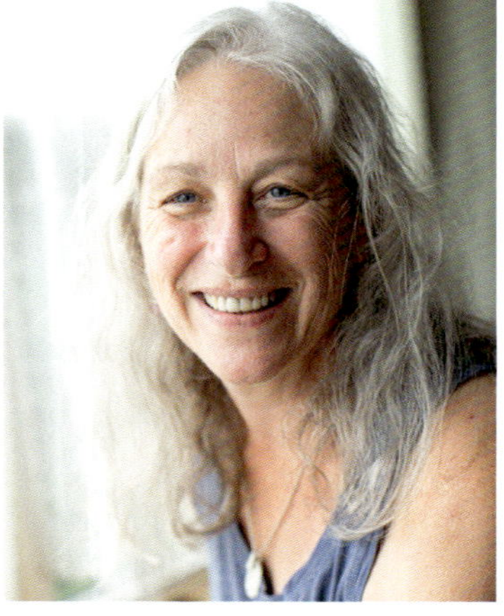

The love we have for our cousins throughout the generations has not changed. Even though a decade may pass between visits, when we do see one another it's as if time has stopped. Nothing has changed. We could have been together yesterday.
— Lenisha Dymond

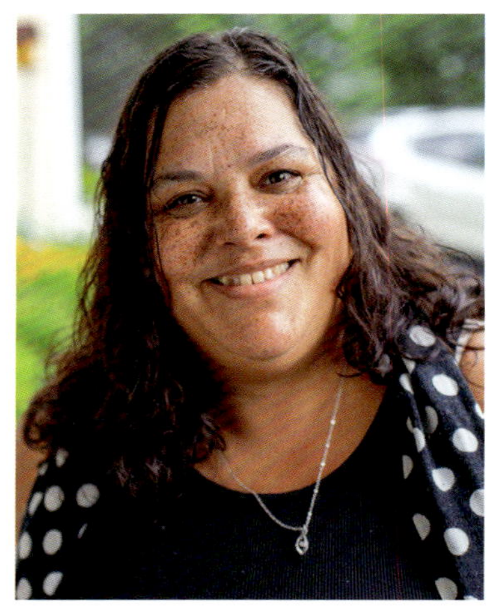

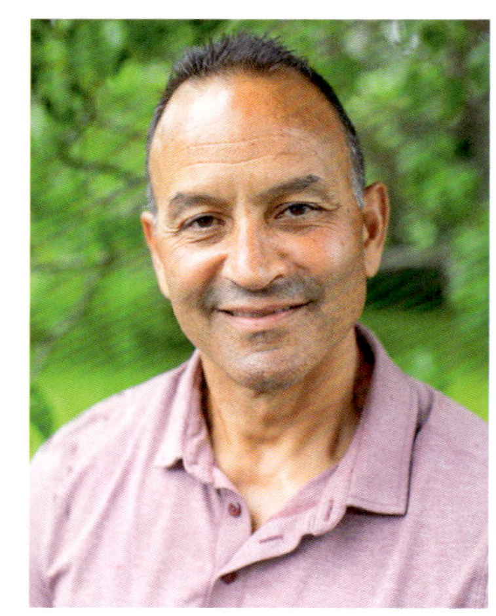

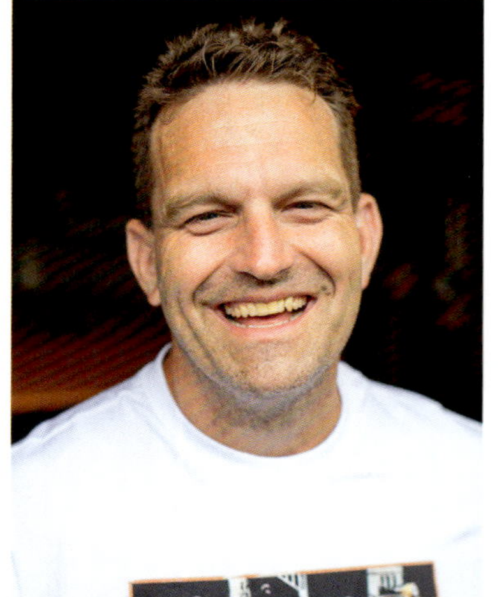

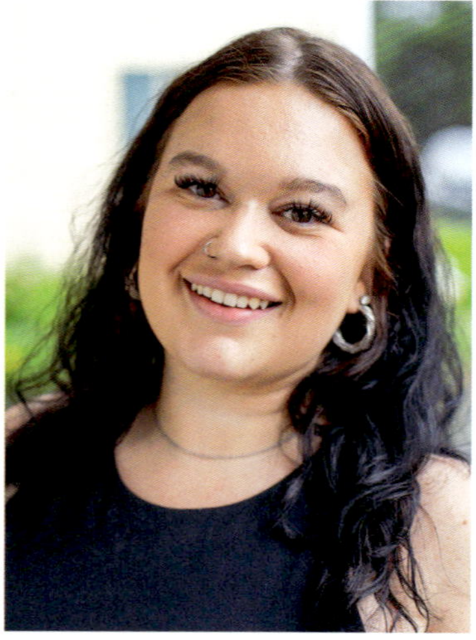

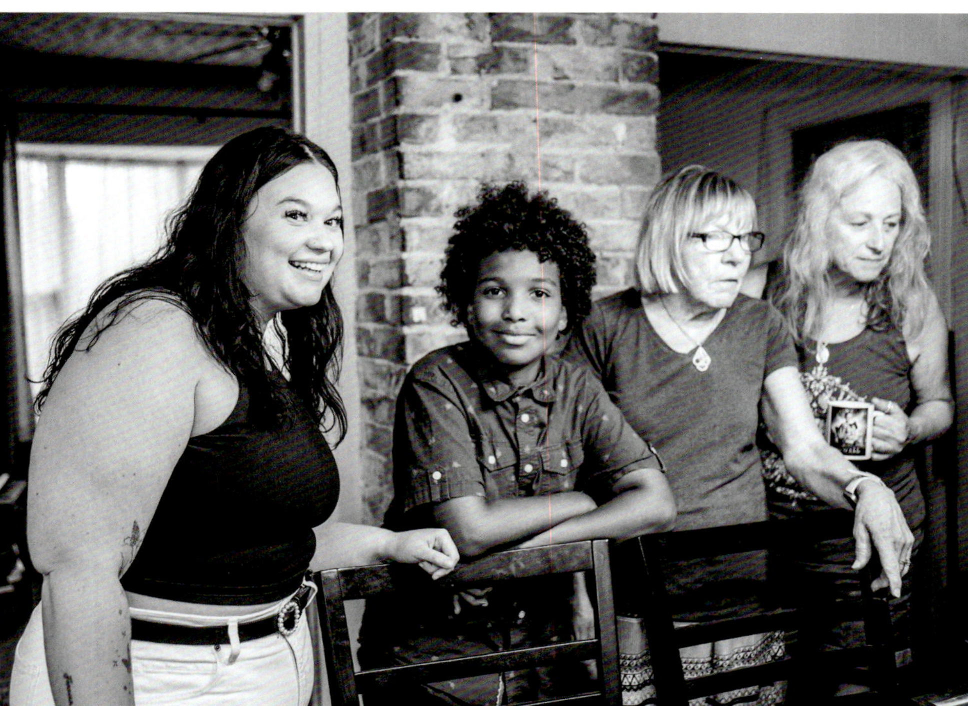

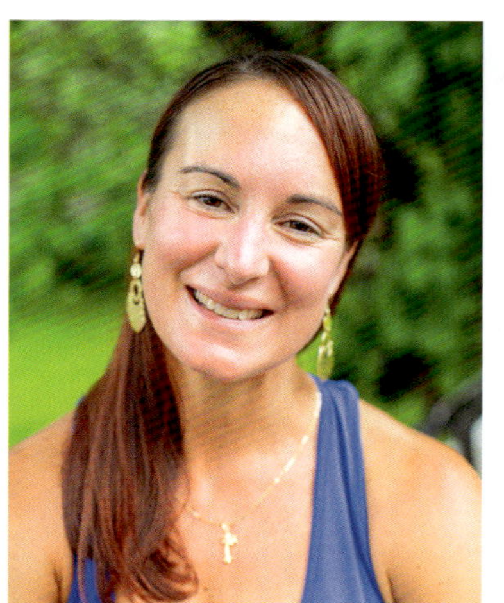

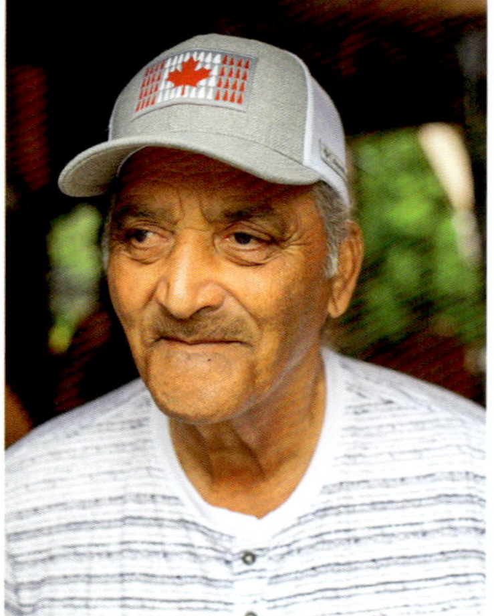

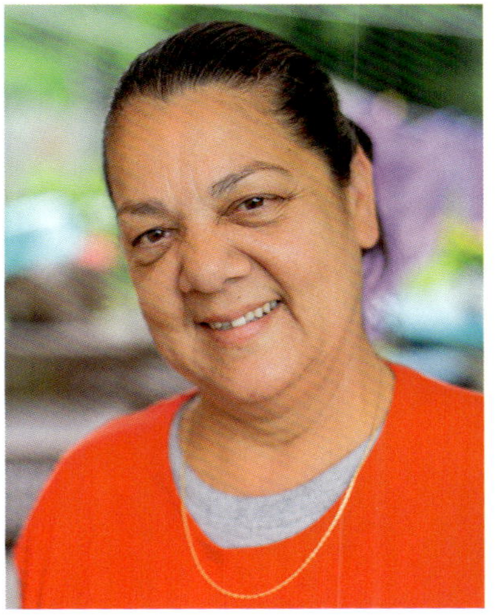

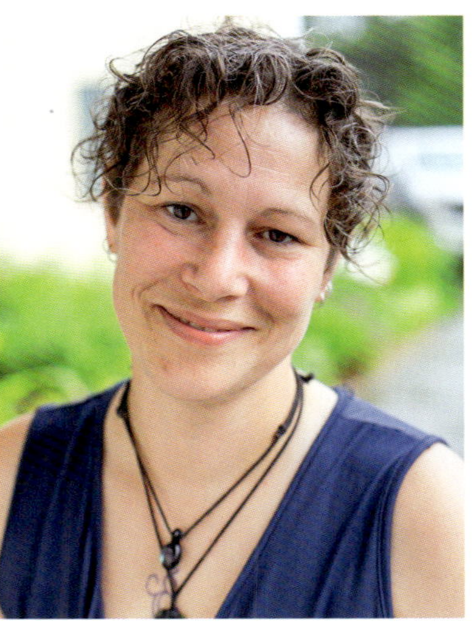

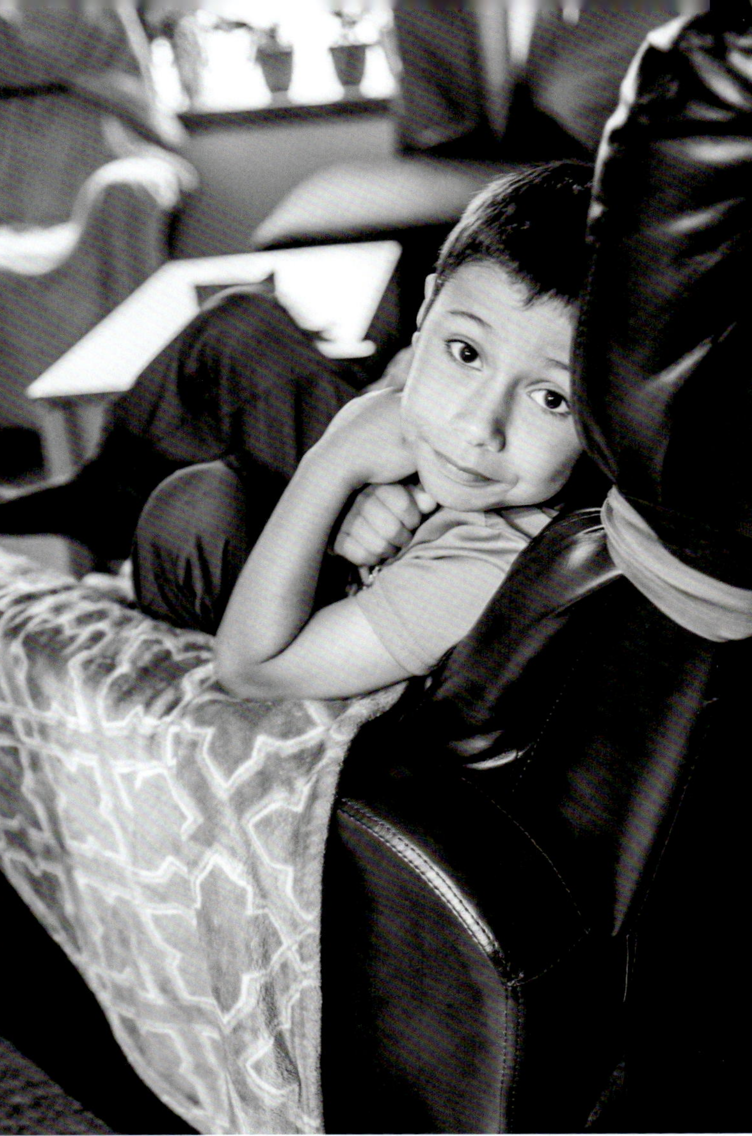

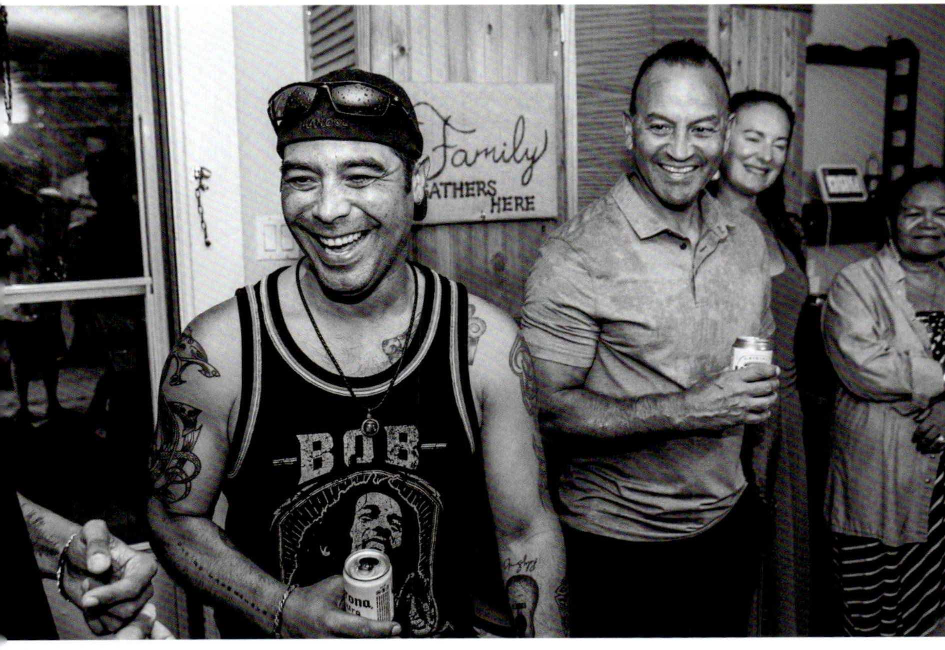
Family
HERE
BOB

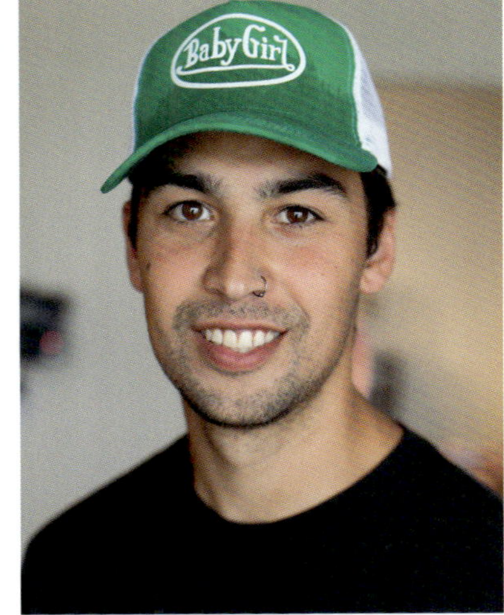
BabyGirl

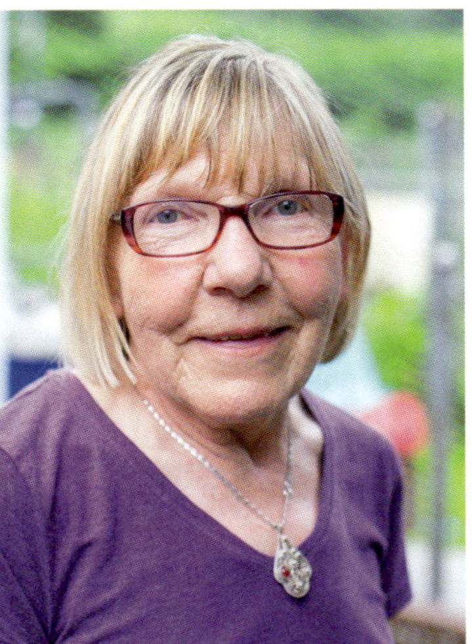

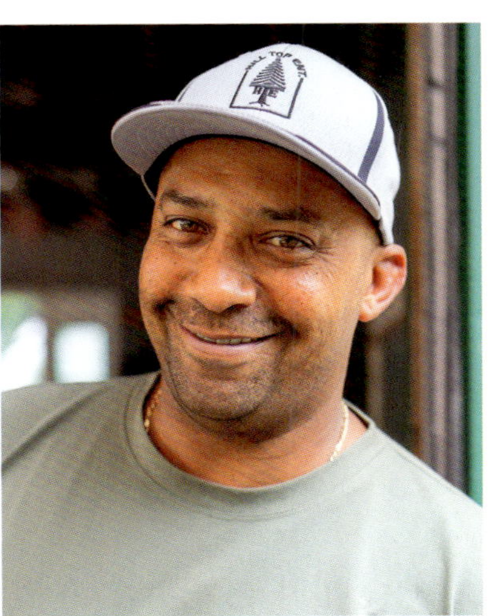

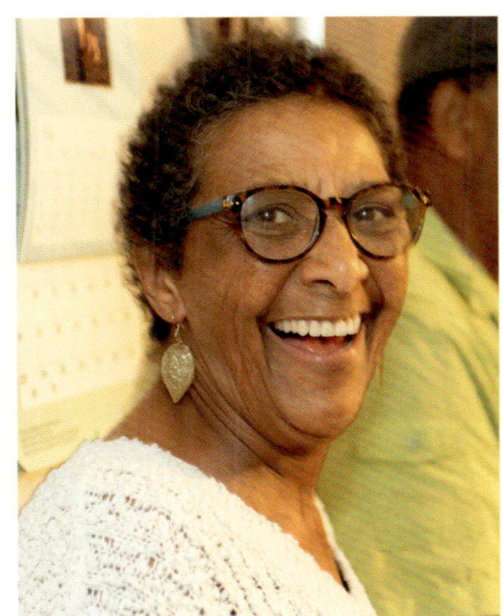

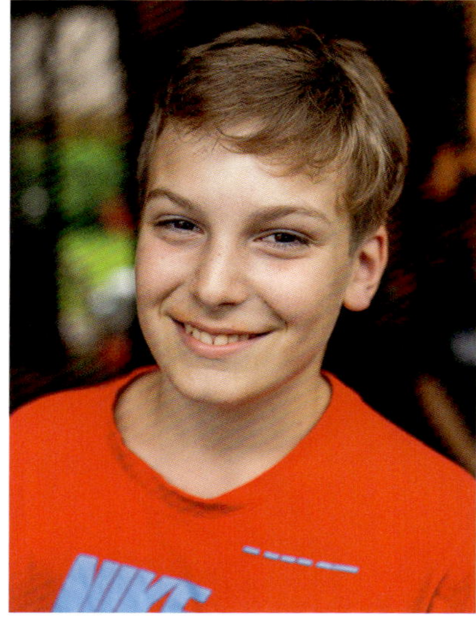

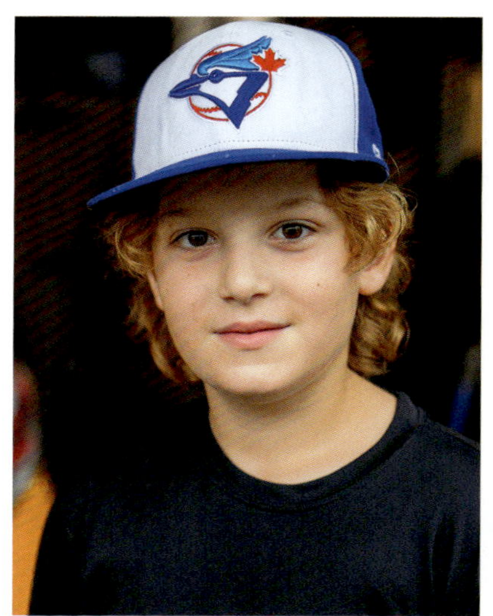

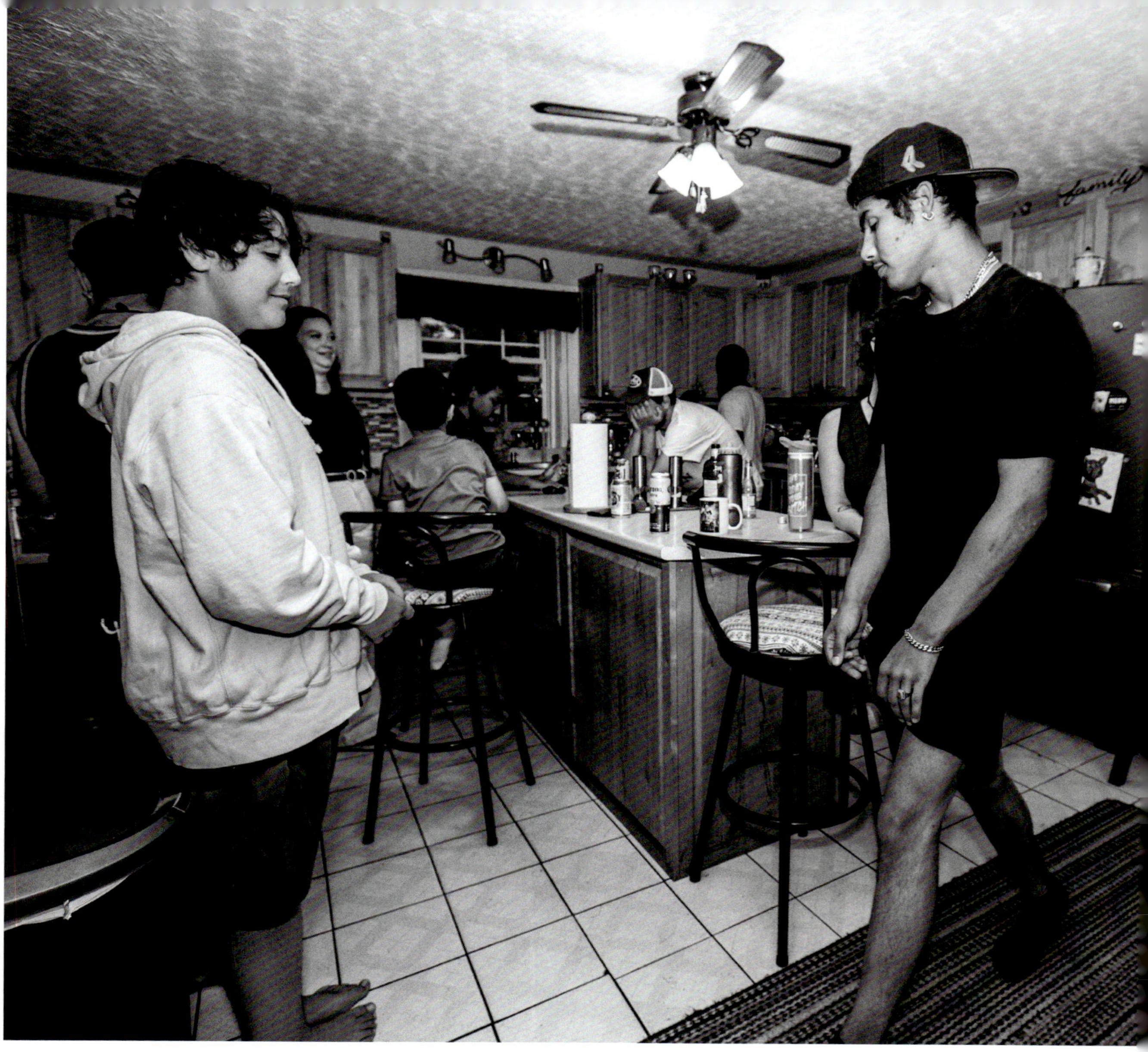

The youngest generation plays with their cousins the same way the older generation did — running through the old orchard, playing tag, trying their hand at a game of cards with their older relatives. Unlike many families who never see one another, our family wants and chooses to be together. Collectively, we know how grateful we should be to our ancestors: We truly are the lucky ones.
— Lenisha Dymond

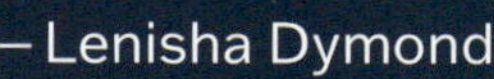

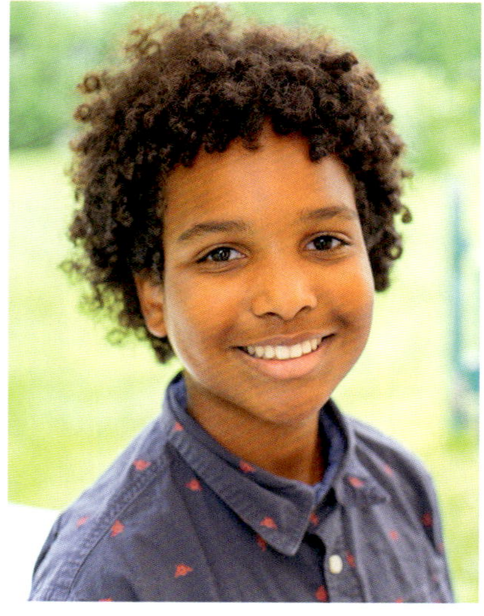

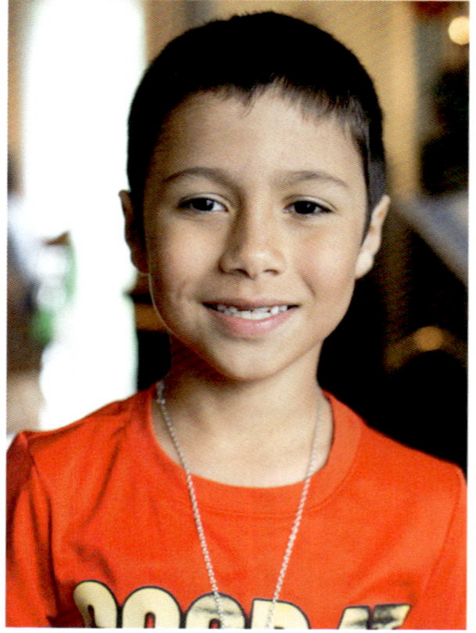

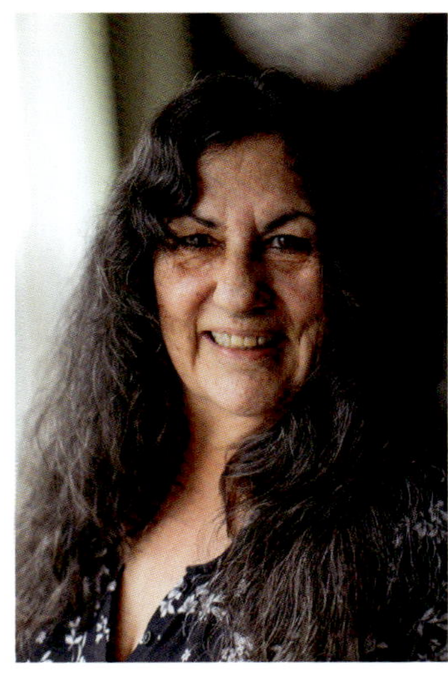

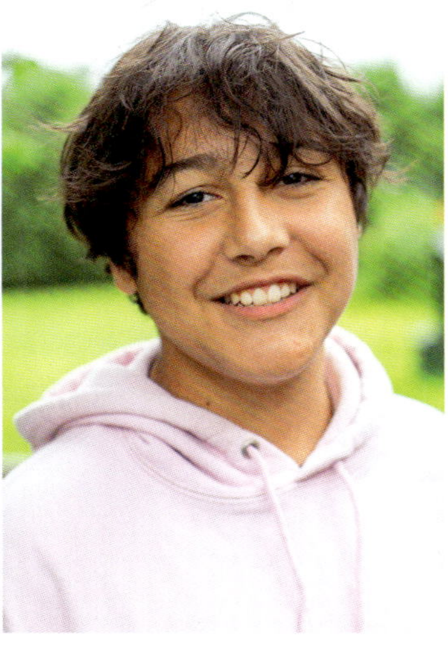

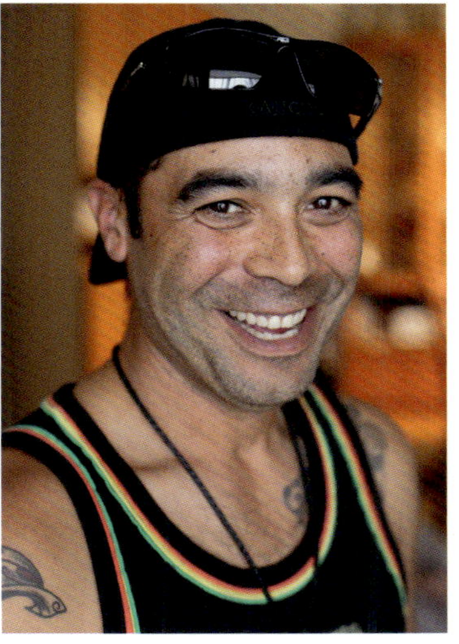

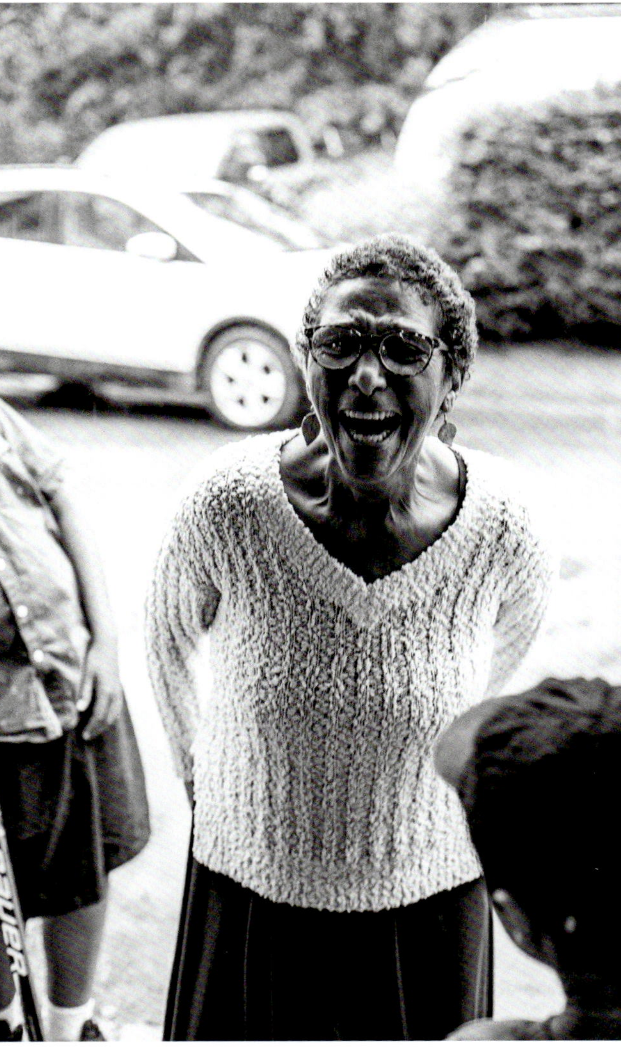

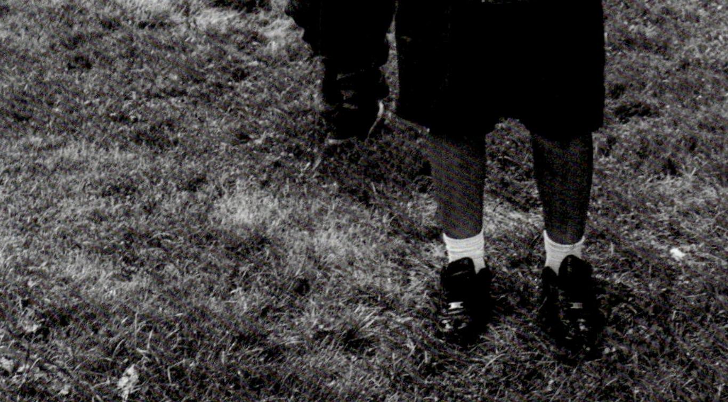

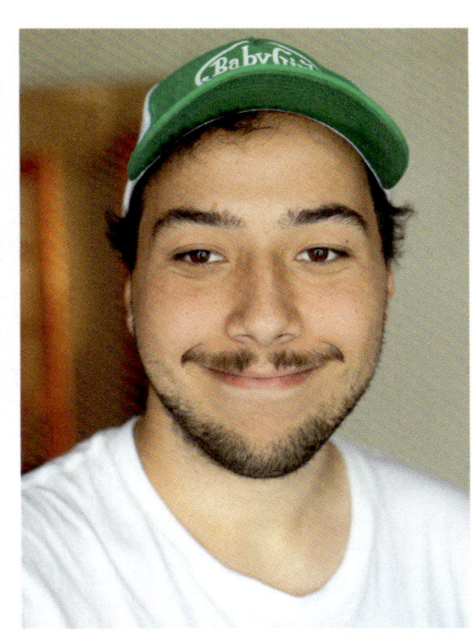

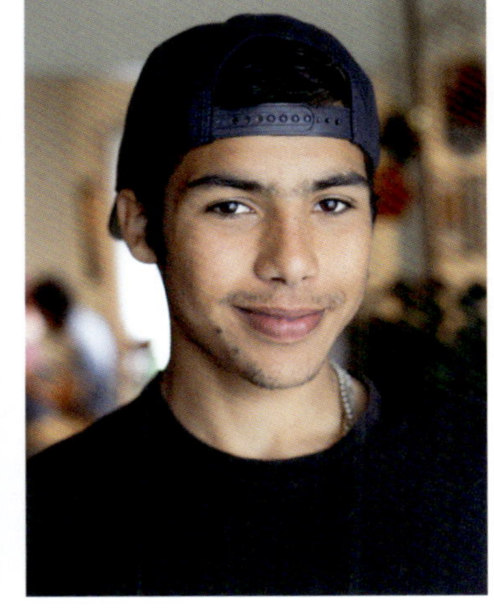

Family dinner on Sunday started years ago, with everyone always gathering at my nanny Florence Dymond's house. These dinners have a magical feeling — the laughter, the stories, the game playing, the dancing and singing — and of course, the food. When Nanny passed away her son Brian and his wife Soili continued the tradition in her home. Everyone always looks forward to family dinner.

— Lenisha Dymond

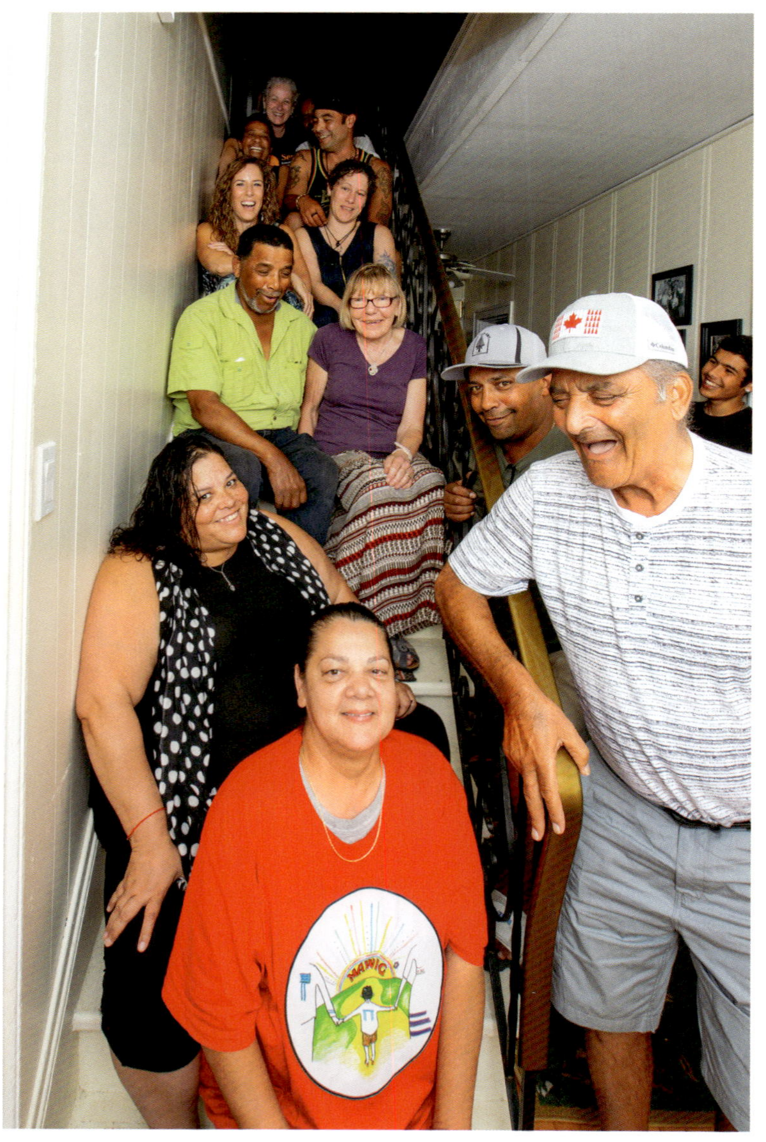

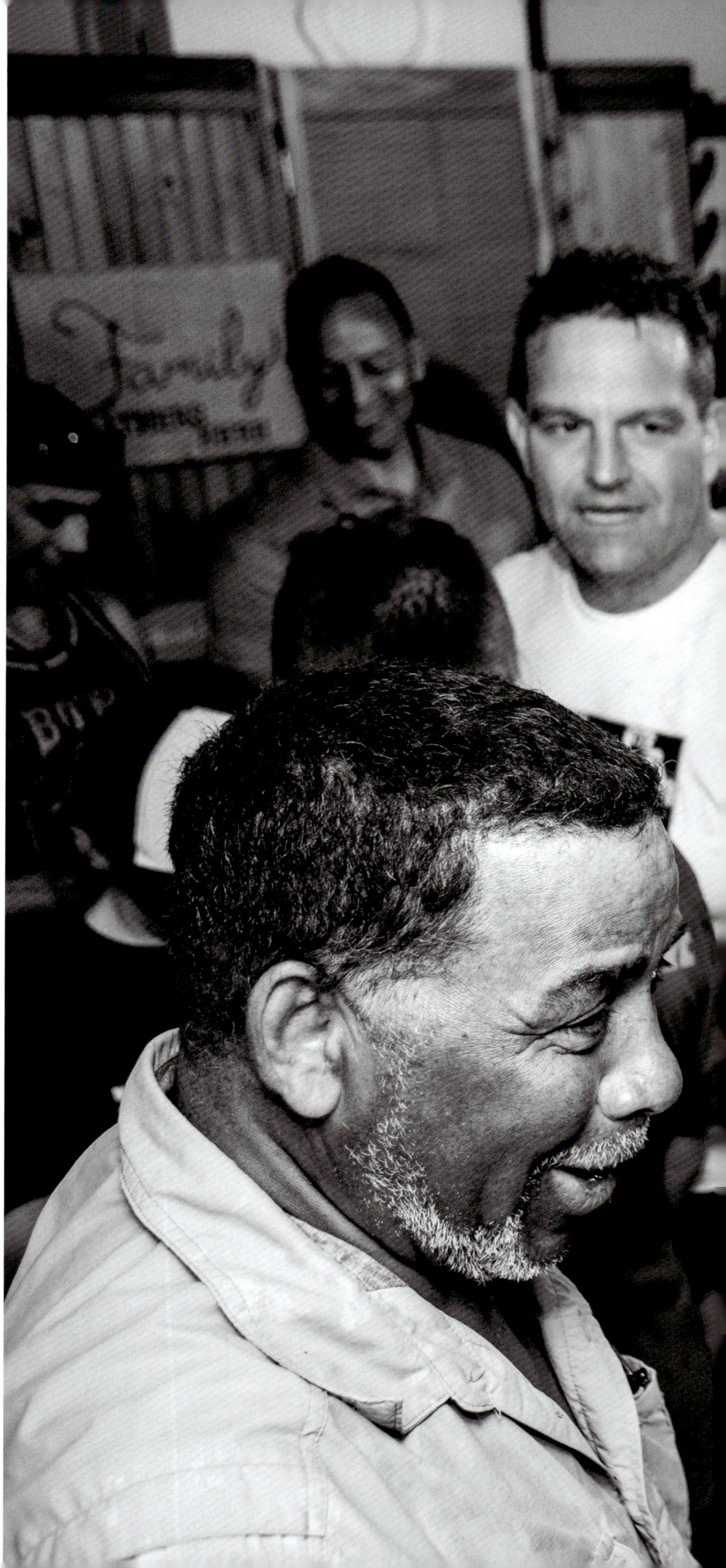

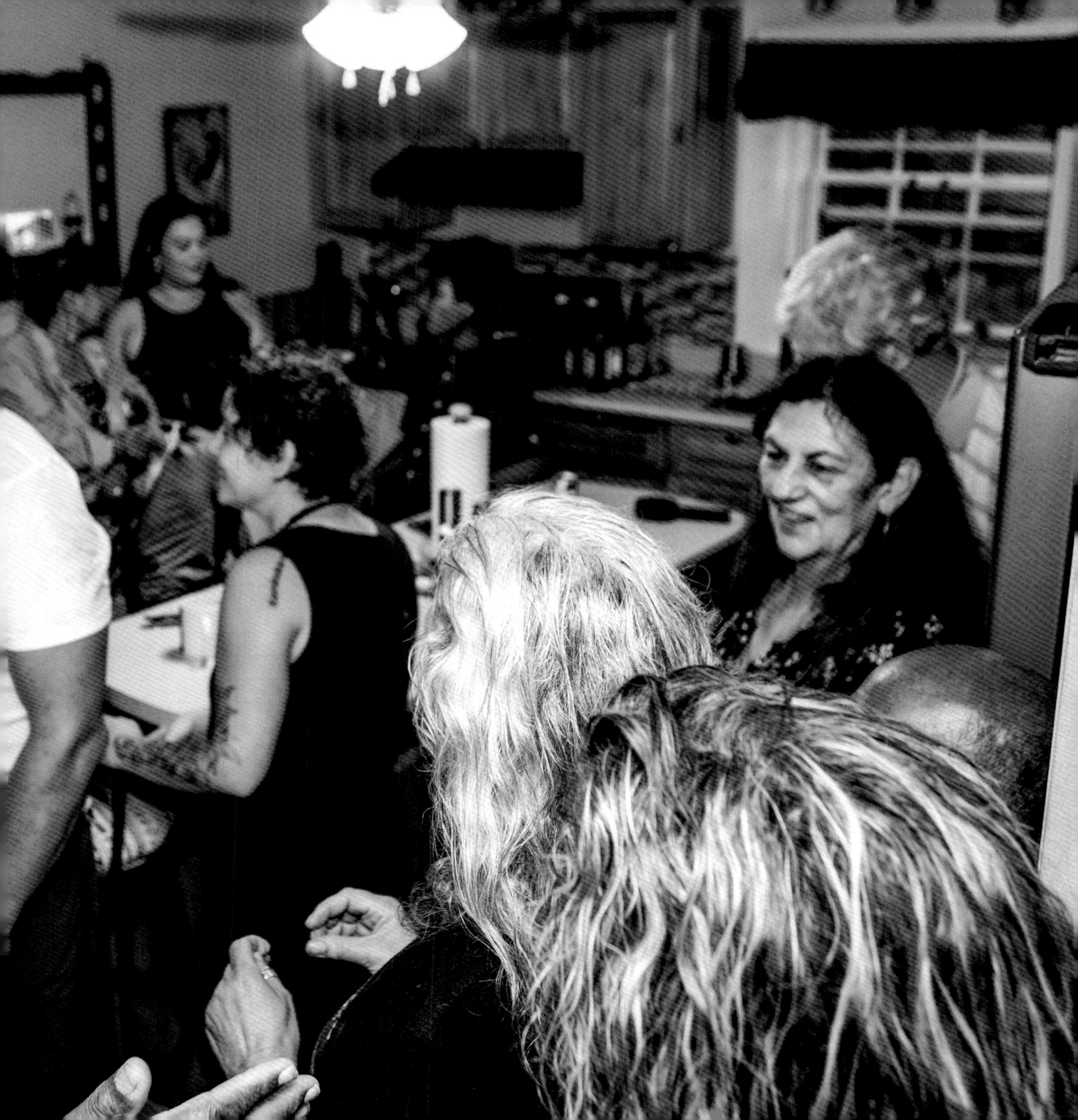

Young / Roche / Hodges / Hector / Snead — Willow Grove and Fredericton

At Willow Grove once again
Is a home built by Caribbean hands.
The house boasts a cabinet parading Black Precious Moments figurines.
A woman who smiles as she remembers
A life dedicated to their appreciation.

More family arrives in a car
To relish the sunlight together.
History covers everyone, near and far,
A quilt, that layer by layer, is woven tougher than leather.

Tensions rise as cousins decide
Around which corners their heritage hides.
Yet every pair of eyes still holds a love
Frustration can never disguise.

Then comes a whisper I've heard too many times
Hidden between shy, cautious replies:
"You should only talk to me about history.
They will only tell you lies."

No one brought their documents out then
So we all skated ice, worn much too thin.
I had to scan documents at another residence
To escape the gravity of gossip's sharp edge.

I left that day wondering.
How can our history heal if never revealed?
How can anyone learn to love and care
If shadows keep our stories from broad sunlight and fresh air?

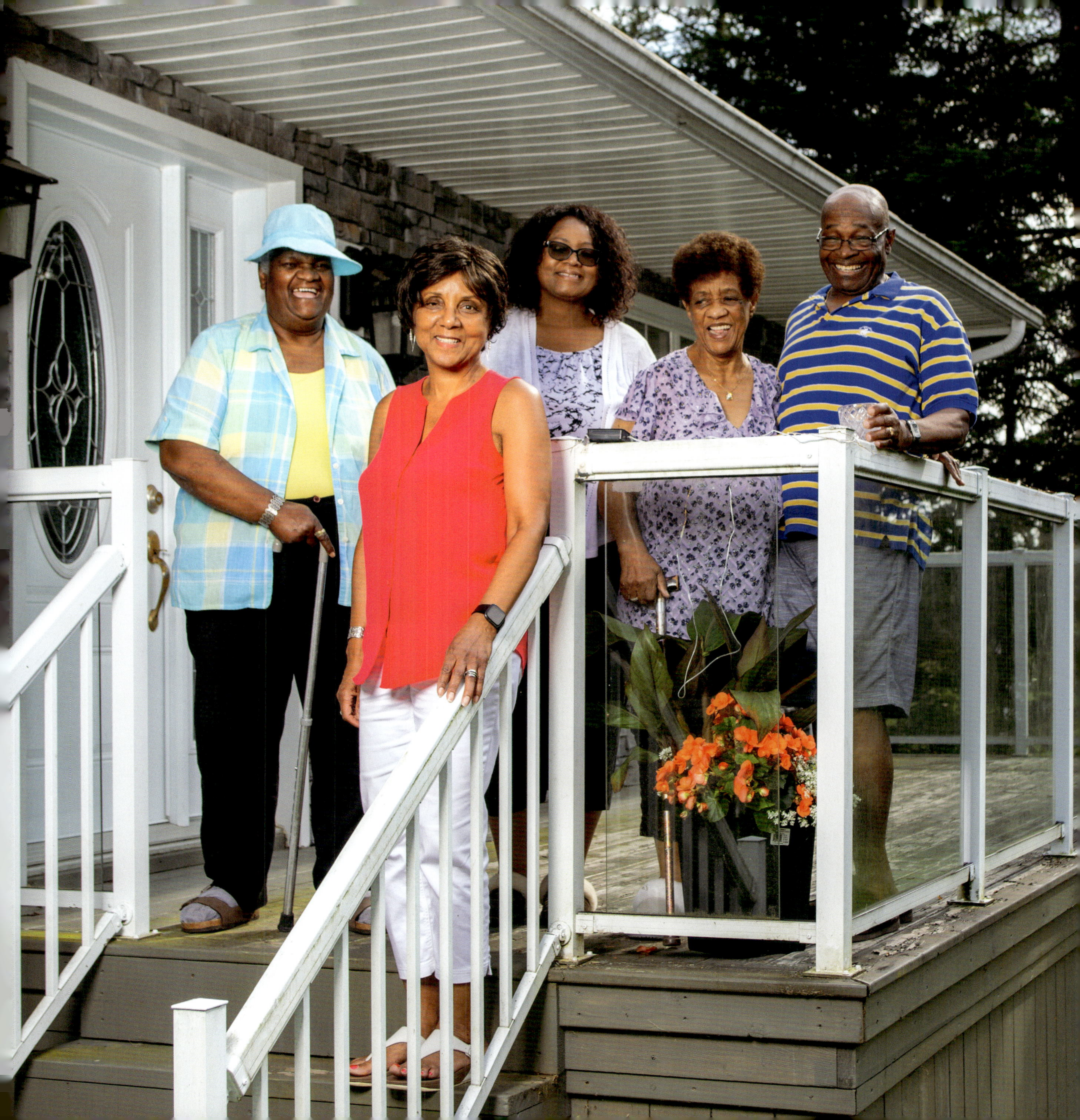

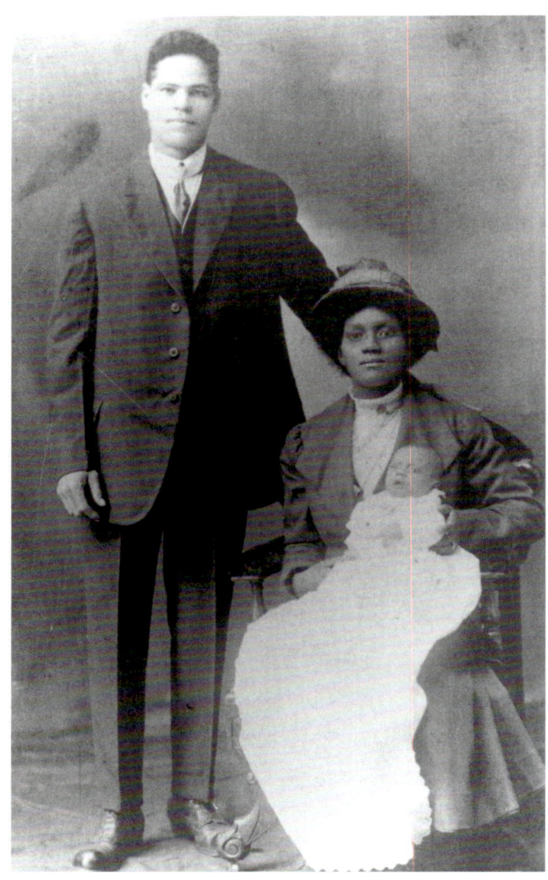

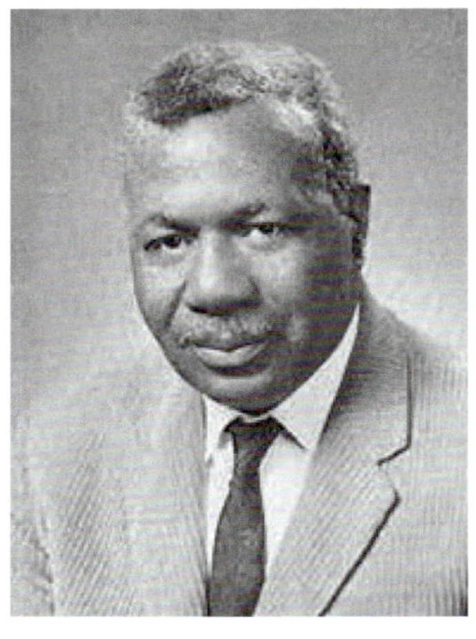

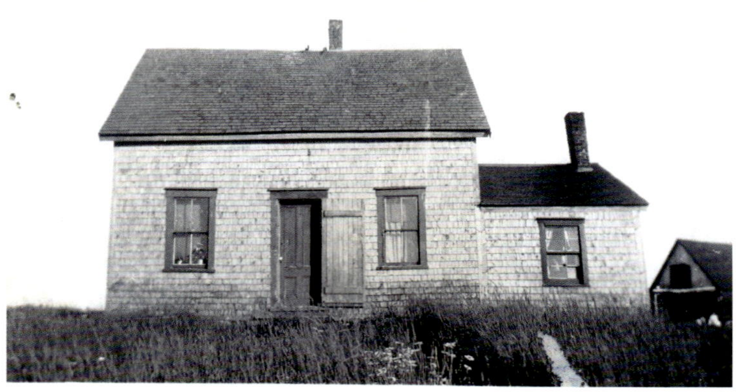

In 1922 Charles and Bertha Sneed granted to their granddaughter's husband, Edward Roche, "the parcel of land that was in the Grant to the Black Refugees so called, dated the 28th day of July AD 1837." This land is where my mother's farm was located, and it still remains in the family today.

— Marsha McGarvie

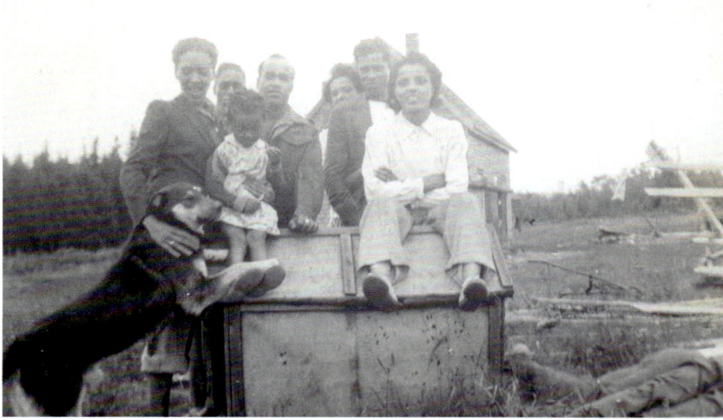

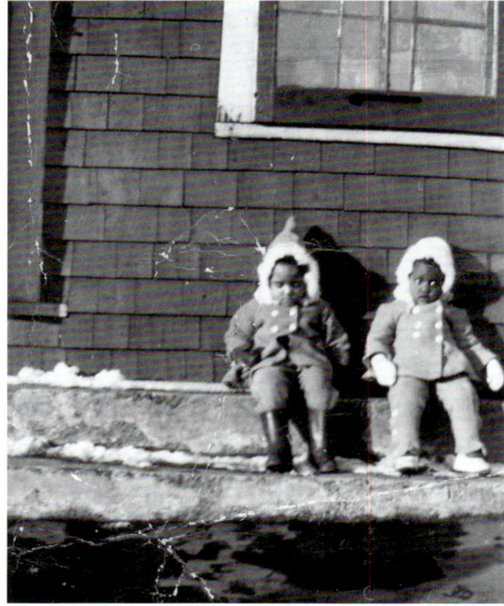

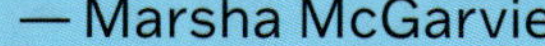

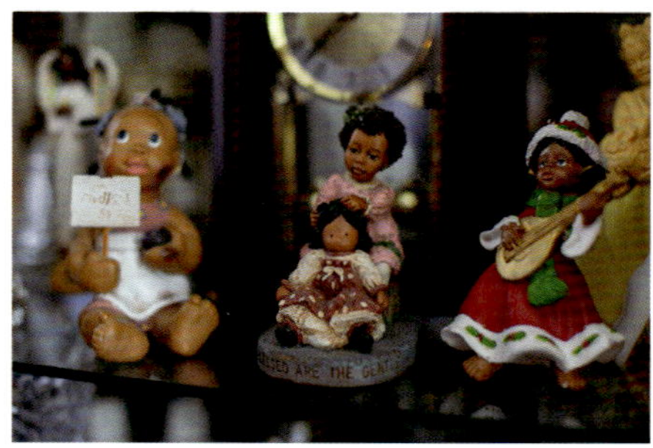

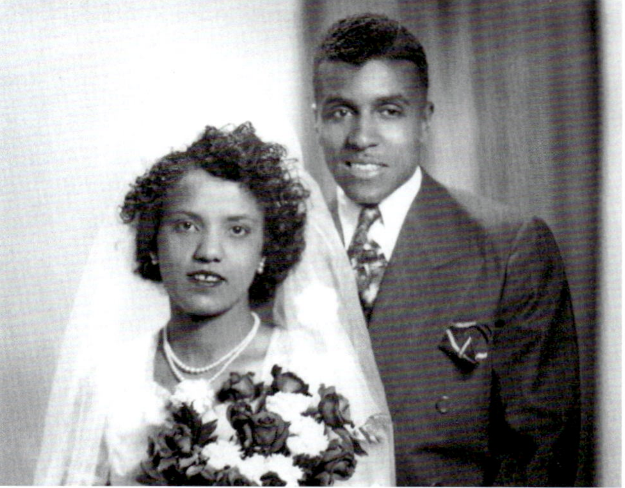

*Fred Hodges portrait courtesy of New Brunswick Black History Society

Marsha McGarvie's mother and father, John and Louise Young, have roots in two of New Brunswick's early Black communities, Willow Grove and Elm Hill.

Marsha's maternal great-grandparents were Bertha and Charles Snead (also Sneed in provincial records). Bertha's birth is recorded as Willow Grove in 1846 and Charles's as Saint John County in 1844. They both died in 1935, when she was eighty-nine and he was ninety-one. Bertha is on record as being buried at Elm Hill.

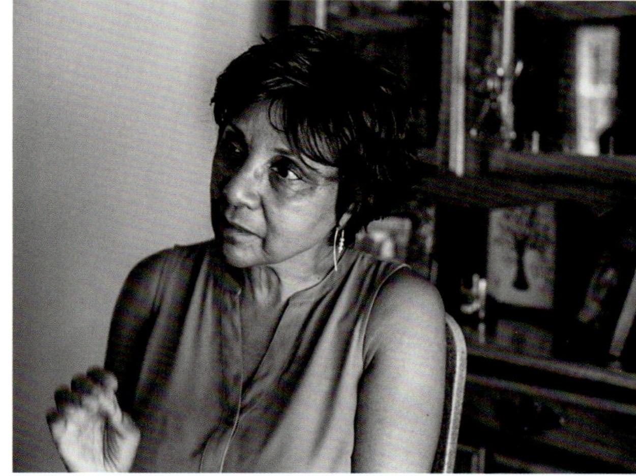

Bertha and Charles's daughter Rachel was born in or around 1872, and in 1890, Rachel Snead and George Hector were married. Following George's death, Rachel married William Harrison in 1900, and when he died too, she married William Hill in 1918.

Marsha's grandparents, Frances Hector and Edward Roche, were married in 1914. Edward Roche was born in Barbados to Samuel and Wilhelmina Roche. Family oral history recounts that he was a stowaway on a boat from Barbados that docked in Saint John. His year of arrival is unknown, but he was a farmer and at times worked as a game warden. Edward Roche died in 1939, prior to the marriages of any of his children.

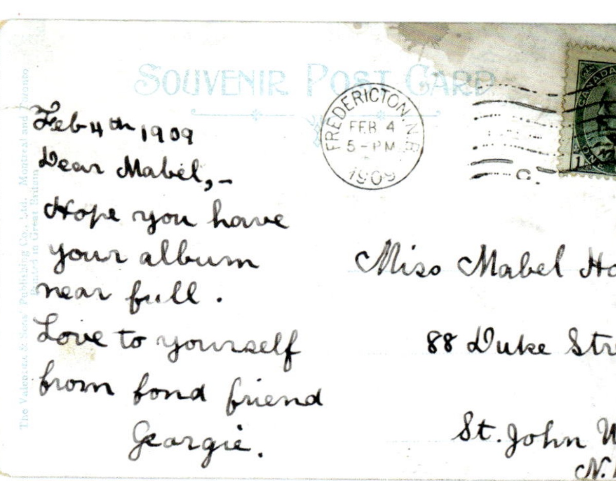

Souvenir Post Card

Feb 4th 1909
Dear Mabel,-
Hope you have
your album
near full.
Love to yourself
from fond friend
Georgie.

Miss Mabel Ho
88 Duke Stre
St. John W
N.B.

Marsha's mother, Louise Wilhelmina Roche, was born in 1920 in Willow Grove and was the fourth of the ten children to survive infancy. Her father, John Murray Noel Young, was born in 1919 to William Ellis Young and Mabel Hodges Young in Saint John, but the Young family had previously lived in Elm Hill. Mabel Hodges was born in Saint John in 1884, and her parents Hiram and Angelina Hodges were early proponents of the importance of education, still present in the Young-Hodges family: Mabel was a graduate of Saint John High School and is believed to have taught school in Elm Hill prior to her marriage.

John's cousin Frederick Hodges, after he left the RCAF in 1946, went on to become the first Black person elected president of the Saint John District Labour Council in 1964. He was a founding member of the New Brunswick Association for the Advancement of Coloured People, in 1969; and he was elected to the city council of Saint John in 1974. Fred received the Queen's Jubilee Medal in 1978, the Order of Canada in 1982, and an Honorary Doctor of Laws from the University of New Brunswick in 1984.

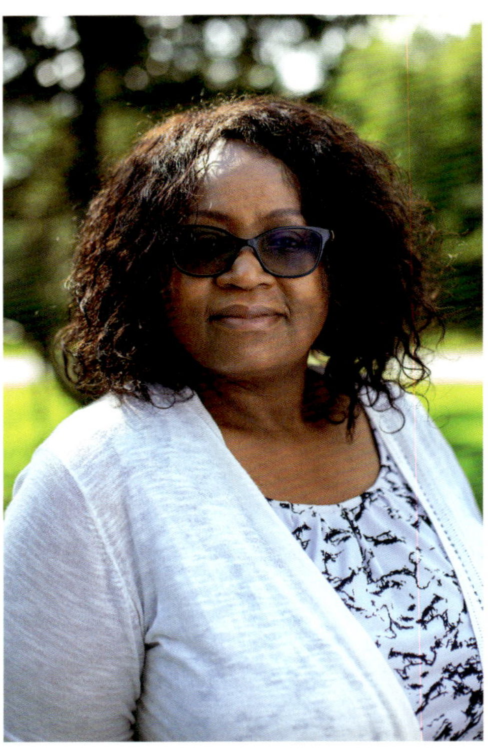

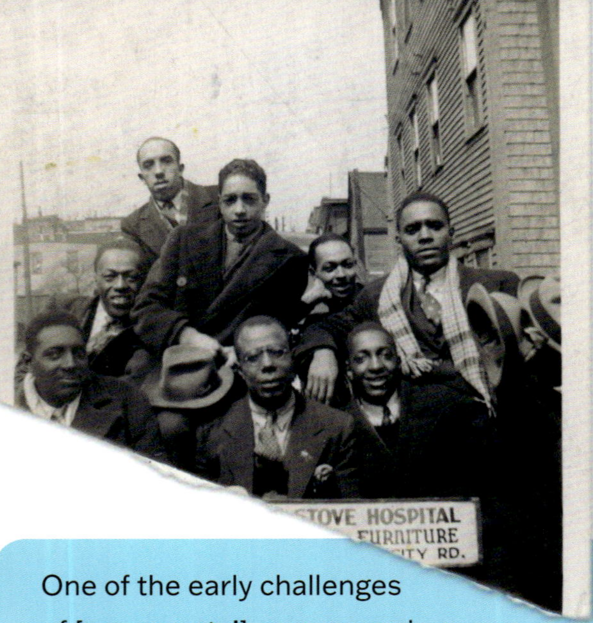

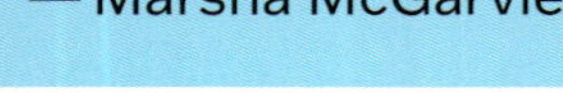

One of the early challenges of [my parents'] young marriage was John's contracting tuberculosis and being admitted to the sanitarium, along with their two children. I'm not sure the length of their stay but my mother must have been under a great deal of stress, staying with her mother in Willow Grove and travelling to Saint John every day to see her family.
— Marsha McGarvie

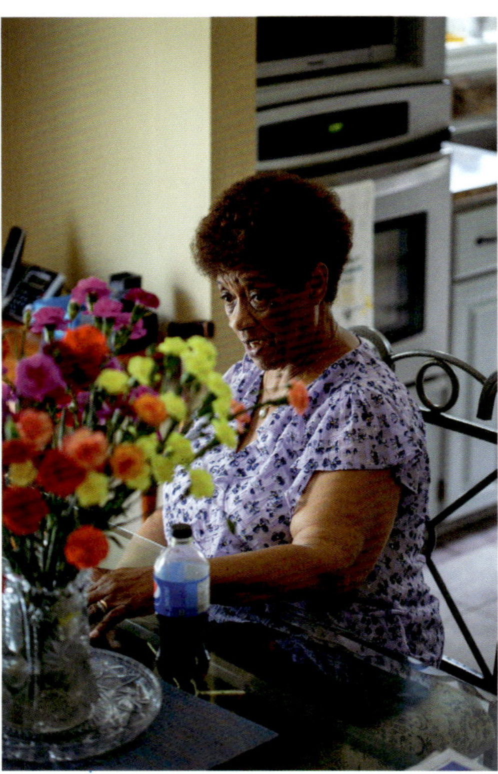

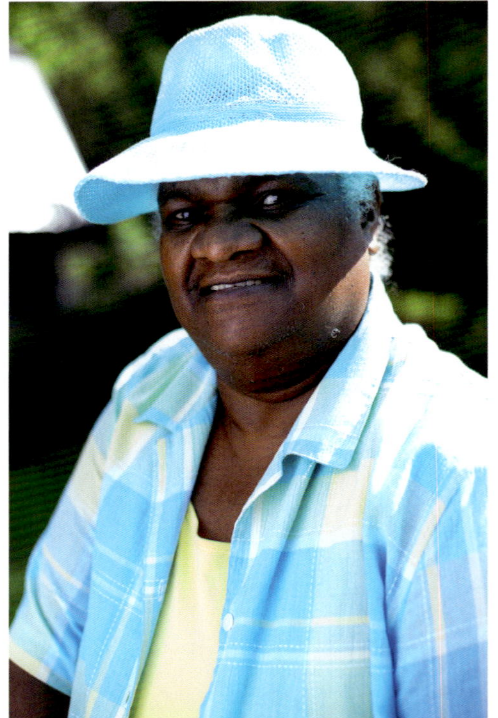

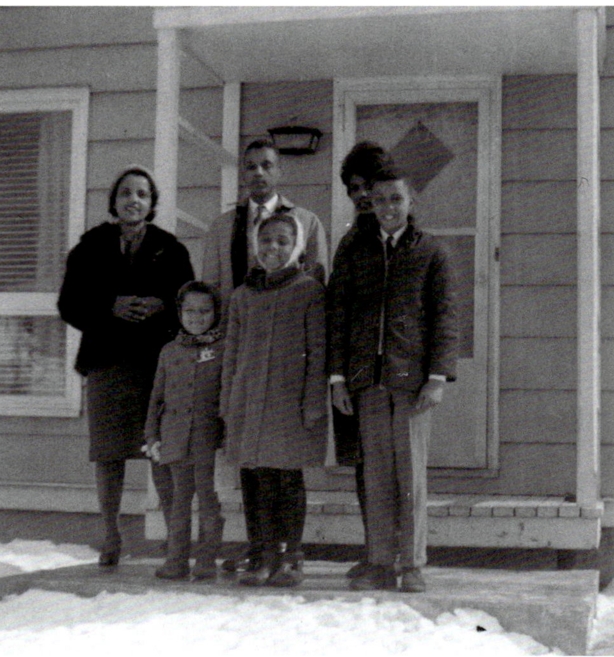

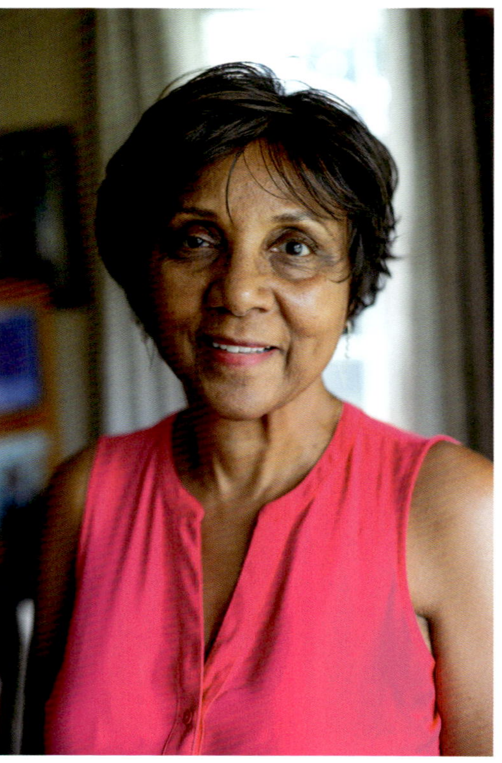

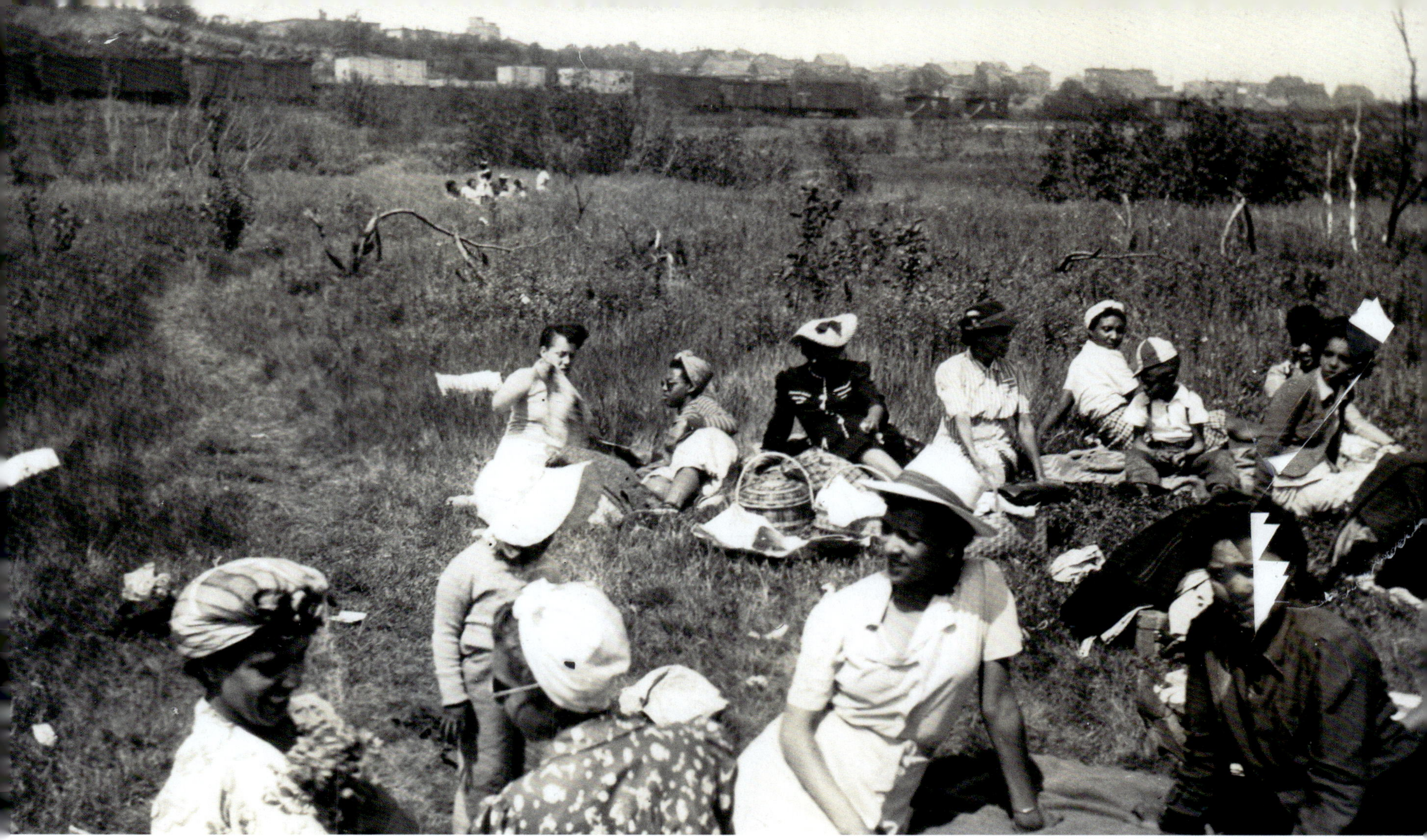

My father's uncle Lloyd Hodges and his father Hiram Hodges were barbers in Saint John. I remember going with my father when he had his hair cut there. It was a gathering place for my father's family, plus Uncle Lloyd's many other Black customers.
— Marsha McGarvie

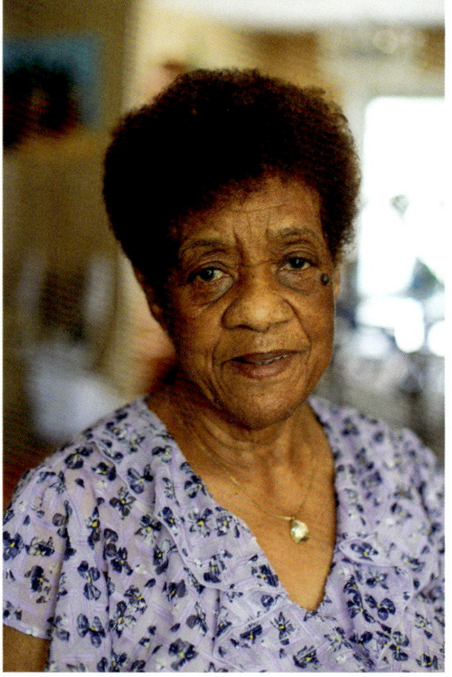

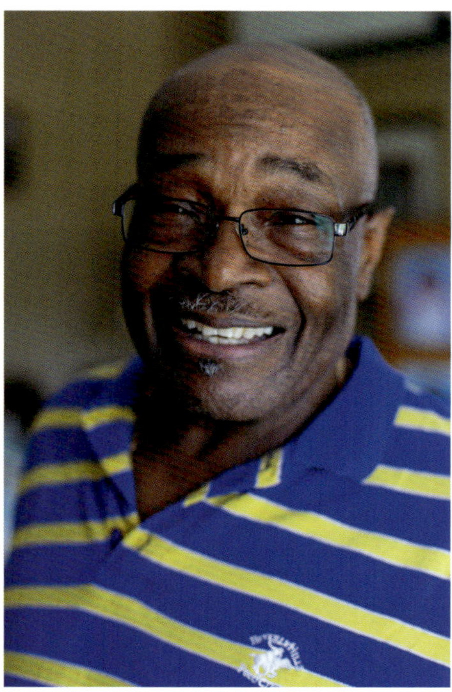

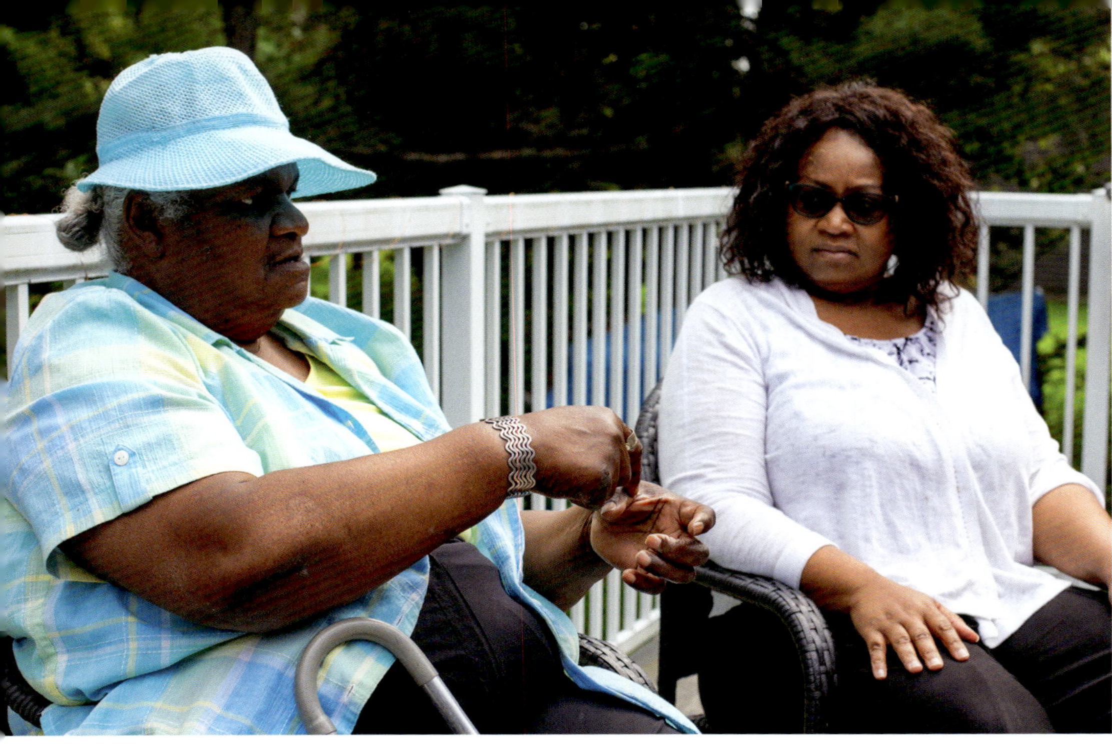

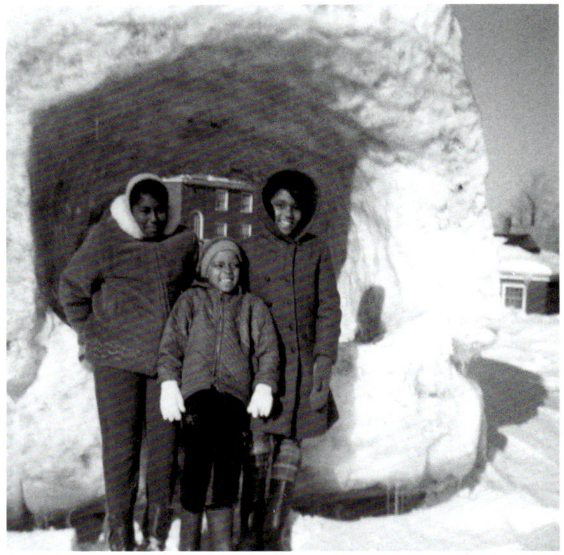

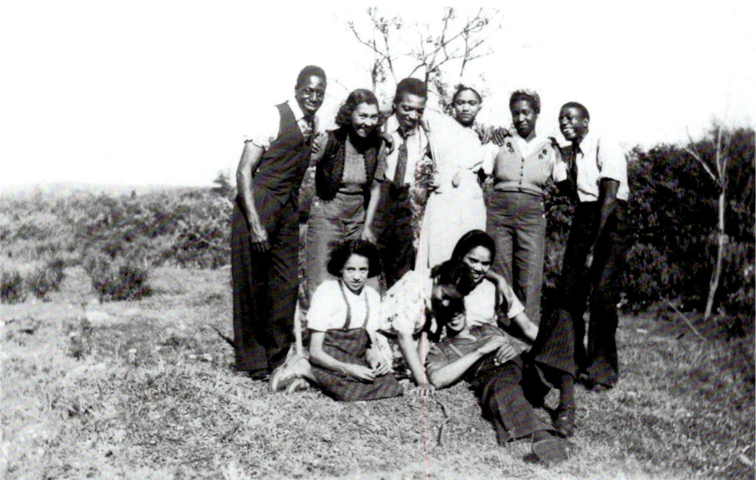

My mother was close to her sisters and it was the best of times when they were all together with their families. There was always abundant good food and stories of growing up on the farm in Willow Grove, their chores, and the people who would visit from Saint John on weekends. They were proud of raising their own vegetables and livestock and having enough to feed anyone visiting.
— Marsha McGarvie

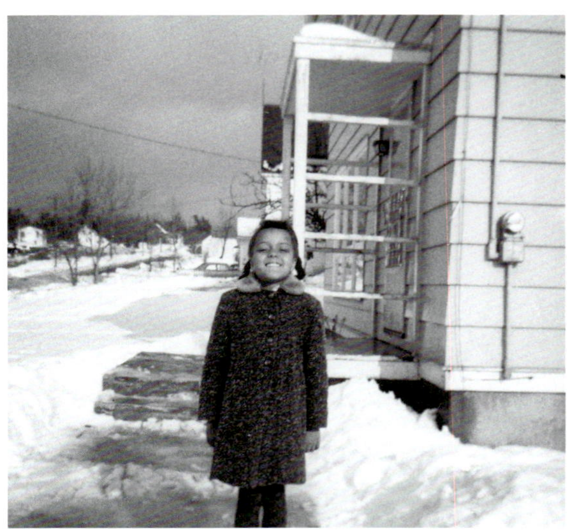

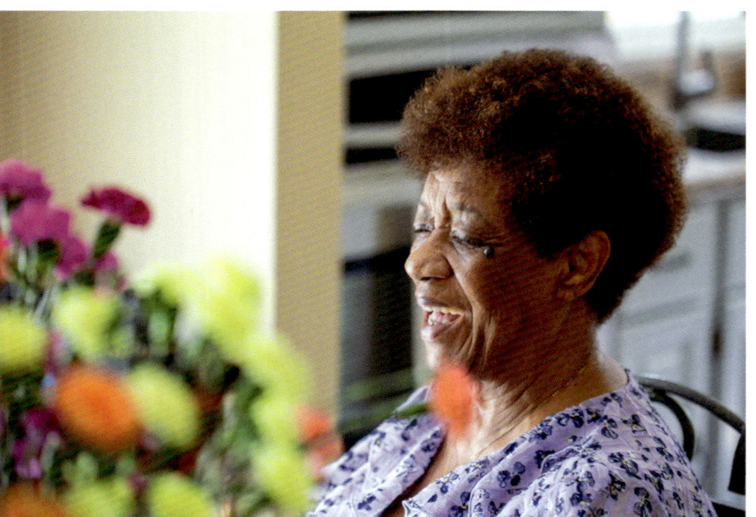

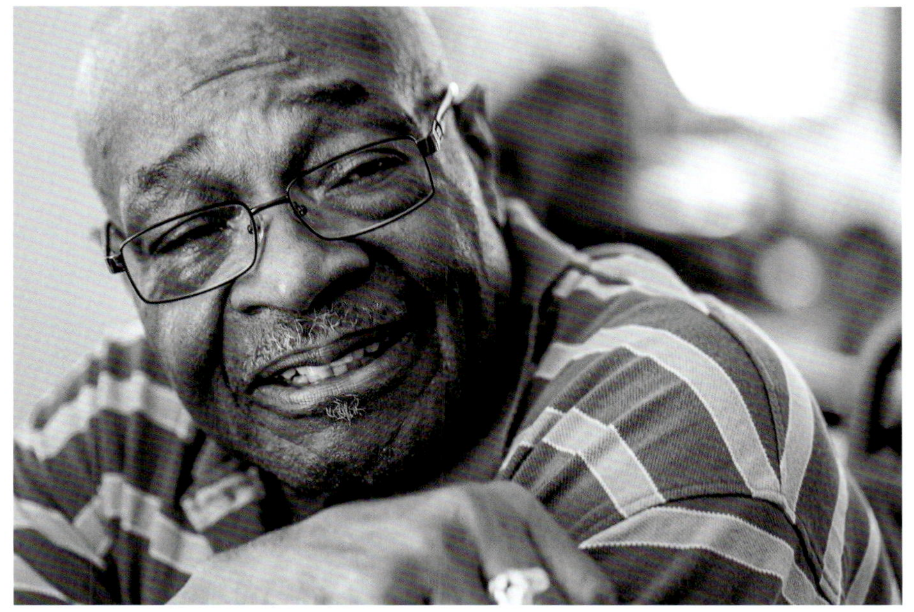

My mother talked about "working out" when she was younger. She and her sisters, prior to marriage, were employed as live-in maids for families in Saint John. My mother would get lonely but on days off would meet up with her sister to spend time together. She once pointed out one of the houses where she'd worked. I wish I had paid more attention.
— Marsha McGarvie

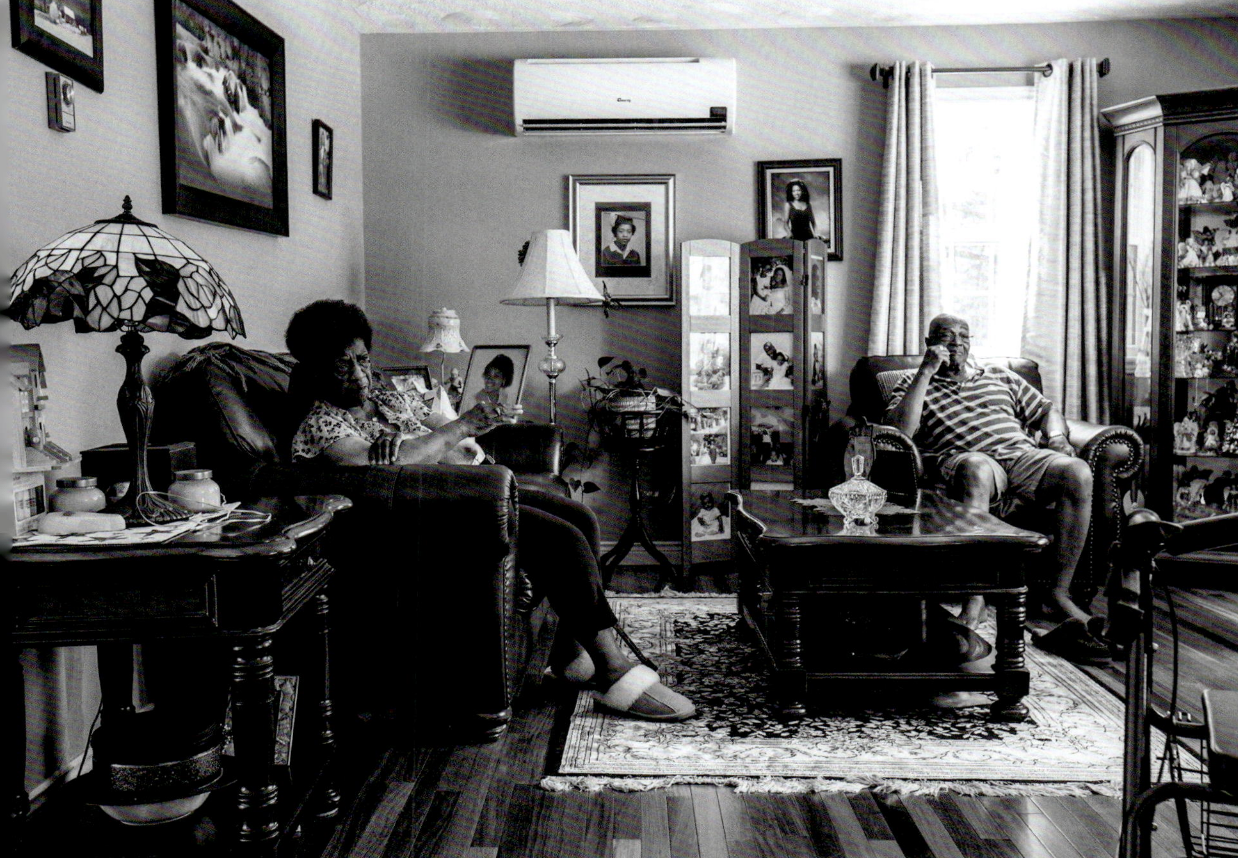

"Nick" Skinner
cordially invites you and your friends
to the Most Outstanding Ball in years at the
LILY LAKE PAVILION, SAINT JOHN
Eastern Canada's Most Modern Dance Hall
with Junior Blizzard's 6 Piece Orchestra
THURSDAY, NOVEMBER 28, 1957
Dancing from 9 p.m. to 1 a.m.
Semi-formal ∴ Admission $1.00 person

An Ideal Chance for Our American Friends
to enjoy their Thanksgiving Holiday.

Skinner / Blizzard — Saint John

At the Skinner family residence
Fresh plates of homemade cookies awaited,
Baked just for us. Meant to be shared.
But the cookies had to wait.

The cookies waited while we listened
To the story of how a family member saved a boy's life
From ending under iced waters' embrace.
The story made teardrops flake from the man's eyes.

Again the cookies waited as we all listened
To a cassette tape of Paula's father
Singing the songs he used to sing to her as a child
This time my eyes found tears.

Those cookies waited while the stories unfolded
Of how Paula's father staged dinner-and-movie nights
Long before TV. He set up a projector in his home.
Kids paid ten cents, adults twenty-five cents, to see the stars up close.

The cookies slowly grew cold
As Paula displayed her quilts, said that every family member got one;
How she crafted handmade purses, sold them at the market.
Her dad's entrepreneurial spirit shining bright.

Oh those cookies had to wait until long after
The tears, laughter, and hugs subsided.
Until we remembered to zip-lock the cold cookies
Eating them on the cold ride home.

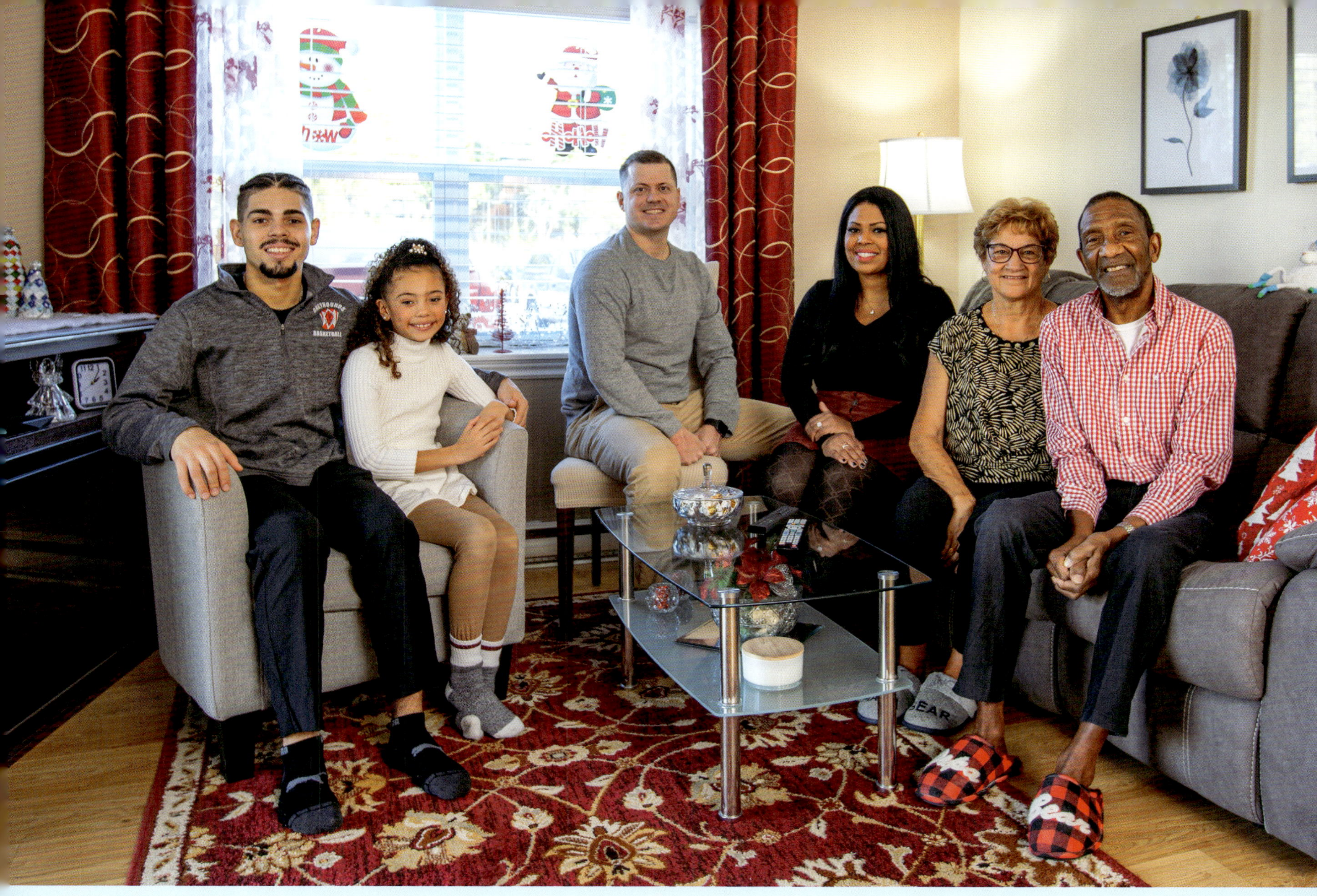

Then after the cookies were finished
It was our turn. To wait.
Until we could see our new friends
Again.

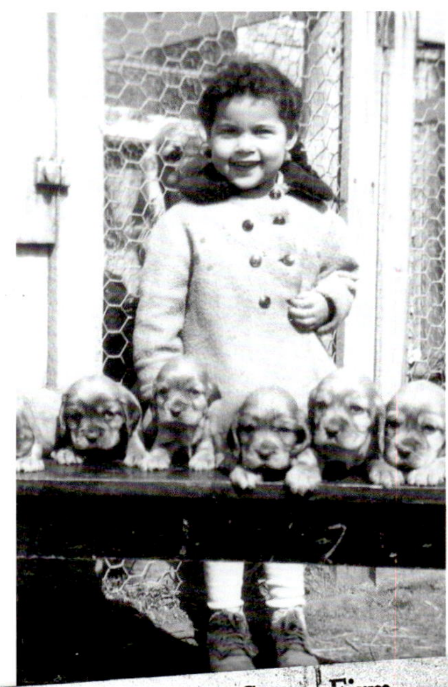

Associated With Stove Firm

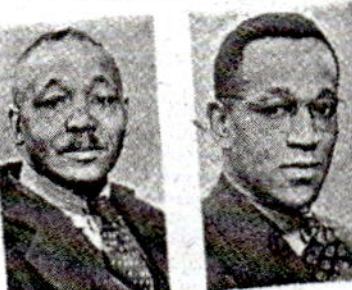 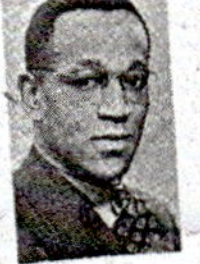 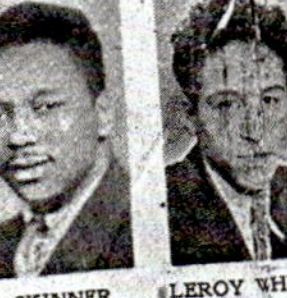 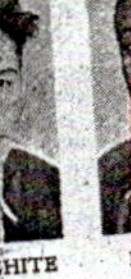

N. D. SKINNER G. SKINNER C. SKINNER LEROY WHITE H. MARTIN

East End Stove Hospital

REMOVAL SALE

—IN—

New Premises - 325 Prince Edward St.

SALE CONTINUES - MAY 1st to MAY 15th

WE SPECIALIZE IN THE BEST USED STOVES AND RANGES!

Our Cooking Stoves are Guaranteed to Bake!

EXTRA LOW PRICES

During This Sale

Make Your Selections from Our

FULL LINE of HOUSEHOLD FURNITURE

Beds, Springs, Mattresses, Tables, Chairs, FLOOR COVERINGS

We have in stock a nice display of

DINING ROOM FURNITURE,
KITCHEN CABINETS, KITCHEN UTENSILS,
DAVENPORTS and CHESTERFIELDS
STUDIO COUCHES
BABIES' and INVALIDS' COMMODE CHAIRS
HALL TREES, SINKS, ELECTRIC LIGHT FIXTURES,
WASHING MACHINES

Repairs and Parts for All Makes of Stoves.
Careful Attention to Welding

BARREL STOVES MADE TO ORDER
STOVE PIPE MADE TO ORDER

RANGE BURNERS FOR SALE, and
HUNDREDS OF OTHER ITEMS AT SPECIAL LOW PRICES
DURING THIS SALE

SALE CONTINUES FOR 15 DAYS, MAY 1st TO MAY 15th, 1941

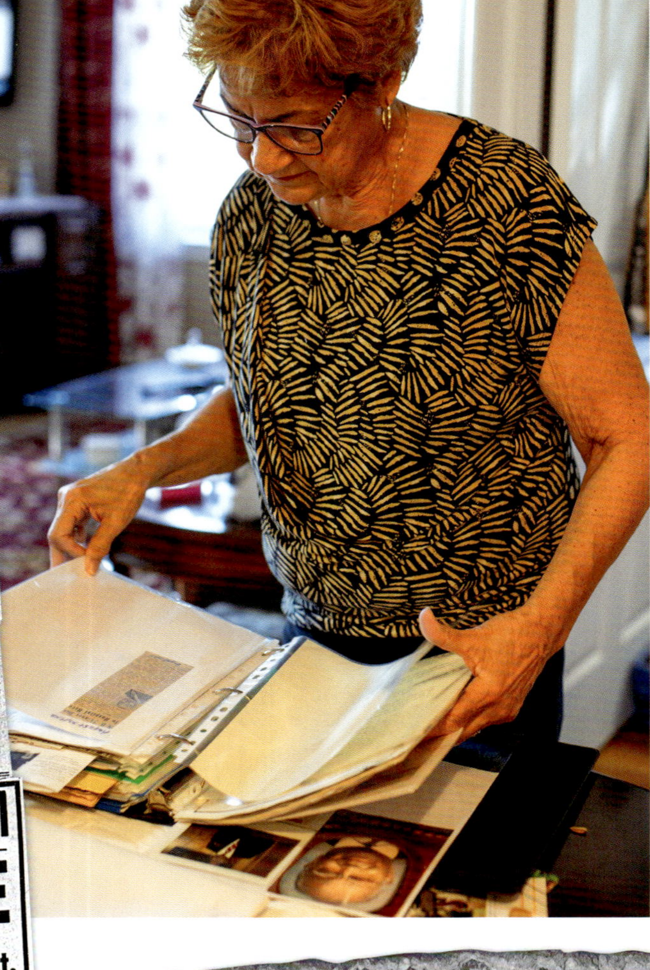

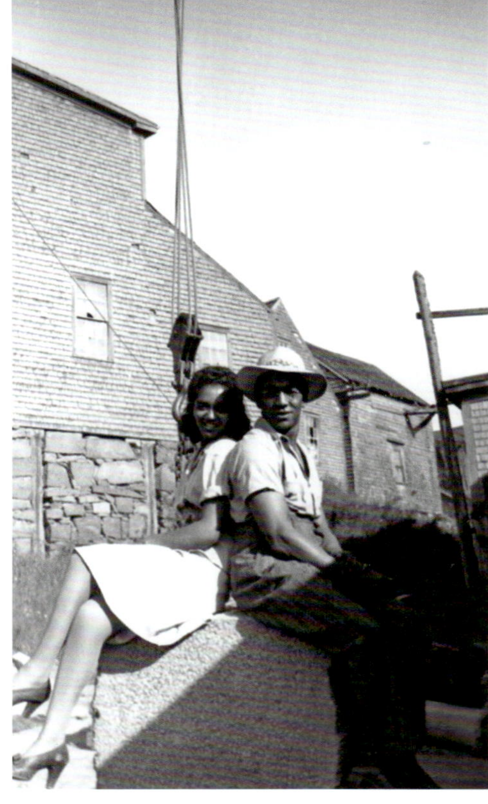

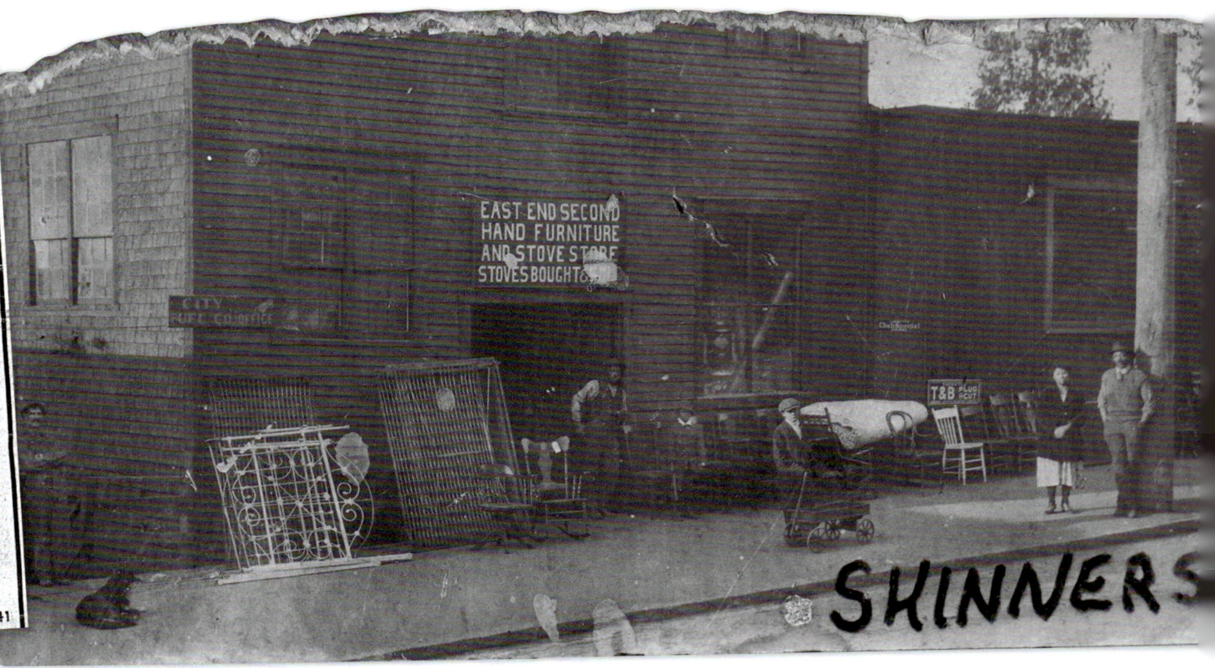

The Skinner family can trace their history back to Nicodemus Skinner (Paula Skinner-Blizzard's grandfather), who was born in Halifax on February 10, 1876, to Demus Moses Skinner and Nancy Clayton. He moved to Saint John, where he married his second wife, Aderine Lillian Bayley (she went by Lillian), who was born in Christ Church, Barbados, on July 29, 1911.

Nicodemus established the East End Stove Hospital, an appliance repair shop and used furniture store, on City Road in Saint John in the early 1900s. By the 1920s, the store was said to be the largest Black-owned business in Atlantic Canada.

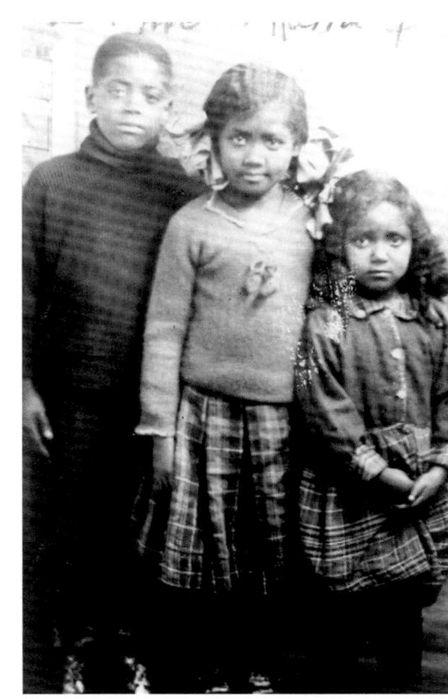

In 1941, Nicodemus bought a building on Prince Edward Street and the business expanded. He also bought a three-storey building on Marsh Street, where he lived along with his son Garfield, Garfield's wife Fern, and their children, Paula and Michael. Garfield worked as the store manager alongside his father while Fern worked as the bookkeeper. Nicodemus retired in 1949, and Garfield took over the business with his mother. When she died, he became the sole owner of the shop, which he renamed Skinner's Stove Hospital.

Skinner's Stove Hospital was expropriated in 1955 when east Saint John underwent urban renewal. Garfield purchased a building on Main Street, in the north of the city, and converted the top floors into apartments over his ground-floor shop.

In 1966, the Stove Hospital closed, and Garfield began working in maintenance at Provincial Hospital of Nervous Diseases, now Centracare psychiatric hospital. Although he went to night school to study engineering, he initially struggled to find employment due to the colour of his skin. Once hired as an engineer, he was underpaid, compared to his White colleagues.

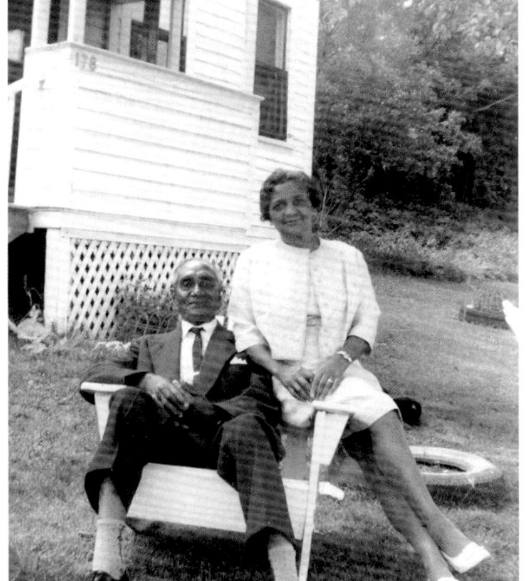

Garfield's brother, Nick Jr., also worked at the stove shop until he started his own business, Nick's Welding and Ornamental Iron Works. An outstanding track star in his youth who held numerous maritime records, Nick Jr. was a founding member of several Black organizations in New Brunswick, including the Colour Progressive Association (founded 1943); Provincial Resources of Black Energy (PROBE, founded 1969); Pride of Race, Unity, Dignity, Education (PRUDE, founded 1981); and the Black Loyalists of New Brunswick Association.

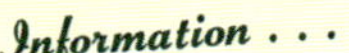

Information . . .

FRIDAY, SEPT. 3rd . . . . Chartered Coach leaves Halifax for Saint John, picking up passengers at all stops en route.

Return trip will leave Saint John Tuesday morning, Sept. 7th.

Take the "A" Train and enjoy the entertainment provided all the way.

Accommodations can be provided for all visitors.

For further information,

Consult the Personnel Director - MR. THEO EBERNE 75 Chapel Street, Phone 3-4105 Saint John, N. B.

Four-Day Programme . . .

FRIDAY
(Evening) Banquet and Dance Party, "The Showboat", Gondola Point.

SATURDAY
(Afternoon) Ball Game.
(Evening) Costume Dance, Lakewood Pavilion.

SUNDAY
(Afternoon) Bus Ride and Picnic.
(Evening) Reserved for Church Service.
(Midnight) Dancing at "The Casablanca"

MONDAY
(Afternoon) Track and Field Sports.
(Evening) Ball Game Finals.
After the Game - The Grand Finale Ball ! !
Our Big "Semi-formal" ; featuring -
The Maritime Beauty Contest
with Presentation of Trophy and Prizes.

Every Dance a Party !
Novelties - Games - Floor Shows - Prizes
Don't Miss
"Labor Day Week End"

Committees . . .

DIRECTOR	GARFIELD SKINNER
Supervisor of Ticket Sales	ALBERT CARTY
Transportation	JOHN YOUNG
Sports	ELIJAH STEWART WILLIAM STEWART
Welcoming Committee	MRS. F. RICHARDS MRS. G. LAUCHNER MRS. G. SKINNER MARGARET EDISON
Refreshments	MRS. P. JOHNSTON MRS. G. CARTY PEGGY MANSFIELD

Judges of Beauty Contest - To be appointed on evening of Contest.

Floor Manager	CHARLES HIGGINS

Orchestras . . .

"HALIFAX COLORED" "OSSIE STEWART'S" "COMMODORES" "ROY MIDDLETON'S"

Chartered Busses to All Distant Points

Support - - - THE CLARION
"YOUR MARITIME PAPER"

YOU *will want to attend the Gala*

LABOR DAY WEEK END
in Saint John, N.B.
September 3 to 6, 1948

FEATURING . . .
The Maritime Beauty Contest

Dancing
Sports
Parties
Picnics
Novelties
Prizes

GARFIELD SKINNER, DIRECTOR

In Aid of
O.F.A.C.P.

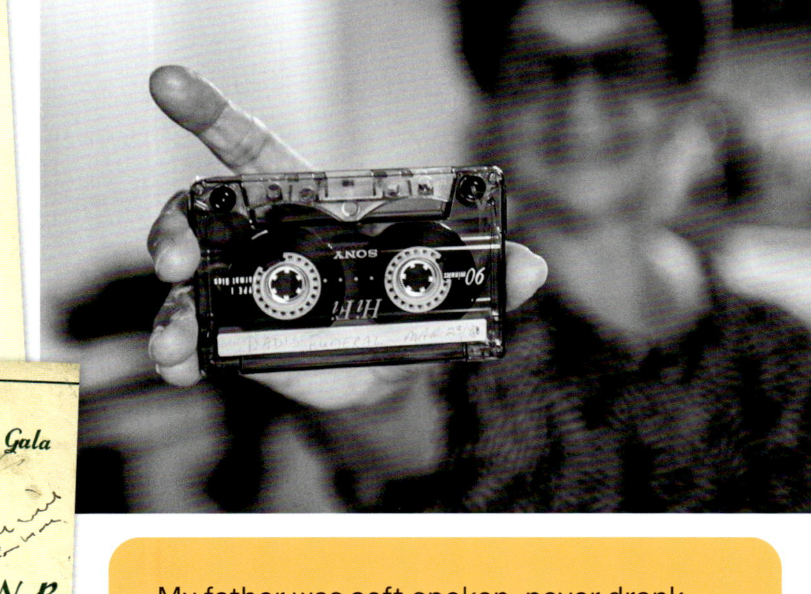

My father was soft-spoken, never drank, smoked, or swore, and was always the first to offer help to anyone in need. After he retired, he lost his sight, but he had a beautiful voice and sang with various groups over the years. On December 23, 1997, he taped me a memory of songs that he loved to sing. He died when he was eighty-three, on March 19, 1998.
— Paula Skinner-Blizzard

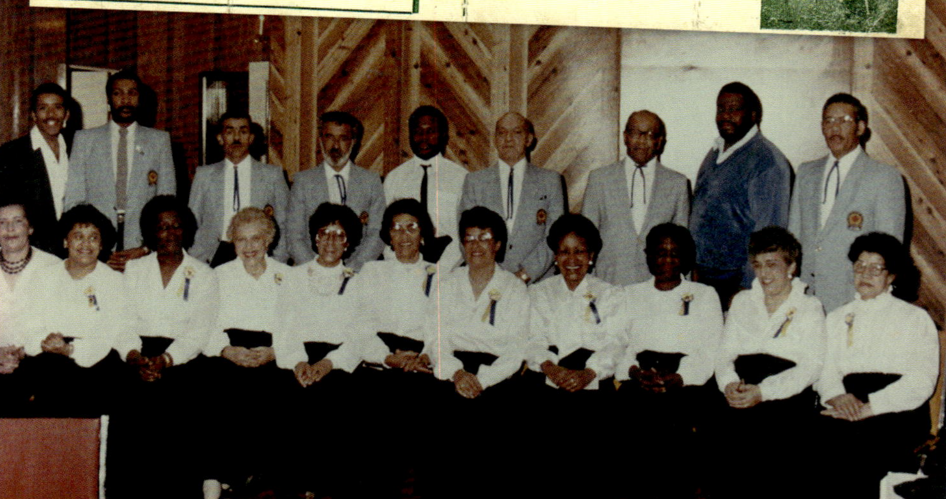

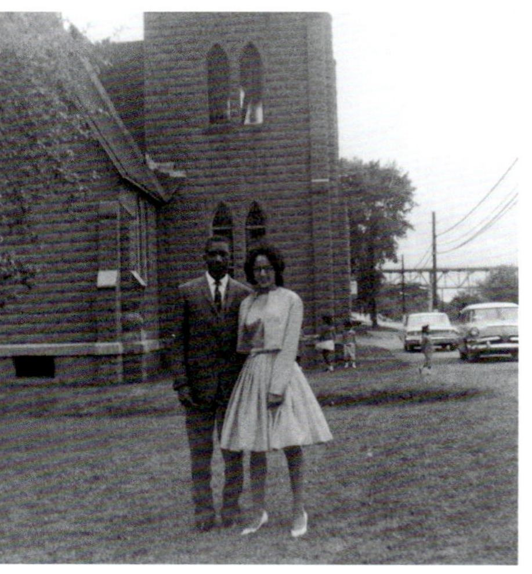

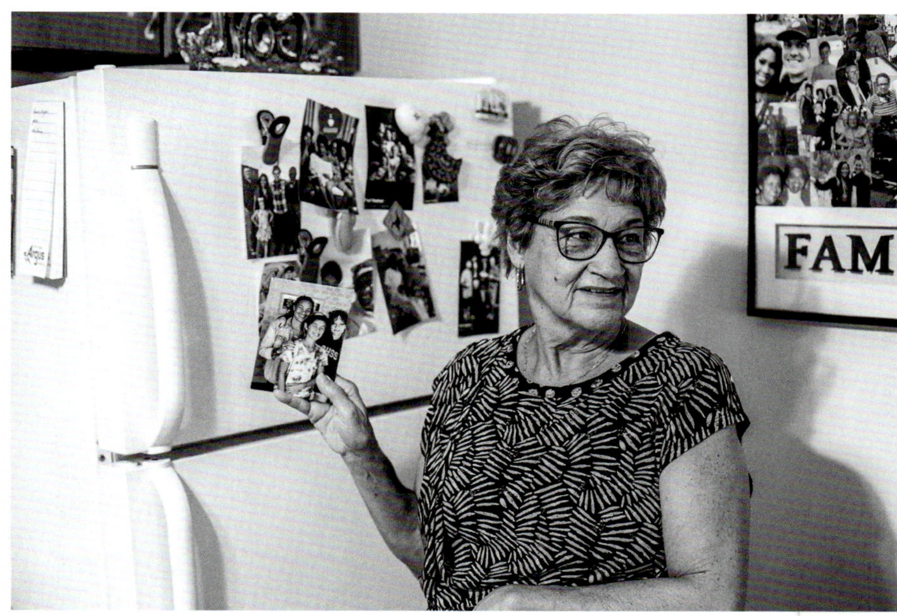

New Brunswick Association
for the
Advancement of Coloured People

J. S. DRUMMOND
Corresponding Secretary

31 Hydro Place
Saint John, N. B.

Dear Member,

There will be a meeting of the Association on Monday, the 19th of June, 1961 at 8 P. M. at the Y.M.C.A. Hazen Ave.

The guest speaker of the evening will be Mr. Ralph Stevens, barrister-at-law. As this is our first invitation to a guest speaker, the Association would more than appreciate a special effort on your part to attend.

Accompanying this notice of meeting, is a copy of the proposed constitution. The Constitution Committee looks forward to you studying the proposed constitution, and to your constructive criticism of this most important document when it is presented for your approval at a future meeting.

We anticipate a good attendance, because of the two-fold importance of the meeting, and look forward to seeing you.

Yours respectfully,

J. S. Drummond,
Corresponding Secretary

JSD/wwp

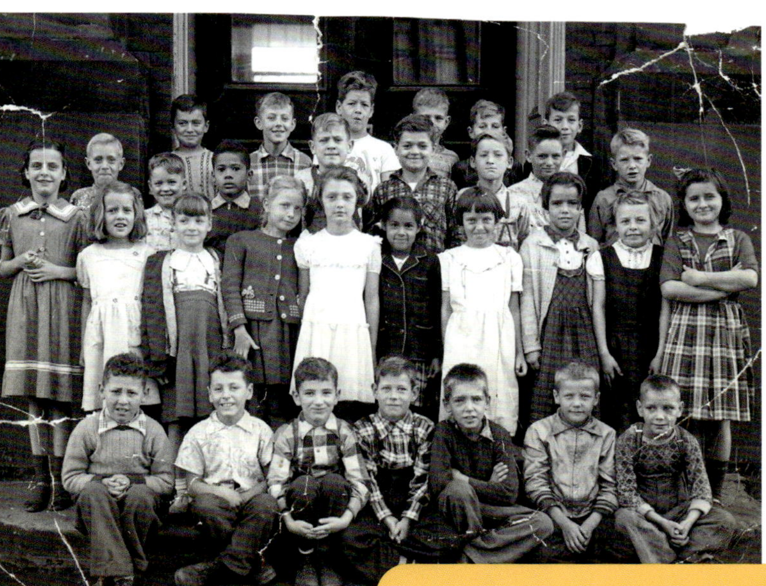

This is to Certify that
Garfield L. Skinner
is a Member of the
NEW BRUNSWICK ASSOCIATION FOR THE ADVANCEMENT OF COLORED PEOPLE
FOR THE YEAR ENDING May 1, 1962
Treasurer.

My father believed in education, and he studied engineering at night to upgrade his skills. But he soon realized what kept him out of top-rated jobs. It was the colour of his skin. The White men he worked with didn't want a Black man as their boss.

A young Lebanese lawyer, Ralph Stephen, helped him fight for work equality. Eventually Dad got the position of chief engineer, but never the right pay grade.
— Paula Skinner-Blizzard

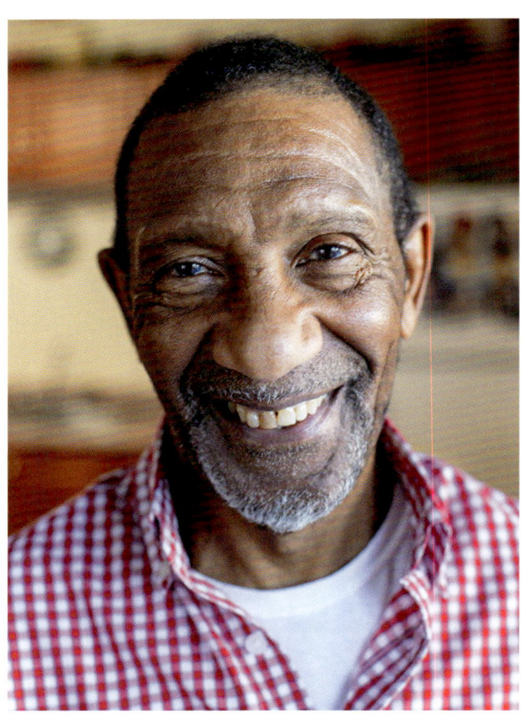

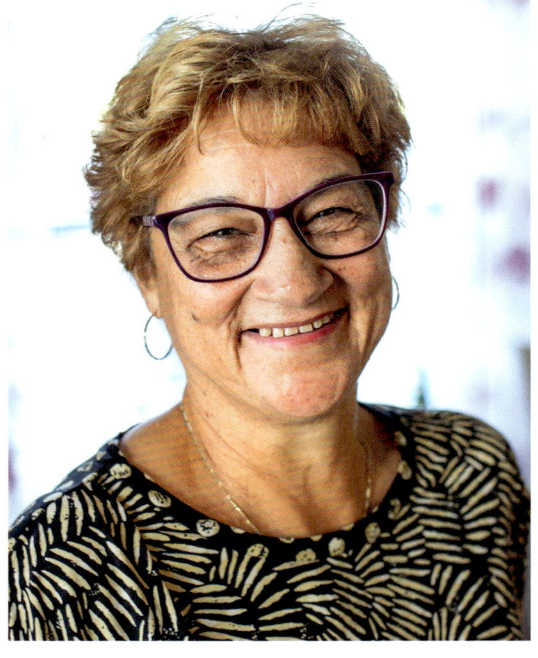

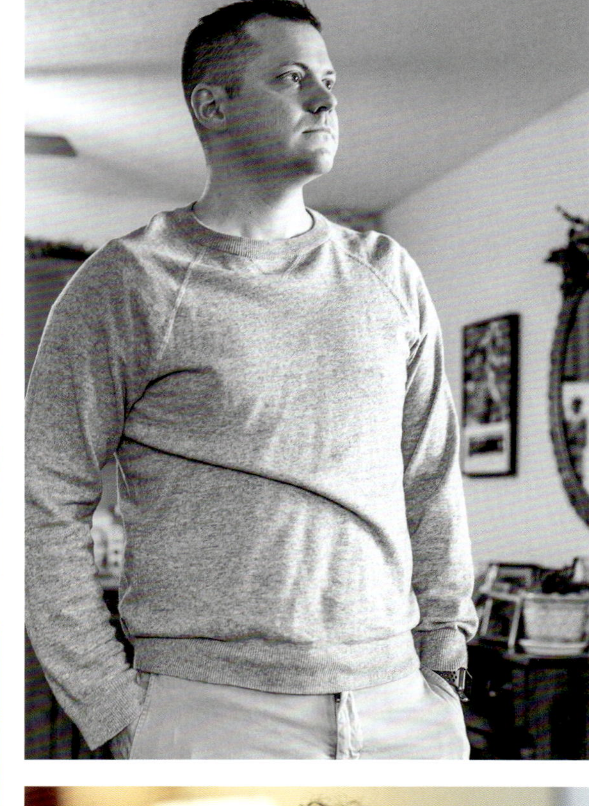

My father always gave good advice, but the most valuable piece was this: the true test of your character is what you do when no one is watching. I've tried to follow that all my life. He also instilled in me that you should treat people how you wanted to be treated.
— Paula Skinner-Blizzard

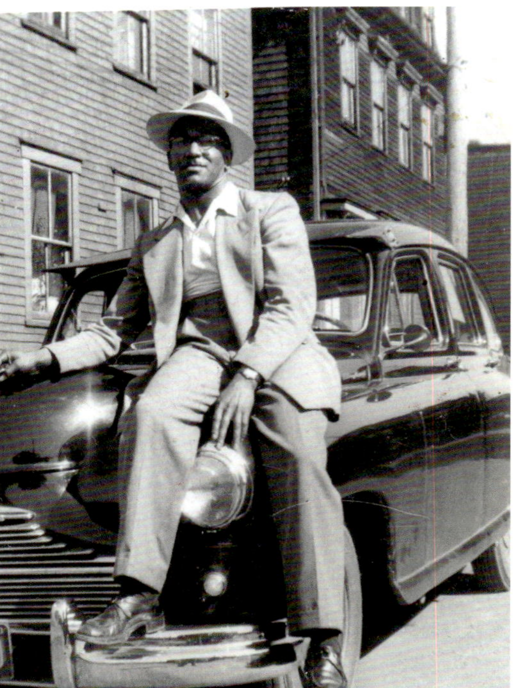

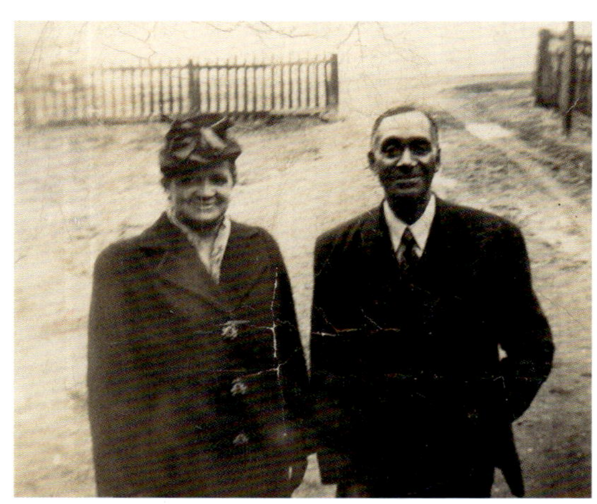

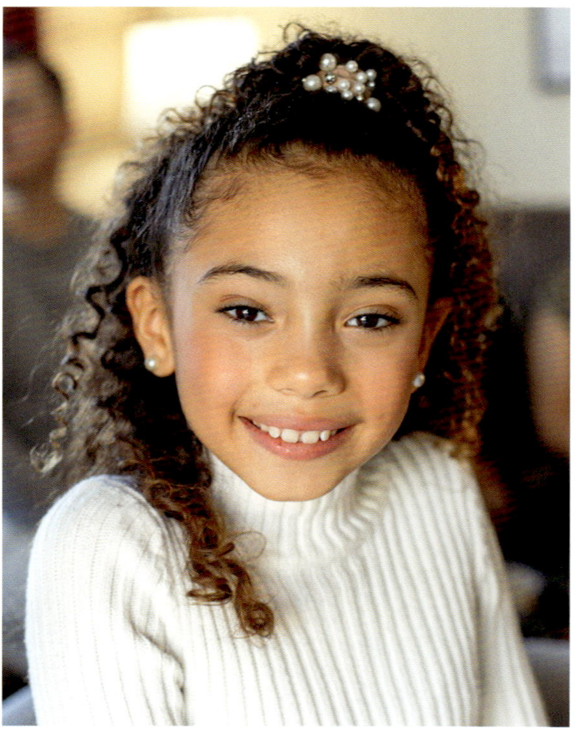

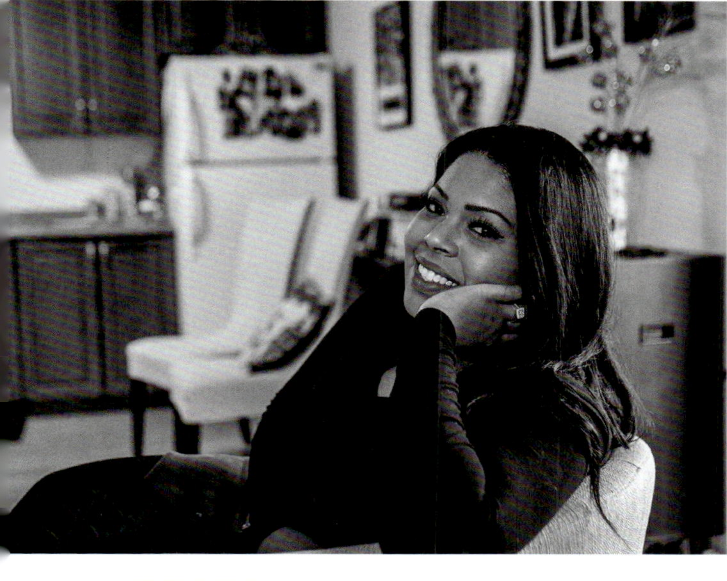

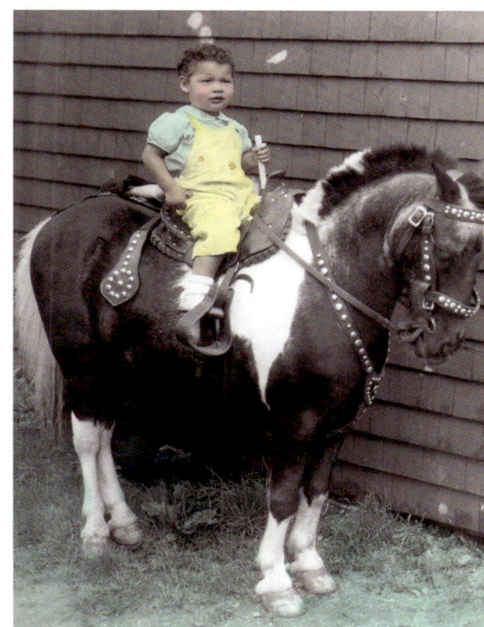

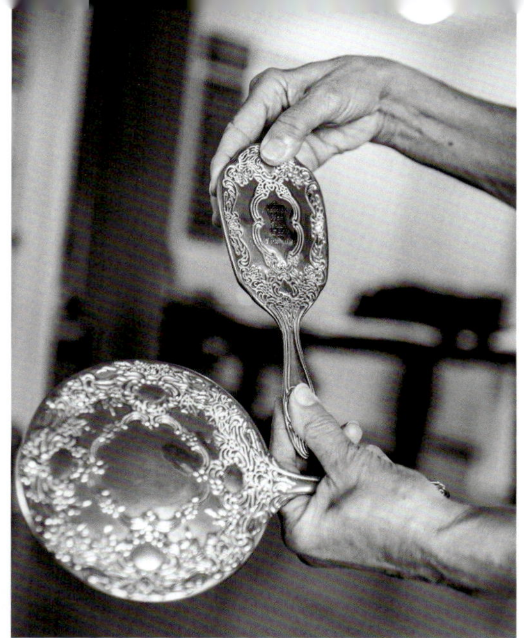

Saturday mornings, I'd go with my mother and my grandmother, Lillian Skinner, to the Saint John City Market. Sometimes people stared at Nannie because she carried her parcels in a basket balanced on her head, but I was always proud to walk with her.
— Paula Skinner-Blizzard

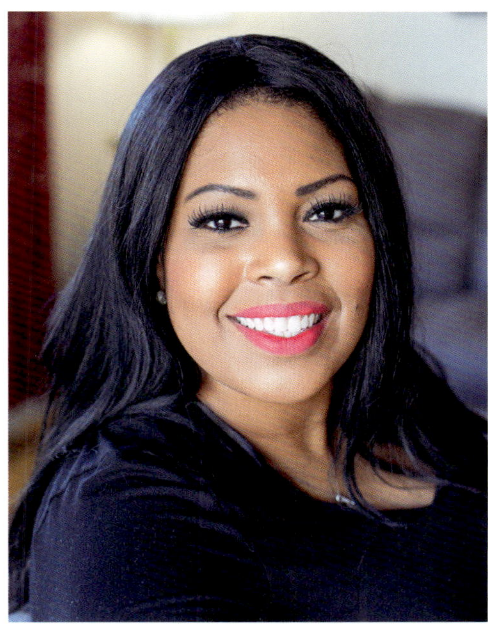

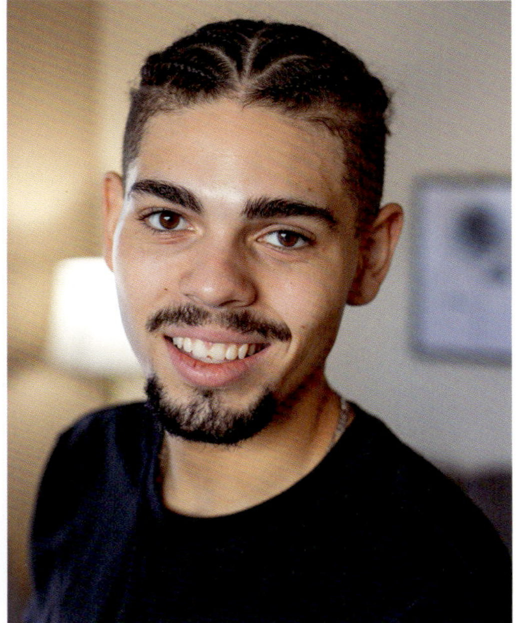

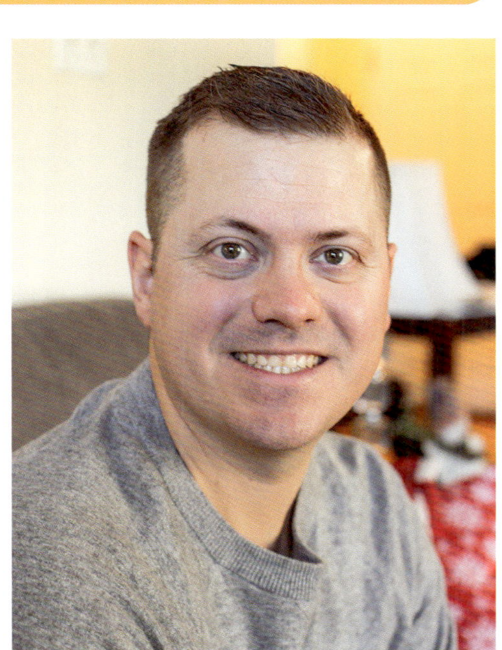

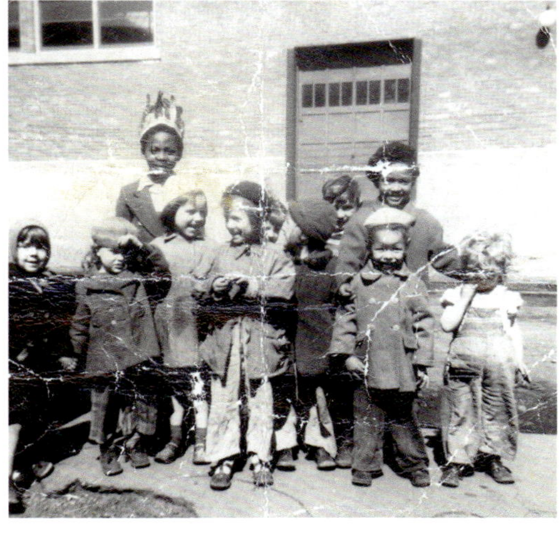

Halfkenny / Cooke — Dorchester, New Brunswick, and Amherst, Nova Scotia

The street that stopped at their property
Doubled as a driveway
An' all the homes around echoed the same family name
A fortress anchoring heritage.

The moment we parked
A tall man threw open the screen door with a wave
That boogied into a handshake.
"Come on in and see the family!"

Inside, the home was alive with laughter.
Ten kids jumping on and off loved ones' laps
Taking breaks from games to have snacks
Then after greetings, the kids ran out, to hopscotch through sun and shade.

The adults unboxed old family records and photos
Harvesting memories down to their roots
Tending the heritage so they can
Pass down timeless stories to the next generation.

Inside the home was a window that showed the kids playing:
A young girl sat in a chair while her cousins lifted it up
Then proceeded to parade her around the courtyard like a queen.
Her giggles wriggled through the walls and triggered smiles.

Children's games of basketball, tag, and mischief made up
All ended in excited shouts and exhausted laughter.
The adults inside the home listened and smiled.
Everyone was winning today.

The first family welcomed us all as kin.
Children poured us water, aunts handed us bug spray, uncles joked about bears.
We were strangers to this family, yet everything from barbecue to bear hugs
Felt so incredibly normal, so wonderfully Black:
That forceful feeling of unforced healing…

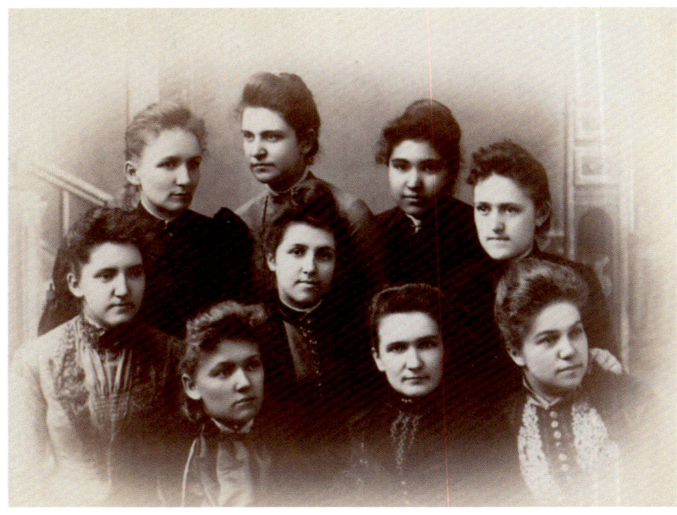

As an eighth-generation descendant of the Halfkenny family, I am constantly learning about the historical significance my ancestors bring into my life. The Halfkenny family has made inroads in various fields, from academia to the music industry. We are a strong, resilient Black family, and the legacy of the Halfkennys continues to inspire us all.
— Elizabeth Cooke-Sumbu

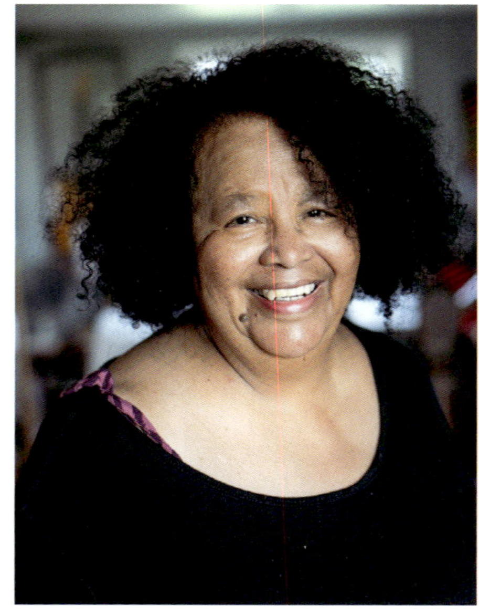

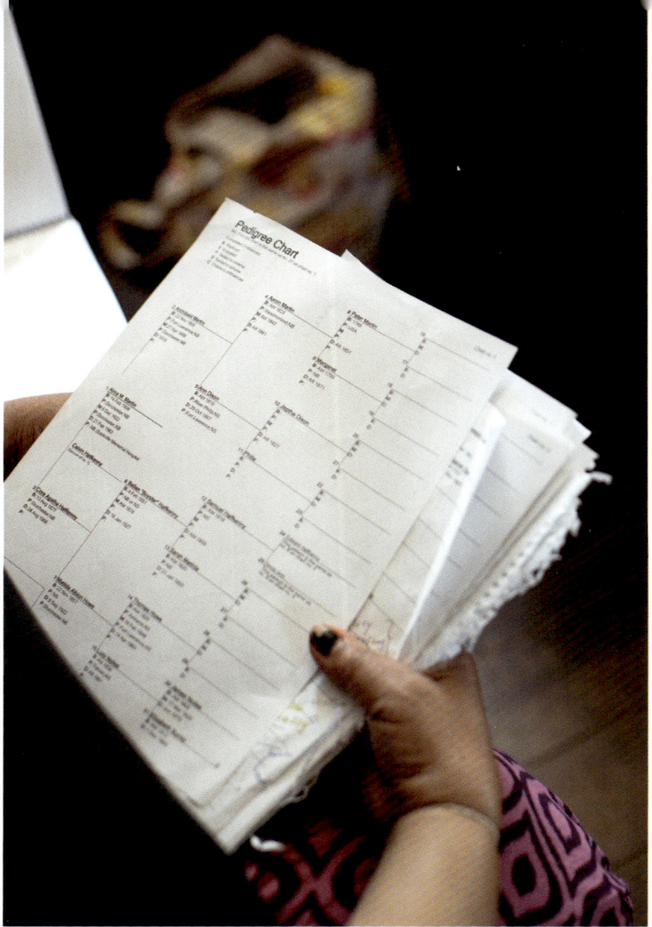

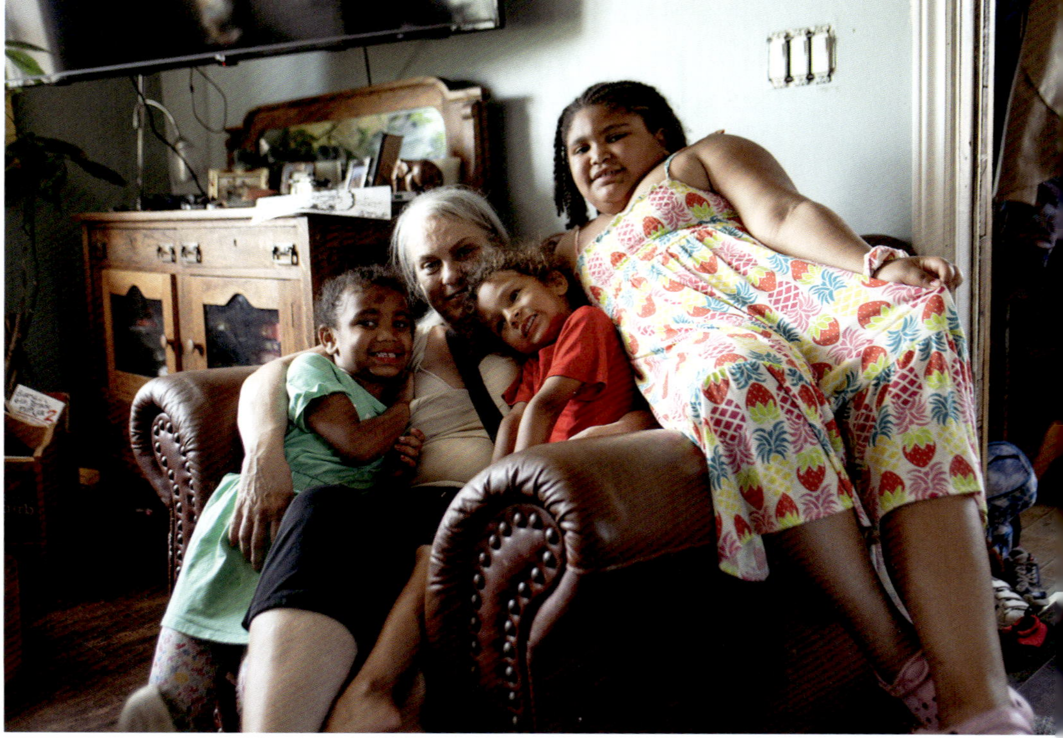

The Halfkenny family's story is one of resilience, entrepreneurial spirit, and a commitment to education, spanning multiple generations. Edward Halfkenny and his wife Simile (in some records spelled Simily, Similie, and Simili) settled in Minudie, Nova Scotia, in the early 1800s. By 1816, Edward, having worked as a tenant farmer, purchased 250 acres of land, marking a significant step toward creating a stable future for his family. His sons, involved in the grindstone industry, eventually migrated to Maine, Boston, and Saint John, New Brunswick, where they worked in the shipping and fishing industries.

The 1851 census recorded Edward's son Samuel and family as "Halfpenny," with a designation of "British American" under Race, which obscures their African Canadian identity during a time of racial categorization and makes tracing their ancestry more challenging. Incomplete and incorrect historical records are a common problem for Black New Brunswickers tracing their roots, as with many populations with histories of oppression and disenfranchisement.

> Each of my ancestors has a story of resilience, triumphing over poverty, homelessness, miseducation, and lack of opportunity. Their struggles became their lifelines, and their challenges turned into their greatest successes.
> — Elizabeth Cooke-Sumbu

Edward prioritized education for the Halfkenny family. His granddaughter Susan Halfkenny attended the segregated School in Elm Hill, as there were no educational institutions available for her in Dorchester. Susan's daughter, Laila Halfkenny, made history as the first African Canadian to graduate from a post-secondary institution in Atlantic Canada, graduating from Acadia Ladies' Seminary in 1889.

William Halfkenny, a landowner of Acadian properties and proprietor of a grindstone, fought several court battles to retain the land legally deeded to him, but he was contested by Acadian families and eventually lost.

More recently, some of the Halfkennys have served in the military. David Robert Halfkenny, born in 1938, enrolled in the Regular Forces as a private in 1955. After posts in northwest Europe in the 1960s, London and Cyprus in the 1970s, and various positions teaching at bases in Ontario and New Brunswick, he became a captain in 1980 and was promoted to major, after thirty years of service, in 1985. When he retired in 1997, he had received a United Nations Medal, a Queen's Jubilee Medal, a Special Service Medal, and the Canadian Forces' Decoration and second clasp, and had been appointed to the rank of Member of the Order of Military Merit.

All four of David's brothers also served in the Canadian Forces, including Lionel, who served in Korea from 1952 to 1953 and was wounded while defending against an attack on Hill 355. In the next generation, David's son followed in his footsteps with a long military career of his own, retiring as a commander in the navy after thirty-six years of service, and his daughter—David's granddaughter—is a navigator on a warship. All exemplify the family's legacy of perseverance.

The Halfkenny family boasts notable accomplishments, including jazz legend Max "the Sax" Lucas, considered an American treasure, who grew up in Harlem, and played with Ella Fitzgerald, Billie Holiday, the Louis Armstrong Orchestra, and even for his own ninety-ninth birthday party in 2010, shortly before he died.

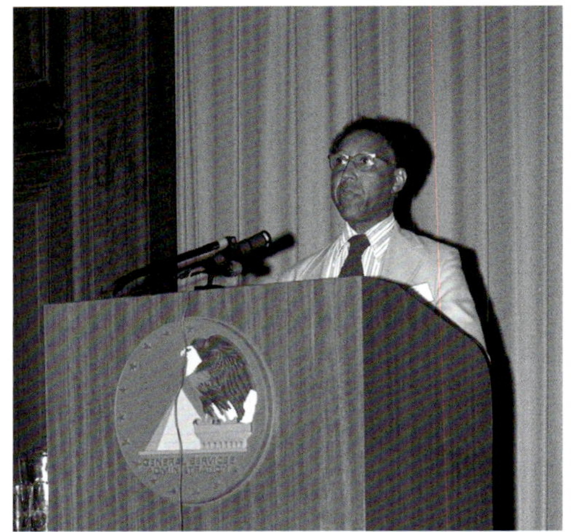

Max's mother, Lena Halfkenny, was the first Black hairdresser to own a salon in Amherst, Nova Scotia. And Roland McConnell (Halfkenny), an African American activist and author, was awarded his PhD from New York University in 1945, further exemplifying the family's contributions to society.

Today, the Halfkenny family's descendants live across Canada, the United States, and beyond, continuing a legacy of community leadership, music, activism, and entrepreneurship that impacts generations worldwide. Their story is a testament to perseverance, education, and making a positive difference.

> Earlier generations of Halfkenny men carried a heavy burden—a chip on their shoulder—but certainly with just cause. Life was not easy for Black people. Yet, in some cases, their families found a way out, determined to overcome the hardships life threw at them.
> —Elizabeth Cooke-Sumbu

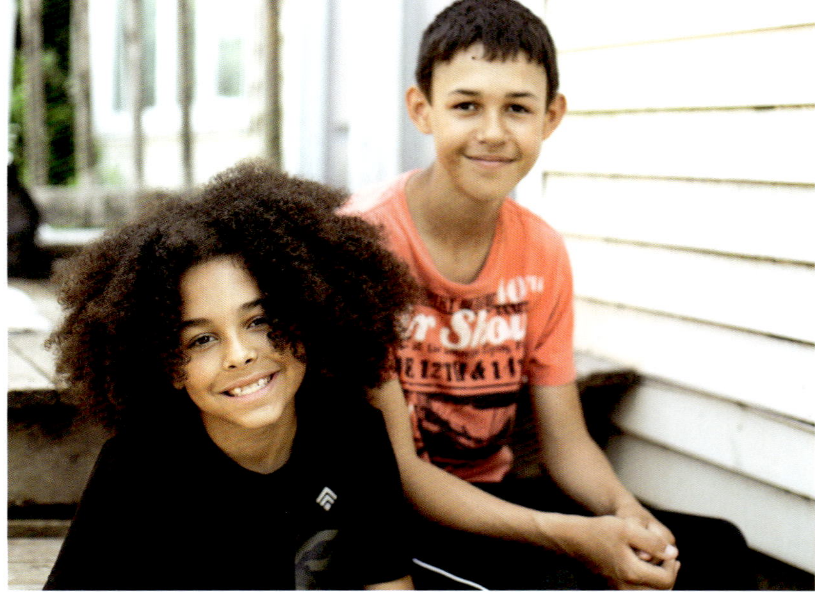

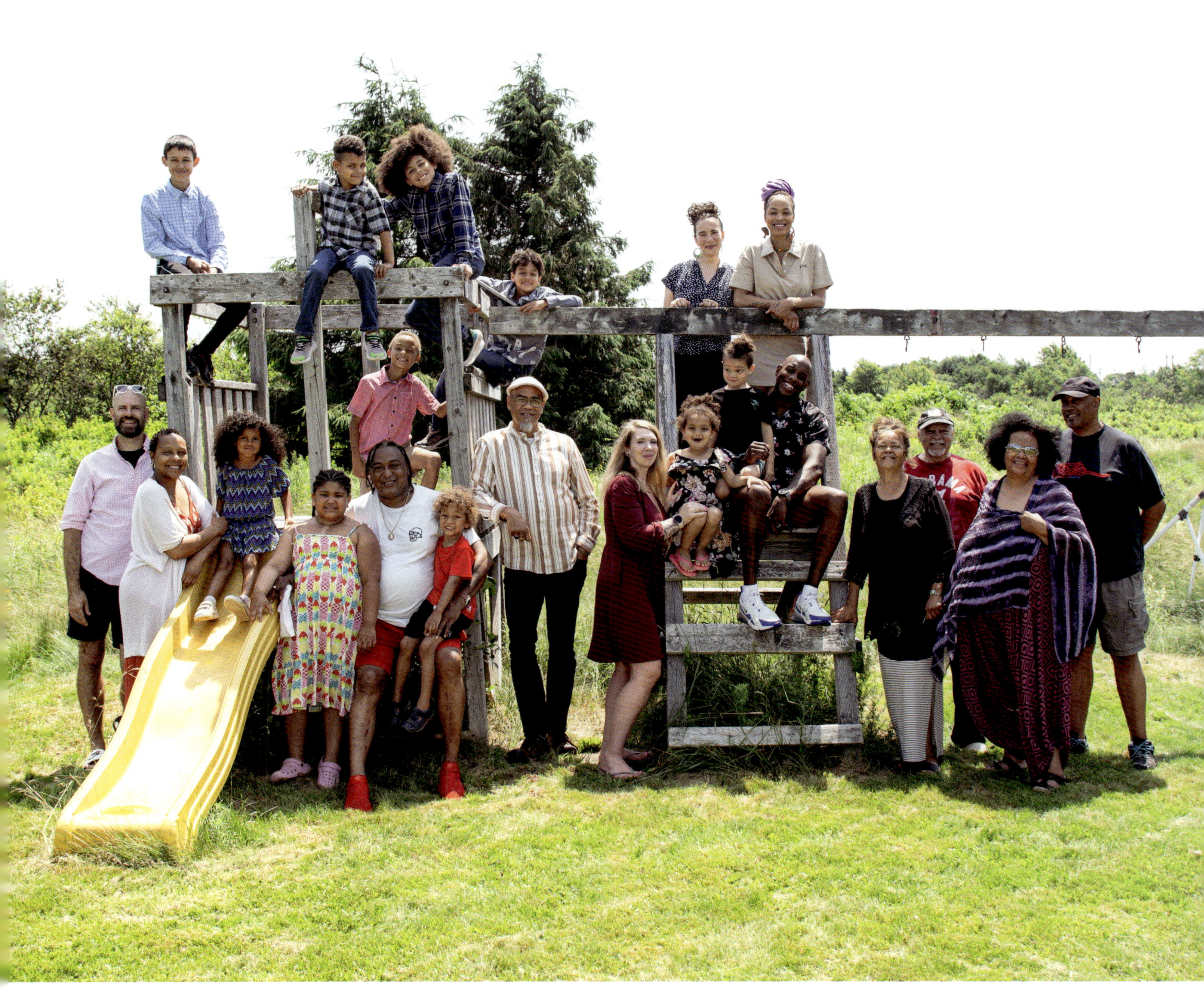

Halfkenny / Cooke — Dorchester, New Brunswick, and Amherst, Nova Scotia

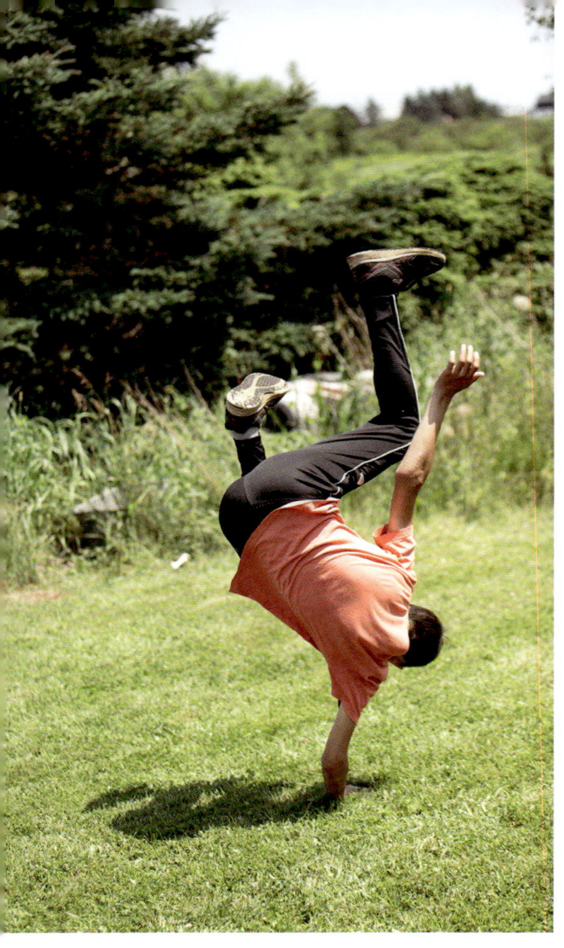

Mom was a favourite among her siblings, and whenever they had the chance, whether on leave from the army or traveling from Ontario or Maine, they would visit my parents' home, which is where I reside today. Although our family had little in the day, a warm home, food, and conversation made their visits pleasant.
— Elizabeth Cooke-Sumbu

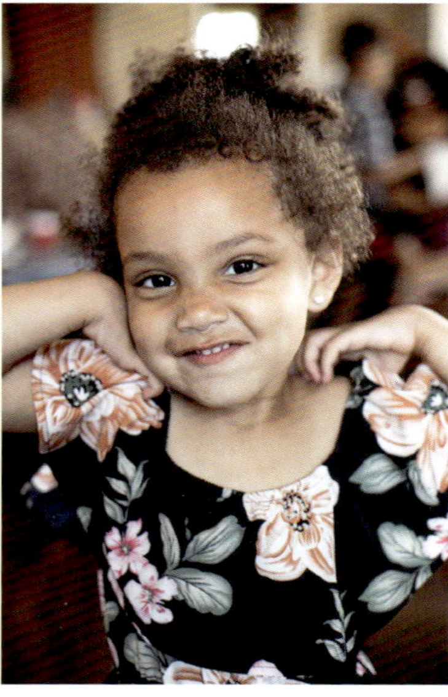

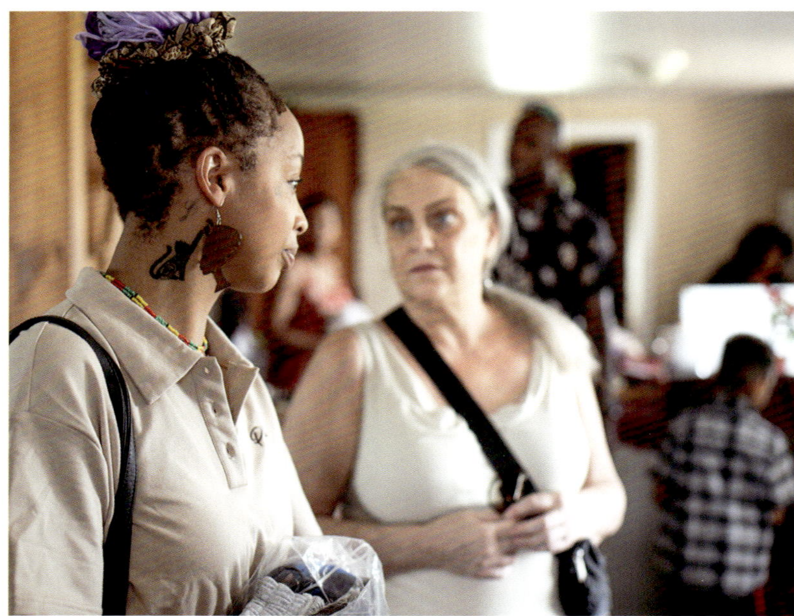

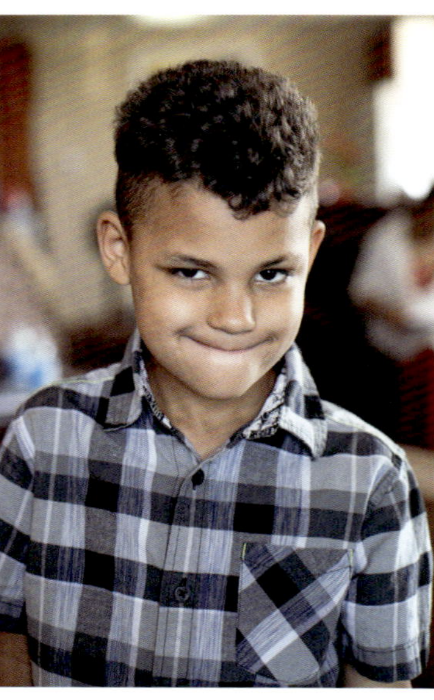

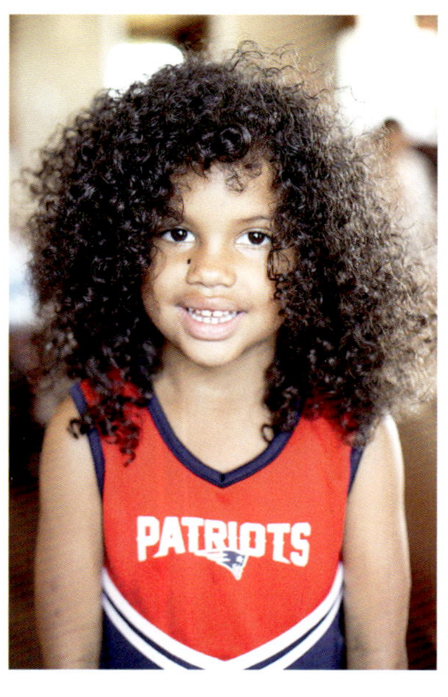

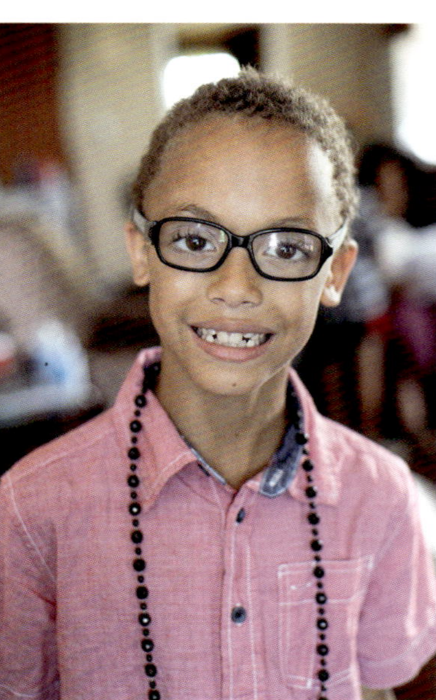

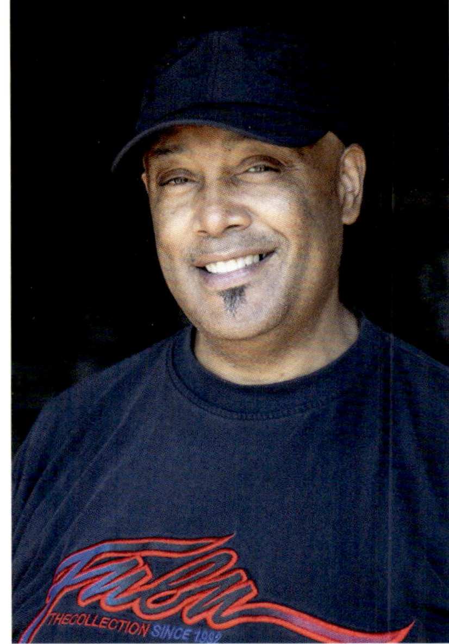

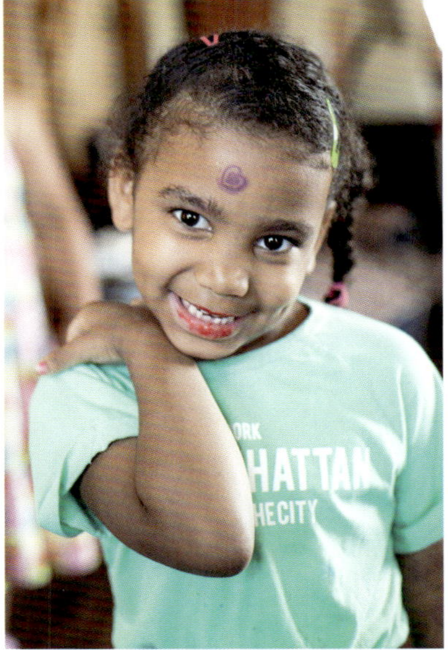

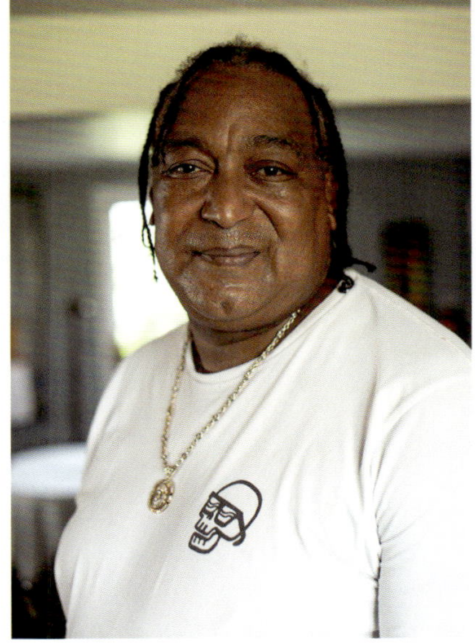

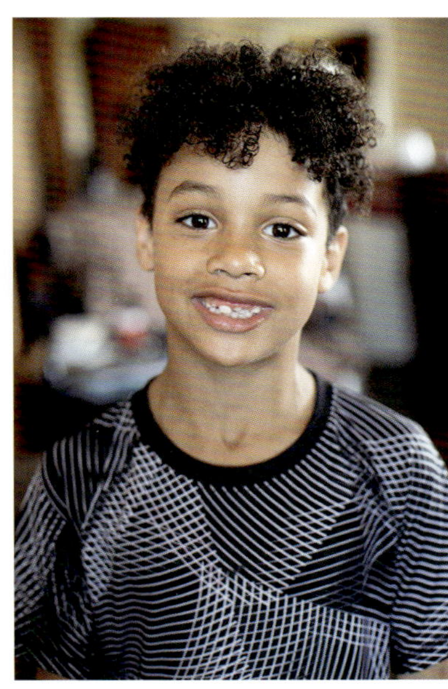

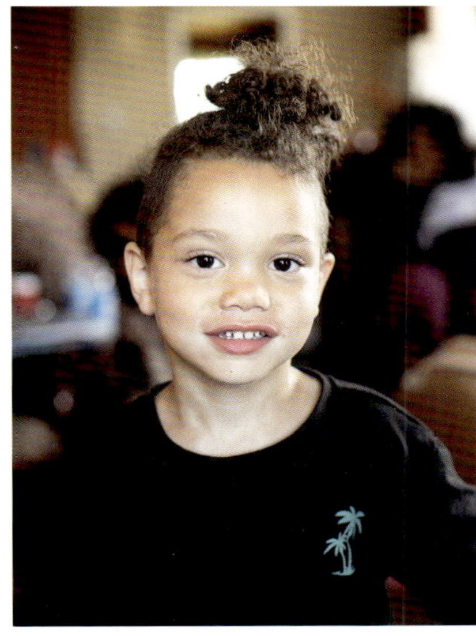

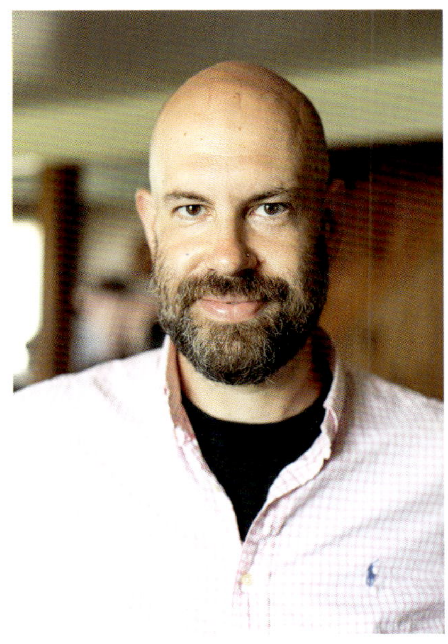

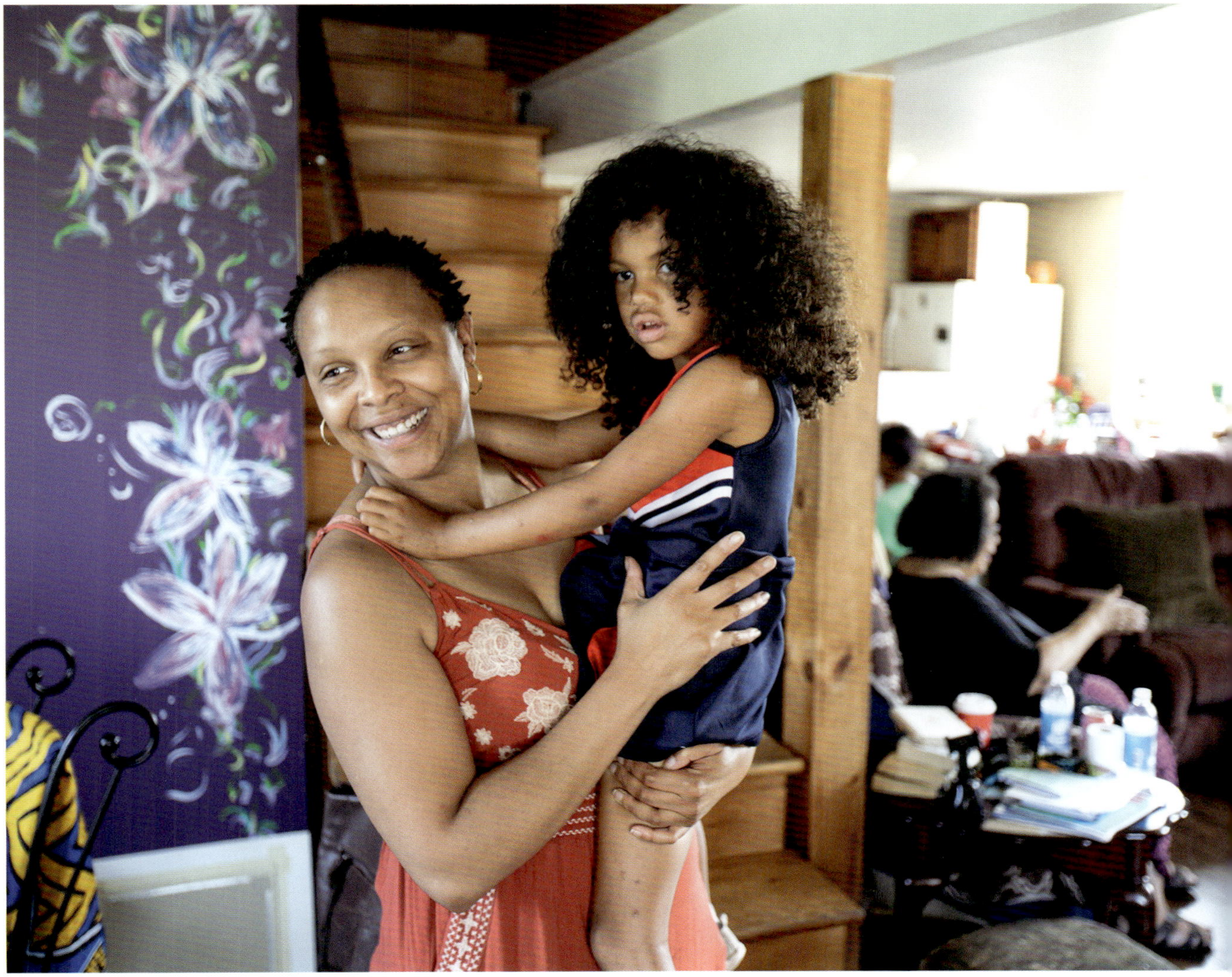

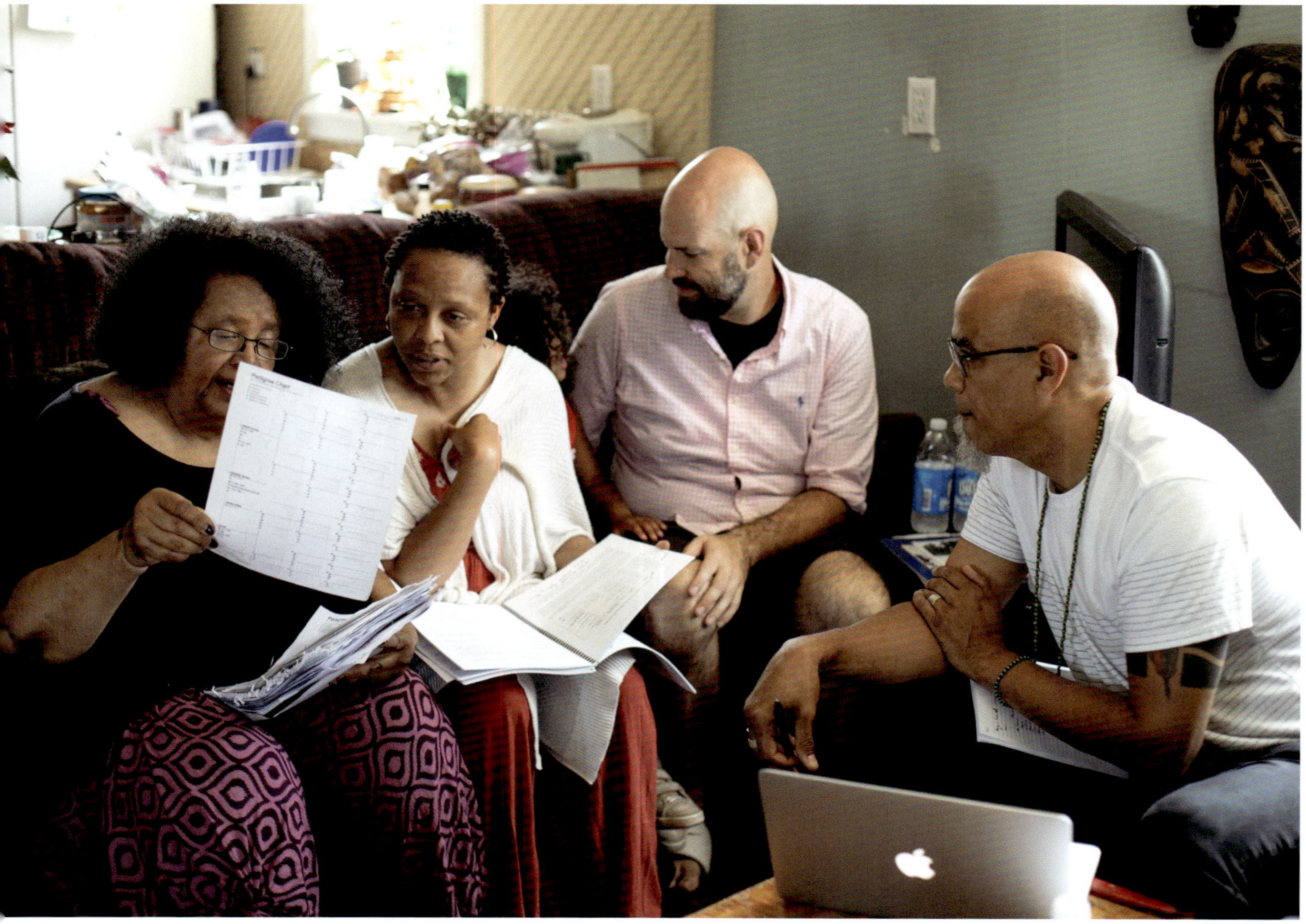

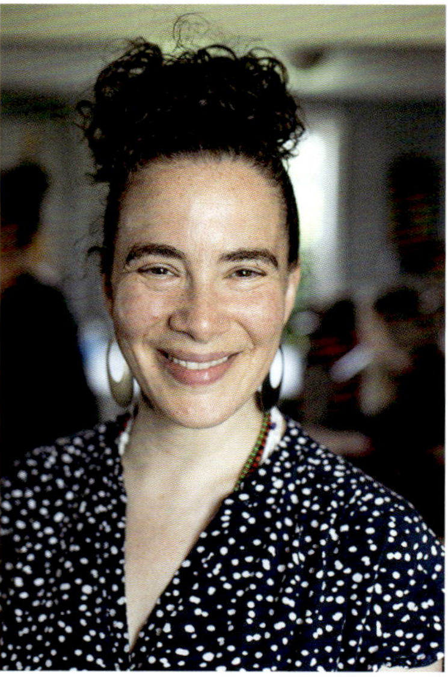

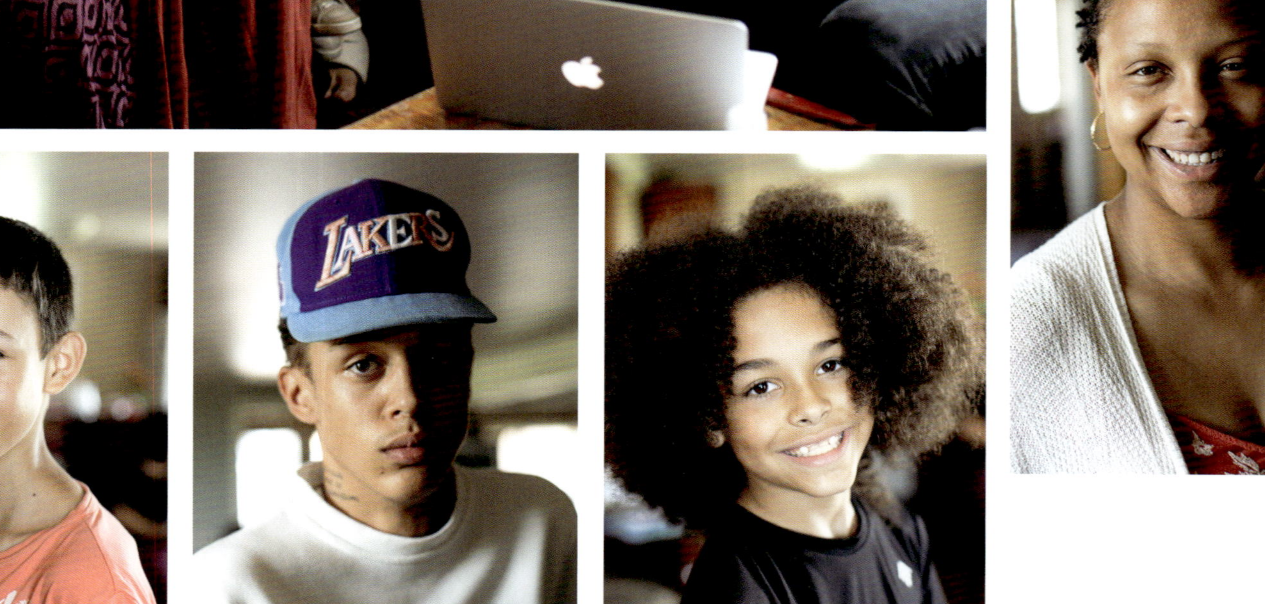
LAKERS

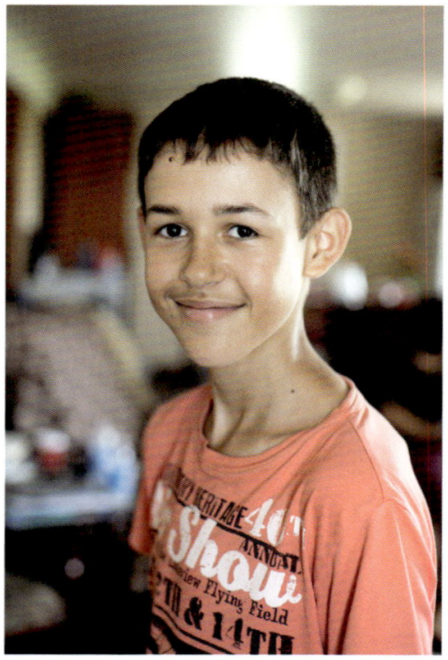

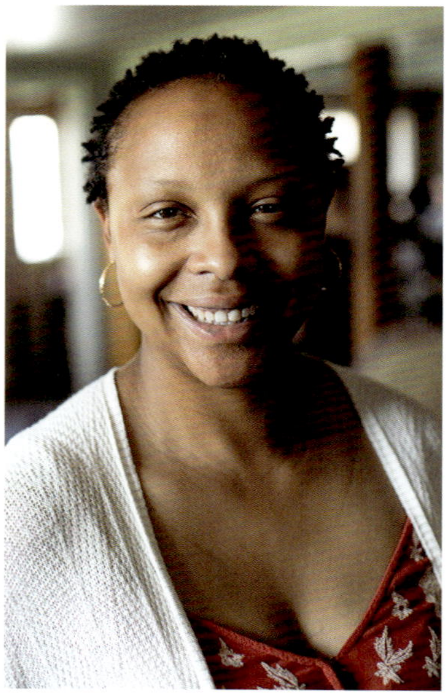

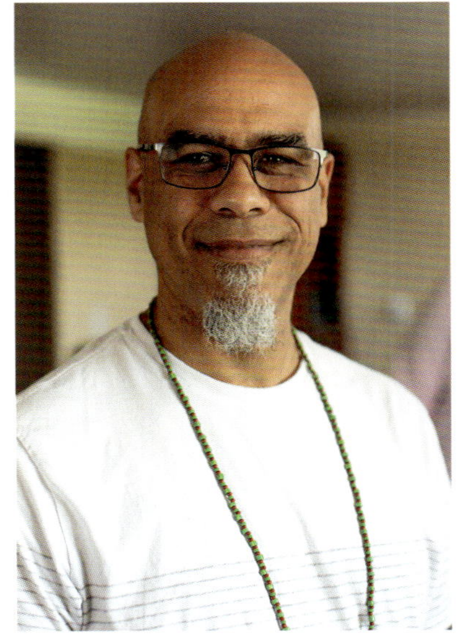
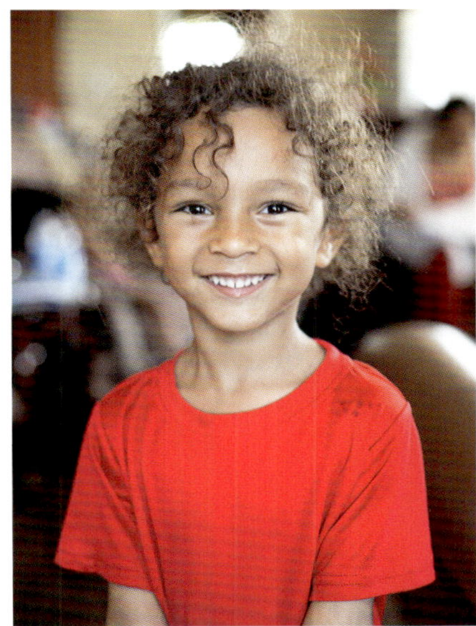
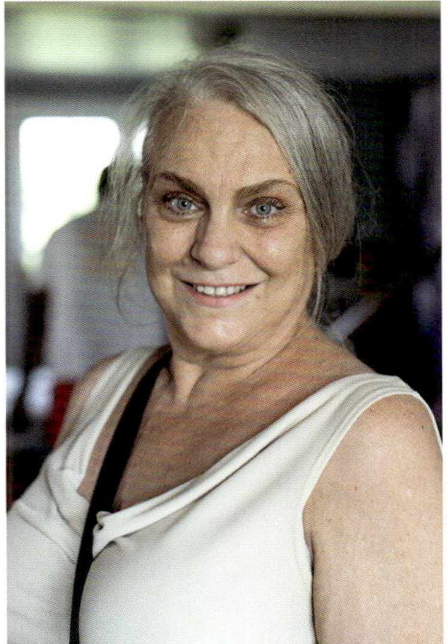
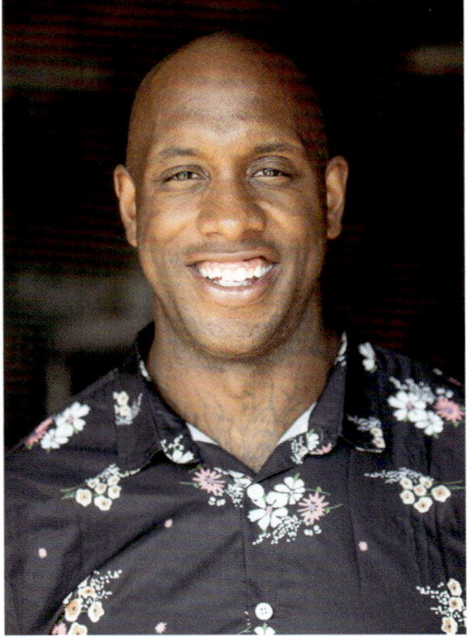
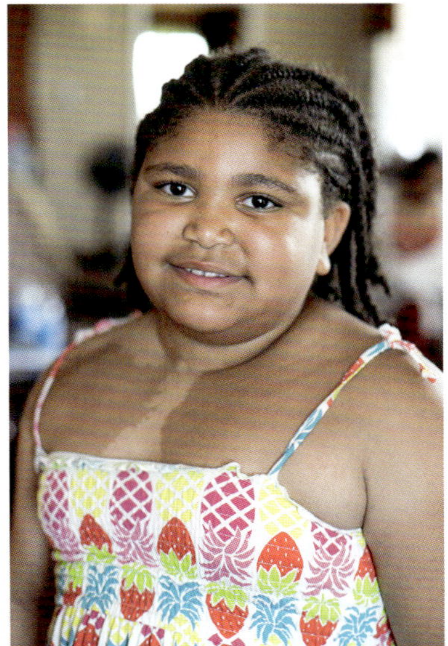
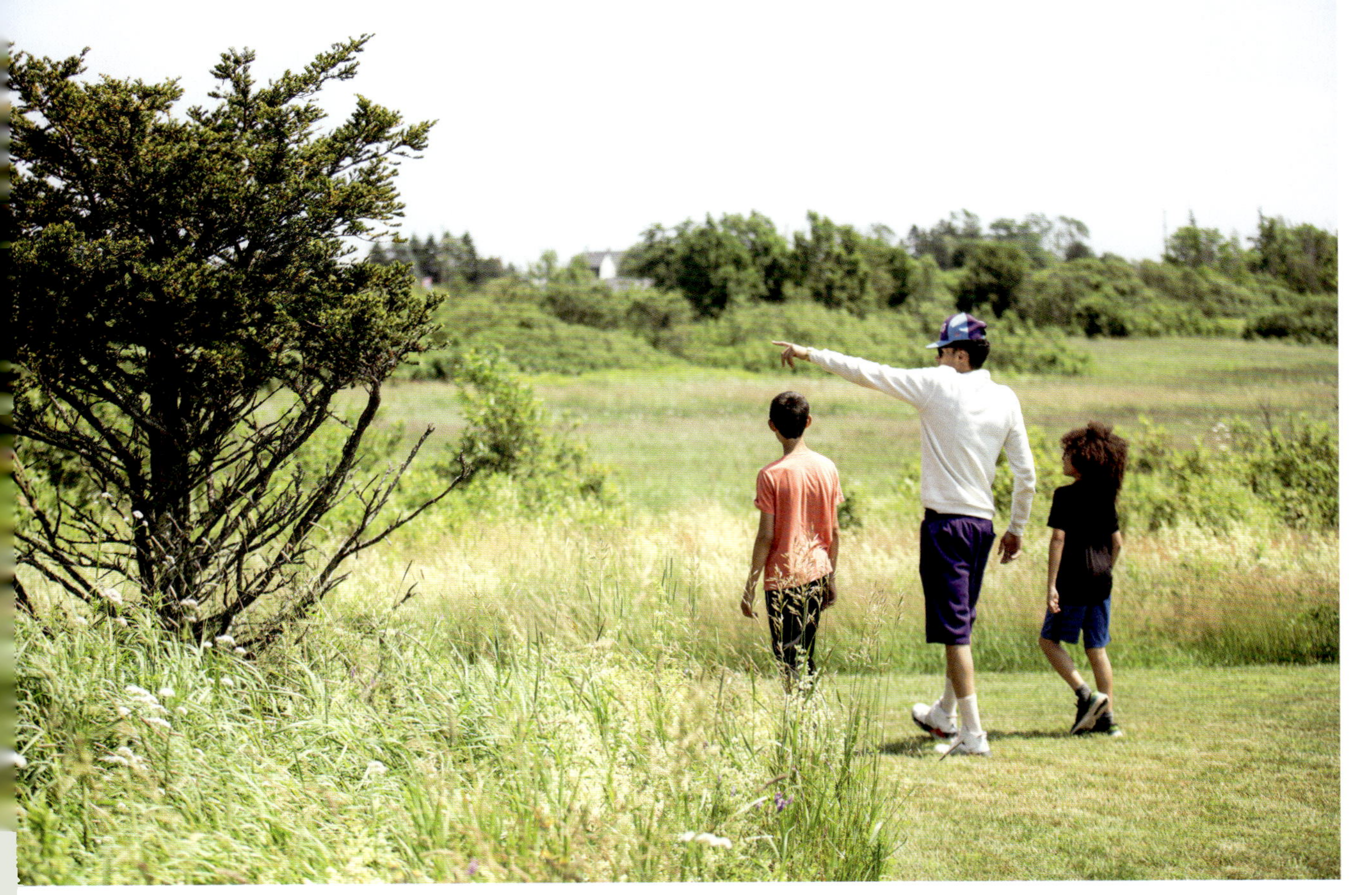
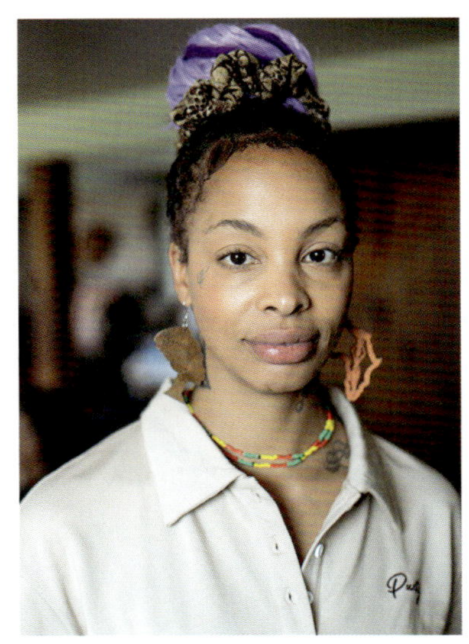

Drummond / Leslie — Willow Grove and Saint John

Deep in Willow Grove, New Brunswick
We thought we were lost.
The road shifted from concrete
To grumbling gravel, then finally to bumpy grass.
This was heritage land.

Three homes: two sisters and two brothers
Settled this street.
A British King had allotted their ancestors this land
Over a century ago.
They still kept the deed.
The sisters had shared a home for decades.
They phoned their brothers every day, and if they didn't pick up?
They'd march down the road to check on their well-being.
To them, family was the holiest blessing.

The photo shoot took over the sisters' home.
The dog and cat wandered outside
Sidling between tree stumps
Decorated with children's toys and figurines.
The front deck was lavishly decorated with chairs and welcome signs.
The porch doubled as a living room
Where everyone was welcome.

The family offered us homemade whiskey and freezies
Stripped family photos from walls for us to scan.
We were treated — indisputably — like kin.

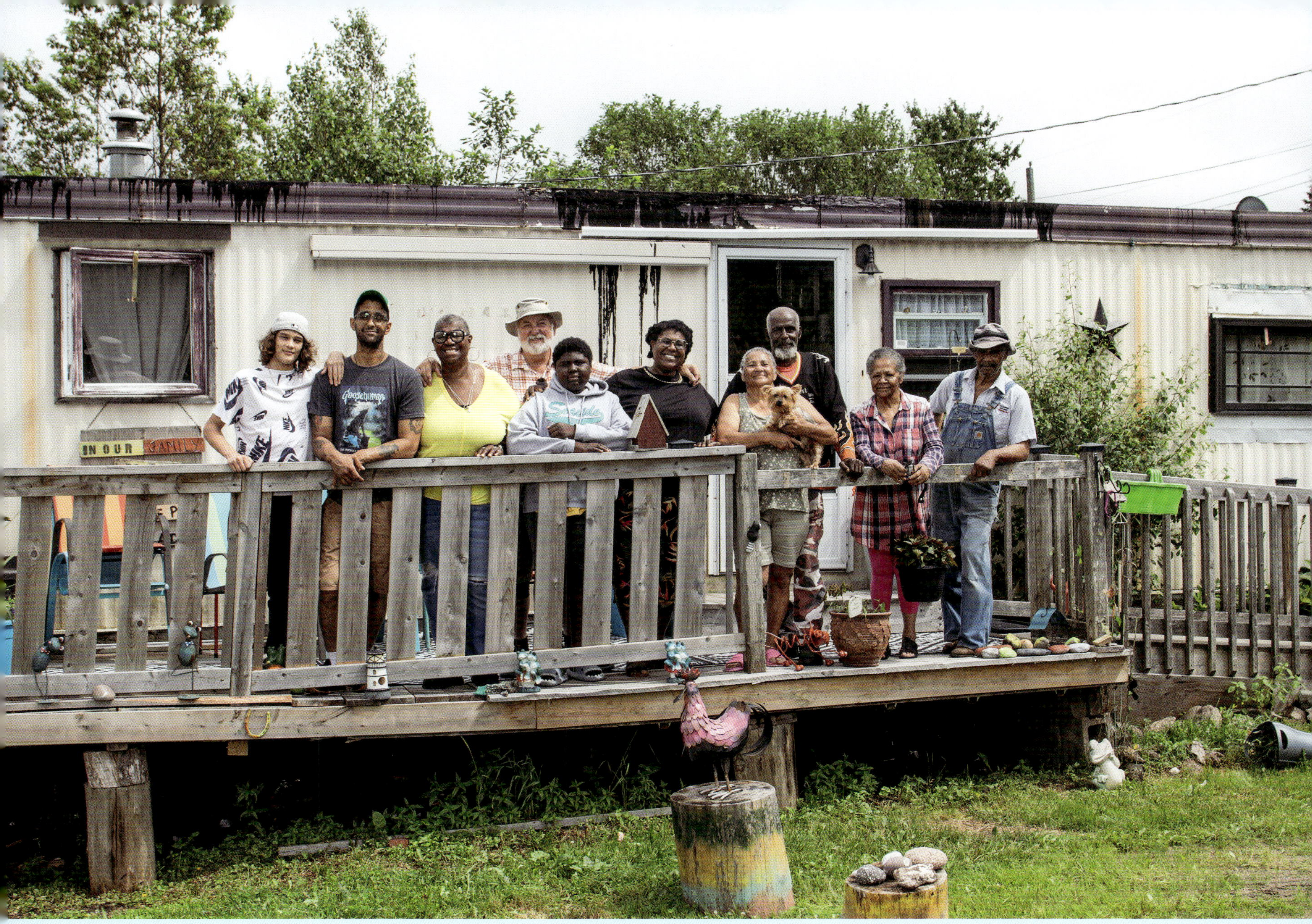

We'd thought we were lost
But we'd merely come home
From concrete to gravel
To grass:
A heritage not yet bulldozed
nor folded away in the archives.

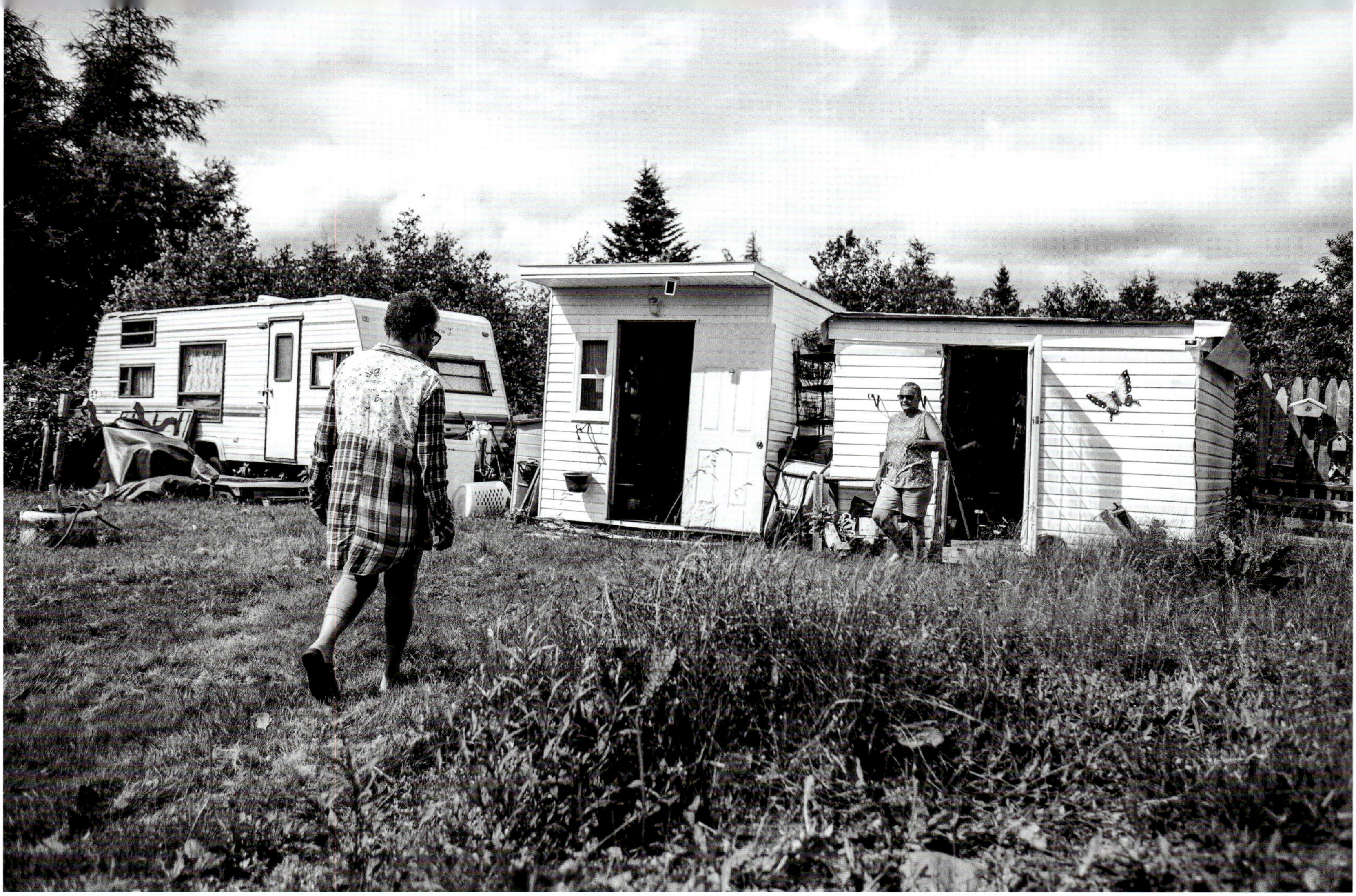

We still reside on the same parcel of land that was granted to Black Loyalists in the 1880s. This land has not left my family's hands since then. We have raised generations of our family on this land. I have walked this land with my father and now I walk it with my son. My son will walk this land with his sons.
— Naomi Drummond

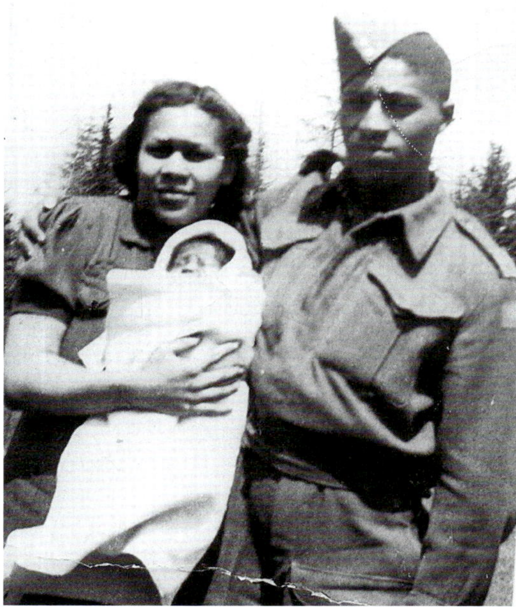

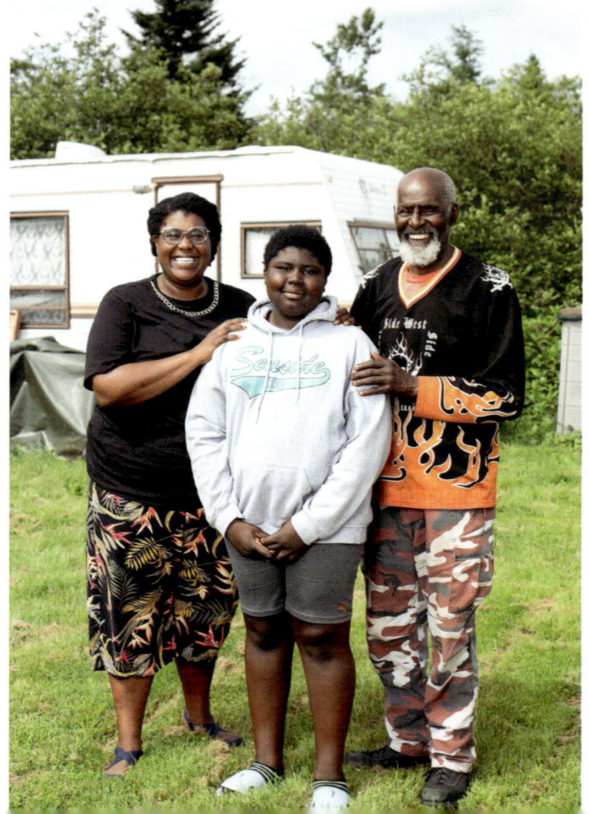

The Leslie side of Naomi Drummond's family are direct descendants of the Black Loyalists who helped build the province, and they can date their history back to the land grants of the early 1800s. Some of the Leslies still live on the property they were granted at Willow Grove. The family is full of scholars and skilled workers who will continue to love and care for their land for generations to come.

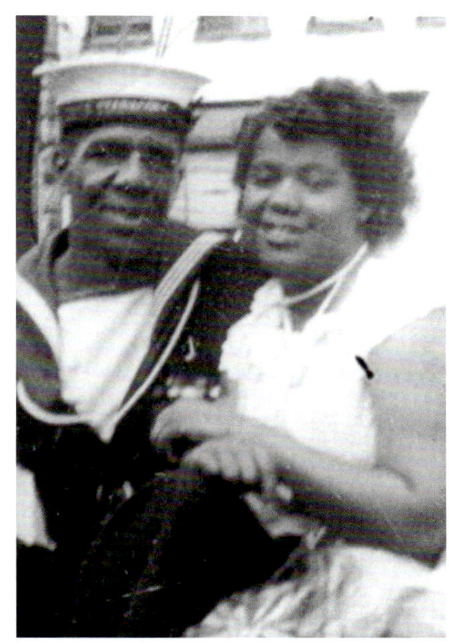

The Drummonds from Saint John are also an integral part of New Brunswick's Black history. Joseph Drummond worked hard to unite the Black community in Saint John, beginning in the 1960s. He cofounded the New Brunswick Association for the Advancement of Coloured People, created the Black Community Phonebook, helped imprisoned members of the community gain employment upon release, and was one of the key researchers—and wrote the foreword—for W.A. Spray's *The Blacks in New Brunswick*. Drummond is perhaps best known for organizing a 1964 sit-in at a Haymarket Square barbershop in Saint John, protesting the owner's refusal to cut the hair of Black customers. Media coverage brought national attention to the need for discussions about systemic racism, which eventually led to legislation regarding fair employment standards.

In the 1970s, Joe and his wife, Verna, began the Annual Black Picnic and Dance. Verna was also a founding member of the Women's Auxiliary of the Black Community (WABC), which hosted harvest dinners and teas. She was a longtime volunteer at Romero House, among other charities, and received the Queen's Jubilee Medal for service.

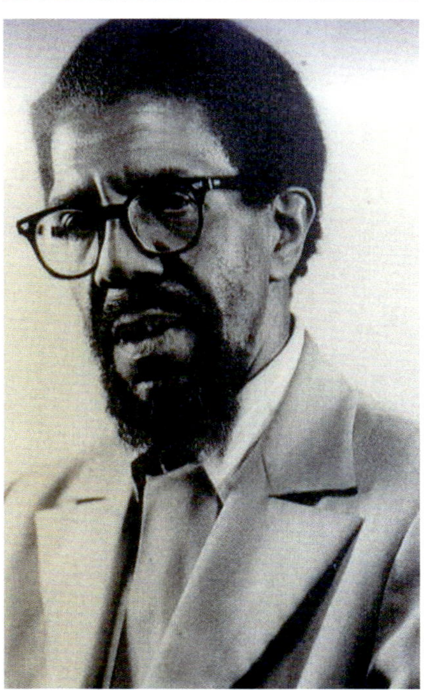

Naomi, Joe and Verna's granddaughter, grew up helping with many of their events from the time she was very young, and she is now a leader, a public speaker, and a proud Black woman who honours her family legacies.

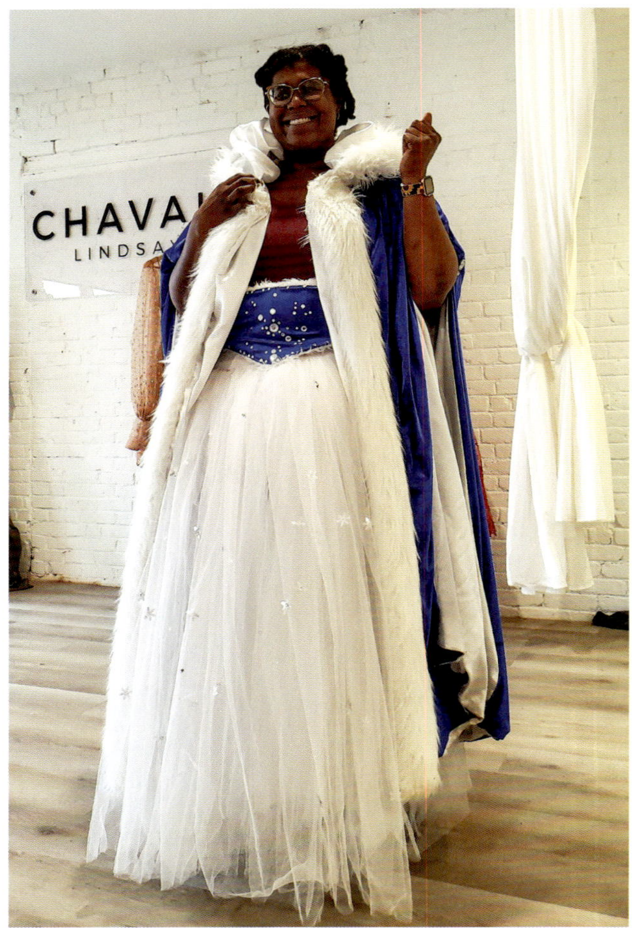

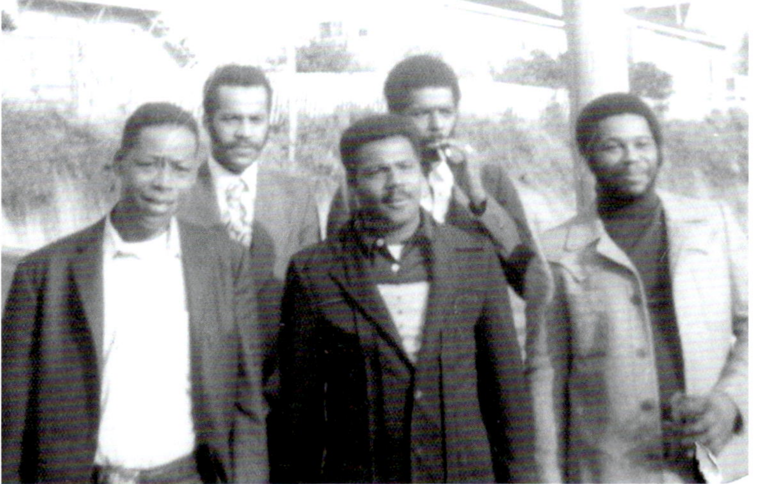

I was the first Black Ms. Sparkles, for Saint John's Uptown Sparkles 2022, ensuring the kids got to see a princess that looked like them. It's important that we see ourselves reflected in our everyday life. I will continue to be an inspiration for future generations the same way I was inspired by my family before me. I am honoured to be a Drummond-Leslie.
— Naomi Drummond

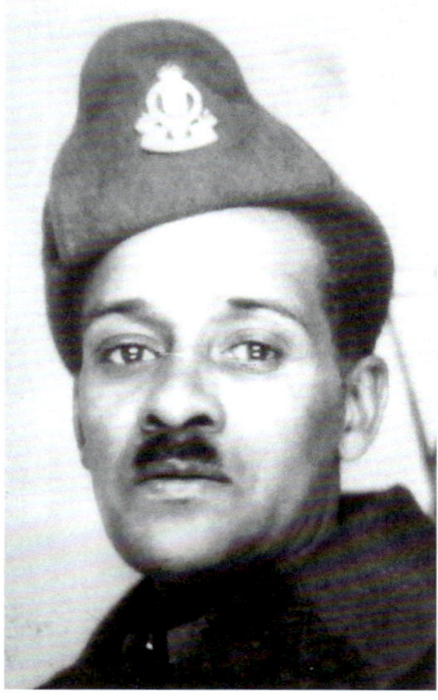

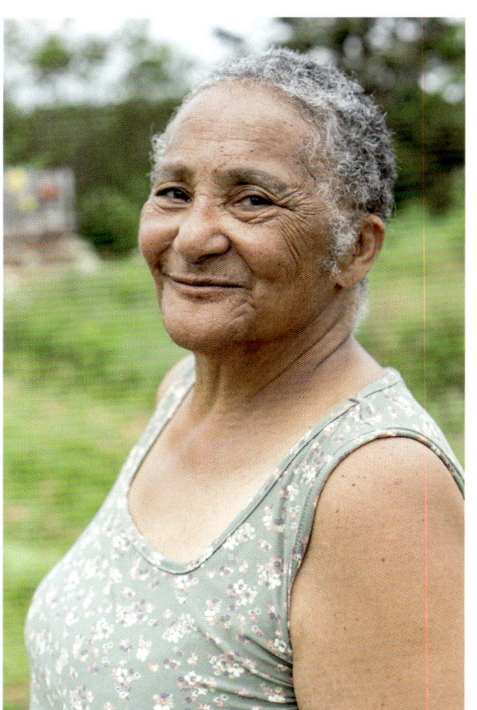

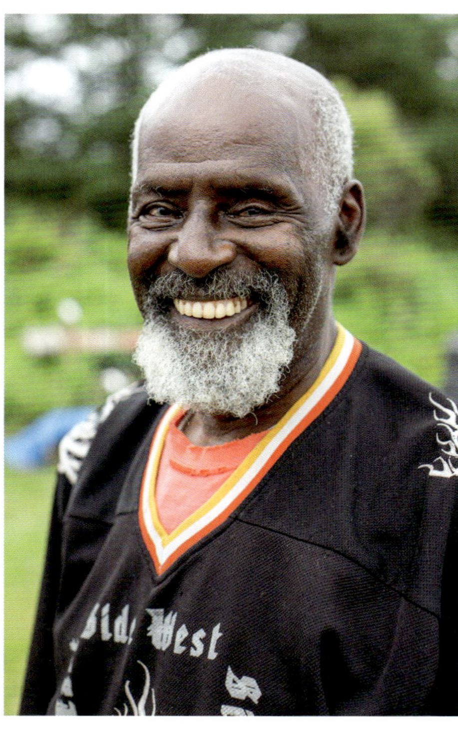

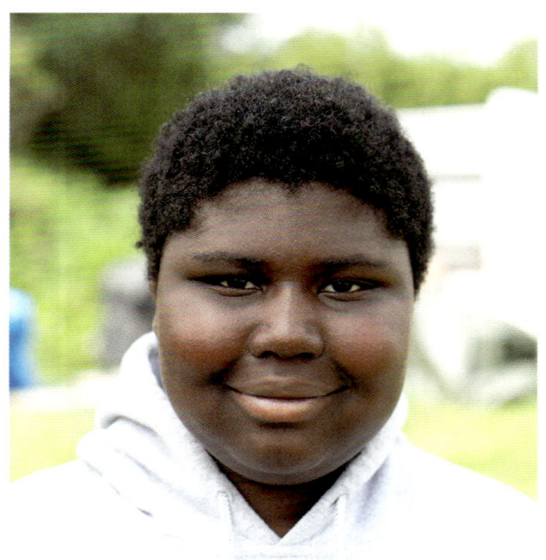

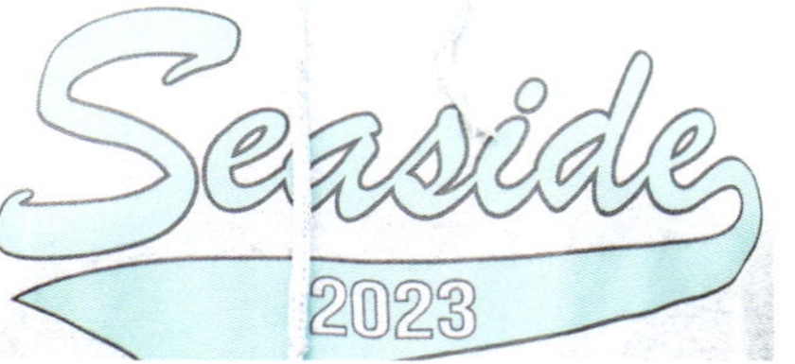

Now that I am older and the original members have passed, I have helped revitalize the WABC, now named the Women's Auxiliary of the Black Community Jr. We promote events like the Annual Black Picnic and Dance and the Senior's Tea, where we celebrate the Black community in Saint John.
— Naomi Drummond

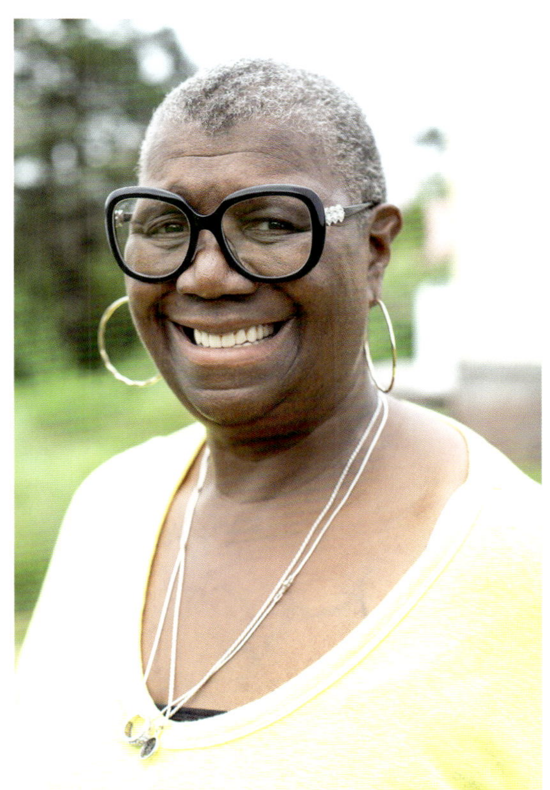

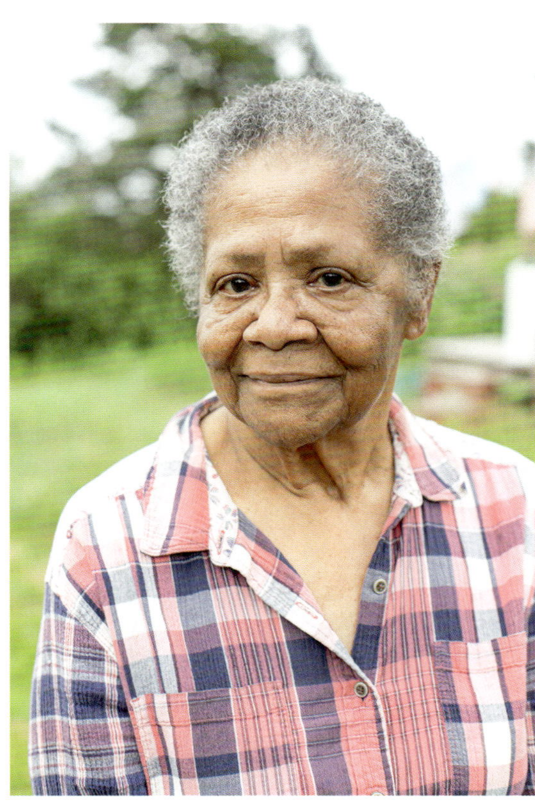

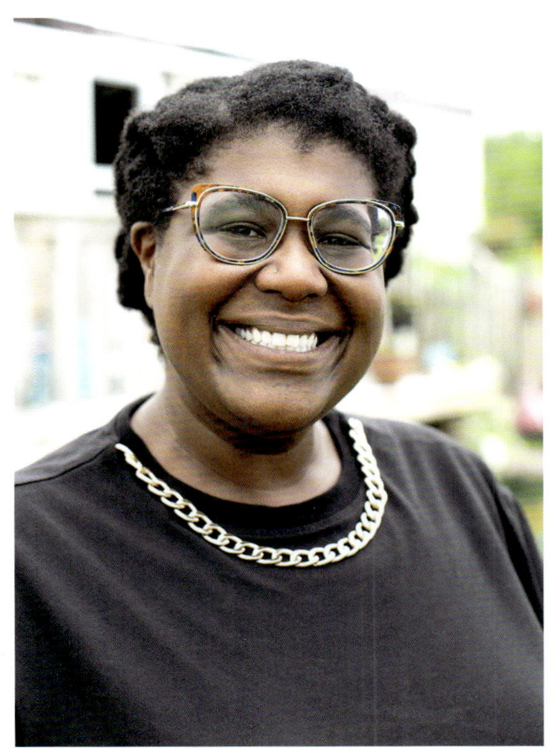

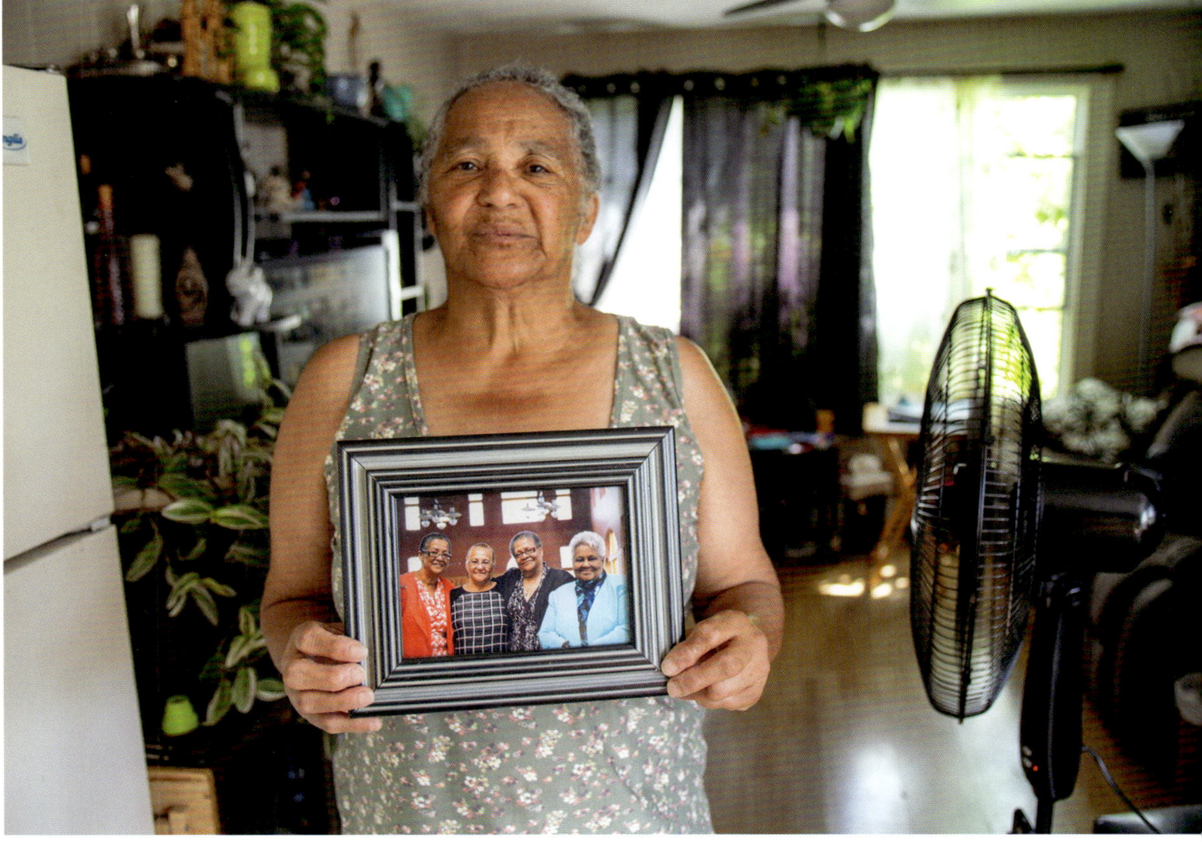

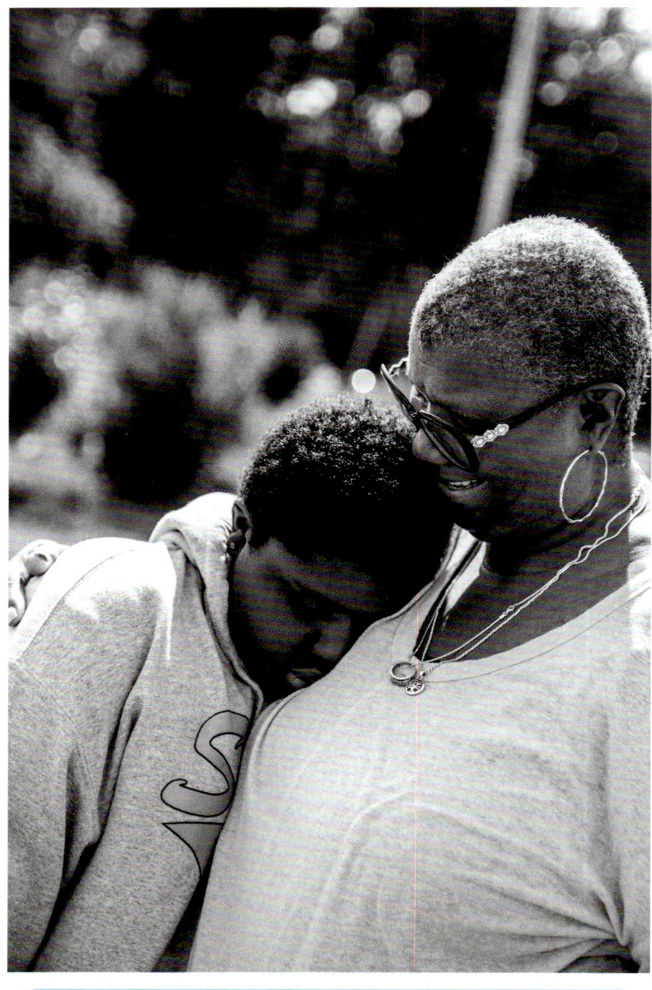

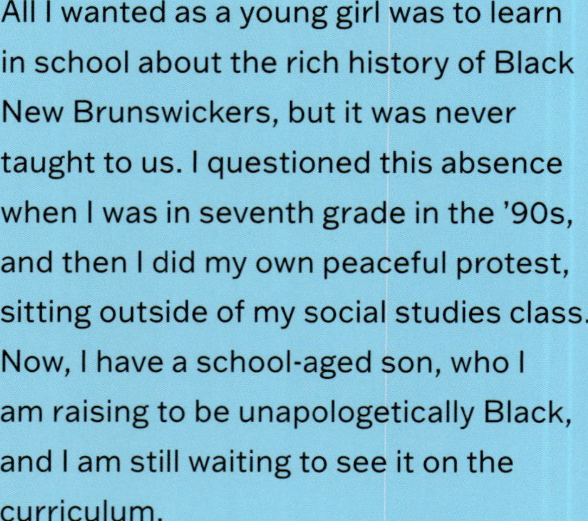

All I wanted as a young girl was to learn in school about the rich history of Black New Brunswickers, but it was never taught to us. I questioned this absence when I was in seventh grade in the '90s, and then I did my own peaceful protest, sitting outside of my social studies class. Now, I have a school-aged son, who I am raising to be unapologetically Black, and I am still waiting to see it on the curriculum.

— Naomi Drummond

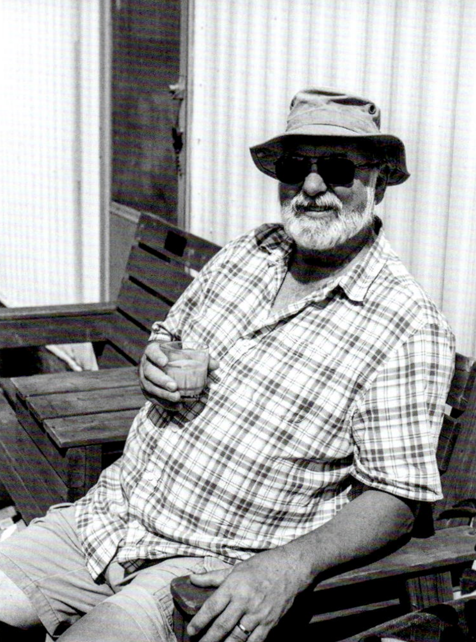

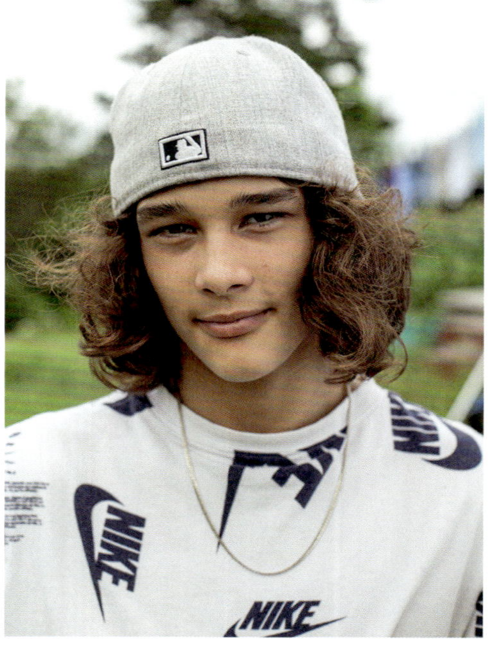

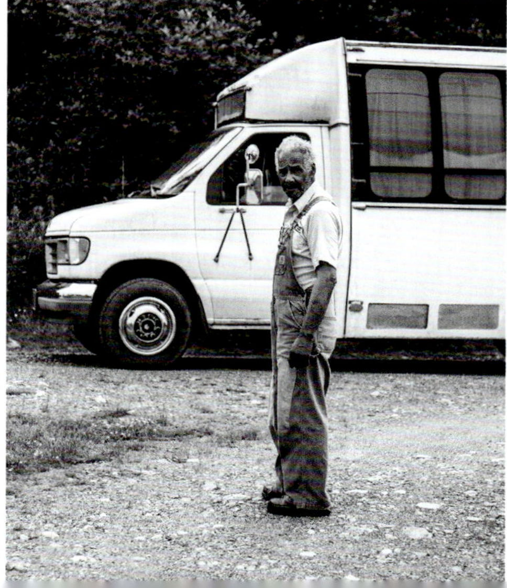

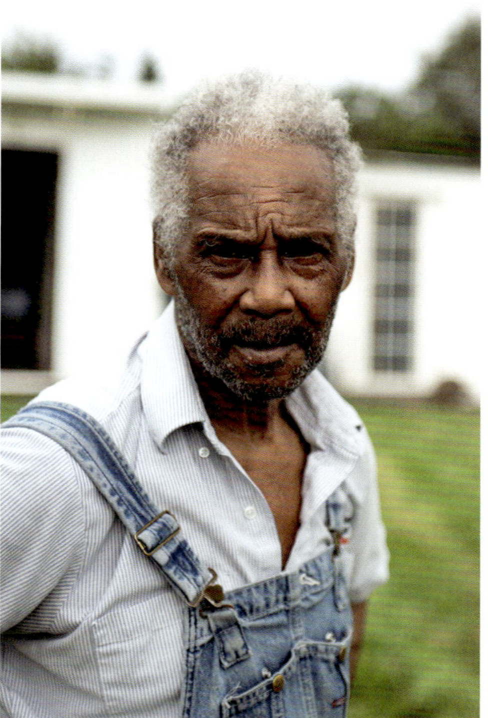

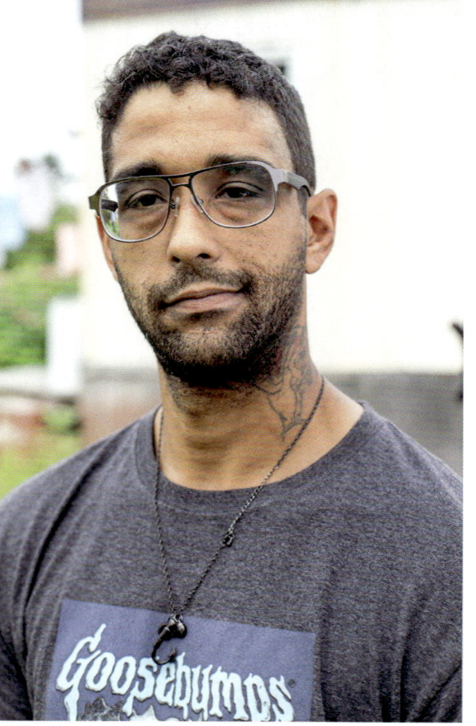

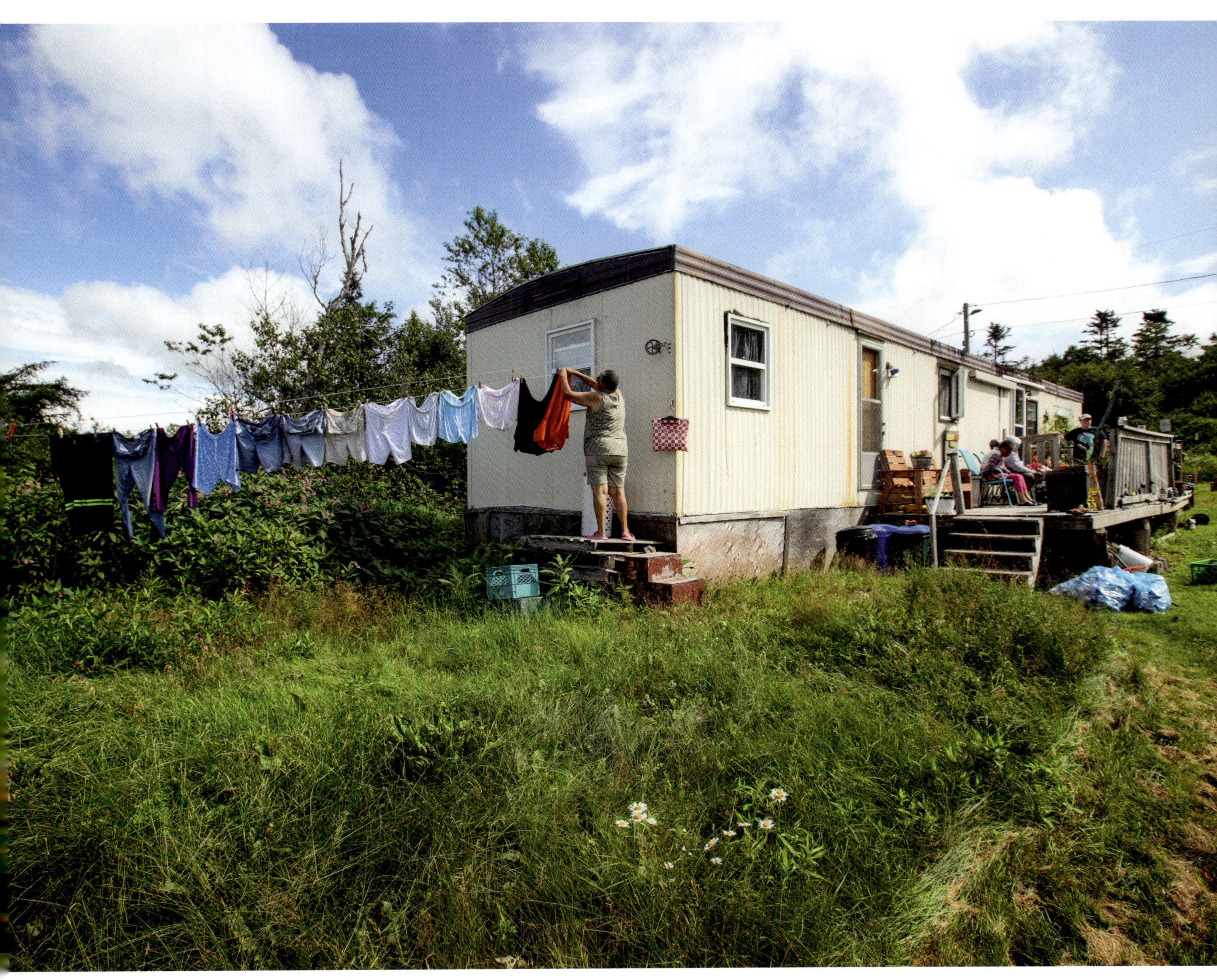

McCarthy / Leek / Dymond / Johnson — Woodstock

The day began with a heist in Woodstock, NB:
A mission to steal a smile from an aunt,
Who now avoids gatherings with family
For fear she'll make uncomfortable waves.

Well, I believe the extinction of a marriage
Is never an eviction notice from a family.
When decades of devotion have been spent
Cherishing in holidays, birthdays, and babysitting children.

When other heritages marry into the family
We must always welcome them to the table.
For if we cannot come together under one love
We are doomed to break apart over any emotion.

Once at the McCarthy home, hugs greeted us,
And the barbeque was fired up as the photo albums came out.
Laughter catches in one corner of the room
Then engulfs the entire home—in a blaze of ivory.

The purple walls tremble with roars of joy,
A high sustained by multiple conversations,
Voices lifting in a giant game of jump rope.
So we hop in and out of banter and belly laughs.

Ain't this what it means to boogie-woogie?
To dance from "Happy Birthday" to "Remember when"?
To feel the shiver down the spine that says,
"We're the right people — at home in the right place."

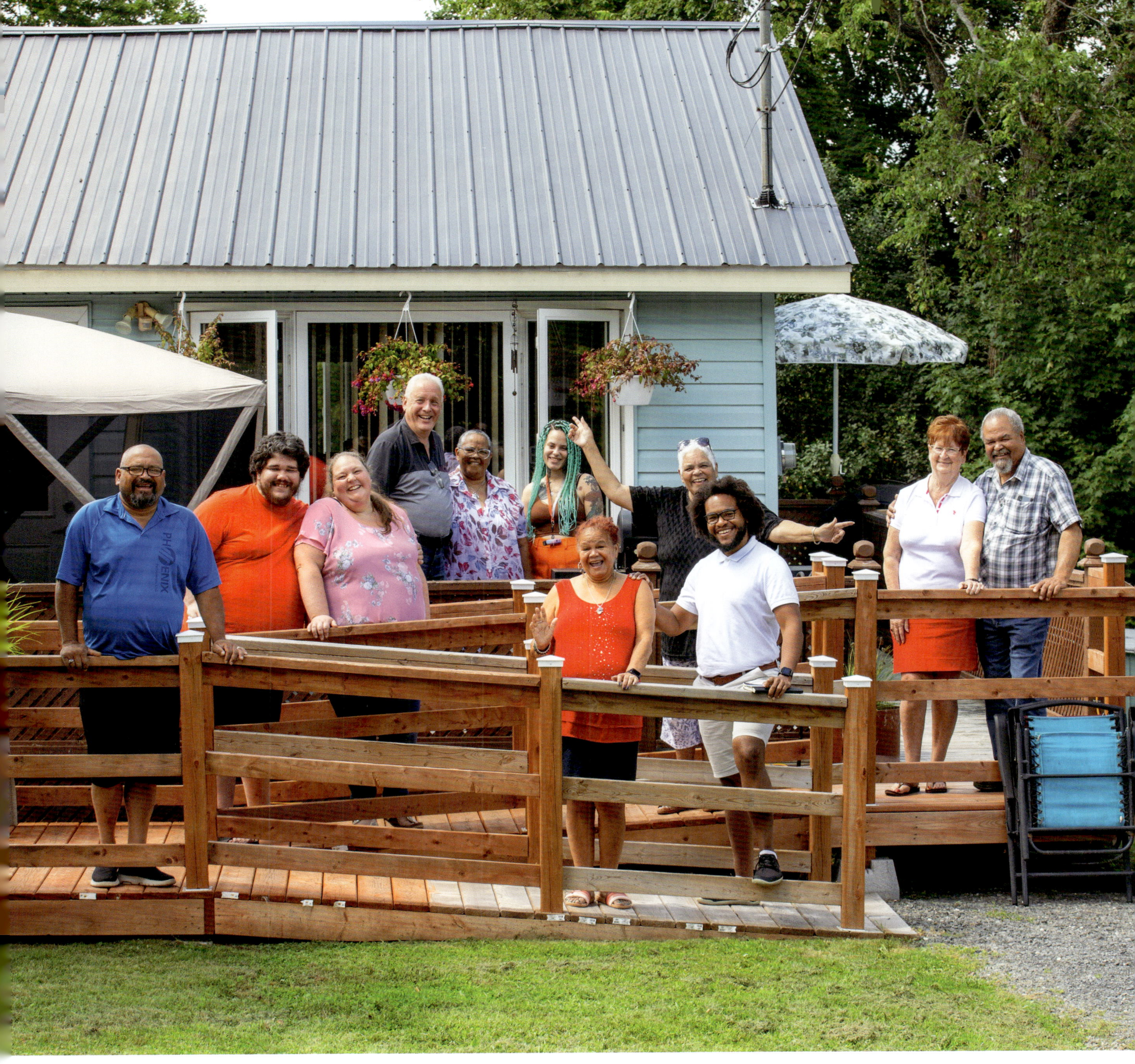

McCarthy / Leek / Dymond / Johnson — Woodstock

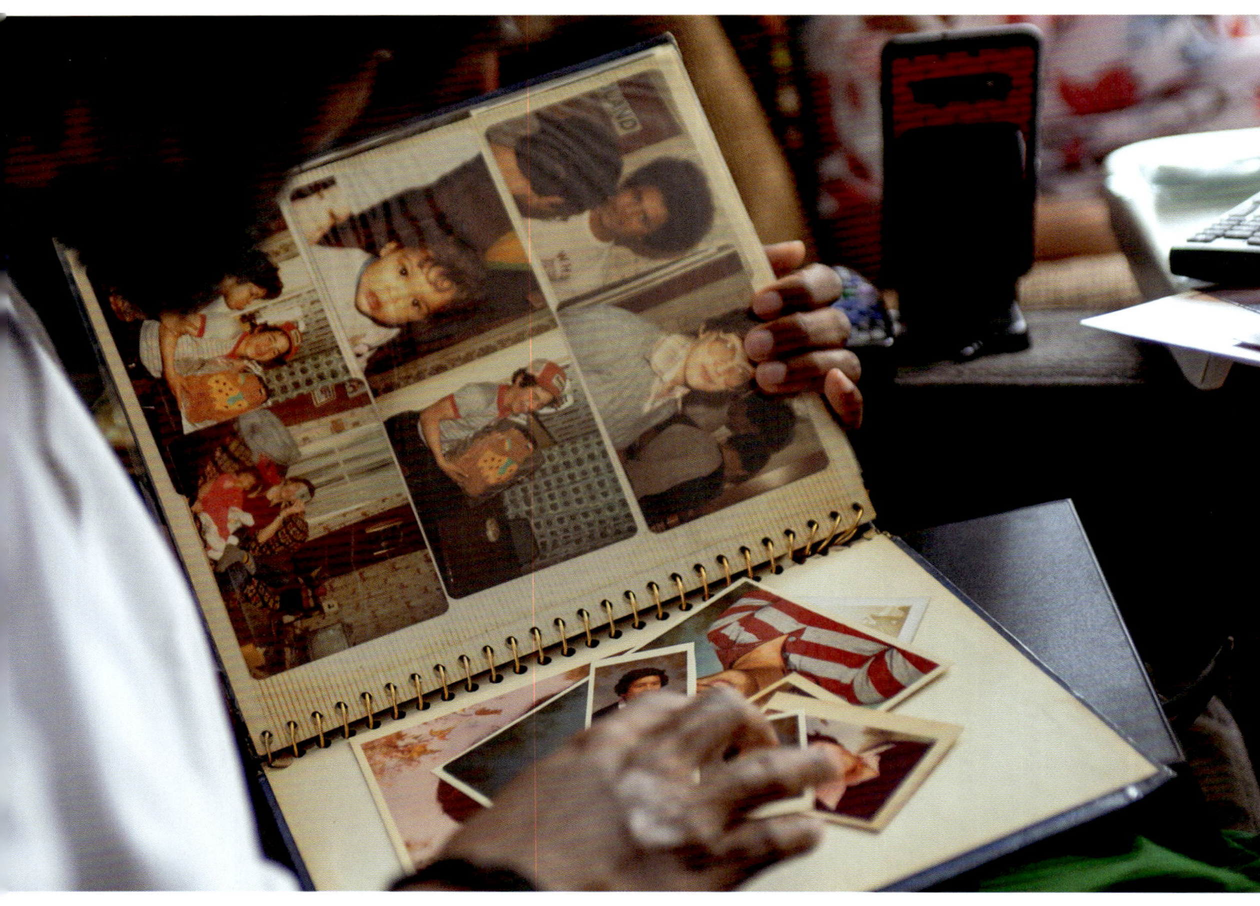

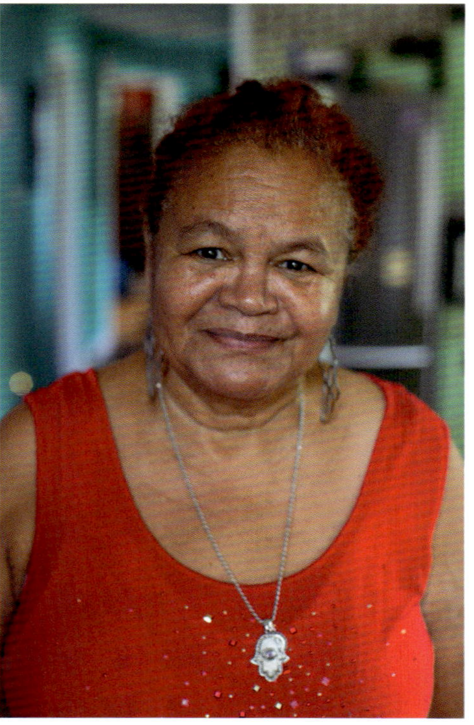

I consider myself sixth-generation African Canadian, and my son is seventh generation. We are a strong family and have grown with the love of our parents, raised to speak with truth and to turn the other cheek.
— Mary Louise McCarthy

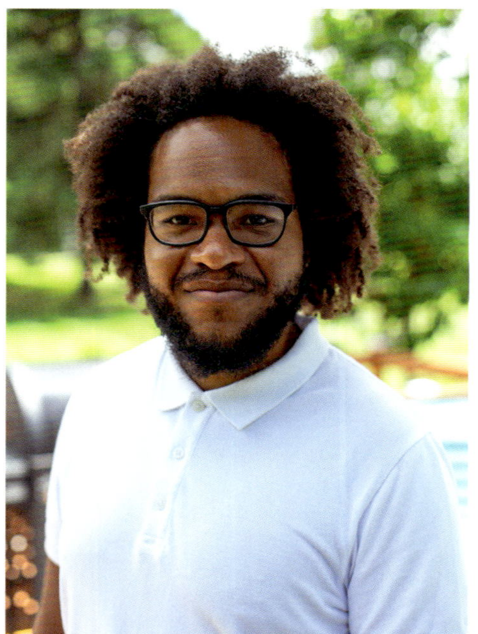

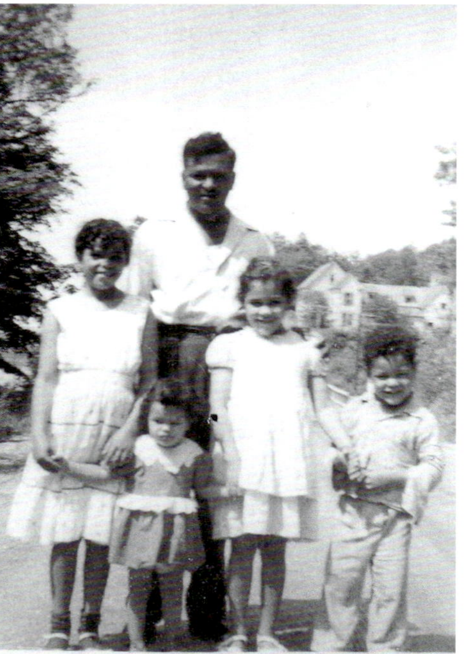

The McCarthy family can date itself back to 1783 on the Leek side, when Sabinah, Mary McCarthy's fifth great-grandmother, arrived in what was then part of Nova Scotia on a ship out of a plantation in Virginia. She was brought to New Brunswick in 1784 as an enslaved person with her owner Sir Isaac Allan, an attorney from New Jersey, when he arrived to settle and to help negotiate the division boundary between New Brunswick and Nova Scotia. As payment for his law skills, he received two thousand acres and was appointed a supreme court judge of the colony of New Brunswick.

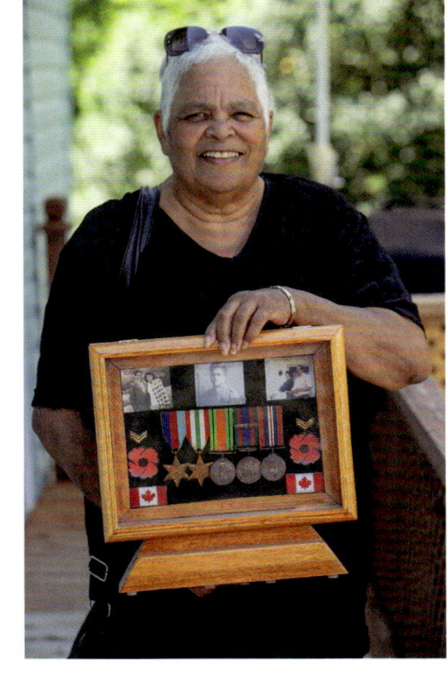

William McCarty and George Leek, Mary's fourth great grandfather, were both children of Sabinah, born in the 1780s, while she was still in servitude to Isaac Allen. According to oral history, Sir Isaac was their father. He was also one of the judges on the "Nancy" Trial in 1800, in which an enslaved woman took her owner, Caleb Jones, to court for cruelty, petitioning to be released from his ownership. Nancy lost the case, but it was so revealing of the atrocities, brutality, and power of the enslavers that, following the court case, Allen went home and released all his enslaved.

George Leek became a master carpenter and was the construction foreman in the building of St. Peter's Anglican Church in Fredericton in the late 1830s.

The Dymond side of the McCarthy family can also be traced back to the late 1700s, to ancestors who were enslaved and later became free and gained a bit of property.

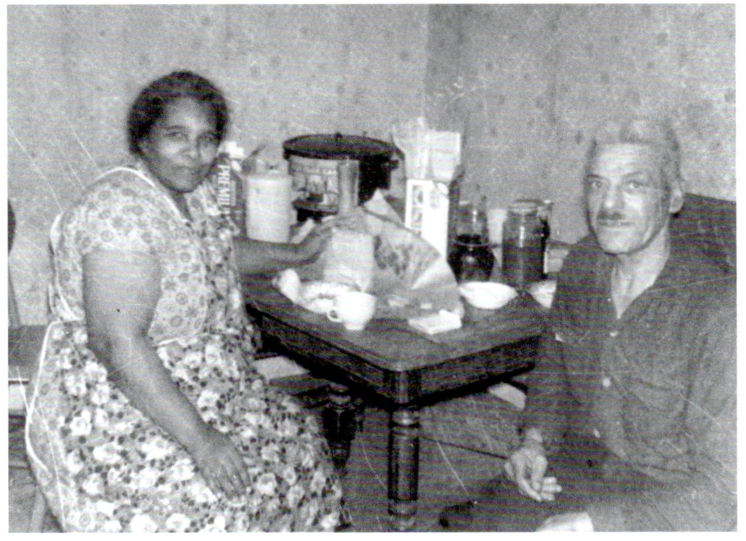

Mary's great grandmother Ada Rae Dymond, born in 1888, was married to Miles Smith Dymond, who was born in 1882. They had a large farm near Jewett's Mill, outside of Fredericton. Miles was a stonecutter and served in the First World War; he was one of the first volunteers to go overseas in October 1914, leaving Ada Rae pregnant at home. At the end of the Second Battle of Ypres, in April 1915, he got word that Ada Rae had given birth to a daughter: they named her Ypres. Miles died in 1933 from chronic endocarditis, which afflicted many First World War veterans.

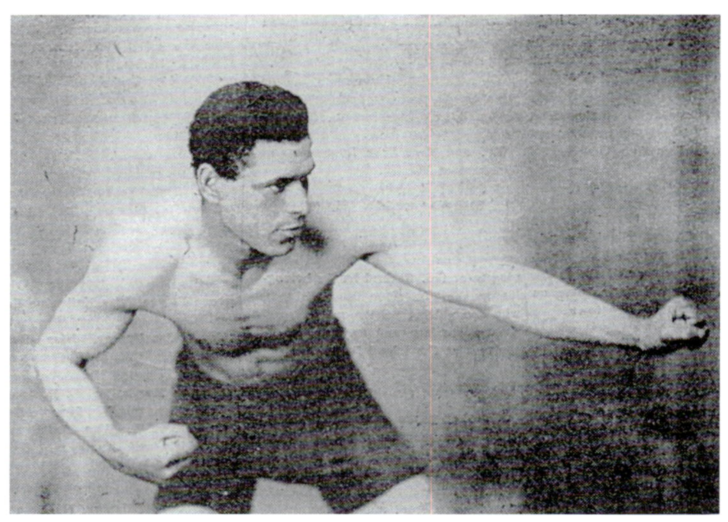

The Dymond family farm was sold during the building of the Mactaquac Dam in the 1960s, and Ada Rae moved to Woodstock. That same Mactaquac Dam project caused the nearly seventy graves of the Old Negro Cemetery to be buried underwater without compensation or acknowledgement.

Mary's grandfather, Reuben Johnson, was a boxer of local fame in the 1930s who once had his jaw broken in a fight but didn't realize it for a week. Reuben's eldest daughter, Althea, married Arthur William McCarthy in 1945.

Mary was raised in a multigenerational family. Mary's mother, Althea, was the eldest child of thirteen and her father, Arthur, was one of eight. The environment she was raised in was very loving and busy. Mary had at least three grandmothers still living, so the home was very matriarchal and always full of cooking, quilting, and multiple family members supporting each other and their descendants.

WINS BY KAYO

JOHNSTON PUTS CAMPBELL AWAY IN 2ND ROUND

Reuben Johnston, Woodstock, knocked out Trueman Campbell, Littleton, Me., in the second round of their scheduled eight round bout at the Vogue Theatre Wednesday evening. Johnston giving away ten pounds, took an awful pasting in the first round, and only his cleverness and ability to take punishment enabled him to last out the round. In the second round he tied up Campbell in a series of clinches and weakened him in the infighting. The end came as a surprise. The two men came together in the centre of the ring and Johnston shot a right hook to Campbell's jaw. Campbell went down and stayed down while Referee Jasper Blake counted him out.

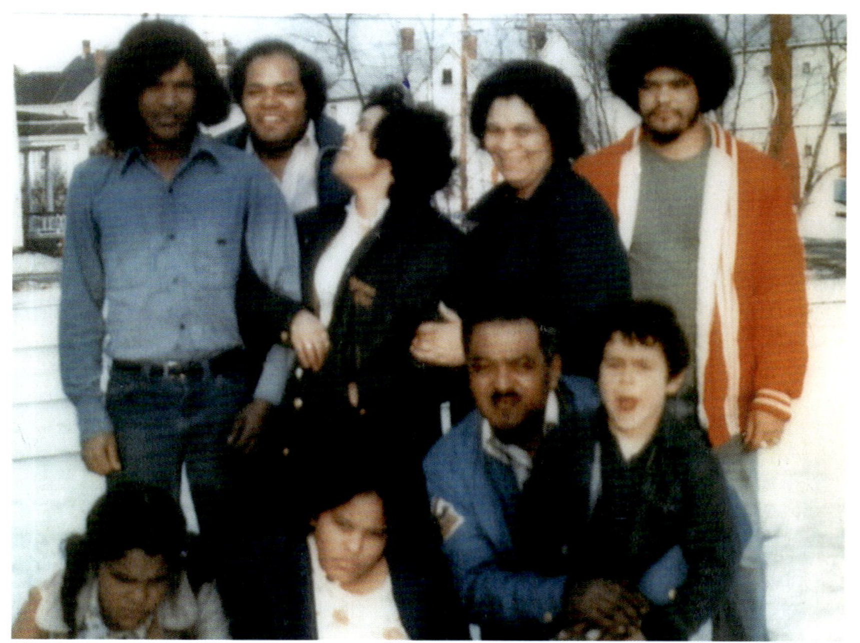

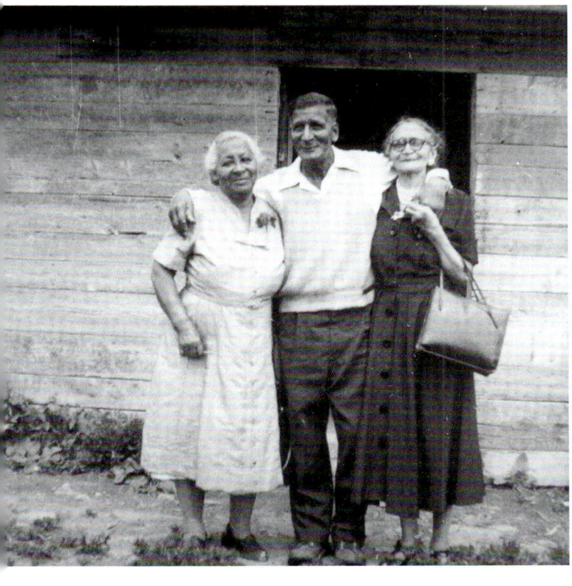

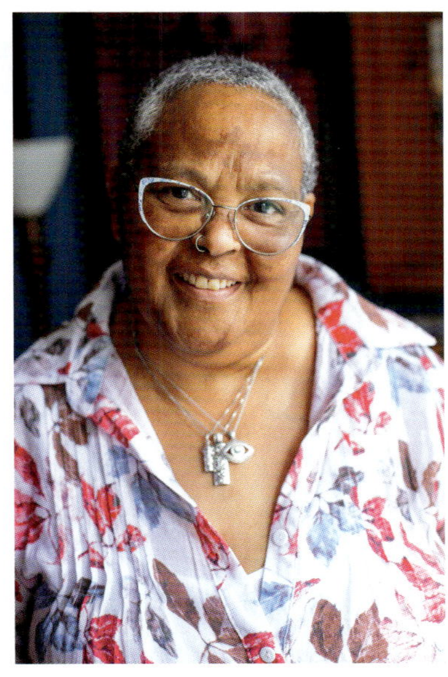

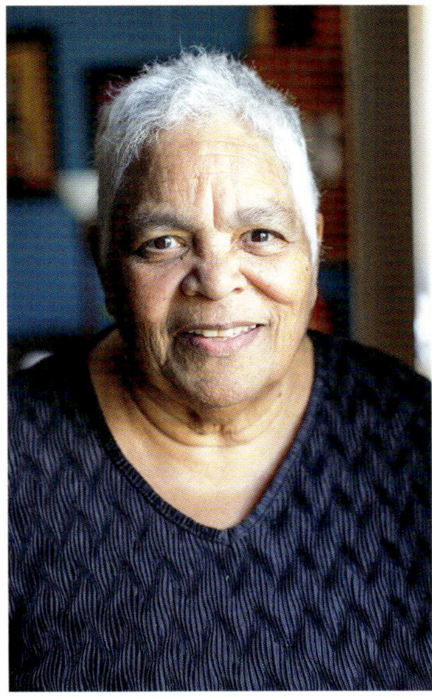

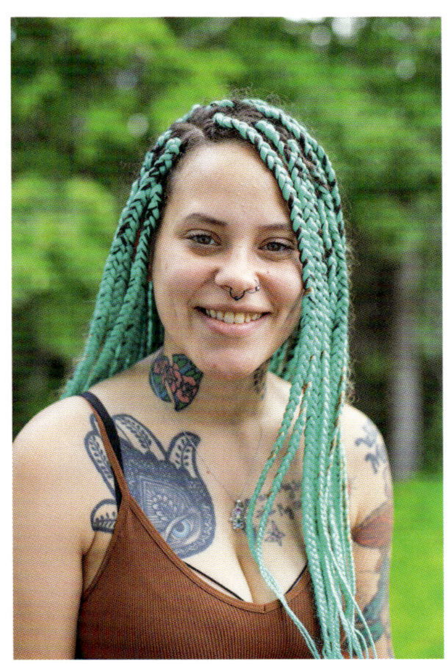

I feel blessed to be the daughter of Althea Jessie Johnson McCarthy, a matriarch bar none. I will always revel in how my mother, in her quiet way, kept peace and love and nourishment flowing both physically and emotionally to our family of nine siblings.

Althea was the glue of our family. She led us in strength and in truths. I am eternally grateful to her for all things inherited. I am because she was. We are because she was.

— Mary Louise McCarthy

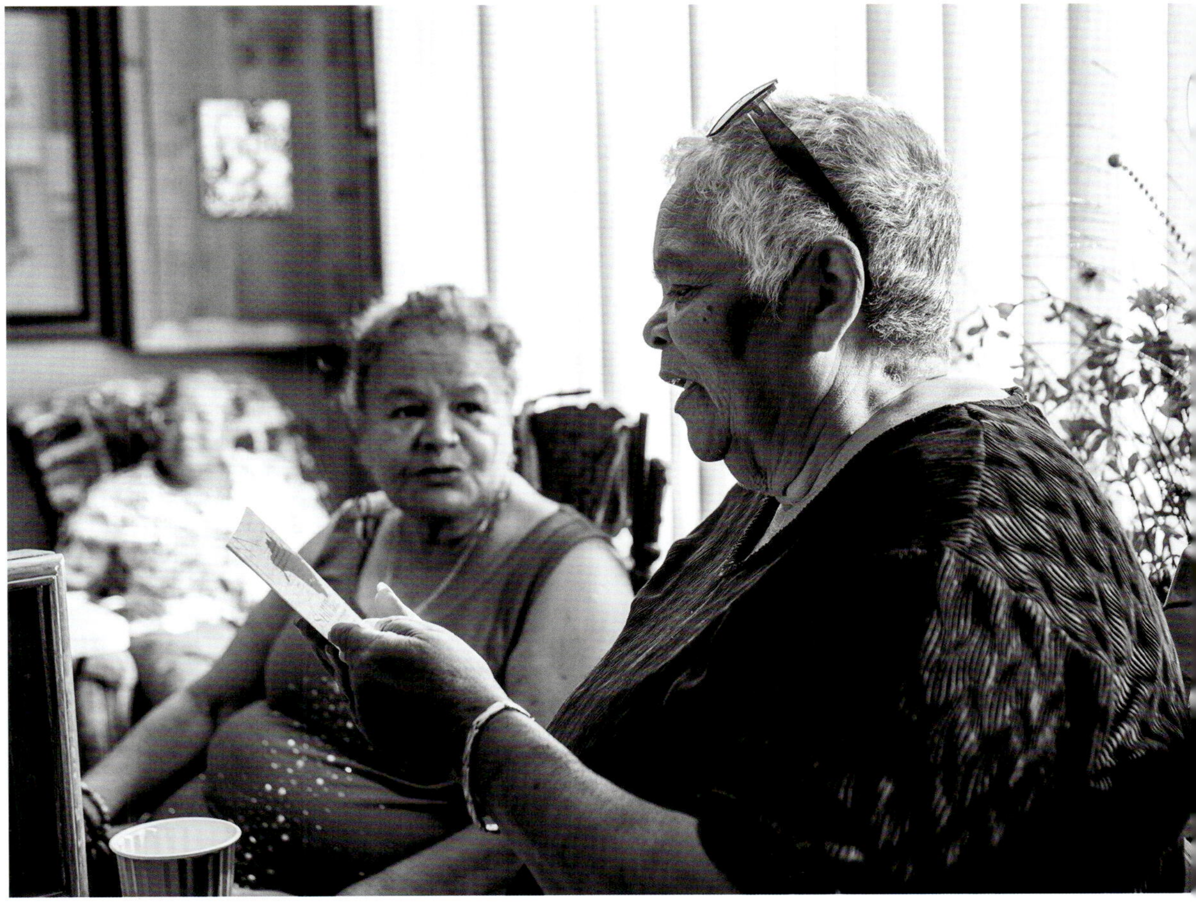

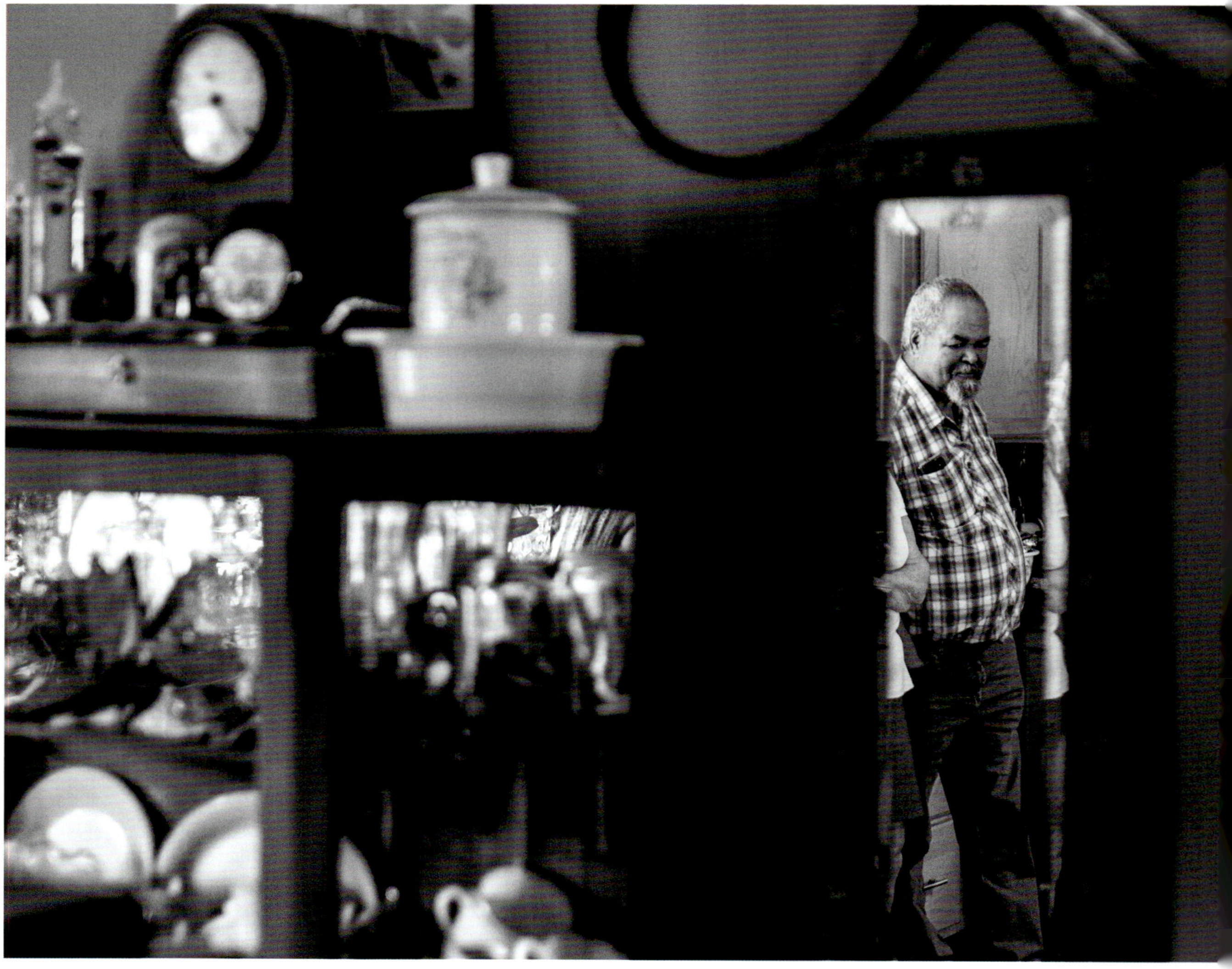

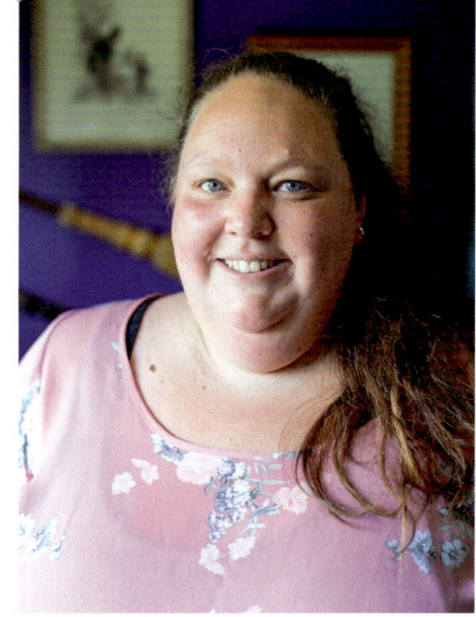
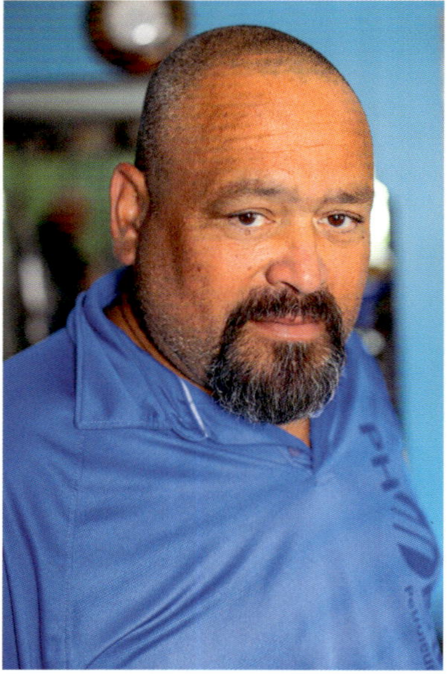
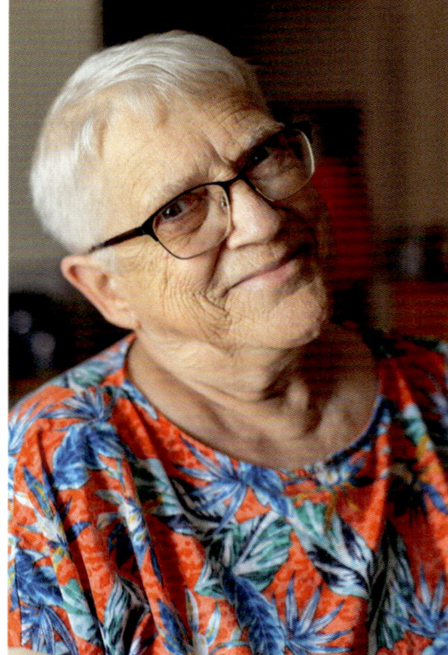
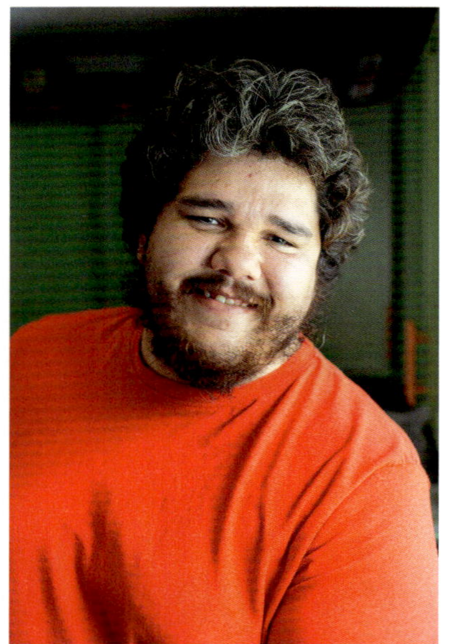
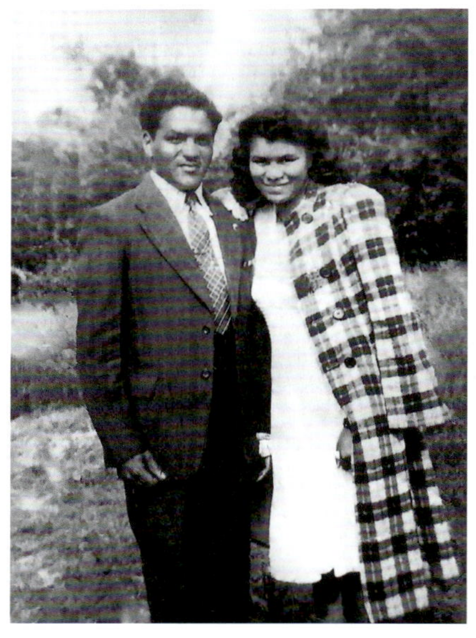
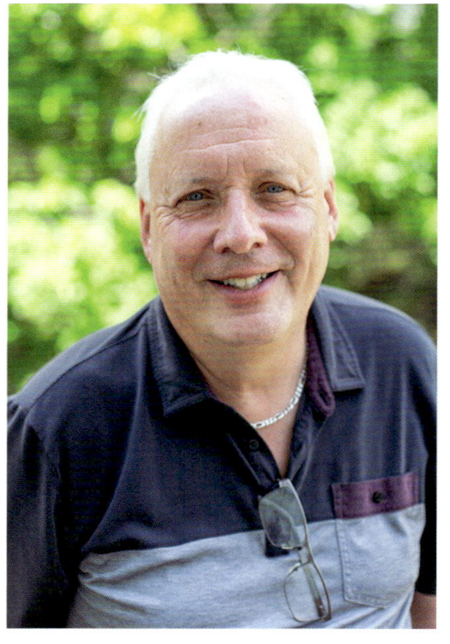

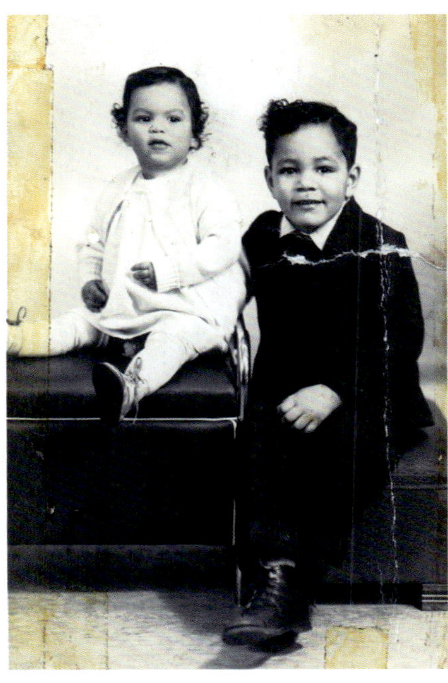

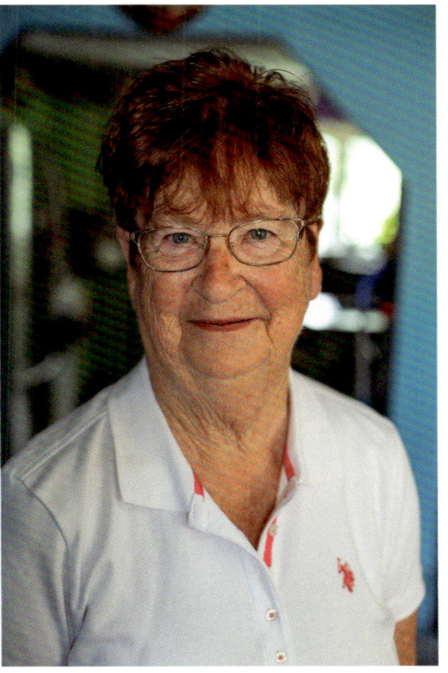

I am blessed to say I come from two lines of strong females, where birth is formulated and growth happens, grandmothers such as Thea Dymond and Martha Leek. I believe in the strength of my ancestors, grandmothers and grandfathers, who have given me the tools to negotiate and live a blessed life in this century.
—Mary Louise McCarthy

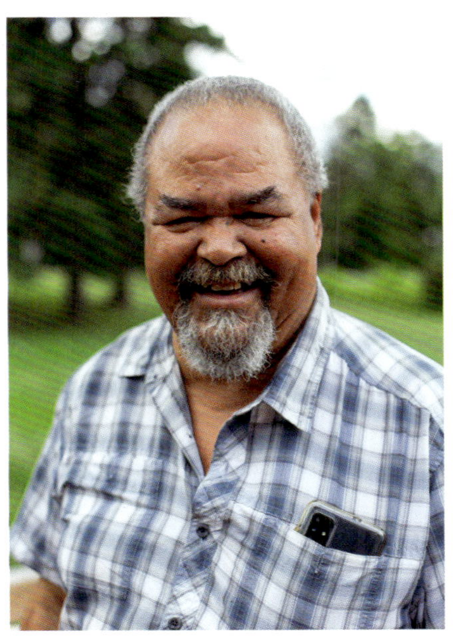

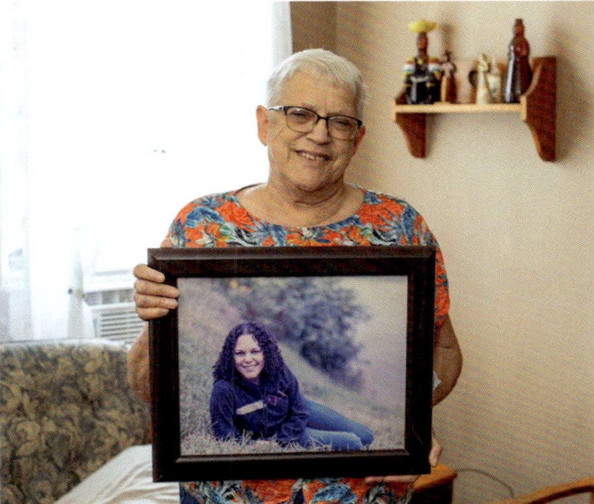

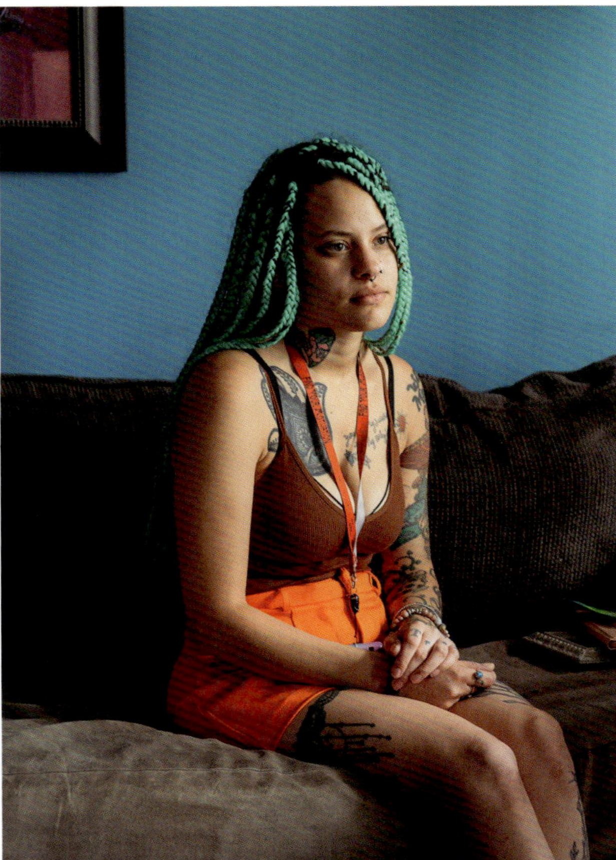

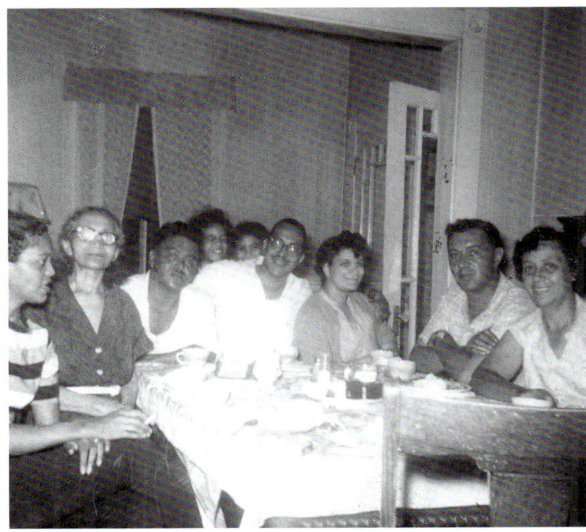

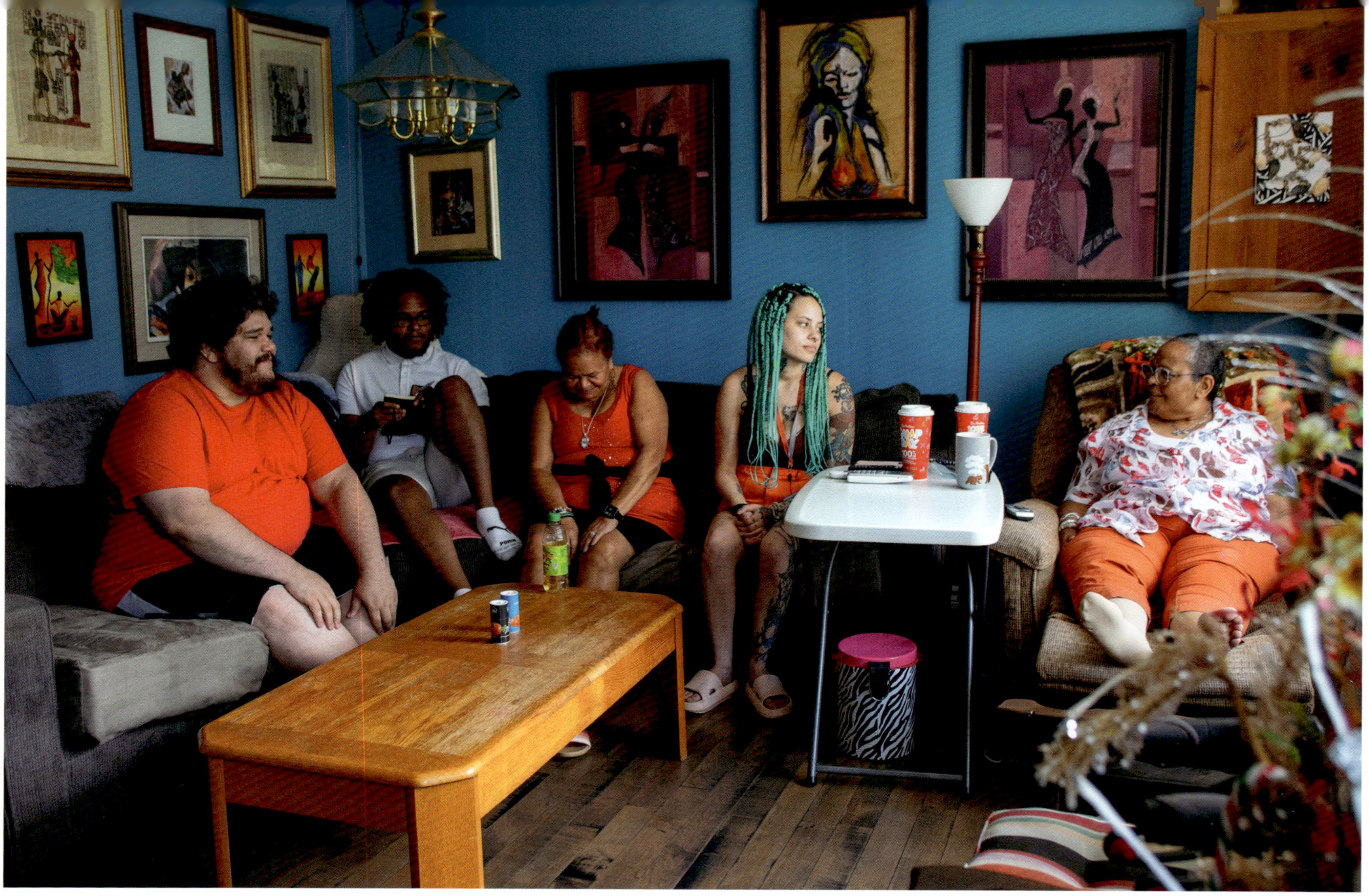

The Mactaquac Dam project that caused my grandmother to sell her house in the 1960s also caused the nearly seventy graves of the Old Negro Cemetery to be lost underwater. At the time of writing, I am currently in negotiations with NB Power to get some form of apology or reparations for the descendants whose ancestors are now buried under the mighty Wolastoq (Saint John River).

— Mary Louise McCarthy

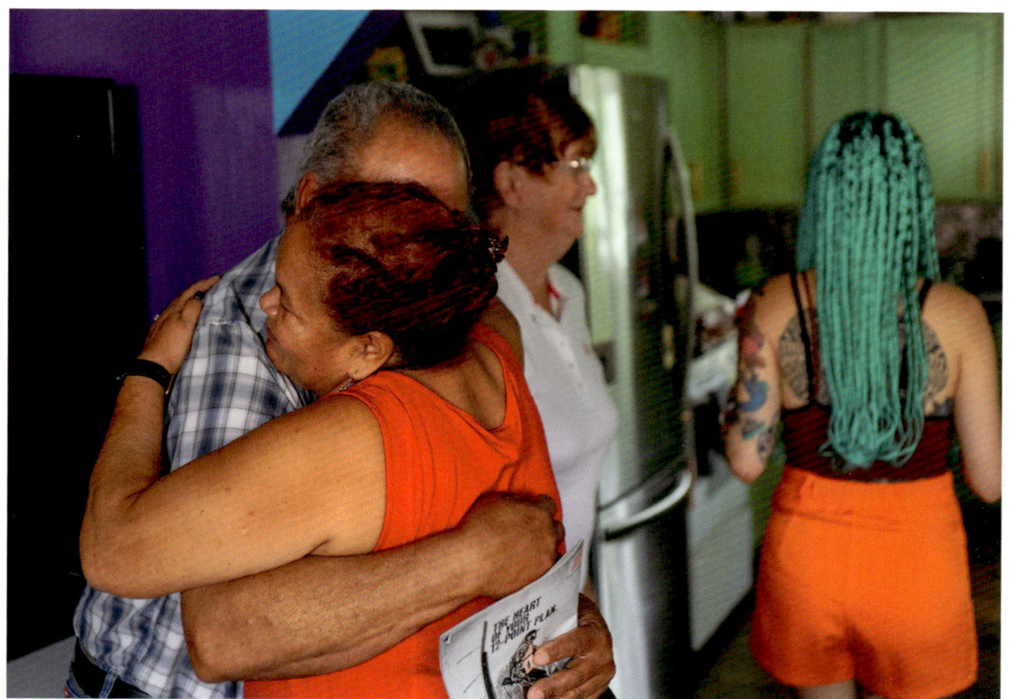

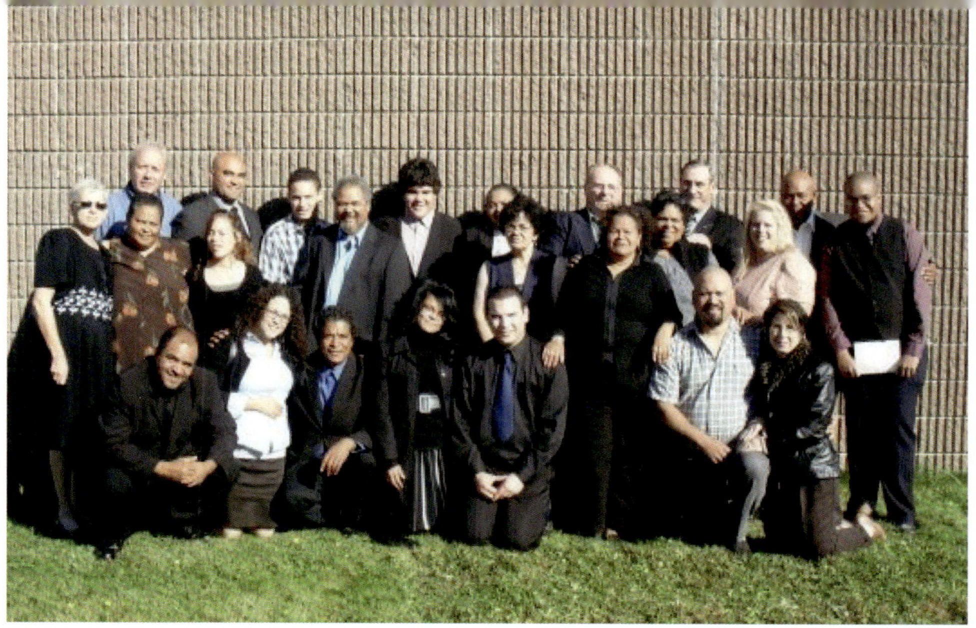

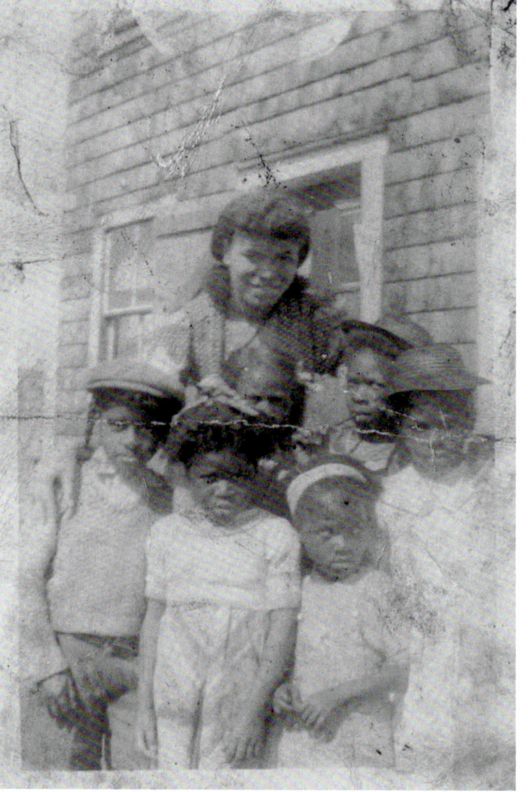

To the Beloved and Dearest Descendants of Althea

Mary Louise McCarthy

I am a Daughter, I am Beloved.
My world is special, encircled with Love.
Althea is our Mother; Her friends call her Beloved
Her friends say we are special as we are Althea's Daughters
We are Althea's offspring, We are Althea's Sons, We are Blessed.
    Althea has a friend, We call her Hazel.
Their friendship is a glue to their precious souls.
Many nights they share devotions, many nights they share smiles.
    Many nights they are together, Feeling blessed and secure that they have each other.
Althea has Sisters, Althea has Brothers. We are surrounded in her love.
We want to say, "We love you." We want to say, "Thank you." We are
    Althea's Descendants, Sons, Daughters, Grandchildren. We cherish that piece of Althea that glues us together.
Like rain on a rainy day, always present,
Ever gentle.
We are very aware of her Light inside of us.

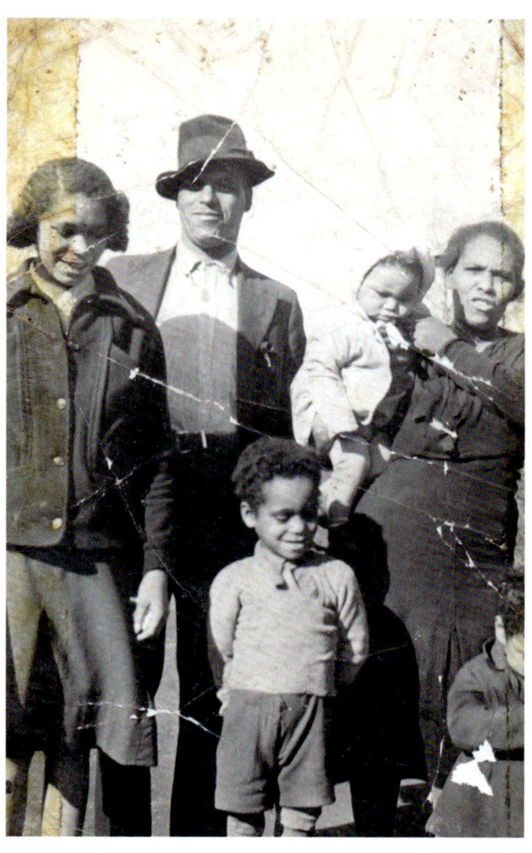

Afterword

> History is a clock that people use to tell their political and cultural time of day. It is a compass they use to find themselves on the map of human geography. It tells them where they have been and what they have been. But most importantly history tells a people where they still must go and what they still must be.
>
> —John Henrik Clarke

Mary McCarthy, Thandiwe McCarthy, and Gary Weekes are very much in tune with these wise words penned by scholar-historian John Henrik Clarke. They have instilled the pages of *Still Here* with emotion, determination, and love. They affirm *presence*.

I first encountered Dr. Mary McCarthy's work in preserving and promoting knowledge of the historical presence of Black/African-descended people in New Brunswick—a *presence* grounded in her own family's long history—ten years ago. At that time, I was researching and preparing the installation, *Excavation: Memory Work* (2018) for the University of New Brunswick Art Centre in Fredericton. The Taylor–Leek Collection at King's Landing (New Brunswick's living history museum), containing precious, ancestral artifacts from Dr. McCarthy's family, was foundational to my project.

The objects in the Taylor–Leek collection represent Dr. McCarthy's legacy and carry the stories of her relatives—proud Black New Brunswickers. One artifact was particularly arresting: a very old, large handmade quilt. Words left me. This quilt bore an astonishing resemblance to my grandmother Ida Grosse Hamilton's quilt, which is a precious part of my own archive. It was a near mirror image, even though they were crafted in different places, decades apart. When I mounted the installation, I positioned the two quilts facing each other in conversation on opposite gallery walls.

Still Here is in keeping with other research-documentary projects launched over the past decades that seek to correct the erasure of Black/African-descended people from Canada's historical narrative. From east to west across Canada, Black history in Canada is being recovered. I think here of works like Dr. Dorothy M. Williams' *The Road to Now: A History of Blacks in Montreal* (still one of the few specific studies on Black Montreal); the work of Dr. Afua Cooper, Adrienne Shadd, and Bryan and Shannon Prince in documenting Ontario's rich Black history; Karina Vernon's *The Black Prairie Archives*, whose writing was motivated by the lack of any information about Black Canadian/Prairie history in her schoolbooks; and

Wayde Compton's capturing of the historic and contemporary creative yield of Black British Columbian writers, poets, advocates, and others in *Bluesprint*.

Closer to home, *Still Here*'s first cousins, the Black Loyalist Heritage Society and the Black Cultural Society of Nova Scotia, document and present companion narratives, stories, and visual representation of Black Atlantic Canadian history—its presence, struggles, and achievements.

Still Here builds on these works, as well as W.A. Spray's foundational text, *The Blacks in New Brunswick*. Writing in 1972, Spray notes: "Today active members of the Black community in New Brunswick are working hard to instill a sense of identity and a feeling of pride in being Black amongst the younger members of the Black community."[1]

These words could have been written about the contemporary efforts of the authors of *Still Here*. They have fully embraced this mission with dedicated work and commitment. With pride, they have erected a marker for Black New Brunswickers and their descendants.

Gary Weekes's joyful photographic vignettes firmly plant the Black families in New Brunswick's soil, while the heartfelt poems crafted by Thandiwe McCarthy voice their experiences, challenges, and fortitude. Dr. Mary asks us to read with attention. Gary's photographs invite us to look closely. Thandiwe insists we listen with our hearts.

Still Here follows the path created by ancestors such as Joseph Drummond of Saint John, New Brunswick, who wrote the foreword to *The Blacks of New Brunswick*, and who Spray thanks in his preface for having shared useful information and suggestions. Drummond's words remain essential:

> Down through the ages the educational institutions of the Western World have been intentionally remiss in not teaching Black People about their culture and their historical traditions.... Therefore, we must rewrite our own history of Black People. We must rewrite it from our knowledge, our genesis, and our deep and abiding love for our Blackness.[2]

To Joseph Drummond, Mary McCarthy, Thandiwe McCarthy, and Gary Weekes, to *Still Here*, I say, "Ashay."

—Sylvia D. Hamilton, CM ONS
Inglis Professor Emeritus, University of King's College

---

1 W.A. Spray, *The Blacks in New Brunswick* (Brunswick Press, 1972), 70.

2 Joseph Drummond, "Foreword," in Spray, *The Blacks in New Brunswick*, 6.

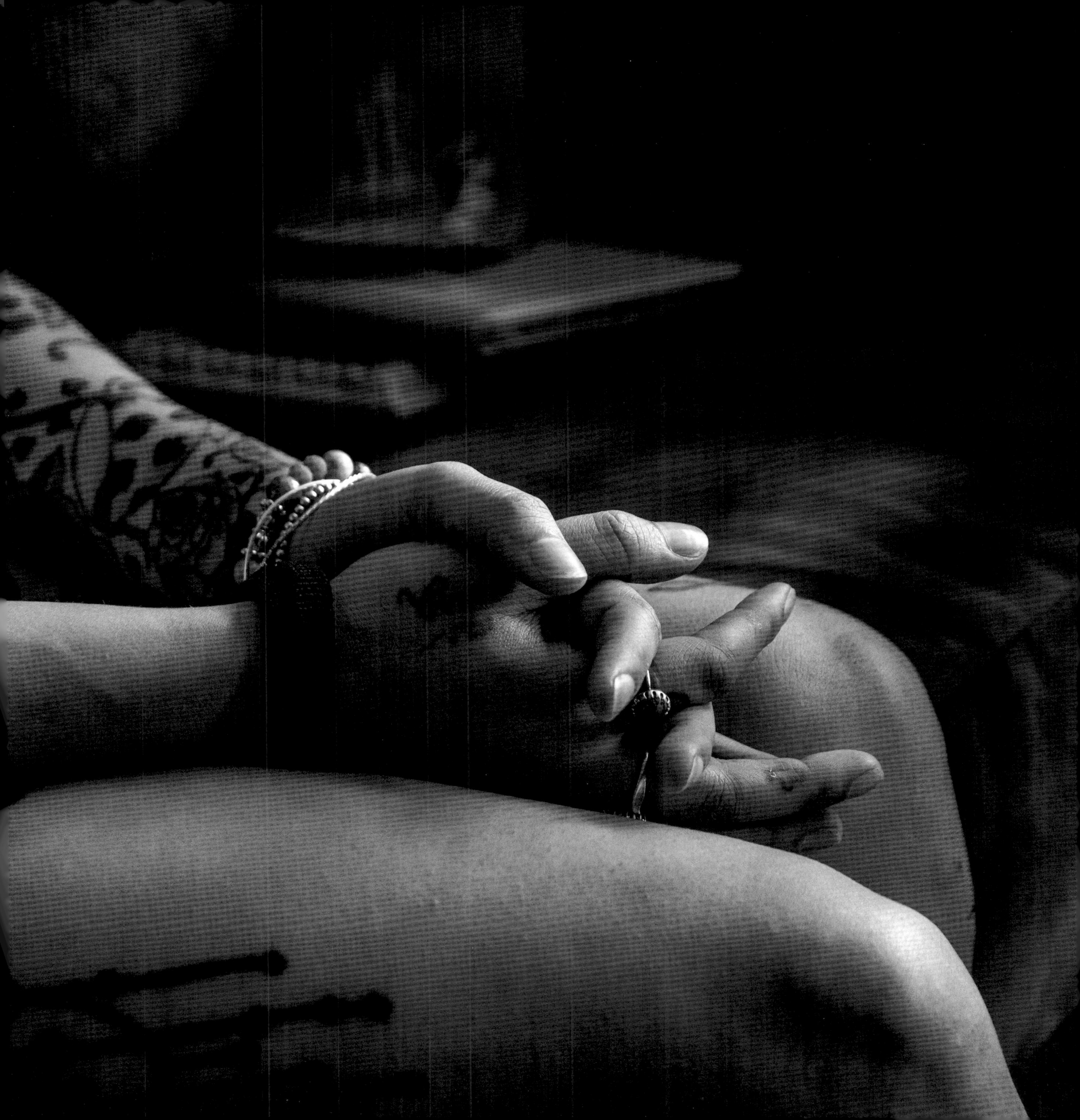

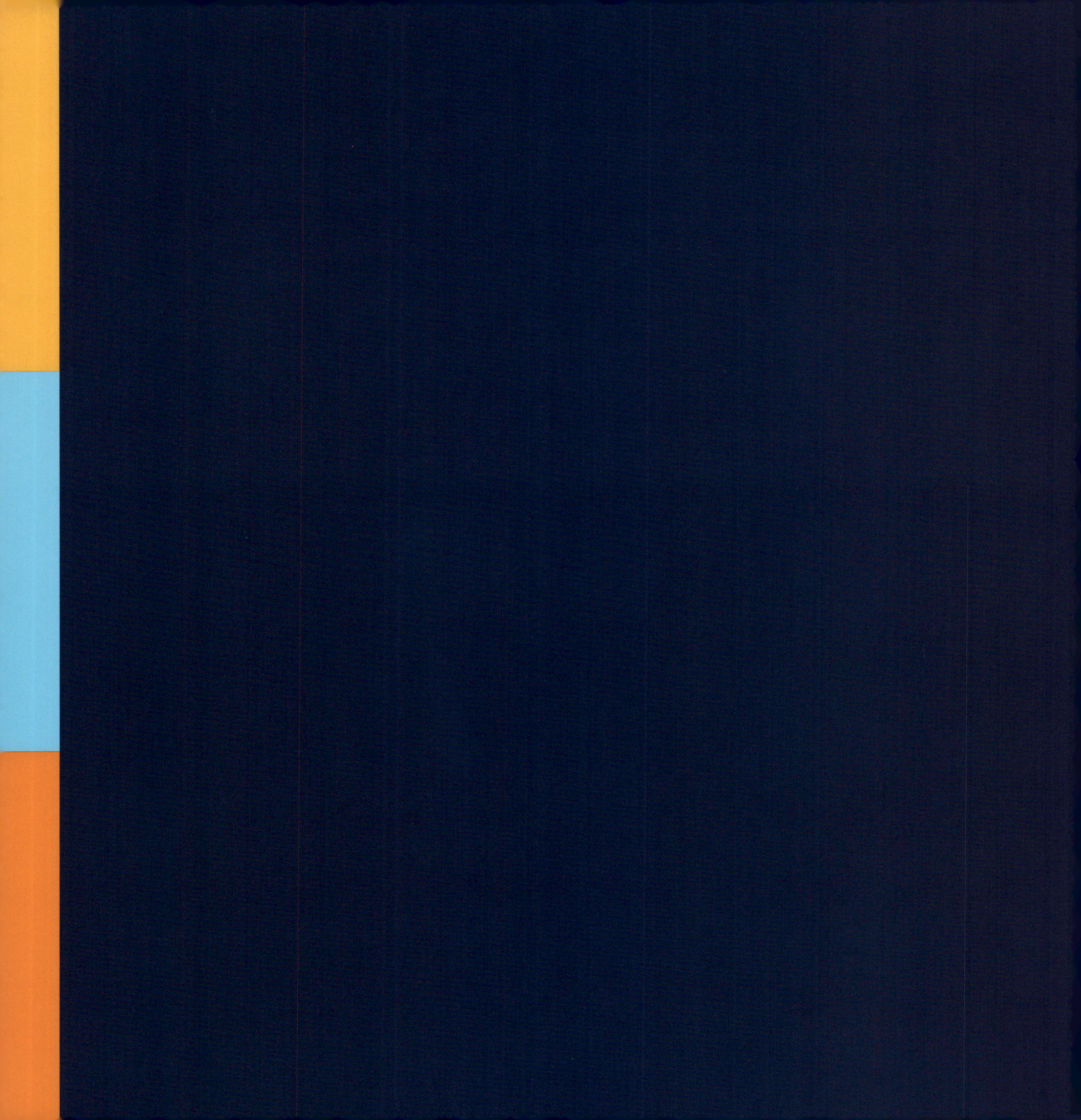

Acknowledgements Thandiwe McCarthy

Still Here owes its first acknowledgement to Karma. This entire project is truly a gift of good energy. Which is why the next round of thanks are for my mother and grandmother, the two people who taught me how to observe and be in relationship with the energy of the universe. Gratitude and kindness are a special kind of currency that trades well in the universal marketplace. It is the hidden reason I was able to barter the powers that be for this project.

This project has changed my DNA. I can't thank the fifteen families enough for the trust and patience they have shown in walking with us. People will never understand the courage these individuals had, to let two strangers walk into a family reunion and take pictures of everyone, telling them to move furniture around. They showed us a level of trust and respect that is engraved into everything we do with this project. Our first rule, before any choice was made, was *respect the families*. We caught fifteen lightning bolts in the same bottle at different times in different places. I am beyond humbled by their collaboration with us. And I'm honoured to say that they are Still Here.

Thank you to the entire *Still Here* team. The greatest team, The Heritage and Culture Justice League. Those who have contributed to the book, and those who have worked behind the scenes.

Still Here would have fallen apart long ago without my best friend, Jeannie Rediker. She has been running beside me on this journey for a long time, and of all the crazy, spur-of-the-moment adventures I've dragged her on, this is the one for which I apologized the most. Her attention to detail and accounting skills are what allowed everyone else on the team to stay true to their strengths, anxiety free.

Gary Weekes is the Superman to my Batman, whose kryptonite is taking compliments and celebrating wins. I know this because when you've slept in enough hotel rooms around the world with someone, you get to know them really well. An' behind the scenes it was Gary's incredible focus and ability to keep cool in the most insane moments of this adventure that were a large part of what helped everyone get to the finish line. An' talking of the finish line, Gary played a crucial role as the designated driver, logging thousands of kilometres across Atlantic Canada and buying the team caffeine and calories to keep everyone alive. Gary is like the older brother I never wanted but clearly needed. He came to this project and captured what I believe to be some of the most stunning images of everyday rural and urban Atlantic life.

Dr. Mary McCarthy is my mother. I love my Mom. If you're reading this you'll know that I constantly tell people I had no idea what Blackness was. It was never forced on me inside the home yet the walls were always covered with gentle reminders. It wasn't until I was ready to learn about my Black heritage that my mother dropped a stack of books in front of me. This began my journey of defining what being Black is to me, which is at the centre of this project—its spiritual core is just that, another step towards my journey of discovery. Also, Mom reached out to all the families, interviewed them, and provided a lot of background research.

Aleya Michaud's professionalism and depth of relationship to the creative spirit is truly inspiring. Her insights on design and creative courage gave the team the energy it needed to keep moving forward, especially as *Still Here* grew beyond our expectations.

•••

Beyond the Still Here team, we need to acknowledge other partners and supporters:

The Owens Art Gallery and Emily Falvey have been key in helping this project get the resources it required, and I am happy this project is one of three of their Black Ark Books, an initiative to help preserve Black New Brunswick culture through the arts.

Many passion projects put people in debt and burnout. But because of the support of the Canada Council for the Arts and the New Brunswick Arts Board we've faced neither. Thank you for pouring enough resources into this project to help the team accomplish what was needed and to be fairly paid for their time.

Long before the book and exhibition, there was a poet, furious at the lack of public acknowledgement of his heritage, who just wanted to write poetry beside archived documents, proving his roots in the province of New Brunswick. I still remember telling the executive director of the Provincial Archives of New Brunswick of my grand vision and her looking deep into my soul and asking me if I had the dedication to see it through. My response seemed to win her over. And over the many years, as this project grew, the entire staff of the provincial archives has dedicated hours to helping us make this project the landmark it is. Thanks to Meredith Batt, Joshua Green, Joanna Aiton Kerr, Keith MacKnight, and the rest of the staff who opened doors clearly labeled "Employees Only" as we worked to bring the history back into the narrative of New Brunswick. The whole provincial archives team found materials, helped us with dates, an' were on call for years. None of this is in their job description, but it is definitely etched in their amazing character. Thanks to each one of you for coming through for Black heritage and my crazy plan to add everything I saw into one book.

Goose Lane Editions or, as the team calls them, "the Goose," had the courage to take on this impossible project and lock in for the long haul. Thanks to Susanne Alexander for being upfront from the first meeting with what it would take for this to get done and being available to chat over many more meetings. This was our team's first time working with a publisher so this level of access to the people working behind the name made all the difference. This is truly a New Brunswick product. Thank you to Julie Scriver for the wonderful book design. It takes a village to make an art book—glad you were part of the team. Special thanks to managing editor Alan Sheppard who was a real delight to work with, and who dreamed up the timeline for the first part of the book, a feature I now couldn't see this project without. And my thanks go to the Goose Lane Editions team as well.

This all started out as a book, and when we told the Beaverbrook Art Gallery about it, they said we should have an exhibition—which shocked everyone on the team. But then they said to reach out to Goose Lane for publishing. So, in a way the Beaverbrook are responsible for the size and multi-faceted nature of the Still Here project! That first meeting with the Beaverbrook Art Gallery amplified everything to do with this project and gave us the industry leverage to approach all the other partners. You'd be surprised by the doors that open if you just mention Goose Lane or the Beaverbrook Art Gallery. Shout out to Ray Cronin, Bernard Doucet, John Leroux, and Adda Mihailescu for believing in this project's potential to tour internationally and make a difference in the national conversation about Black Canadian heritage and culture.

Thank you to Kings Landing for offering actual artifacts of Black Loyalists from the 1800s for the exhibition.

The CBC short documentary on the project by Aniekan Etuhube won an RTDNA Canada award for local news. CBC has since filmed and promoted more of these videos and I am humbled by their support. Thanks for all the radio interviews and for capturing the key points of this project in a tangible way that could be shared with the world.

Many people helped make this happen, way too many to name. But I'm going to try: Jennifer Dow, Karrie Nash, El Jones, David Woods, George Elliott Clark, Pamela Edmonds, Roger Paul Nason (RIP), W.A. Spray (RIP), Ralph Thomas, Carlos Anthony, Paulina O'Kieffe-Anthony, Mutiat Adeleke, Joana Joachim, Erin Morton, Martha Langford, Graham Nickerson, Greg Marquis, various personnel from Concordia University, and many, many more.

And of course, we thank the readers who pick up this book and are inspired to look into their own heritage. Don't let anything stop you from being your own historian and archivist, preserving your family history with the tools you have. These stories are important and I appreciate you supporting this creative project telling ours.

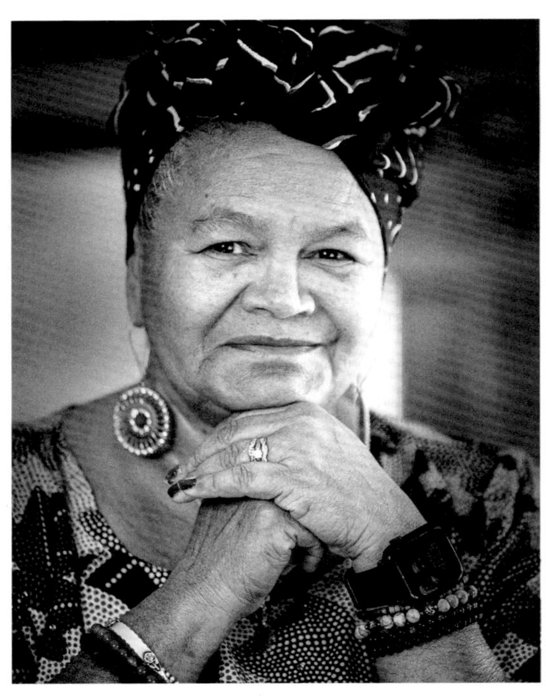

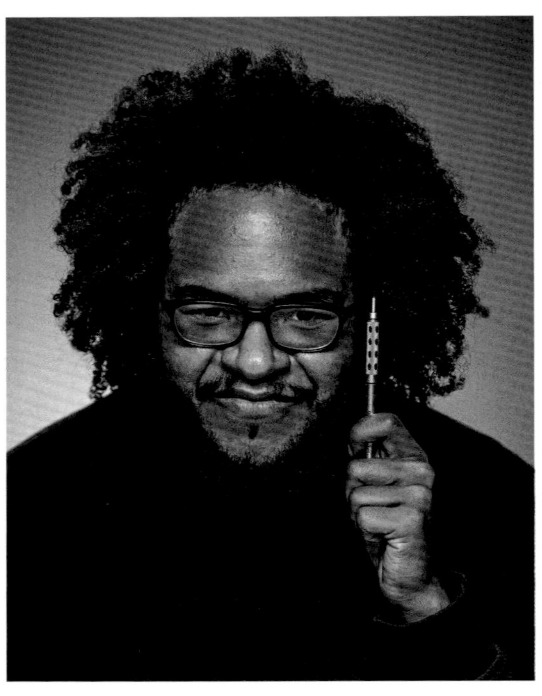

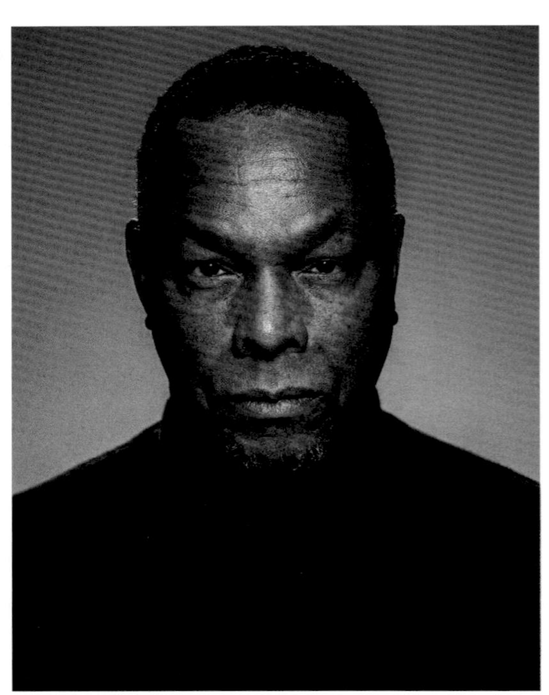

Contributors

Mary McCarthy is a sixth-generation woman of African descent. A writer, educator, and historian, she is dedicated to preserving the histories of Black New Brunswickers. McCarthy holds a PhD from the University of Toronto's Ontario Institute for Studies in Education, where her scholarly research focused on segregated and forgotten graveyards in New Brunswick. She has been featured in *Chatelaine* as one of "33 Black Canadians Making Change Now" for her work identifying systemic and anti-Black racism and was awarded an Honorary Doctorate of Letters from St. Thomas University in Fredericton for her social justice work in May 2022.

Thandiwe McCarthy is a seventh-generation African Canadian and a renowned spoken-word poet and writer. His unique narrative style interweaves the rich history of Black New Brunswick with contemporary experiences, emphasizing the significance of storytelling in preserving cultural heritage. A cofounder of the New Brunswick Black Artists Alliance, an advocate for the recognition of August 1 as Emancipation Day, and an organizer for the New Brunswick Emancipation Celebration event, Thandiwe was recognized by the CBC in 2023 as one of "20 Black Changemakers in Atlantic Canada." He is the culture correspondent for [*EDIT*] magazine and author of the poetic memoir, *Social Oblivion: Raised Black in Canada*.

Gary Weekes is a Fredericton-based documentary filmmaker and acclaimed photographer whose work explores alternative methods of visual storytelling and offers profound visual narratives of Black life in New Brunswick, his upbringing in the UK, the ten years spent in New York, and his constantly changing role as a father of three young women. In 2022, Weekes became the first Black New Brunswicker to have a solo show at the Beaverbrook Art Gallery, and several of his photographs are now in the gallery's permanent collection. Weekes's recent recognition as a CBC "Black Changemaker" underscores his pivotal role in highlighting the community's vibrant culture and history.

Edited by Alan Sheppard and Alison Taylor.
Copy edited by Martin Ainsley.
Cover and page design by Julie Scriver.
Printed in Canada by Friesens.
10 9 8 7 6 5 4 3 2 1

Still Here: Preserving Our Legacy is part of Black Ark Books, a publishing initiative of the Owens Art Gallery (Mount Allison University) devoted to Black creative practices in the Maritime Provinces. This project, which received generous funding from the Canada Council for the Arts, borrows its name from the monumental sculpture *Black Ark* by the artist Oluseye.

Goose Lane Editions acknowledges the generous support of the Government of Canada, the Canada Council for the Arts, and the Government of New Brunswick.

Library and Archives Canada Cataloguing in Publication

Title: Still here : preserving our legacy / Mary McCarthy, Thandiwe McCarthy, and Gary Weekes.
Names: McCarthy, Mary (Mary L.), author. | McCarthy, Thandiwe, 1987- author. | Weekes, Gary, photographer.
Description: Includes bibliographical references.
Identifiers: Canadiana 2025028930X | ISBN 9781773104522 (hardcover)
Subjects: LCSH: Black people—New Brunswick—History. | LCSH: Black people—New Brunswick—Portraits. | LCSH: Black people—New Brunswick—Biography. | LCSH: Families, Black—New Brunswick—History. | CSH: Black Canadians—New Brunswick—History.
Classification: LCC FC2500.B6 M33 2026 | DDC 971.5/100496071—dc23

Goose Lane Editions is located on the unceded territory of the Wəlastəkwiyik whose ancestors along with the Mi'kmaq and Peskotomuhkati Nations signed Peace and Friendship Treaties with the British Crown in the 1700s.

Goose Lane Editions
500 Beaverbrook Court, Suite 330
Fredericton, New Brunswick
CANADA E3B 5X4
gooselane.com